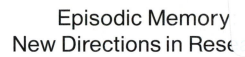

Episodic Memory
New Directions in Research

Episodic Memory:
New Directions in Research

Edited by

ALAN BADDELEY
Centre for the Study of Learning and Memory
University of Bristol, Bristol

JOHN P. AGGLETON
School of Psychology
University of Cardiff, Cardiff

and

MARTIN A. CONWAY
Department of Psychology
University of Durham, Durham

Originating from a Discussion
Meeting of the Royal Society

THE ROYAL
SOCIETY

OXFORD
UNIVERSITY PRESS

OXFORD

UNIVERSITY PRESS

Great Clarendon Street, Oxford OX2 6DP

Oxford University Press is a department of the University of Oxford.
It furthers the University's objective of excellence in research, scholarship,
and education by publishing worldwide in

Oxford   New York

Auckland   Bangkok   Buenos Aires   Cape Town   Chennai
Dar es Salaam   Delhi   Hong Kong   Istanbul   Karachi   Kolkata
Kuala Lumpur   Madrid   Melbourne   Mexico City   Mumbai   Nairobi
Sao Paulo   Shanghai   Singapore   Taipei   Tokyo   Toronto

Oxford is a registered trade mark of Oxford University Press
in the UK and in certain other countries

Published in the United States
by Oxford University Press Inc., New York

British Library Cataloging in Publication Data

Data available

Library of Congress Cataloguing in Publication Data

ISBN 0 19 850879 4 (hardback)
ISBN 0 19 850880 8 (paperback)

10 9 8 7 6 5 4 3 2

Printed in Great Britain
on acid-free paper by
T. J. International Ltd, Padstow

Preface

The term episodic memory was proposed by Endel Tulving in the early 1970s to refer to the capacity to recollect specific events or episodes in our lives. This provided a contrast with semantic memory, the system assumed to store factual knowledge of the world. At a pragmatic level, this created a useful distinction that has now become universally accepted. More controversial, however, was the question of whether these two concepts referred to separate memory systems or to a single system operating under different constraints. More recently, Tulving has sharpened the question by emphasizing the importance of the phenomenological experience of remembering as a distinguishing feature of episodic memory.

After a number of years of relative theoretical quiescence, the nature of episodic memory has attracted renewed interest as a result of conceptual and methodological developments in a range of interrelated fields. The Discussion Meeting was called to review such developments and to facilitate further interaction and progress. Contributors addressed both behavioural and phenomenological issues using data and techniques from cognitive psychology, behavioural analysis, neuroimaging and computational modelling. Data discussed derive from 'normal' subjects, from patients with neuropsychological deficits and from animal studies. A concluding discussion is provided by Endel Tulving. While important questions remain, the combination of interdisciplinary expertise to neuroscience has, in recent years, resulted in considerable progress towards an understanding of this central concept in memory. This is illustrated by the contributions that follow.

Alan Baddeley[1]   *August 2001*
John Aggleton[2]
Martin Conway[3]

[1]*Centre for the Study of Learning and Memory, University of Bristol, Bristol BS8 1TN, UK*
[2]*School of Psychology, University of Cardiff, Cardiff CF10 3YG, UK*
[3]*Department of Psychology, University of Durham, Durham DH1 3LE, UK*

Contents

Contents

Contributors

John P. Aggleton   School of Psychology, University of Cardiff, UK

Alan Baddeley   Centre for the Study of Learning and Memory, University of Bristol, UK

Suzanna Becker   Department of Psychology, McMaster University, Canada

Neil Burgess   Institute of Cognitive Neuroscience, University College London, UK

N. S. Clayton   Department of Experimental Psychology, University of Cambridge, UK

Martin A. Conway   Department of Psychology, University of Durham, UK

Anthony Dickenson   Department of Experimental Psychology, University of Cambridge, UK

Chad S. Dodson   Department of Psychology, Harvard University, USA

N. J. Emery   Department of Experimental Psychology, University of Cambridge, UK

David G. Gadian   Radiology and Physics Unit, Institute of Child Health, University College London, UK

John M. Gardiner   Psychology Group, School of Cognitive and Computing Sciences, University of Sussex, UK

Kim S. Graham   MRC Cognition and Brain Sciences Unit, Cambridge, UK

D. P. Griffiths   Department of Experimental Psychology, University of Cambridge, UK

John R. Hodges   MRC Cognition and Brain Sciences Unit, Cambridge, UK

Narinder Kapur   Department of Clinical Neuropsychology, Wessex Neurological Centre, Southampton General Hospital, UK

John A. King   Institute of Cognitive Neuroscience, University College London, UK

Michael D. Kopelman   University Department of Psychiatry and Psychology, King's College London, UK

Eleanor A. Maguire   Wellcome Department of Cognitive Neurology, Institute of Neurology, University College London, UK

Andrew R. Mayes   Department of Psychology, Eleanor Rathbone Building, University of Liverpool, UK

Mortimer Mishkin   Laboratory of Neuropsychology, National Institute of Mental Health, Bethesda, USA

Richard G. M. Morris   Department of Neuroscience, The University of Edinburgh, UK

John O'Keefe   Institute of Cognitive Neuroscience, University College London, UK

John M. Pearce   School of Psychology, University of Cardiff, UK

Neil Roberts   Magnetic Resonance and Image Analysis Centre, University of Liverpool, UK

Daniel L. Schacter   Department of Psychology, Harvard University, USA

Endel Tulving   Rotman Research Institute, Baycrest Centre for Geriatric Care, Toronto, Canada

Fareneh Vargha-Khadem   Cognitive Neuroscience Unit, Institute of Child Health, University College London, UK

Andrew P. Yonelinas   Department of Psychology, University of California, USA

The concept of episodic memory

Alan Baddeley

Over the last half century, the experimental study of human memory has departed from the earlier concept of a unitary faculty, with the increase in knowledge leading to differentiation between subsystems of memory, often based on the study of neuropsychological patients.

Although foreshadowed by the classic work of William James (1890), the current approach to the fractionation of memory probably began with Hebb's (1949) proposal of a distinction between short-term memory (STM), based on temporary electrical activity within the brain, and long-term memory (LTM), based on the development of more permanent neurochemical changes. He even proposed a learning mechanism, a concept that continues to be influential in neurobiological theorizing (see Burgess *et al.* 2001). Experimental evidence for a distinction between STM and LTM began to appear a decade later with the demonstration by Brown (1958) and Peterson & Peterson (1959) of the rapid forgetting of small amounts of material when ongoing rehearsal was prevented. They proposed that this forgetting reflected the decay of a short-term trace, a process they distinguished from long-term forgetting, which was attributed to interference among long-term memory representations. This view was resisted, with the counter claim made that all forgetting could be interpreted within a single stimulus–response association framework (Melton 1963). The question of whether short-term forgetting reflects trace decay or interference remains unresolved (Cowan *et al.* 2000; Service 1998).

During the 1960s, however, experimental evidence from a range of sources seemed to point increasingly strongly to the need to distinguish between STM and LTM on grounds other than type of forgetting. Neuropsychological evidence was particularly influential, with patients suffering from the classic amnesic syndrome showing grossly impaired LTM, coupled with total preservation of performance on a range of tasks associated with STM (Baddeley & Warrington 1970). Anatomically, the amnesic syndrome has most strongly been associated with damage to the hippocampus (Milner 1966), although it could result from damage to a series of structures that broadly make up the Papez circuit (see Aggleton & Pearce 2001). The STM–LTM distinction was further supported by patients showing the opposite dissociation, with STM performance impaired and LTM preserved (Shallice & Warrington 1970).

By the late 1960s, a range of two-component models was being proposed, of which the most influential was that of Atkinson & Shiffrin (1968). In this model, information was assumed to come in from the environment, be processed by a short-term storage system and then fed into LTM. Probability of learning was assumed to depend on time held within the short-term store. STM was also assumed to act as a working memory, a system responsible for the temporary maintenance of information demanded by the performance of such complex tasks as reasoning and comprehension. Amnesic patients were assumed to have a deficit in LTM, while the second type of patient was assumed to have an STM deficit.

Although it appeared to give a good account of the available data, and still figures prominently in many cognitive psychology textbooks, the Atkinson–Shiffrin model rapidly encountered major problems. The simple unitary STM proposed had difficulty accounting for the neuropsychological evidence. The model would suggest that patients with STM deficits should have substantial further problems in using LTM and, moreover, should have extensive further problems in complex information processing. In fact such patients often have remarkably few problems outside the range of their specific STM deficit (Vallar & Shallice 1990). Baddeley & Hitch (1974) therefore proposed replacing the concept of a unitary STM with a multicomponent working memory (WM) model. This attributed the STM patient's deficit to a subcomponent of WM, the phonological loop, suggesting that other components of WM were intact in these patients, hence allowing their comparatively normal cognitive function. The phonological loop, on the other hand, was proposed to function principally as a mechanism to facilitate the acquisition of language through its impact on phonological LTM and vocabulary learning (Baddeley *et al.* 1998), although it probably also has a further role in the verbal control of action (Baddeley *et al.* 2001; Luria 1959*a,b*; Vygotsky 1962).

The Atkinson–Shiffrin model also encountered problems as a result of its simple assumption that the longer an item was held in STM, the more likely was its transfer to LTM. Simply maintaining an item in short-term store is a very poor method of long-term learning. Craik & Lockhart (1972) showed LTM to be dependent on the nature of the processing of the incoming material, with 'deeper' and more semantically based processing leading to much better subsequent learning than 'shallow' visual or phonological processing.

At about this time, computer scientists were attempting to programme machines to understand language. They rapidly encountered the problem of how meaning might be stored, a problem that was tackled by a Massachusetts Institute of Technology (MIT) graduate student, Ross Quillian, who developed a program he called TLC (the teachable language comprehender). At the heart of the system was a series of assumptions about the way in which meaning was stored, using hierarchical organization to minimize storage demand. Psychologists began to use this model in order to investigate the way in which humans store knowledge, resulting in a series of experimental investigations into the speed at which statements or features of the world can be accessed and verified (Collins & Quillian 1969; Landauer & Freedman 1968).

This new line of research was well represented in a conference organized by Tulving & Donaldson (1972) on the role of organization in human memory. The conference prompted Endel Tulving to ponder the relationship between this new approach to human memory and the more traditional approach reflected in the remaining conference papers, resulting in his writing a concluding chapter to the proceedings in which he proposed to distinguish between what he termed 'semantic memory' and 'episodic memory'.

Semantic memory was assumed to reflect our knowledge of the world; knowing the meaning of the word 'bottle', how many yards there are in a mile, or what is the colour of a ripe banana. Semantic memory held generic information that is probably acquired across many different contexts and is able to be used across many different situations. The term episodic memory, in contrast, was assumed to refer to the capacity to recollect individual events, for example, meeting an old sea captain on holiday last year, or remembering what you had for breakfast. The essence of this type of memory is its specificity, its capacity to represent a specific event and to locate it in time and space. The proposed distinction was widely accepted, though principally I suspect because it allowed the separate conceptualization of knowledge of the world, an important area of investigation that had hitherto been largely neglected by experimental psychologists. At this point, most people probably regarded the term 'episodic memory' as applying to virtually everything else, although, as we shall see, Tulving himself developed a much more specific interpretation.

At first sight, the neuropsychological evidence also appeared to support a clear distinction between semantic and episodic memory. Amnesic patients clearly have a gross deficit in their capacity for storing new episodic memories in the absence of any obvious semantic memory deficit; they can use language perfectly normally, and typically can answer questions about the world and its ways. However, this is not a fair comparison as it involves contrasting new episodic learning with old semantic knowledge. Subsequent research de-confounded these two variables; Baddeley & Wilson (1986) and Wilson & Baddeley (1988) showed that densely amnesic patients could have well-preserved and apparently normal episodic memories of incidents in their earlier lives, while such patients would experience considerable difficulty in adding to their store of semantic knowledge. Such densely amnesic patients would, for example, typically be unaware of who is the current prime minister or president, and fail to know the meaning of words such as AIDS that were introduced into the language after the onset of their amnesia (Gabrieli et al. 1988). While the possibility remains that semantic and episodic memory reflect different storage systems, perhaps relying on a common episodic input system, it seemed simpler to assume that semantic memory merely represents the residue of many episodes. Features that the episodes hold in common would be well learned, in contrast to the individual features of an episode that allow one experience to be separated from another, presumably by its association with a specific context.

A third important dissociation began to be emphasized during the 1970s, namely that between implicit and explicit memory. Once again the strongest evidence came from neuropsychology, where it became increasingly clear that densely amnesic patients were capable of certain types of learning, including priming, the acquisition of motor skills, classical conditioning and habit learning. An example of priming is the capacity to enhance the perception of stimuli under degraded conditions by prior presentation (for a review, see Squire et al. 1993). In all these cases, learning is reflected through enhanced performance of the task in question, with the amnesic patient typically denying ever having encountered that task before. Although this array of tasks was initially interpreted as reflecting a unitary capacity, it now seems likely that they reflect a range of different learning mechanisms dependent upon different brain systems, and having in common the fact that they do not depend upon the recollective or episodic system that is typically impaired in amnesic patients. By the 1990s, there was growing agreement for fractionation in LTM along the lines shown in Figure 1.1, based on Squire (1992) but also supported by a range of other theorists (see Baddeley 1997, ch. 20).

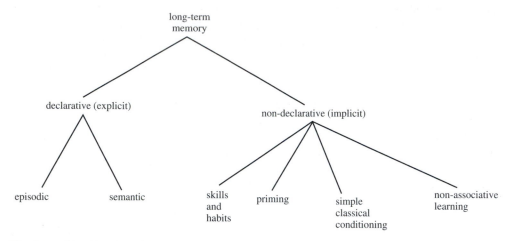

Fig. 1.1. Classification of long-term memory. Declarative (explicit) memory refers to conscious recollection of events (episodic) and facts (semantic). Non-declarative (implicit) memory refers to a heterogeneous collection of abilities whereby experience alters behaviour non-consciously without providing access to any memory content. (Based on Squire (1992).)

The classic amnesic syndrome therefore played a major role in the conceptual fragmentation of the human memory. However, attempts to understand amnesia in more detail proved less satisfactory. A number of attempts were made to attribute the amnesic deficit to cognitive failures of one type or another, including failure to encode sufficiently deeply (Cermak & Reale 1978), excessive sensitivity to interference between memory traces (Warrington & Weiskrantz 1968) and failure to use environmental context adequately (Huppert & Piercy 1978). None of these, however, has been convincingly shown to be responsible for the amnesic syndrome, leaving a more basic neurobiological interpretation in terms of some function such as trace consolidation as a plausible baseline hypothesis (Baddeley 2001).

Attempts to fractionate amnesia into a number of subtypes have also had little sustained success. The proposal that patients with amnesia resulting from temporal lobe damage forget at a different rate from those in which the deficit is diencephalic (Parkin 1992) was not supported by subsequent research, while the proposal that some patients showed impaired recall but preserved recognition memory (Aggleton & Shaw 1996; Hirst *et al.* 1986) was criticized on the grounds that the recognition tests were simply intrinsically easier than those testing recall (Shallice 1988; Reed & Squire 1997).

By the 1990s, there was broad, although not universal, agreement that it was valuable to distinguish between LTM and working memory, that working memory itself was fractionable, and that a broad distinction should be made between implicit and explicit LTM. Anatomically, it seemed well established that episodic memory depended crucially on the hippocampus, while working memory reflected systems in the temporo-parietal and frontal lobes. There was general agreement that semantic memory served a different function and operated in a different way from episodic memory, although there was disagreement as to whether the two depended upon fundamentally different learning and memory systems. Other unresolved issues concerned the question of whether recall and recognition reflected different retrieval mechanisms applied to the same memory systems, or were basically different processes. Although a number of single case studies hinted at the possibility of a range of different types of amnesia (Aggleton & Brown 1999), there was no generally accepted subcategorization. Finally, the concept of episodic memory itself was showing signs of potential fractionation.

The core of the potential separation stemmed from a feature of episodic memory that was increasingly emphasized by Tulving himself, namely the central importance of the phenomenological experience of remembering. This did not play an important role in the general use of the concept in its initial years, when the term episodic memory was commonly used to refer to all memory other than semantic or working memory. Indeed, in the 1970s, suspicion of phenomenology was such that emphasis on this aspect might well have militated against its general use. Increasingly, however, Tulving began to emphasize what he referred to as the 'autonoetic' character of episodic memory, with the recollective experience being regarded as a *sine qua non* of episodic memory (Tulving 1985). He suggested that subjects be questioned as to whether an item recognized or recalled was 'remembered' or simply 'known'. 'Remembering' requires the capacity to recollect some specific feature of the learning experience. For example, when remembering the word 'dachshund', a subject might recollect that, when shown the word, it evoked the memory of a particular dachshund belonging to a friend, or perhaps that it suggested the possibility of an association with an earlier word such as 'sausage'. Other words could confidently be attributed to the previously presented list but had no such specific recollected experience. Tulving suggests that this capacity to 'relive' the experiences associated with the initial episode is crucial in allowing us to reinvestigate our past and use it to predict the future; 'episodic memory does exactly what the other forms of memory do not and cannot do—it enables the individual to mentally travel back into her personal past' (Tulving 1998, p. 266). As the contribution by Gardiner (2001) indicates, despite its phenomenological nature, a regular and meaningful pattern of empirical results has resulted from asking subjects recognizing a previously presented item whether they 'remember' it, in that they recollect the circumstances under which it was previously encountered, or simply 'know' that it was presented.

The remember–know distinction is only one of a series of techniques suggesting that explicit recognition and recall memory may reflect more than one underlying system or process. Mandler (1980) suggested that recognition may be based on at least two separate processes, one analogous to recollection, while the other is based on a feeling of familiarity. Jacoby (1994) has developed a series of ingenious techniques for separating such components of memory using what has come to be known as the 'process dissociation procedure'. The extent to which this procedure and the remember–know distinction reflect equivalent underlying systems has been a topic of some controversy in recent years (Baddeley 1997; Joordens & Merikle 1993; Jacoby *et al.* 1993). Yonelinas (2001) describes some elegant work that attempts to resolve this issue.

Mayes & Roberts (2001) describe a range of new findings resulting from increasingly sophisticated methods of investigation that are questioning earlier interpretations of the amnesic syndrome, while the application of new technology and novel methodology is throwing fresh light on the nature of normal memory—and of the ways in which it breaks down, as is well illustrated by Schacter & Dodson (2001).

A crucial feature of the concept of episodic memory is the role of the rememberer. The concept therefore bears very centrally on theorizing about the self, and the extent to which one's self concept is based on the accumulation of episodic experience. This problem forms the focus of the contribution by Conway (2001), who makes a distinction between the term 'episodic memory', which he limits to relatively recent recollective experience, and the longer-term accumulation of personal knowledge that he refers to as 'autobiographical memory'. The next two chapters use data from neuropsychological patients to investigate further the nature of the accumulated memories that play such an important role in allowing us to function. Kopelman & Kapur (2001) provide a valuable review of the area of retrograde amnesia, the loss of memory for events preceding a memory deficit. In this review they examine the range of factors that influence retrograde amnesia at the level of both recollecting specific episodes and retrieving knowledge about one's early life, sometimes known as semantic autobiographical memory (Kopelman *et al.* 1989).

Despite the excitement generated by the concept of semantic memory in the 1970s, research on normal subjects proved frustratingly inconclusive (Kintsch 1980) in that the experimental methods available, based principally on the complex task of sentence verification, did not appear able to decide between the various models proposed. A breakthrough in this area came from the observation that certain dementia patients showed a progressive deterioration in the knowledge of the meaning of even common words (Warrington & McCarthy 1987). The decline was typically lawful in that detailed information was lost first. Hence a patient who had had an accident, when asked to name a picture of a greyhound, might first of all lose the specific term but still know that it was a dog, subsequently only being able to classify it as an animal and eventually potentially losing even this capacity. This syndrome became known as 'semantic dementia' (Snowden *et al.* 1989) and, as Hodges & Graham (2001) illustrate, is beginning to throw considerable light not only on semantic memory but also on its relationship to episodic and autobiographical memory.

The contributions so far can be described as stretching and elaborating the status quo, rather than challenging it directly. In my own view, the greatest challenge to the status quo is offered by the group of patients described by Vargha-Khadem *et al.* (2001). In particular the case of the young man 'Jon' challenges received wisdom in that despite being amnesic, apparently from birth, he has nevertheless acquired normal intelligence, language and semantic memory. If semantic memory is simply the accumulation of episodes, then his impaired episodic memory surely ought to have led to substantial developmental deficits. A second challenge to the status quo is the observation that his recognition memory appears to be entirely normal, whereas his recall capacity is seriously impaired. This may provide a clue as to how he has been able to acquire normal knowledge of the world but the underlying principles remain obscure. Interestingly, Jon appears to lack the normal capacity to 'remember', in the sense of failing to recollect the experience of learning, the autonoetic component that is central to Tulving's concept of episodic memory. It is, of course, difficult to argue strongly from a failure of the experimenter to elicit a particular type of introspective response. Fortunately, the great strides made recently in functional brain imaging offer a possible solution. Maguire (2001) gives an excellent overview of this development, and has in fact used such techniques to study Jon's episodic memory, producing evidence suggesting that he is capable of episodic recollection but that this does not occur under standard recognition conditions. Neuroanatomically, Jon's memory deficit appears to be associated principally with reduced hippocampal volume. This again casts doubt on the status quo, since hippocampal damage was typically regarded as associated with the classic amnesic syndrome, which shows impairment in both recall and recognition. Indeed, Squire and co-authors have demonstrated very clearly a deficit in recognition in a group of their own patients whose damage is principally associated with the hippocampus (Manns & Squire 1999; Reed & Squire 1997).

As Aggleton & Pearce (2001) illustrate, however, the development of increasingly sophisticated neurobiological techniques has cast doubt on the earlier assumption of the simple and central role of the hippocampus. They present a convincing case for the need to assume a much more complex relationship between the various anatomical structures whose damage is classically associated with the amnesic syndrome in humans and impaired learning and memory in animals.

Animal studies clearly allow a much wider range of investigative techniques than those applicable to the study of either normal human subjects or neuropsychological patients. The question therefore arises as to whether it is possible, or even conceivable, to study episodic memory in animals. Certainly, using Tulving's definition, episodic memory would only be possible if animals were assumed to have consciousness, something that is very difficult to establish. However, as Aggleton and Pearce point out, one feature of episodic memory is the pulling together in a single episode of 'what', 'where' and 'when' something happened, and its subsequent recall. This issue is taken up and discussed in much more detail by Morris (2001), while the capacity for such episodic-like memory is elegantly illustrated by Clayton *et al.* (2001), who study the remarkable capacity of scrub jays to store food (the 'where') while successfully remembering the nature of the food (the 'what') and allowing for its perishability in deciding which to eat first (the 'when').

Finally, one important aspect of recent work in this area is its interdisciplinary nature. This is illustrated particularly well by Burgess *et al.* (2001), who combine neurophysiological and behavioural evidence from animals with neuropsychological and neuroradiological evidence from humans to develop and elaborate a computational model that attempts to give an account of how episodic memories are acquired, and lost following brain damage.

In the 30 years since the concept of episodic memory was first proposed, it has proved to be highly durable, suggesting its inherent usefulness as a theoretical concept. At the same time, it has also proved to be extremely productive in raising important questions and stimulating new research, a characteristic that is well illustrated by the contributions in this issue that follow. Indeed, since this Discussion Meeting was planned, the concept has spread to working memory, in the form of a fourth component, the 'episodic buffer' (Baddeley 2000). This is assumed to be a temporary storage system that binds together information from the phonological and visuo-spatial subsystems of WM with information from LTM. As such, it provides an interface with episodic LTM, using conscious awareness as a retrieval process. I was tempted to crash the episodic memory party with a presentation on the buffer, but the programme was full, and at under 1 year old, the episodic buffer is a little young for parties. We have therefore limited the discussion to episodic long-term memory, a concept that was initiated almost 30 years ago by Endel Tulving, who continues to develop and refine our understanding of memory, and who, in a final discussion (Tulving 2001), appropriately has the last word.

References

Aggleton, J. P. & Brown, M. W. 1999 Episodic memory, amnesia, and the hippocampal–anterior thalamic axis. *Behav. Brain Sci.* **22**, 425–490.

Aggleton, J. P. & Pearce J. M. 2001 Neural systems underlying episodic memory: insights from animal research. *Phil. Trans. R. Soc. Lond.* B **356**, 1467–1482.

Aggleton, J. P. & Shaw, C. 1996 Amnesia and recognition memory: a reanalysis of psychometric data. *Neuropsychologia* **34**, 51–62.

Atkinson, R. C. & Shiffrin, R. M. 1968 Human memory: a proposed system and its control processes. In *The psychology of learning and motivation: advances in research and theory*, vol. 2 (ed. K. W. Spence), pp. 89–195. New York: Academic Press.

Baddeley, A. D. 1997 *Human memory: theory and practice*, revised edn. Hove, UK: Psychology Press.

Baddeley, A. D. 2000 The episodic buffer: a new component of working memory? *Trends Cogn. Sci.* **4**, 417–423.

Baddeley, A. D. 2001 Developmental amnesia: a challenge to current models? In *The neuropsychology of memory*, 3rd edn (ed. L. R. Squire & D. Schacter). New York: Guilford Press. (In the press.)

Baddeley, A. D. & Hitch, G. J. 1974 Working memory. In *Recent advances in learning and motivation*, vol. 8 (ed. G. A. Bowers), pp. 47–89. New York: Academic Press.

Baddeley, A. D. & Warrington, E. K. 1970 Amnesia and the distinction between long- and short-term memory. *J. Verbal Learn. Behav.* **9**, 176–189.

Baddeley, A. D & Wilson, B. A. 1986 Amnesia, autobiographical memory and confabulation. In *Autobiographical memory* (ed. D. C. Ruben), pp. 225–252. Cambridge University Press.

Baddeley, A. D., Gathercole, S. & Papagno, C. 1998 The phonological loop as a language learning device. *Psychol. Rev.* **105**, 158–173.

Baddeley, A. D., Chincotta, D. & Adlam, A. 2001 Working memory and the control of action: evidence from task switching. *J. Exp. Psychol. Gen.* (In the press.)

Brown, J. 1958 Some tests of the decay theory of immediate memory. *Q. J. Exp. Psychol.* **10**, 12–21.

Burgess, N., Becker, S., King, J. A. & O'Keefe, J. 2001 Memory for events and their spatial context: models and experiments. *Phil. Trans. R. Soc. Lond.* B **356**, 1493–1503.

Cermak, L. S. & Reale, L. 1978 Depth of processing and retention of words by alcoholic Korsakoff patients. *J. Exp. Psychol. Hum. Learn. Mem.* **4**, 165–174.

Clayton, N. S., Griffiths, D. P., Emery, N. J. & Dickinson, A. 2001 Elements of episodic-like memory in animals. *Phil. Trans. R. Soc. Lond.* B **356**, 1483–1491.

Collins, A. M. & Quillian, M. R. 1969 Retrieval time from semantic memory. *J. Verbal Learn. Behav.* **8**, 240–247.

Conway, M. A. 2001 Sensory-perceptual episodic memory and its context: autobiographical memory. *Phil. Trans. R. Soc. Lond.* B **356**, 1375–1384.

Cowan, N., Nugent, L. D. & Elliott, E. M. 2000 Memory search and rehearsal processes and the word length effect in immediate recall: a synthesis in reply to service. *Q. J. Exp. Psychol.* A **53**, 666–670.

Craik, F. I. M. & Lockhart, R. S. 1972 Levels of processing: a framework for memory research. *J. Verbal Learn. Behav.* **11**, 671–684.

Gabrieli, J. D. E., Cohen, N. J. & Corkin, S. 1988 The impaired learning of semantic knowledge following bilateral medial temporal-lobe resection. *Brain Cogn.* **7**, 157–177.

Gardiner, J. M. 2001 Episodic memory and autonoetic consciousness: a first-person approach. *Phil. Trans. R. Soc. Lond.* B **356**, 1351–1361.

Hebb, D. O. 1949 *Organization of behavior*. New York: Wiley.

Hirst, W., Johnson, M. K., Kim, J. K., Phelps, E. A., Risse, G. & Volpe, B. T. 1986 Recognition and recall in amnesics. *J. Exp. Psychol.* **12**, 445–451.

Hodges, J. R. & Graham, K. S. 2001 Episodic memory: insights from semantic dementia. *Phil. Trans. R. Soc. Lond.* B **356**, 1423–1433.

Huppert, F. A. & Piercy, M. 1978 The role of trace strength in recency and frequency judgements by amnesic and control subjects. *Q. J. Exp. Psychol.* **30**, 246–254.

Jacoby, L. L. 1994 Measuring recollection: strategic versus automatic influences of associative context. In *Attention and performance XV: conscious and non-conscious processing* (ed. C. Umilta & M. Moscovitch), pp. 661–680. Cambridge, MA: MIT Press.

Jacoby, L., Toth, J. P. & Yonelinas, A. P. 1993 Separating conscious and unconscious influences of memory: measuring recollection. *J. Exp. Psychol. Gen.* **122**, 139–154.

James, W. 1890 *The principles of psychology*. New York: Holt, Rinehart & Winston.

Joordens, S. & Merikle, P. M. 1993 Independence or redundancy? Two more models of conscious and unconscious influences. *J. Exp. Psychol. Gen.* **122**, 462–467.

Kintsch, W. 1980 Semantic memory: a tutorial. In *Attention and performance VIII* (ed. R. S. Nickerson), pp. 595–620. Hillsdale, NJ: Lawrence Erlbaum Associates, Inc.

Kopelman, M. D. & Kapur, N. 2001 The loss of episodic memories in retrograde amnesia: single-case and group studies. *Phil. Trans. R. Soc. Lond.* B **356**, 1409–1421.

Kopelman, M. D., Wilson, B. A. & Baddeley, A. D. 1989 The autobiographical memory interview: a new assessment of autobiographical and personal semantic memory in amnesic patients. *J. Clin. Exp. Neuropsychol.* **11**, 724–744.

Landauer, T. K. & Freedman, J. L. 1968 Information retrieval from long-term memory: category size and recognition time. *J. Verbal Learn. Behav.* **7**, 291–295.

Luria, A. R. 1959a The directive function of speech in development and disillusion. Part I. *Word* **15**, 341–352.

Luria, A. R. 1959b The directive function of speech in development and disillusion. Part II. *Word* **15**, 453–464.

Maguire, E. A. 2001 Neuroimaging studies of autobiographical event memory. *Phil. Trans. R. Soc. Lond.* B **356**, 1441–1451.

Mandler, G. 1980 Recognising: the judgement of previous occurrence. *Psychol. Rev.* **87**, 252–271.

Manns, J. R. & Squire, L. R. 1999 Impaired recognition memory on the Doors and People test after damage limited to the hippocampal region. *Hippocampus* **9**, 495–499.

Mayes, A. R. & Roberts, N. 2001 Theories of episodic memory. *Phil. Trans. R. Soc. Lond.* B **356**, 1395–1408.

Melton, A. W. 1963 Implications of short-term memory for a general theory of memory. *J. Verbal Learn. Behav.* **2**, 1–21.

Milner, B. 1966 Amnesia following operation on the temporal lobes. In *Amnesia* (ed. C. W. M. Whitty & O. L. Zangwill), pp. 109–133. London: Butterworths.

Morris, R. G. M. 2001 Episodic-like memory in animals: psychological criteria, neural mechanisms and the value of episodic-like tasks to investigate animal models of neurodegenerative disease. *Phil. Trans. R. Soc. Lond.* B **356**, 1453–1465.

Parkin, A. J. 1992 The functional significance of etiological factors in human amnesia. In *The neuropsychology of memory* (ed. L. R. Squire & N. Butters), pp. 122–129. New York: Guilford Press.

Peterson, L. R. & Peterson, M. J. 1959 Short-term retention of individual verbal items. *J. Exp. Psychol.* **58**, 193–198.

Reed, J. M. & Squire, L. R. 1997 Impaired recognition memory in patients with lesions limited to the hippocampal formation. *Behav. Neurosci.* **111**, 667–675.

Schacter, D. L. & Dodson, C. S. 2001 Misattribution, false recognition and the sins of memory. *Phil. Trans. R. Soc. Lond.* B **356**, 1385–1393.

Service, E. 1998 The effect of word length on immediate serial recall depends on phonological complexity, not articulatory duration. *Q. J. Exp. Psychol.* A **51**, 283–304.

Shallice, T. 1988 *From neuropsychology to mental structure*. Cambridge University Press.

Shallice, T. & Warrington, E. K. 1970 Independent functioning of verbal memory stores: a neuropsychological study. *Q. J. Exp. Psychol.* **22**, 261–273.

Snowden, J. S., Goulding, P. J. & Neary, D. 1989 Semantic dementia: a form of circumscribed cerebral atrophy. *Behav. Neurol.* **2**, 167–182.

Squire, L. R. 1992 Declarative and non-declarative memory: multiple brain systems supporting learning and memory. *J. Cogn. Neurosci.* **4**, 232–243.

Squire, L. R., Knowlton, B. & Musen, G. 1993 The structure and organisation of memory. *A. Rev. Psychol.* **44**, 453–495.

Tulving, E. 1985 Memory and consciousness. *Can. Psychol.* **26**, 1–12.

Tulving, E. 1998 Neurocognitive processes of human memory. In *Basic mechanisms in cognition and language* (ed. C. von Euler, I. Lundberg & R. Llinas), pp. 261–281. Amsterdam: Elsevier.

Tulving, E. 2001 Episodic memory and common sense: how far apart? *Phil. Trans. R. Soc. Lond.* B **356**, 1505–1515.

Tulving, E. & Donaldson, W. 1972 *Organization of memory*. New York: Academic Press.

Vallar, G. & Shallice, T. 1990 The impairment of auditory-verbal short-term storage. In *Neuropsychological impairments of short-term memory* (ed. G. Vallar & T. Shallice), pp. 11–53. Cambridge University Press.

Vargha-Khadem, F., Gadian, D. & Mishkin, M. 2001 Dissociations in cognitive memory: the syndrome of developmental amnesia. *Phil. Trans. R. Soc. Lond.* B **356**, 1435–1440.

Vygotsky, L. S. 1962 *Thought and language*. Cambridge, MA: MIT Press.

Warrington, E. K. & McCarthy, R. 1987 Categories of knowledge: further fractionation and an attempted integration. *Brain* **110**, 1273–1296.

Warrington, E. K. & Weiskrantz, L. 1968 New methods of testing long-term retention with special reference to amnesic patients. *Nature* **217**, 972–974.

Wilson, B. A. & Baddeley, A. D. 1988 Semantic, episodic and autobiographical memory in a post-meningitic amnesic patient. *Brain Cogn.* **8**, 31–46.

Yonelinas, A. P. 2001 Components of episodic memory: the contribution of recollection and familiarity. *Phil. Trans. R. Soc. Lond.* B **356**, 1363–1374.

2

Episodic memory and autonoetic consciousness: a first-person approach

John M. Gardiner

Episodic memory is identified with autonoetic consciousness, which gives rise to remembering in the sense of self-recollection in the mental re-enactment of previous events at which one was present. Autonoetic consciousness is distinguished from noetic consciousness, which gives rise to awareness of the past that is limited to feelings of familiarity or knowing. Noetic consciousness is identified not with episodic but with semantic memory, which involves general knowledge. A recently developed approach to episodic memory makes use of 'first-person' reports of remembering and knowing. Studies using this approach have revealed many independent variables that selectively affect remembering and others that selectively affect knowing. These studies can also be interpreted in terms of distinctiveness and fluency of processing. Remembering and knowing do not correspond with degrees of confidence in memory. Nor does remembering always control the memory response. There is evidence that remembering is selectively impaired in various populations, including not only amnesic patients and older adults but also adults with Asperger's syndrome. This first-person approach to episodic memory represents one way in which that most elusive aspect of consciousness, its subjectivity, can be investigated scientifically. The two kinds of conscious experiences can be manipulated experimentally in ways that are systematic, replicable and intelligible theoretically.

2.1. New concepts and a first-person approach

It is almost thirty years since Endel Tulving introduced the concept of episodic memory and contrasted it with semantic memory (Tulving 1972). Episodic memory corresponded roughly with autobiographical memory, i.e. with memory for personally experienced events, remembered as such. Semantic memory corresponded roughly with knowledge of the world, without any autobiographical context. Thus, I can well remember the last time I visited Paris, and having a particularly self-indulgent dinner at a famous brasserie on the left bank. But if asked what is the capital of France, I may simply say 'Paris' without experiencing any personal recollections of the many times I know I have been there. Memory for the dinner is episodic. Knowledge that Paris is the capital of France is semantic, as is knowledge that I have visited Paris many times in the past.

In introducing this distinction, Tulving (1972) was making the point that up until that time the experimental study of memory had been essentially confined to the study of episodic memory. Standard laboratory tasks involved presenting lists of verbal materials and then asking subjects to recall or to recognize the materials to which they had been exposed. This does not test knowledge of the materials but memory for their occurrence in a particular personal context: that of the experiment. Thus, initially, the concept of episodic memory was closely identified with certain kinds of memory tasks, in contrast with other tasks that were being introduced at that time which involved tests of general knowledge.

In *Elements of episodic memory*, Tulving (1983) introduced new concepts of episodic and semantic memory. Instead of being defined in terms of a distinction between memory tasks, these new concepts were defined in terms of memory systems. The proposal was that episodic and semantic memory corresponded with functionally distinct, though overlapping, mind–brain systems. Moreover, Tulving suggested that a defining property of these mind–brain systems was the phenomenal subjective experience that accompanied retrieval from them. He proposed a distinction between two kinds of consciousness, which he termed autonoetic (self-knowing) consciousness and noetic (knowing) consciousness. Autonoetic consciousness is a defining property of episodic memory. It is expressed in experiences of mental time travel, as in the mental reinstatement of personal experiences of previous events at which one was present. Noetic consciousness is expressed without any such self-recollection but simply in awareness of familiarity, of knowing. In a clear departure from previous usage and from common parlance, Tulving used the term 'remembering' to refer to expressions of autonoetic consciousness and the term 'knowing' to refer to expressions of noetic awareness. Thus, in what follows, the words 'remember' (or 'remembering') and 'know' (or 'knowing') are used in this restricted, technical sense to refer to the two subjective states of awareness. Used in this sense, I remember that particular dinner, but I know that Paris is the capital of France and that I have been there many times.

A year or two later, Tulving (1985) showed that subjects could readily understand the distinction between the two kinds of awareness and could report them, using remember and know responses. For example, he asked subjects to study a list of words which were then re-presented for a recognition test, randomly mixed with other unstudied words. For each test word, subjects first made a 'Yes or No' decision about whether it had appeared in the study list. If the decision was 'Yes', then subjects additionally responded with 'remember' or with 'know'. A remember response meant that they could consciously recollect something they experienced at the time that word was studied. A know response meant that they could not do that, but recognized the word 'on some other basis' (see Tulving 1985, p. 8). In most subsequent research using this paradigm, that 'other basis' has been defined more specifically. For example, subjects are often instructed that for a know response they must be confident that the test word was in the study list because it gives rise to strong feelings of familiarity in the experimental context (see Gardiner & Richardson-Klavehn 2000). This definition of knowing emphasizes feelings of familiarity that are associated with a recent but unremembered occurrence, as distinct from 'just knowing' in the sense that one just knows that Paris is the capital of France. Though this phenomenological difference is not unimportant, knowing in each sense is an expression of noetic rather than autonoetic consciousness (see Conway *et al.* 1997; Gardiner & Conway 1999).

From a conventional point of view, recognition decisions are objective (third-person), and remember–know judgements are subjective (first-person). On this view, these two successive stages in the remember–know paradigm cross the boundary between data that are open to science and data that are not. But I think this view is mistaken not only in the light of all the evidence, as I shall shortly illustrate, but even in principle. The objective accuracy of remember and know judgements can be just as readily checked as can the accuracy of the recognition decisions into which they summate. Moreover, it is possible to check that remember and know judgements have been made in a valid way by asking subjects to describe the bases of those judgements, after they have been made.

Gardiner *et al.* (1998) described a database of descriptions of remember and know judgements elicited after the recognition test had been completed. Two such remember and know judgements were randomly selected for each of the forty-eight subjects in the experiment. The descriptions provided for remember responses always included specific contextual details connected with the study-list presentation of the test word. Examples included, for the word 'president', 'Yesterday I associated this word with the word "minister". Today I automatically remembered that association', and, for the word 'harp', 'On Friday I was in a restaurant with a harpist. I remember thinking of that yesterday.' In contrast, descriptions of know responses never included such detailed contextual information. Examples included, for the word 'gun', 'I just know that I knew it' and, for the word 'butterfly', 'It was just one of those words that rang a bell'. Such post-test checks are useful in supporting the inference that subjects are using remember and know responses according to instructions. Converging evidence for the validity of remember and know responses has also been provided by studies of 'source memory', e.g. by showing that subjects are able to judge with some accuracy presentation details such as relative position or spatial location for items they claim to remember but not for items they claim to know (see Perfect *et al.* 1996; see also Mather *et al.* 1997).

In the fifteen years or so since Tulving's (1985) initial demonstration that subjects could use remember and know responses to report autonoetic and noetic awareness of memory, a great many studies have made use of the remember–know paradigm, especially in recognition memory tasks. These studies have been directed at a number of questions. The most general question concerns the extent to which remembering and knowing can be dissociated by different independent variables. More specific theoretical issues include the extent to which alternative processing frameworks can account for the evidence, the relation between remembering, knowing, and confidence or trace strength, and the relation between remembering, knowing and conscious control of the memory task. There is also the question of how remembering and knowing might differ in different populations. The remainder of this review provides illustrative evidence relating to each of these issues.

2.2. Some general effects of independent variables

Illustrated in Table 2.1 are results from four different experiments. The first column of data shows the overall proportions of correct recognition scores, which are then partitioned between proportions of correct remember and know responses in the second and third columns. The experiments have been chosen to illustrate four possible kinds of relationship between remembering and knowing. Error data are not shown but do not affect these relationships. The first experiment is a level-of-processing experiment (Gardiner *et al.* 1996, experiment 1). In the semantic condition, when each studied word was presented, subjects had to produce a meaningful associate of the word. In the graphemic condition, when each studied word was presented subjects had to produce any two letters not present in the word. This difference in level of processing had a very

Table 2.1. Examples of functional relations between remembering and knowing in recognition memory.

(Proportions of correct responses only.)

variable	condition	overall	remember	know
level of processing	semantic	0.90	0.72	0.18
	graphemic	0.35	0.15	0.20
study/test modalities	visual/visual	0.63	0.11	0.52
	visual/auditory	0.37	0.10	0.27
materials	words	0.44	0.28	0.16
	non-words	0.49	0.19	0.30
study trials	three	0.69	0.37	0.32
	one	0.35	0.14	0.21

large effect on correct recognition performance and this effect occurred in remembering, not in knowing.

In the conditions shown from the next experiment, study/test modality was manipulated (Gregg & Gardiner 1994, experiment 2). Subjects either studied words presented visually and then the words were presented visually in the recognition test, in an identical format, or subjects studied words presented visually and then the words were presented auditorially in the recognition test. Following normal study conditions, recognition performance is not usually much affected by this same versus different study/test modality manipulation, as indeed we showed in other conditions in this experiment. But the data shown here were from unusual study conditions that had a perceptual focus and were intended to prevent more meaningful, elaborative encoding. The words were presented very rapidly and subjects were led to believe that the experiment was concerned with visual perception, not with memory. They were told to count the number of words in the list in which some of the letters were blurred and to report this number at the end of the list. It was emphasized that they did not have to remember the actual words, only keep track of the number. In fact, none of the words had any blurred letters in them, as subjects duly reported. Following these unusual study conditions there was quite a large effect of same versus different study/test modality. This effect, however, occurred in knowing, not in remembering.

The third experiment was one in which subjects studied a mixed list of words and pseudo-words, or non-words, under usual learning conditions (Gardiner & Java 1990, experiment 2). The words and non-words were all one syllable long and pronounceable, though they were presented visually. Here, there was very little effect of the manipulation on overall recognition performance. But the manipulation did have quite a strong effect on the reported states of awareness. Words gave rise to more remembering than knowing. Non-words gave rise to more knowing than remembering.

The last experiment was one in which subjects heard melodies taken from English or from Polish folk songs presented vocally, as single line melodies, without words (Gardiner & Radomski 1999). The subjects themselves were either English or Polish and they were very familiar with the melodies from folk songs in their own culture. The melodies from the other culture were foreign to them and sounded not merely novel but rather strange. Both English and Polish subjects heard both English and Polish melodies either presented once or three times in succession before the recognition test. The scores in Table 2.1 show the effect of study trials for the melodies that were strange to the subjects, the Polish songs for the English folk, and the English songs for the Polish folk. Three study trials, compared with one, increased overall recognition substantially. But here the effect occurs not only in remembering but also in knowing. Interestingly, this parallel effect of increased study trials on remembering and knowing occurred only with the strange melodies. Additional study trials with subjects' own folk songs increased remembering but did not increase knowing.

Thus some independent variables affect remembering but not knowing. Other independent variables affect knowing and not remembering. Still others affect remembering and knowing in opposite ways and some affect remembering and knowing in parallel ways. Functionally, then, these two subjective states of awareness are independent in the sense that they are susceptible to this pattern of experimental manipulation.

In Tulving's (1983, 1985) theory, events have first to be registered in the semantic system before they can be registered in the episodic system; they can be stored in parallel in both systems and retrieval from both systems is independent (see Tulving 1995). If remembering and knowing, respectively, reflect retrieval from episodic and semantic systems this evidence clearly implies that both systems contribute to recognition memory. Just as certain autobiographical facts are known as such—I know I have visited Paris many times without any remembrance of a particular visit— so too can study list events be known to have occurred without any remembrance of them. Indeed, under certain conditions, such as those in the experiment by Gregg & Gardiner (1994), recognition memory may largely reflect the semantic rather than the episodic system. Presumably, the unusual study conditions in that experiment were sufficient to allow encoding into the semantic system but largely precluded encoding into the episodic system. Encoding into the episodic system seems to depend on the more conscious elaboration of meaning, as is also suggested by the other findings illustrated in Table 2.1.

These findings did not, of course, stem from any strong tests of that hypothesis or, more broadly, even of the interpretation of them provided by the distinction between episodic and semantic memory. Rather, this interpretation is supported by other kinds of converging evidence, which includes evidence from amnesic patients (for a discussion of some of this evidence, see Mishkin *et al.* 1998; Squire & Zola 1998; Tulving & Markowitsch 1998). It also includes evidence from recent studies of patterns of brain activity. This evidence points clearly to both temporal and spatial differences in activations associated, respectively, with remembering and knowing (e.g. Curran 2000; Düzel *et al.* 1997; Eldridge *et al.* 2000; Henson *et al.* 1999).

2.3. An alternative processing framework

At a cognitive–behavioural level, an alternative processing account of remembering and knowing has been developed by Suparna Rajaram (Rajaram 1993, 1996). This approach is complementary to the systems approach; it does not contradict it. Nor has research been much concerned in contrasting the two approaches within any given experiments. Rather, this processing account provides another framework for integrating the various findings, one that has the advantage of allowing quite specific predictions about the conditions that are likely to influence the two states of awareness.

The initial proposal (Rajaram 1993) was that the two states of awareness mapped onto a distinction between conceptual processing and perceptual processing (see e.g. Roediger *et al.* 1989). Early evidence did seem to support this possibility. Conceptual variables like level of processing were found to influence remembering. Perceptual variables like same versus different study/test modality were found to influence knowing. More recently, however, a number of studies have shown that there are perceptual variables that influence remembering (e.g. Rajaram 1996) and conceptual variables that influence knowing (e.g. Mantyla 1997). The relationship between the process distinction and the states of awareness therefore now seems to be more of an orthogonal one. Rajaram (1996) revised this processing account and proposed instead that remembering depends largely on the distinctiveness of the processing, which could be more or less distinctive, either conceptually or perceptually, and that knowing depends largely on processing fluency, which could be more or less fluent, either perceptually or conceptually. By this account, a deeper level of processing leads not only to more conceptual encoding but also to more distinctive encoding. Such distinctive encoding is more difficult to achieve in the unusual study conditions used by Gregg & Gardiner (1994), or for non-words compared with words, or for melodies from a foreign musical culture. Following those sorts of conditions the study list encounter is more likely to increase the fluency with which studied items are perceived in the test, and hence affect knowing rather than remembering.

One of the findings that led to the distinctiveness–fluency framework had to do with recognition memory for pictorial materials, specifically for line drawings of familiar everyday objects (Snodgrass & Vandervart 1980). Picture recognition memory is affected by size congruence at study and at test. If there are larger and smaller versions of the same picture, then presenting the picture in the same size at study and test leads to higher recognition than presenting the picture in different sizes at study and test. Rajaram (1996) found that this perceptual manipulation of size congruence occurred in remembering but not in knowing. Presumably, the distinctiveness of picture encoding is likely to be more fully reinstated at test when the picture at test is the same size as the picture at study.

An orthogonal view of the relationship between the states of awareness and the kind of processing, however, suggests that if encoding conditions were impoverished, hence reducing the opportunity to achieve distinctive encoding, then the same effect might influence processing fluency. If so, the effect might then occur partially, or even wholly, in knowing (compare with Gregg & Gardiner 1994).

We investigated this possibility in an experiment that replicated Rajaram's (1996) experiment but used photographs of faces rather than pictures of everyday objects (Gardiner *et al.* 2001*a*, experiment 2). The faces were presented for study in one of two sizes, a larger or a smaller version. At test, half the faces were presented in the same larger or smaller size, and half in the alternate size. To manipulate encoding, subjects were given a level-of-processing task. For deeper processing, subjects had to rate the reliability of the person (1 = very reliable; 5 = very unreliable). For shallow processing, subjects had simply to report whether the face belonged to a female or to a male person. The results are shown in Table 2.2.

Table 2.2. Proportions of recognition responses as a function of level of processing and size congruence.

response category	reliability rating			gender assignment		
	same size	different size	unstudied	same size	different size	unstudied
overall	0.76	0.53	0.10	0.43	0.23	0.09
remember	0.54	0.33	0.04	0.12	0.10	0.04
know	0.22	0.20	0.06	0.31	0.13	0.05

The overall scores are shown in the first row of the table. These scores show clear effects of level of processing and of size congruence. Recognition was higher following reliability ratings and it was higher when the faces were presented in the same size at study and at test. Reports of the states of awareness, however, reveal a more complex pattern. Following the reliability ratings, the effects of size congruence occurred in remembering which replicates the results found by Rajaram (1996). Following gender assignment, however, the effects of size congruence occurred in knowing, not in remembering. Thus, in keeping with the processing framework, similar effects may occur either in remembering or in knowing, depending on encoding conditions. If those conditions foster more distinctive processing, the effects are likely to occur in remembering. If those conditions largely preclude more distinctive processing, the effects are likely to occur in knowing.

Of course, these findings can also be accommodated within the systems framework. The effects of encoding conditions may influence the relative ease, or difficulty, of encoding events into the episodic system. Encoding into the episodic system may depend on the distinctiveness of the encoded event and the amount of attention paid to it.

This result has been replicated in another experiment on the size congruence effect (Gardiner et al. 2001a, experiment 1), but it is not known whether similar results might be found for other kinds of effect. They might be restricted to certain kinds of perceptual effects. In line with that possibility, Curran & Hildebrandt (1999) showed that remembering is greatly reduced by alcohol but that a level-of-processing effect did not as a result then appear in know responses. That result too suggests that the appearance of the size congruence effect in know responses was not simply due to the lower level of performance in the more impoverished encoding conditions, rather than due to the qualitative nature of the encoding. Nor have lower levels of performance been shown to lead to the appearance in knowing of other effects that have been found normally to occur in remembering (see e.g. Dewhurst & Anderson 1999; Gardiner & Radomski 1999). Further evidence on this problem is clearly desirable.

But, for now, the important point is that the size congruence effect itself, as distinct from its influence on subjective awareness, was quite unaffected by level of processing. And this is the first demonstration that, at least under some circumstances, exactly the same effect (rather than two different effects, such as those illustrated in Table 2.1) may occur independently either in remembering or in knowing.

2.4. Remembering, knowing and confidence

Remembering and knowing must clearly be related to confidence in memory. Indeed, Tulving (1985, p. 10) had suggested that 'the adaptive value of episodic memory and autonoetic consciousness lies in the heightened subjective certainty with which organisms endowed with such memory and consciousness believe, and are willing to act upon, information retrieved from memory.'

In contrast with the idea that it is subjective states of awareness that give rise to varying degrees of confidence in memory, it has also been suggested that the subjective states of awareness might be explained in terms of confidence (Donaldson 1996; see also Hirshman & Master 1997; Inoue & Bellezza 1998). On this view, remembering and knowing do not reflect different sources of memory, but different response criteria for the same memory trace. Remember responses reflect stricter response criteria; know responses reflect more lenient response criteria. Using these assumptions, it is possible that remembering and knowing could be accounted for by a signal detection model that provides separate estimates of the strength of the memory trace and of response criteria.

For example, Donaldson (1996) described a meta-analysis of some eighty different experimental conditions from remember–know studies and used this database for some critical tests of a detection model. A crucial prediction for this model is that the strength of the memory trace should be the same whether estimated from only remember responses (the strict criterion) or from remember-plus-know responses (the more lenient criterion, that is, overall yes–no recognition). In a re-analysis of Donaldson's (1996) database, Gardiner & Gregg (1997) showed that, though the differences were small, memory strength was consistently greater when estimated from know and remember responses than when estimated from only remember responses. Moreover, estimates of memory strength have been shown sometimes to be considerably higher when know responses are added to remember responses in individual experiments. This is the case in the conditions from the Gregg & Gardiner (1994) study in Table 2.1, and also in the conditions from the Gardiner *et al.* (2001*a*) study in Table 2.2 (for details, see Gardiner & Gregg 1997; Gardiner *et al.* 2001*a*). These tests of the model indicate that know responses do reflect an additional source of memory.

A number of studies that have directly compared results obtained from remember and know responses with results obtained from confidence judgements have found different patterns of results for the two kinds of responses (e.g. Gardiner & Java 1990; Parkin & Walter 1992; Rajaram 1993). These findings show that remember and know responses are not equivalent to confidence judgements. One example of this is shown in Table 2.3. The data here are for the words and non-words in the second experiment by Gardiner & Java (1990), together with data for the same words and non-words in a third experiment. This third experiment was identical to the second experiment in all respects except for the test instructions. Instead of being instructed for remember and know responses, subjects were instructed to give binary confidence judgements, 'sure' and 'unsure'. With these confidence judgements, the proportions of correct responses form quite a different pattern. In contrast with remember and know responses, sure and unsure judgements did not differ much between the words and the non-words. Notice too that the proportion of sure judgements for studied non-words was considerably higher than the proportion of remember responses.

Table 2.3. Proportions of recognition responses for words and nonwords as a function of response category.

response category	studied		unstudied	
	words	non-words	words	non-words
remember	0.28	0.19	0.04	0.03
know	0.16	0.30	0.11	0.12
sure	0.33	0.39	0.13	0.07
unsure	0.28	0.28	0.22	0.22

Compared with remember and know responses, sure and unsure judgements seem to have induced more lenient response criteria, as indicated by the relatively high proportions of unsure judgements to unstudied words and non-words. But similar kinds of outcomes would be observed for know responses if subjects elected to use know responses as if they were unsure confidence judgements instead of reports of noetic awareness. Subjects could use know responses in this more strategic way (Gardiner *et al.* 1997; Strack & Forster 1995). Indeed, noetic awareness could be completely obscured if know responses were used as if they were unsure confidence judgements and response criteria were very lenient and subjects responded 'yes' to many of the unstudied items.

Most remember–know studies have controlled for this by strongly emphasizing that know responses are not low confidence judgements and by discouraging guessing. In quite a few recent studies, another approach to this problem has been adopted. In addition to reporting remember and know responses, subjects are also instructed to report guesses. Guesses are defined as having some other reason to believe, or suspect, that a test item was encountered in the study list—some reason other than remembering or knowing. Such reasons might include strategies based on memory for the proportions of studied to unstudied items in the test, or on memory for a particular category of items that was studied, such as names of musical instruments, rather than for the particular instances from that category that were presented.

Following Donaldson (1996), we have recently put together another database of some eighty-six different experimental conditions from remember–know studies (Gardiner *et al.* 2001*b*). All of these conditions included guess responses, as well as remember and know responses. None of these conditions appeared in Donaldson's (1996) database; no condition in his database included guess responses. Thus our database is completely independent of his. Also, in our database we replicated the finding that memory strength was significantly greater when estimated from know and remember responses than when estimated from only remember responses. In addition, in our database, when guess responses were added to remember and know responses, the estimated strength of memory slightly but significantly decreased.

The reason for this is shown in Figure 2.1, where, following Donaldson (1996), the strength of the memory trace is estimated by the A′ values plotted against the vertical axis. These A′ values were here estimated separately (not cumulatively) for remember

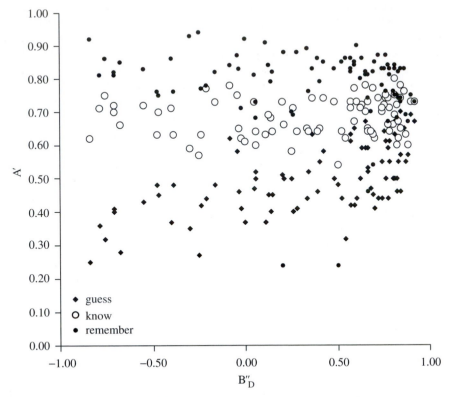

Fig. 2.1. Separate A' estimates of memory from remember, know and guess responses as a function of overall recognition response criteria, B''_D.

responses, for know responses and for guess responses. They indicate the extent to which each of the different kinds of responses, taken alone, reflects memory for the studied lists. An A' estimate of 1.0 represents perfect memory; 0.5 represents chance. Along the horizontal axis, these A' estimates are shown as a function of overall yes–no recognition response criteria, moving from the most strict response criteria on the right to the most liberal response criteria on the left.

Note that not only A' estimates for remember responses but also A' estimates for know responses were consistently and appreciably above chance. Also, neither remember nor know responses were correlated with yes–no recognition response criteria. Guess responses, however, on average did not differ from chance and they fell away to well below chance as response criteria become more lenient. They did so because as yes–no response criteria become more lenient, there tended to be more guesses for unstudied than for studied items. Thus, there was a significant positive correlation between yes–no response criteria and guessing. Donaldson (1996) predicted, and found, just such a correlation between yes–no response criteria and knowing in his database. We found no such correlation for knowing, but instead found the correlation in guessing. The implication is that the correlation in Donaldson's (1996) database did not reflect noetic awareness, but guessing. Thus, our results provide further evidence that the detection model does not fit remembering and knowing.

There are other difficulties in an approach of this kind. These include its lack of explanatory value and the question of whether such an approach to trying to understand the subjective states of awareness measured by remember and know responses is even appropriate methodologically. It is hard to see much explanatory value in the concept of trace strength, or how an approach based on this concept could accommodate the evidence from amnesic patients and from studies of brain activation. Also, as Tulving (1985) suggested, it is surely the subjective state of awareness that gives rise to confidence in memory, not confidence that gives rise to the state of awareness. Methodologically, tests of the detection model require response criteria to be manipulated, but manipulating response criteria risks invalidating remember and know responses as measures of autonoetic and noetic awareness. The main point made here, however, is that even if it is accepted at face value, without taking such broader considerations into account, this trace strength model does not fit the data, except under exceptional circumstances (for more discussion, see Gardiner 2000; Gardiner & Conway 1999; Gardiner *et al.* 2001*a*).

There is a final cautionary note. Although some studies have shown dissociations between remember and know responses and confidence judgements (e.g. Gardiner & Java 1990), some other studies have found evidence of convergence between these two kinds of data (e.g. Yonelinas *et al.* 1998). It is possible that evidence of such convergence may simply mean that remember and know responses (particularly know responses) are being used as confidence judgements.

2.5. Remembering, knowing and conscious control

In another approach to recognition memory, strong assumptions are made about the relation between subjective states of awareness and conscious control. This is a dual-process model that distinguishes between two independent processes: recollection and familiarity (e.g. Jacoby 1991; Mandler 1980). It is additionally assumed that recollection is a relatively slow, effortful process, depending on conscious control, and that familiarity is a relatively fast, automatic process, not dependent upon conscious control. And the processes of recollection and familiarity have also been assumed to give rise to the corresponding subjective states of awareness, as measured by remember and know responses (see e.g. Jacoby *et al.* 1997).

A useful way of at least partially separating the relative contributions of recollection and familiarity to recognition memory is provided by a response deadline procedure in which subjects are trained to respond rapidly to each test item after either a short or a long response deadline. For example, Toth (1996) trained subjects to respond at one of two response deadlines. The shorter deadline was 500 ms after the presentation of the test item. The longer deadline was 1500 ms after the presentation of the test item. On the given signal to respond, subjects then had to make their yes–no recognition decision within 400 ms. The training phase involved a lexical decision task unrelated to the recognition memory experiment and it was interpolated between the presentation of the study list and the recognition test.

The argument is that at the shorter response deadline recognition will depend largely on the faster, more automatic, familiarity process. With the longer response deadline, recognition will depend more on the slower, more effortful, recollection process. Using this procedure, Toth (1996) found that at the shorter but not at the longer response deadline, there was an effect of same-versus-different study-test modalities, rather like the effect found by Gregg & Gardiner (1994) shown in Table 2.1. This sensitivity of the speeded recognition decisions to perceptual match at study and test supports the argument that they largely reflected the familiarity process. Toth (1996) also found that there were level-of-processing effects at the shorter, as well as at the longer, response deadlines. That level-of-processing effects occurred at both deadlines suggests that familiarity, as well as recollection, is influenced by conceptual processing.

In contrast with the assumed effects of level of processing on the familiarity process, level-of-processing effects have not generally been found in know responses (see Table 2.1). Toth's (1996) findings raised the question of whether level-of-processing effects might be found in know responses at shorter response deadlines. More generally, they raised the question of how shorter and longer response deadlines relate to remembering and knowing. For example, one might expect that know responses should predominate at the shorter deadline and remember responses should predominate at the longer deadline. Similarly, one might expect that remember but not know responses should increase considerably with the longer deadline.

Table 2.4 summarizes the results from an experiment designed to test these predictions (Gardiner et al. 1999, experiment 1). The semantic study task was to rate the ease of generating an associate of each studied word. The phonemic study task was to rate the ease of generating a rhyme for each studied word. Replicating the results obtained by Toth (1996), the overall recognition results show that there were level-of-processing effects at both the shorter and the longer response deadlines. However, these level-of-processing effects occurred only in remember responses, even at the shorter deadline. Know responses did not show any level-of-processing effects, nor did they predominate at the shorter response deadline. In fact, both know and remember responses increased at the longer compared with the shorter deadline. As Table 2.4 shows, there were also guess responses in this experiment, though guessing was discouraged in the test instructions in order to avoid any speed–accuracy trade-off. (False alarm rates were similar at each response deadline.) There was also little difference between the proportions of guess responses to unstudied and studied words.

Table 2.4. Proportions of recognition responses as a function of level of processing and response deadline.

response category for each delay (ms)	studied				unstudied	
	semantic		phonemic			
	500	1500	500	1500	500	1500
overall	0.56	0.77	0.48	0.59	0.12	0.13
remember	0.43	0.59	0.28	0.32	0.01	0.02
know	0.09	0.15	0.10	0.21	0.05	0.07
guess	0.04	0.03	0.10	0.06	0.06	0.04

Because the two processes of recollection and familiarity are assumed to be independent, the raw proportions of know responses underestimate the familiarity process. In an 'independence remember–know' model (see e.g. Jacoby *et al.* 1997), the recollection process is estimated by the proportions of correct remember responses (there are usually extremely few incorrect remember responses). However, the familiarity process is given by dividing the proportion of correct know responses by 1 minus the proportion of correct remember responses. Applying this model to the data in Table 2.4 gives familiarity estimates of 0.16 and 0.14 for the semantic and phonemic conditions at the shorter response deadline. For the longer response deadline, the corresponding familiarity estimates are 0.37 and 0.31. Thus, even with this independence remember–know model, familiarity estimates do not show level-of-processing effects at the shorter deadline, nor do they indicate that recognition at the shorter deadline largely reflects the familiarity process.

These findings, among others (for more discussion see Gardiner 2000; Gardiner & Richardson-Klavehn 2000; Richardson-Klavehn *et al.* 1996), support the conclusion that remembering and knowing do not correspond with recollection and familiarity processes as conceived in this dual-process model. Granted that the longer response deadline allows more conscious control, it then seems that knowing, as well as remembering, increases with conscious control. Conversely, granted that the shorter response deadline allows less conscious control, it then seems that remembering, as well as knowing, can occur in a relatively automatic way.

There are situations other than speeded recognition in which remembering does not seem to control the memory response. For example, there is evidence, both at a behavioural level and at the level of brain activity, of dissociations between retrieval volition and memorial awareness, i.e. between whether or not subjects consciously intended to retrieve studied words and their awareness that some of the words retrieved were studied (e.g. Java 1994; Richardson-Klavehn & Gardiner 1996; Richardson-Klavehn *et al.* 2000). This evidence shows awareness of memory in incidental (or 'implicit') tests, such as word-stem completion, under circumstances in which it can be shown that there was no conscious intention to retrieve words from the study list, only to retrieve the first words brought to mind by the incidental retrieval instructions and test cues (for a review, see Gardiner *et al.* 2001c).

The general conclusion is that remembering should not be identified with conscious control in the way that it has been in some theoretical models.

2.6. Remembering and knowing in adults with Asperger's syndrome

There is considerable evidence that remembering and knowing differ systematically in certain special populations compared with the normal population. Most of this evidence relates to amnesic patients compared with matched controls and to older adults compared with younger adults. In both amnesia and in normal ageing, remembering is substantially reduced, if not, in some cases, essentially absent (see e.g. Tulving *et al.* 1991). In contrast, knowing has been found to remain relatively unimpaired in amnesia, with one or two exceptions (e.g. Knowlton & Squire 1995), and in old age.

There is also some evidence that a reduced capability for autonoetic consciousness is characteristic of some other problems that—unlike amnesia, or the effects of normal ageing—have not traditionally been thought of in connection with memory impairment. It has been discovered, for example, that schizophrenia is associated with a reduction in autonoetic awareness. Huron *et al.* (1995) found that schizophrenic patients showed impaired recognition memory in their remember responses but not in their know responses.

We have recently begun to investigate remembering and knowing in another population—adults with Asperger's syndrome (Bowler *et al.* 2000*b,c*). Asperger's syndrome is now regarded as part of a wider spectrum of autistic disorders. This syndrome includes problems common to the wider spectrum, such as problems in social communication, an inability to relate fully to others, and to understand fully what is required, or what is meant, in a given social situation. Its distinguishing characteristics are the lack of any evidence of impaired language function and the existence of intellectual abilities that fall within the normal range. Adults with Asperger's syndrome have also been observed to display remarkably good rote memories for highly specialized information, such as bus or train timetables.

There have been relatively few experimental studies of memory within the autistic spectrum and most of these have been of memory in children rather than in adults. For example, Boucher & Warrington (1976) found that, unlike matched controls, children with autism were unable to make much use of category relations among studied words (compared with unrelated words) to improve their recall. Bowler *et al.* (1997) replicated this finding in adults with Asperger's syndrome. There is also some evidence of poorer source monitoring in children with autism, in that they have been found to recall more words from previously studied lists, rather than from the currently studied list, than matched controls (Bennetto *et al.* 1996). However, Farrant *et al.* (1998) did not find evidence of poorer source monitoring when children with autism had to identify which of two experimenters had spoken the words from a study list.

In contrast with evidence of impaired free recall and source memory in individuals with autism, there is little evidence of significant memory impairment in cued recall and in recognition, at least in high-functioning individuals, including adults with Asperger's syndrome. For example, Bowler *et al.* (1997) found that both word-stem completion and word-stem cued recall were unimpaired in adults with Asperger's syndrome. And in two different experiments, Bowler *et al.* (2000*b,c*) found no significant impairments in recognition. The absence of any significant impairment in recognition, however, does not necessarily mean the absence of any impairment in autonoetic awareness. A decrease in remember responses can sometimes be offset by an increase in know responses (see e.g. Blaxton & Theodore 1997).

Table 2.5 summarizes some results from the experiment by Bowler *et al.* (2000*c*, experiment 2). The adults with Asperger's syndrome in this experiment were individually matched with subjects in a control group by age and verbal intelligence quotient (IQ). The average age of both these adults and those in a control group was about 27 (range 21–35), and their verbal IQ scores were on average about 87 (range 79–133). The experiment used a version of a converging-associates paradigm introduced by Deese (1959) and subsequently developed by Roediger & McDermott (1995). This paradigm has been widely used to study false recall and false recognition—'illusions' of memory for items that were not actually presented in the study list.

Table 2.5. Proportions of recognition responses for adults with Asperger's syndrome and for a matched control group.

item and response category	Asperger group (n = 10)	control group (n = 10)
true targets:		
overall	0.68	0.79
remember	0.51	0.72
know	0.17	0.07
false targets:		
overall	0.28	0.46
remember	0.27	0.43
know	0.01	0.03
non-target lures:		
overall	0.06	0.08
remember	0.01	0.03
know	0.05	0.05

In our experiment, subjects studied five sets of nine words. Each set consisted of the nine next most highly associated words for three other words that were not presented. For example, one set might be 'frigid, chilly, heat, weather, hot, air, shiver, arctic, frost' for the three non-presented associates 'winter, ice, wet'. Words within sets were blocked at study and each set was presented in succession. In the test, the words were randomly ordered and there were true and false targets. The true targets were three words that had been presented in each of the nine associated sets. The false targets were the three non-presented associates for each of the nine sets. Illusions of memory occur to the extent that subjects recognize the false targets. These illusions can be compelling— Roediger & McDermott (1995) showed that they tend to occur more in remember than in know responses.

Thus, the experiment was also designed to determine the extent to which adults with Asperger's syndrome are susceptible to illusions of memory. Other populations have been found to be differentially susceptible. For example, there is some evidence that amnesic patients are less susceptible to memory illusions (Schacter *et al.* 1996) but that adults become more susceptible to them with normal ageing (Schacter *et al.* 1997).

Remember and know responses were defined somewhat more abstractly in this experiment as 'type A' and 'type B' memories (see also Bowler *et al.* 2000*b*) and the subjects explained their remember and know responses after they made each recognition decision. This enabled the experimenter to monitor subjects' understanding and use of these responses online, throughout the test. There was no evidence from this monitoring procedure, or from the explanations given for remember and know responses, that the adults with Asperger's syndrome were using these responses any differently from subjects in the control group.

First, in Table 2.5, consider overall recognition of true targets, the associates that were actually presented. Recognition is somewhat lower in the adults with Asperger's syndrome, though not significantly so. However, they made significantly fewer remember responses, and more know responses, than did the matched control subjects, replicating results found by Bowler *et al.* (2000*b*). Consider next false recognition of those associates that were not presented. Both groups show quite high levels of false recognition, the control group more so than the adults with Asperger's syndrome, though that difference was not significant statistically either. And in contrast with veridical recognition, false recognition in each group was essentially restricted to remembering.

Additional signal detection analyses of these data, of the sort described earlier in this paper (§ 2.4), confirmed that overall A' estimates of memory strength, for both true and false targets, did not differ significantly between groups. They were, however, significantly higher for overall recognition (remember-plus-know responses) than for remember responses alone. Nor were there any between-group differences in the corresponding estimates of response criteria.

Some conclusions from this experiment are obviously qualified by the implications of the relatively small group sizes, which mean that failure to find significant differences must be accepted with caution. In contrast with our results, Beversdorf *et al.* (2000) found that high-functioning adults with autism (the distinction between the various forms of autism spectrum disorder was not clear in this group) showed significantly less false recognition in a similar converging associates paradigm. (They found no significant between-group differences in recognition of true targets.) However, in a free recall experiment Bowler *et al.* (2000*c*, experiment 1) also found no significant between-group differences in the false recall of non-presented associates, despite significantly lower recall of presented associates in the adults with Asperger's syndrome. Further evidence is needed to establish whether or not adults with Asperger's syndrome really might be less susceptible to memory illusions of this kind.

The evidence of reduced autonoetic awareness in adults with Asperger's syndrome does not suffer from this limitation. Thus the main conclusion is that there is indeed episodic memory impairment in adults with Asperger's syndrome. In terms of the distinctiveness–fluency framework, it seems that adults with Asperger's syndrome are less likely to encode items in an elaborative, distinctive way, and hence may be more likely to rely on processing fluency in recognition memory. We are currently evaluating some hypotheses as to the reasons for this impairment, including the possibility is that it may reflect attentional problems, both at encoding and at retrieval (Bowler *et al.* 2000*a*). More broadly, it may be that reduced autonoetic awareness in adults with Asperger's syndrome may have consequences for their self-awareness generally, and be related to their difficulties in goal-directed and social behaviour.

2.7. Conclusions

In this paper, I have illustrated a first-person approach to understanding episodic memory and consciousness, as exemplified by the remember–know paradigm. Episodic memory is identified with autonoetic awareness, measured by remember responses. Semantic memory is identified with noetic awareness, measured by know responses. Both memory systems may contribute to performance in episodic memory tasks. I have illustrated the approach by making five main points:

(i) Remembering is readily dissociable from knowing, particularly in recognition memory.
(ii) Remembering and knowing can also be interpreted within a distinctiveness or fluency of processing framework.
(iii) Remembering and knowing do not correspond with differences in confidence in memory or trace strength.
(iv) Nor does remembering correspond with conscious control of the memory task.
(v) Populations in which remembering is impaired include adults with Asperger's syndrome.

At a much broader theoretical level, it is necessary to abandon the old view of consciousness and memory that distinguished only between conscious and non-conscious forms of memory (for a review, see Toth 2000). Instead, there is a need for finer distinctions within consciousness, as evidenced by the distinction between remembering and knowing. There is also a need to distinguish between these different kinds of memorial awareness and consciousness in the sense of conscious control of the task. Remembering does not control the memory response either in speeded recognition or in some incidental tests of memory.

This approach also demonstrates one way in which the subjectivity of conscious experience, long thought to be intractable to science, can be tackled scientifically. Doing this depended on classifying conscious experiences into at least two different natural kinds, autonoetic and noetic, that could then be manipulated experimentally. It also depended on treating these natural kinds at the level of populations of experiences, not at the level of individual experiences, which are inevitably idiosyncratic. Other classifications of subjective conscious experiences of memory are undoubtedly possible and may even prove more useful, in the longer run, than this one. But they will have to retain these two essential features. And the ultimate fate, theoretically, of any such classification, including this one, will depend more on the convergence of three major sources of evidence—behaviour, mind and brain—than on any one or even any two such sources of evidence considered in isolation.

Supported by grants from the Economic and Social Research Council (ESRC) (in collaboration with Alan Richardson-Klavehn) and from the Wellcome Trust (in collaboration with Dermot Bowler).

References

Bennetto, L., Pennington, B. F. & Rogers, S. J. 1996 Intact and impaired memory function in autism. *Child Development* **67**, 1816–1835.

Beversdorf, D. Q. (and 10 others) 2000 Increased discrimination of 'false memories' in autism spectrum disorder. *Proc. Natl Acad. Sci. USA* **97**, 8734–8737.

Blaxton, T. A. & Theodore, W. H. 1997 The role of the temporal lobes in recognizing visuo-spatial materials: Remembering versus knowing. *Brain Cogn.* **35**, 5–25.

Boucher, J. & Warrington, E. 1976 Memory deficits in early infantile autism: Some similarities to the amnesic syndrome. *Br. J. Psychol.* **67**, 73–87.

Bowler, D. M., Matthews, N. J. & Gardiner, J. M. 1997 Asperger's syndrome and memory: Similarity to autism but not amnesia. *Neuropsychologia* **35**, 65–70.

Bowler, D. M., Gardiner, J. M. & Berthollier, N. 2000*a Source memory in high-functioning children with autism*. Annual Meeting of the Cognitive Neuroscience Society, San Francisco.

Bowler, D. M., Gardiner, J. M. & Grice, S. 2000*b* Episodic memory and remembering in adults with Asperger's syndrome. *J. Autism Dev. Disord.* **30**, 305–316.

Bowler, D. M., Gardiner, J. M., Grice, S. & Saavalainen, P. 2000*c* Memory illusions: False recall and recognition in adults with Asperger's syndrome. *J. Abnorm. Psychol.* **109**, 663–672.

Conway, M. A., Gardiner, J. M., Perfect, T. J., Anderson, S. J. & Cohen, G. M. 1997 Changes in memory awareness during learning: The acquisition of knowledge by psychology undergraduates. *J. Exp. Psychol. Gen.* **126**, 393–413.

Curran, H. V. & Hildebrandt, M. 1999 Dissociative effects of alcohol on recollective experience. *Conscious. Cogn.* **8**, 497–509.

Curran, T. 2000 Brain potentials of recollection and familiarity. *Mem. Cognit.* **28**, 923–938.

Deese, J. 1959 On the prediction of occurrence of particular verbal intrusions in immediate recall. *J. Exp. Psychol.* **58**, 17–22.

Dewhurst, S. A. & Anderson, S. J. 1999 Effects of exact and category repetition in true and false recognition memory. *Mem. Cognit.* **27**, 665–673.

Donaldson, W. 1996 The role of decision processes in remembering and knowing. *Mem. Cognit.* **24**, 523–533.

Düzel, E., Yonelinas, A. P., Mangun, G. R., Heinze, H.-J. & Tulving, E. 1997 Event-related brain potential correlates of two states of conscious awareness in memory. *Proc. Natl Acad. Sci. USA* **94**, 5973–5978.

Eldridge, L. L., Knowlton, B. J., Furmanski, C. S., Bookheimer, S. Y. & Engel, S. A. 2000 Remembering episodes: A selective role for the hippocampus during retrieval. *Nature Neurosci.* **3**, 1149–1152.

Farrant, A., Blades, M. & Boucher, J. 1998 Source monitoring in children with autism. *J. Autism Dev. Disord.* **28**, 43–50.

Gardiner, J. M. 2000 On the objectivity of subjective experiences of autonoetic and noetic consciousness. In *Memory, consciousness, and the brain: The Tallinn conference* (ed. E. Tulving), pp. 159–172. Philadelphia: Psychology Press.

Gardiner, J. M. & Conway, M. A. 1999 Levels of awareness and varieties of experience. In *Stratification of consciousness and cognition* (ed. B. H. Challis & B. M. Velichkovsy), pp. 237–254. Amsterdam/Philadelphia: John Benjamin Publishing Company.

Gardiner, J. M. & Gregg, V. H. 1997 Recognition memory with little or no remembering: Implications for a detection model. *Psychon. Bull. Rev.* **4**, 474–479.

Gardiner, J. M. & Java, R. I. 1990 Recollective experience in word and nonword recognition. *Mem. Cognit.* **18**, 23–30.

Gardiner, J. M. & Radomski, E. 1999 Awareness of recognition memory for Polish and English folk songs in Polish and English folk. *Memory* **7**, 461–470.

Gardiner, J. M. & Richardson-Klavehn, A. 2000 Remembering and knowing. In *Handbook of memory* (ed. E. Tulving & F. I. M. Craik), pp. 229–244. New York: Oxford University Press.

Gardiner, J. M., Java, R. I. & Richardson-Klavehn, A. 1996 How level of processing really influences awareness in recognition memory. *Can. J. Exp. Psychol.* **50**, 114–122.

Gardiner, J. M., Richardson-Klavehn, A. & Ramponi, C. 1997 On reporting recollective experiences and 'direct access to memory systems'. *Psychol. Sci.* **8**, 391–394.

Gardiner, J. M., Ramponi, C. & Richardson-Klavehn, A. 1998 Experiences of remembering, knowing, and guessing. *Conscious. Cogn.* **7**, 1–26.

Gardiner, J. M., Ramponi, C. & Richardson-Klavehn, A. 1999 Response deadline and subjective awareness in recognition memory. *Conscious. Cogn.* **8**, 484–496.

Gardiner, J. M., Gregg, V. H., Mashru, R. & Thaman, M. 2001*a* Impact of encoding depth on awareness of perceptual effects in recognition memory. *Mem. Cognit.* **29**, 433–440.

Gardiner, J. M., Ramponi, C. & Richardson-Klavehn, A. 2001*b* Recognition memory and decision processes: A meta-analysis of remember, know, and guess responses. *Memory* (In the press.)

Gardiner, J. M., Richardson-Klavehn, A., Ramponi, C. & Brooks, B. M. 2001*c* Involuntary level-of-processing effects in perceptual and conceptual priming. In *Perspectives on human memory and cognitive aging: Essays in honour of Fergus Craik* (ed. M. Naveh-Benjamin, M. Moscovitch & H. L. Roediger). Philadelphia: Psychology Press. (In the press.)

Gregg, V. H. & Gardiner, J. M. 1994 Recognition memory and awareness: A large effect of study-test modalities on 'know' responses following a highly perceptual orienting task. *Eur. J. Cogn. Psychol.* **6**, 137–147.

Henson, R. N. A., Rugg, M. D., Shallice, T., Josephs, O. & Dolan, R. J. 1999 Recollection and familiarity in recognition memory: An event-related functional magnetic resonance imaging study. *J. Neurosci.* **19**, 3962–3972.

Hirshman, E. & Master, S. 1997 Modeling the conscious correlates of recognition memory: Reflections on the remember-know paradigm. *Mem. Cognit.* **25**, 345–351.

Huron, C., Danion, J.-M., Giacomoni, F., Grange, D., Robert, P. & Rizzo, L. 1995 Impairment of recognition memory with, but not without, conscious recollection in schizophrenia. *Am. J. Psychiatry* **152**, 1737–1742.

Inoue, C. & Bellezza, F. S. 1998 The detection model of recognition using know and remember judgements. *Mem. Cognit.* **26**, 299–308.

Jacoby, L. L. 1991 A process-dissociation framework: separating automatic from intentional uses of memory. *J. Mem. Language*, **30**, 513–541.

Jacoby, L. L., Yonelinas, A. P. & Jennings, J. M. 1997 The relation between conscious and unconscious (automatic) influences: A declaration of independence. In *Scientific approaches to the question of consciousness* (ed. J. D. Cohen & J. W. Schooler), pp. 13–47. Hillsdale, New Jersey: Lawrence Erlbaum Associates.

Java, R. I. 1994 States of awareness following word stem completion. *Eur. J. Cogn. Psychol.* **6**, 77–92.

Knowlton, B. J. & Squire, L. L. 1995 Remembering and knowing: Two different expressions of declarative memory. *J. Exp. Psychol. Learn. Mem. Cogn.* **21**, 699–710.

Mandler, G. 1980 Recognizing: the judgement of previous occurrence. *Psychol. Rev.* **87**, 252–271.

Mantyla, T. 1997 Recollections of faces: Remembering differences and knowing similarities. *J. Exp. Psychol. Learn. Mem. Cogn.* **23**, 1203–1216.

Mather, M., Henkel, L. A. & Johnson, M. K. 1997 Evaluating characteristics of false memories: Remember/know judgements and memory characteristics compared. *Mem. Cogn.* **25**, 826–837.

Mishkin, M., Vargha-Khadem, F. & Gadian, D. G. 1998 Amnesia and the organisation of the hippocampal system. *Hippocampus* **8**, 212–216.

Parkin, A. J. & Walter, B. 1992 Recollective experience, normal aging, and frontal dysfunction. *Psychol. Aging* **7**, 290–298.

Perfect, T. J., Mayes, A. R., Downes, J. J. & Van Eijk, R. 1996 Does context discriminate recollection from familiarity in recognition memory? *Q. J. of Exp. Psychol.* A **49**, 797–813.

Rajaram, S. 1993 Remembering and knowing: Two means of access to the personal past. *Mem. Cogn.* **21**, 89–102.

Rajaram, S. 1996 Perceptual effects on remembering: Recollective processes in picture recognition memory. *J. Exp. Psychol. Learn. Mem. Cogn.* **22**, 365–377.

Richardson-Klavehn, A. & Gardiner, J. M. 1996 Cross-modality priming in stem completion reflects conscious memory, but not voluntary memory. *Psychon. Bull. Rev.* **3**, 238–244.

Richardson-Klavehn, A., Gardiner, J. M. & Java, R. I. 1996 Memory: Task dissociations, process dissociations, and dissociations of consciousness. In *Implicit cognition* (ed. G. Underwood), pp. 85–158. Oxford University Press.

Richardson-Klavehn, A., Düzel, E., Schott, B., Heinrich, J., Hagner, T., Gardiner, J. M. & Heinze, H.-J. 2000 *Electromagnetic brain activity during incidental and intentional retrieval shows dissociation of retrieval mode from retrieval success.* Annual Meeting of the Cognitive Neuroscience Society, San Francisco, USA.

Roediger, H. L. & McDermott, K. B. 1995 Creating false memories: Remembering words not presented in lists. *J. Exp. Psychol. Learn. Mem. Cogn.* **21**, 803–814.

Roediger, H. L., Weldon, M. S. & Challis, B. H. 1989 Explaining dissociations between implicit and explicit measures of retention: A processing account. In *Varieties of memory and consciousness: Essays in Honour of Endel Tulving* (ed. H. L. Roediger & F. I. M. Craik), pp. 3–41. Hillsdale, New Jersey: Lawrence Erlbaum Associates.

Schacter, D. L., Verfaellie, M. & Praedere, D. 1996 The neuropsychology of memory illusions: false recall and recognition in amnesic patients. *J. Mem. Language* **35**, 319–334.

Schacter, D. L., Koutstaal, W., Johnson, M. K., Gross, M. S. & Angell, K. E. 1997 False recollection induced by photographs: a comparison of older and younger adults. *Psychol. Aging*, **12**, 203–215.

Snodgrass, J. G. & Vandervart, M. 1980 A standardised list of 260 pictures: norms for name agreement, image agreement, familiarity, and visual complexity. **6**, 174–215.

Squire, L. R. & Zola, S. M. 1998 Episodic memory, semantic memory, and amnesia. *Hippocampus* **8**, 205–211.

Strack, F. & Forster, J. 1995 Reporting recollective experiences: direct access to memory systems? *Psychol. Sci.* **6**, 352–358.

Toth, J. P. 1996 Conceptual automaticity in recognition memory: levels of processing effects on familiarity. *Can. J. Exp. Psychol.* **50**, 123–138.

Toth, J. P. 2000 Nonconscious forms of human memory. In *Handbook of memory* (ed. E. Tulving & F. I. M. Craik), pp. 245–261. New York: Oxford University Press.

Tulving, E. 1972 Episodic and semantic memory. In *Organization of memory* (ed. E. Tulving & W. Donaldson), pp. 381–403. New York: Academic Press.

Tulving, E. 1983 *Elements of episodic memory*. Oxford University Press.

Tulving, E. 1985 Memory and consciousness. *Canadian Psychology*, **26**, 1–12.

Tulving, E. 1995 Organization of memory: Quo vadis? In *The cognitive neurosciences* (ed. M. S. Gazzaniga), pp. 839–847. Cambridge, MA: MIT Press.

Tulving, E. & Markowitsch, H. J. 1998 Episodic and declarative memory: Role of the hippocampus. *Hippocampus* **8**, 198–204.

Tulving, E., Hayman, C. A. G. & Macdonald, C. A. 1991 Long-lasting perceptual priming and semantic learning in amnesia: A case experiment. *J. Exp. Psychol. Learn. Mem. Cogn.* **17**, 595–617.

Yonelinas, A. P., Kroll, N. E. A., Dobbins, I., Lazzara, M. & Knight, R. T. 1998 Recollection and familiarity deficits in amnesia: Convergence of remember-know, process dissociation, and receiver operating characteristic data. *Neuropsychology* **12**, 323–339.

3

Components of episodic memory:
the contribution of recollection and familiarity

Andrew P. Yonelinas

The examination of recognition memory confidence judgements indicates that there are two separate components or processes underlying episodic memory. A model that accounts for these results is described in which a recollection process and a familiarity process are assumed to contribute to recognition memory performance. Recollection is assumed to reflect a threshold process whereby qualitative information about the study event is retrieved, whereas familiarity reflects a classical signal-detection process whereby items exceeding a familiarity response criterion are accepted as having been studied. Evidence from cognitive, neuropsychological and neuroimaging studies indicate that the model is in agreement with the existing recognition results, and indicate that recollection and familiarity are behaviourally, neurally and phenomenologically distinct memory retrieval processes.

3.1. Introduction

The notion that episodic memory consists of distinct components dates back at least to Aristotle. In the 1970s and early 1980s, cognitive psychologists formalized this notion and developed dual-process models that assumed that there were two separate processes, recollection and familiarity, that contributed to episodic recognition memory (e.g. Atkinson & Juola 1974; Jacoby & Dallas 1981; Mandler 1980; Tulving 1985). The idea was that previously studied items would be more familiar than new items, thus subjects could accept the more familiar items as having been studied. However, in addition to assessments of familiarity, if subjects could retrieve some aspect of the study event, such as when or where it occurred, this could also be used as a basis for recognition judgements.

Despite the introspective appeal of the dual-process models and their initial success in accounting for a variety of behavioural results, the dominant theories of that period assumed that recognition memory reflected only a single familiarity process, and recollection was not thought to play a significant, if any, role in recognition memory judgements. In these single process models, recognition was generally assumed to be well described by signal-detection theory (see Figure 3.1). The basic idea is that studied items are on average more familiar than new items, but because the old and new item familiarity distributions overlap it is necessary to set a response criterion and accept only the items above that level of familiarity as having been studied. The advantage of the model is that it uses only a single memory component, thus recognition memory accuracy can be characterized using a single parameter (i.e. d', which is the distance between the old and new item distributions). Over the past 20 years, single process models have become more sophisticated and have included additional assumptions

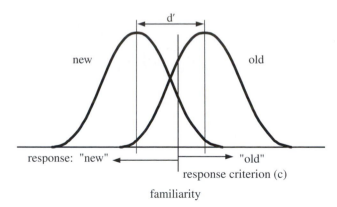

Fig. 3.1. Familiarity distributions for old and new items for an equal-variance signal-detection model.

about how items are represented and how these items are stored in the memory. These include global memory models such as episodic or instance models (e.g. MINERVA, Hintzman 1986), as well as connectionist or distributed models (e.g. TODAM, Murdock 1982). Although the specific assumptions of these models differ, they all maintain that recognition memory judgements rely on the assessment of a single familiarity measure.

Over the past 10 years, however, the limitations of the single process models have become increasingly obvious (see, for example, Clark & Gronlund 1996; Hockley 1991; Ratcliff *et al.* 1992; Yonelinas 1994), and there has been a renewed interest in dual-process theories of recognition memory. The aim of the current paper is to review some of the recognition memory work that my colleagues and I have conducted over the past 10 years. I will first describe a set of findings that demonstrate that there are at least two distinct components of episodic recognition memory. I will argue that these two components reflect the operation of two distinct retrieval processes: recollection and familiarity. I will then describe a dual-process model that was designed to account for these results and review the empirical studies that have been conducted to test the underlying assumptions of that model. I will conclude by discussing the limitations of that model and raise questions for future studies of episodic memory.

3.2. Recognition receiver operating characteristics

One area of research that turns out to be particularly problematic for the current single process models of episodic memory is the study of receiver operating characteristics (ROCs). A ROC is the function that relates the proportion of correct recognitions (i.e. the hit rate) to the proportion of incorrect recognitions (i.e. the false alarm rate). Typically, performance is examined across levels of response confidence. For example, after studying a list of words, subjects are presented with a mixture of old and new words and are required to make recognition judgements on a scale ranging from 'sure it was studied' to 'sure it was not studied'. The ROC is plotted as a function of confidence

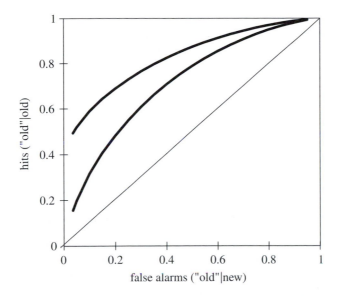

Fig. 3.2. Symmetrical (lower function) and asymmetrical (upper function) receiver operating characteristics.

such that the leftmost point includes only the most confidently recognized items and subsequent points include less and less confident responses.

Figure 3.2 shows two hypothetical recognition memory ROCs. The lower function is generated by the signal-detection model illustrated in Figure 3.1. The function is produced by plotting the hits against the false alarms as the response criterion is varied. This function is curvilinear and symmetrical along the diagonal. It is curvilinear because of the continuous nature of the Gaussian familiarity distributions, and it is symmetrical because the old and new item's familiarity distributions are the same shape (i.e. they have equal variance).

Early memory studies indicated that recognition memory ROCs were curvilinear and approximately symmetrical (e.g. Murdock & Dufty 1972). This lent support to the notion that episodic memory reflected only a single component, and justified the practice of measuring recognition accuracy using a single parameter (e.g. d', A', or proportion correct). However, subsequent studies demonstrated that recognition ROCs were not generally symmetrical but rather took the form of the top function in Figure 3.2. The ROC is curvilinear but it is asymmetrical, and appears to be pushed up along the left y-axis. In terms of signal-detection theory, this asymmetry indicates that the old item familiarity distribution must be associated with more variance (i.e. a fatter distribution) than the new item distribution.

The fact that ROCs are asymmetrical is not necessarily a problem for single component views of recognition memory. For example, if the degree of asymmetry were always the same, then one could assume that the old item variance was always some constant amount greater than the new item variance, and thus it would still be possible to measure recognition accuracy using a single d' parameter. Alternatively, if the degree of asymmetry were directly related to accuracy (e.g. as accuracy increased, the degree of asymmetry always increased) then one could still measure recognition performance using a single accuracy parameter.

However, recognition accuracy and the degree of ROC asymmetry are functionally independent (e.g. Ratcliff *et al.* 1992; Glanzer *et al.* 1999; Yonelinas 1994), indicating that recognition memory reflects at least two separate memory components. That is, in some studies, increases in accuracy are accompanied by increases in ROC asymmetry, whereas in other studies the degree of ROC asymmetry remains relatively constant as accuracy increases. Thus, there is no way to characterize the existing ROCs using fewer than two separate memory components or parameters.

Using the signal-detection framework, one needs one component to account for increases in accuracy (i.e. d′) and another component to account for the changes in ROC asymmetry (i.e. the variance of the old item distribution relative to the new item variance). This 'unequal-variance signal-detection model' can produce the data pattern just described but, as we will see later, it fails to account for the ROCs observed in recognition memory tests.

This simple pattern of results turns out to be extremely problematic for current single process models, even multiple parameter models such as MINERVA and TODAM. The models either predict that the ROC asymmetry should always remain constant or that it should always increase as accuracy increases and thus they cannot account for the fact that both patterns are observed. The problem is that these models do not have separate parameters that are tied to accuracy and ROC asymmetry and it is not possible to introduce separate components without restructuring these models (see Ratcliff *et al.* 1992).

3.3. The dual-process signal-detection model

The important question arising from the ROC literature is, 'why are these dissociations observed in simple recognition memory tests?'. The explanation provided by dual-process theory is that the dissociations occur because there are two retrieval processes, rather than just one, that contribute to recognition performance. That is, recognition memory judgements can be based either on the assessment of familiarity or on a recollection process whereby subjects retrieve qualitative information about a study event. I will argue that the familiarity process produces an ROC that is curvilinear and symmetrical, whereas the recollection process leads the ROC to become asymmetrical. Because the relative contributions of recollection and familiarity can vary, accuracy and ROC asymmetry can vary independently.

These assumptions form the basis of a simple quantitative model that I will refer to as the dual-process signal-detection model. The model assumes that familiarity is well described by the classical signal-detection model illustrated in Figure 3.1 (i.e. an equal-variance model). In contrast, recollection is assumed to reflect a fundamentally different form of memory retrieval—a threshold retrieval process. Describing recollection as a threshold process means that for any given item a subject either succeeds at retrieving some information about the study event or they fail to. That is, for some items they may retrieve information about when or where the item was presented, but there will be some items that fall below the threshold, and for these items subjects will be unable to retrieve any accurate qualitative information about the study event.

If performance relies exclusively on familiarity then the model predicts a curvilinear ROC that is symmetrical along the diagonal (e.g. the lower function in Figure 3.2 that is generated by an equal variance signal-detection model). If subjects recollect some proportion of the studied items then this will increase the hit rate and influence the shape of the ROC. However, in order to know exactly how it will influence the ROC it is necessary to make assumptions about how recollection and familiarity combine. The model assumes that the two processes make independent contributions to recognition, and that recollection leads to relatively high confidence recognition responses. Thus recollection will add high confidence hits, and the leftmost point on the ROC will move up. Because the ROC is cumulative across confidence, the entire ROC will be shifted up and thus become asymmetrical (e.g. the top function in Figure 3.2).

The model can be represented by the following equations:

$$P(\text{'old'}|\text{old}) = R + (1 - R)F_o \tag{3.1}$$

$$P(\text{'old'}|\text{new}) = F_n \tag{3.2}.$$

Old items will be correctly recognized if they are recollected (R), or if they are familiar (F_o) in the absence of recollection $(1 - R)$. New items will be incorrectly accepted as old if they are familiar (F_n). If familiarity is assumed to reflect a signal-detection process then F_o and F_n will be a function of d' (the distance between the means of the old and new item distributions) and c (the response criterion), such that $F_o = \Phi(d'/2 - c)$ and $F_n = \Phi(-d'/2 - c)$. These functions represent the proportion of the old and new item distributions that exceed the response criterion given that the distance between the means of the two normal distributions is d' (see Macmillan & Creelman 1991). The model requires two free memory parameters to generate an ROC; R, which represents the probability that a studied item is recollected, and d', which represents the average increase in familiarity associated with studying an item.

Given that there are two processes that differentially contribute to the shape of the recognition ROC, the dual-process model can account for the observed dissociations between accuracy and asymmetry. That is, according to the model the asymmetry typically seen in recognition ROCs reflects the fact the recollection is contributing to performance. If recollection increases and familiarity remains relatively constant then accuracy should increase and the ROC should become more asymmetrical. Thus the model can account for cases in which increases in accuracy are accompanied by increases in ROC asymmetry (e.g. Donaldson & Murdock 1968). The model can also account for cases in which increases in accuracy do not influence the degree of asymmetry (e.g. Ratcliff et al. 1992). That is, if recollection and familiarity increase approximately equally then the increase in asymmetry caused by recollection will be offset by the increase in symmetry caused by additional familiarity (see Yonelinas 1994 for an illustration of these predictions).

Further support for the model comes from the finding that the shape of the recognition ROC is directly related to the contribution of recollection and familiarity. For example, Jacoby's process dissociation procedure (Jacoby 1991) was used to estimate the contribution of recollection and familiarity, in order to determine the relationship between the shape of the ROC and the contribution of these two processes (Yonelinas 1994). Subjects were required to make both recognition confidence judgements, and list discrimination judgements indicating from which of two study lists the test items originated. The confidence responses were used to plot ROCs. Recollection was then estimated as the ability to determine list membership accurately and familiarity was estimated as the probability of recognizing an item, given that it was not accurately recollected. As expected, the results across several experiments showed that when recollection increased but familiarity was unchanged, accuracy increased while the ROCs became more asymmetrical. Moreover, when both recollection and familiarity increased together, accuracy increased while the ROC asymmetry remained constant. Finally, estimates of recollection and familiarity derived from the process dissociation procedure were found to predict the observed recognition confidence ROCs accurately. The results indicate that the shape of recognition ROCs is directly related to the contribution of recollection and familiarity.

The dual-process model can therefore account for the existing recognition memory ROC results that are problematic for earlier models, and it shows that the shape of the recognition ROC is directly related to the contribution of recollection and familiarity. Although these results provide support for the model, one would like to be able to test the individual assumptions underlying the model directly. One advantage of the model is that it is based on a relatively small number of assumptions, and thus it is possible to assess each of these assumptions in turn. The model assumptions are: (i) recollection is a threshold process; (ii) familiarity is a signal-detection process; (iii) recollection supports relatively high confidence recognition responses; and (iv) these two processes are independent. Next, I will review the studies that have directly assessed these assumptions.

3.4. Does recollection reflect a threshold process?

If recollection is a threshold process, then subjects either retrieve qualitative information about a previous study event or they fail to. They can, of course, retrieve different aspects of an event or different amounts of information, but if they relax their response criterion below the recollective threshold, accurate levels of recollection will not increase. Figure 3.3 illustrates the strength distributions of a high threshold model and the predicted ROC if performance relies exclusively on this threshold process. The ROC is generated by moving the response criterion from the right to the left along the strength continuum and accepting the items to the right of the response criterion as having been studied. The threshold is the point at which the new item distribution ends (i.e. the right side of the new item distribution). Note that threshold models with more than a single threshold may be appropriate under some conditions (e.g. Yonelinas 1997), but this single threshold model appears to be sufficient to describe recollection in standard recognition paradigms. The recollection distributions are discrete or square rather than continuously varying, thus, unlike signal-detection theory, the model generates a linear ROC. However, note that, strictly speaking, the predicted ROC is actually a kinked line; when the response criterion moves to the right of the threshold, the ROC intersects the y-axis and drops. However, as long as the subject places each of their response criteria at—or to the left of—the threshold, the ROC should be a straight line.

One way of determining whether recollection reflects a threshold process is to look for tests of recognition that rely primarily on recollection and determine whether linear

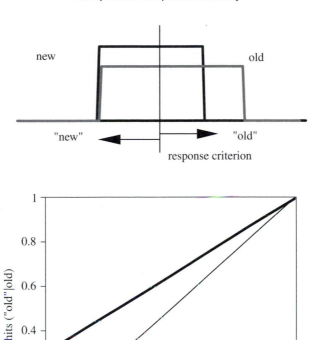

Fig. 3.3. Strength distributions of a high threshold model and the predicted ROC if performance relies exclusively on this threshold process.

ROCs are obtained. Five years ago, it seemed that this assumption must be incorrect because the previous 20 years of recognition memory research had not produced a single linear ROC. However, these studies almost always examined only standard old–new recognition judgements, tests in which familiarity could be used to discriminate between studied and non-studied items.

In order to test the threshold assumption it is necessary to find experimental conditions under which familiarity plays only a limited role in recognition performance. Such conditions were found in tests of associative recognition, in which subjects studied pairs of words and were then required to discriminate between previously presented pairs and rearranged pairs (Yonelinas 1997). Because all the studied and rearranged pairs consisted of familiar items (i.e. they had been studied), familiarity was expected to be less useful than in tests of single item recognition in which the studied items were familiar and the non-studied items were novel. If associative recognition relies primarily on recollection, then the ROCs should be relatively linear. Figure 3.4 presents the average ROCs for associative and single item recognition (from Yonelinas 1997,

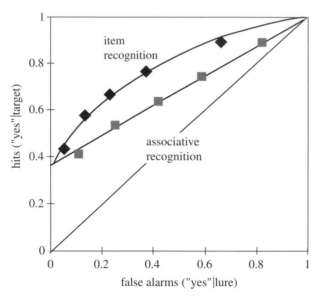

Fig. 3.4. Recognition memory ROCs for item and associative information (Yonelinas 1997, experiment 1).

experiment 1). Unlike the curvilinear item ROC, the associative ROC is relatively linear. The same results were found in two other experiments in that study and similar results have since been reported using a variety of different materials (e.g. Kelley & Wixted 1998; Rottello *et al.* 2000; Yonelinas *et al.* 1999*b*).

The threshold assumption was further verified in tests of source memory (Yonelinas 1999*a*), in which subjects were required to discriminate between items that had originated from two different sources (e.g. words spoken by two different experimenters and words presented in different locations). Under test conditions in which the familiarity of items from the two different sources were not expected to differ, the ROCs were relatively linear.

The results of these source and associative memory studies are important in providing support for the assumption that recollection reflects a threshold process. Moreover, they indicate that a simple signal-detection model is not consistent with the ROC data, i.e. signal-detection theory always predicts curvilinear ROCs, as long as performance is above chance. Even a two-component signal-detection model that has separate accuracy and variance parameters (i.e. the unequal-variance signal-detection model) cannot generate linear ROCs.

3.5. Does familiarity reflect a signal-detection process?

A second critical assumption of the dual-process model is that familiarity reflects an equal-variance signal-detection process. The most critical aspect of this model is that the old and new item familiarity distributions are assumed to have equal variance. There is no *a priori* reason why this assumption must be true and there are reasons to think that it might be violated. For example, if there is a great deal of variability in the degree to which studied items increase in memory strength due to encoding, then one would expect the old item distribution to be associated with greater variance than the new item distribution. Alternatively, there may be some upper limit on the familiarity level that an item can reach, and this could lead the variance of the old item distribution to be less than that of the new item distribution.

A way to test the signal-detection assumption directly is to examine recognition performance under conditions in which performance relies exclusively on familiarity. If familiarity reflects a signal-detection process then the ROC should be curvilinear and symmetrical. One way to test this assumption is to examine recognition ROCs in amnesic patients (e.g. patients with medial temporal lobe damage). Because amnesics are unlikely to recollect previous events but are able to make recognition responses based on assessments of item familiarity (Huppert & Piercy 1976; Mandler 1980; Mayes 1988), their ROCs should reflect the contribution of familiarity in the absence of recollection. If the current dual-process model is correct, and amnesics are making their recognition judgements based on familiarity alone, then their recognition ROCs should be curvilinear and symmetrical, in contrast to the asymmetrical functions observed in healthy subjects. This prediction was tested by examining recognition memory for previously studied words in amnesics and healthy control subjects (Yonelinas *et al.* 1998). Figure 3.5 shows that, in contrast to control subjects who exhibited curved asymmetrical recognition ROCs, the amnesics' functions were curved and symmetrical. Note that even when overall recognition performance was equated between the two groups by decreasing the study duration of the study items for the control subjects, the controls still exhibited asymmetrical ROCs in contrast to the amnesics. Similar results have also been observed when recognition memory for faces was tested (Dobbins *et al.*

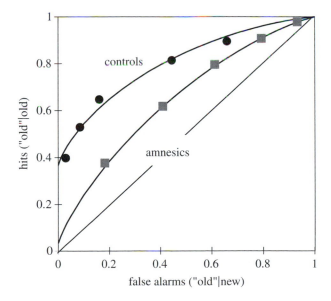

Fig. 3.5. Recognition memory ROCs from amnesics and aged-matched controls (Yonelinas *et al.* 1998).

1998). These results provide support for the claim that familiarity is well described as an equal-variance signal-detection process, and demonstrate that the model is useful in understanding the memory performance of healthy and memory impaired populations.

Additional support for the threshold and signal-detection assumptions comes from studies using the remember–know procedure (Gardiner 1988; Tulving 1985) to examine the ROCs associated with familiarity and recollection (e.g. Yonelinas 2001). In the remember–know procedure, subjects are instructed to indicate when a recognition judgement is based on recollection (i.e. respond 'remember' if you can recollect any qualitative aspect of the study event) and when it is based on familiarity in the absence of recollection (i.e. respond 'know' if the item is familiar and you know it was studied but you cannot recollect anything about the study event). If subjects are required to make confidence judgements and remember–know judgements for each test item, then remember and know responses can be used to examine separately the ROCs associated with recollection and familiarity.

Figure 3.6a shows a recognition ROC derived on the basis of confidence judgements (Yonelinas 2001, experiment 1). In agreement with previous studies, the recognition ROC is curvilinear and asymmetrical. Figure 3.6b shows the separate ROCs for the remembered items and the items accepted on the basis of familiarity. The figure shows that the probability of a remember response remained constant as the response criterion was relaxed, indicating that relaxing the response criterion below the recollection threshold did not lead to an increase in accurate recollection. Familiarity was estimated using the independence remember–know method of analysis (Yonelinas & Jacoby 1995), i.e. because subjects were instructed to respond 'know' whenever an item was familiar but not recollected $(F(1-R))$, familiarity was estimated as the probability of making a 'know' response given that the item was not recollected $(F = K/(1-R))$. The figure shows that familiarity increased gradually and formed a curved and symmetrical function, as expected if it reflected an equal-variance signal-detection process. Similar results have also been reported using the process dissociation procedure (Yonelinas 1994), i.e. when recollection is estimated as the ability to determine list membership, recollection is found to remain relatively constant as the recognition response criterion is relaxed, whereas familiarity estimates increase gradually and form symmetrical ROCs.

The important point of these studies is that they indicate that the asymmetrical ROCs that are observed in recognition memory tests arise because both recollection and familiarity contribute to performance. When the recollection-based responses are separated from the familiarity-based responses, familiarity is found to behave like a classical signal-detection process (i.e. as the response criterion relaxes, familiarity increases and produces a symmetrical curved ROC), whereas recollection behaves as a threshold process (i.e. recollection remains relatively constant across changes in response criteria).

3.6. Does recollection support relatively high confidence responses?

A third assumption underlying the dual-process model is that recollection leads to high confidence recognition responses relative to familiarity. This assumption is meant to capture the notion that when subjects retrieve qualitative information about a study

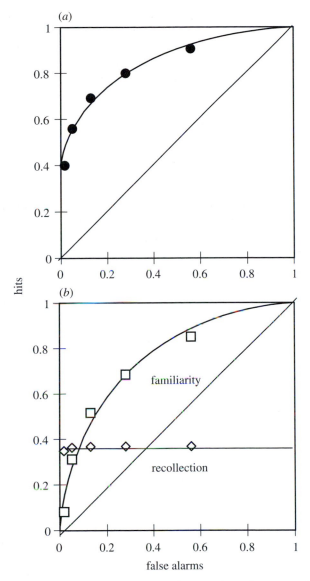

Fig. 3.6. (*a*) Recognition memory ROC, and (*b*) estimates of recollection and familiarity derived from remember–know responses (Yonelinas 2001, experiment 1).

event they should be confident that the event actually occurred. In contrast, accepting items on the basis of familiarity should be more error prone because of the overlapping familiarity distributions of old and new items, thus subjects are expected to be less sure about familiarity-based responses than recollection-based responses. The assumption that recollection supports high confidence responses is reflected in the manner in which the two components combine in the dual-process model. That is, the model assumes that response criterion should influence only familiarity while recollection should be relatively invariant as the response criterion is relaxed. The assumption that recollection leads to high confidence responses can of course be violated. For example, if one were to instruct subjects that they would be fined $1000 every time they false alarmed to a new item, they would probably adopt such a strict response criterion that they would respond 'no' to all the familiar items and all the recollected items. The critical question, however, is whether recollection, in general, leads to higher confidence responses than does familiarity.

The results in the remember–know study described earlier suggest that recollection does lead to high confidence responses, i.e. remembered items did not increase appreciably as the response criterion was varied, indicating that recollection did not contribute to the lower confidence responses. However, to assess this assumption more directly it is useful to examine the distribution of recognition confidence responses for remember and know responses. Figure 3.7a presents the proportion of remember and know responses to studied items for each level of recognition memory confidence. It shows that most of the remembered items (94%) led to the highest confidence recognition responses. In contrast, the know responses were distributed across the range of response confidence categories. Note, however, that familiarity based responses were in many cases associated with high confidence responses, and thus confidence in itself cannot be used as an index of recollection and familiarity (for similar arguments, see Gardiner & Java 1990; Rajaram 1993).

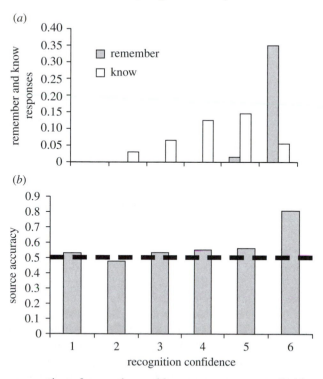

Fig. 3.7. (a) The proportion of remember and know responses to studied items for each level of recognition memory confidence (Yonelinas 2001, experiment 1). (b) The proportion of studied items leading to correct source judgements for each level of recognition memory confidence (Yonelinas 1999, experiment 3).

Similar results were observed in a study in which subjects made recognition confidence judgements and source memory judgements (i.e. 'was it in list 1 or list 2?') for each test item (Yonelinas 2001). In this study, recollection was measured, not on the basis of subjective reports of remembering but on the basis of accurate source memory, i.e. if the subject can accurately determine when or where the item was studied, it can be assumed that the item was recollected. In this way, accurate source memory was used as an index of recollection. Figure 3.7b shows the source accuracy associated with each level of recognition confidence. It indicates that items receiving recognition confidence scores of less than six were associated with source memory performance that was close to chance (i.e. 50%), whereas items that were recognized with the highest level of confidence were associated with highly accurate source memory judgements.

These studies indicate that whether recollection is measured as 'remember' responses or as the ability to determine source accurately, items that are recollected are associated with high levels of recognition confidence, whereas familiarity based responses are associated with a wide range of confidence responses.

3.7. Are recollection and familiarity independent?

A fourth critical assumption of the dual-process model is that recollection and familiarity are independent retrieval processes. This assumption is supported by numerous behavioural studies indicating that recollection and familiarity are functionally dissociable (for a review see Jacoby et al. 1997). For example, several variables such as amnesia, aging, response dead-lining, dividing attention and list length have been found to have disproportionately large effects on recollection compared with familiarity (e.g. Jacoby 1991; Jennings & Jacoby 1993; Toth 1996; Yonelinas 2001; Yonelinas & Jacoby 1994; Yonelinas et al. 1998). In contrast, variables such as response bias, massed priming, and study–test lag have disproportionately large effects on familiarity (e.g. Rajaram 1993; Yonelinas 1994; Yonelinas & Levy 2001). It is of course possible to find manipulations that have similar effects on both processes. For example, increasing study duration and varying the size of items between study and test appear to influence both recollection and familiarity (e.g. Yonelinas 1994; Yonelinas & Jacoby 1995). It is important, however, to realize that these latter findings do not indicate that the two processes are dependent, only that some variables play important roles in both processes.

Other evidence for the independence of recollection and familiarity comes from electrophysiological studies of recognition. For example, remember and know responses are correlated with independent event related potentials (ERPs). In a study of recognition memory for words, knowing responses were found to be associated with an early temporo-parietal positivity in the N400 range and a late fronto-central negativity (Düzel et al. 1997). In contrast, remembering responses were associated with a widespread late bifrontal and a left parieto-temporal positivity. Similar recollection and familiarity ERPs have been observed in a study in which recollection was measured as the ability to recollect the plurality of the studied items (Curran 2000), i.e. when subjects were able to determine accurately whether the word was studied in a singular or plural form, a late temporo-parietal positivity was observed. In contrast, familiar items compared with new items, regardless of plurality, led to a early positivity in the

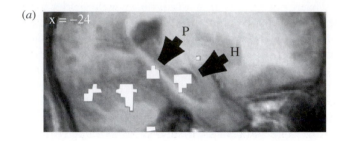

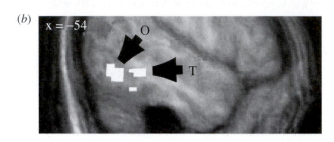

Fig. 3.8. Regions of activation overlaid on the average normalized T1 structural images. (*a*) Bilateral hippocampal [H] and parahippocampal [P] regions were more active during associative recognition than old item recognition (the left hemisphere activations are shown here). (*b*) Regions in the left middle occipital gyrus [O] and left middle temporal gyrus [T] were more active for old compared with new item recognition.

N400 range. Although the ERP results do not clearly indicate the brain regions supporting recollection and familiarity, the fact that the recollection and familiarity ERPs are temporally distinct and exhibit distinct scalp topographies suggest that recollection and familiarity rely on partially independent neural generators.

Three recent studies using functional magnetic resonance imaging (fMRI) have provided further evidence that recollection and familiarity involve partially independent brain regions. For example, we examined the temporal lobe regions contributing to recognition memory for line drawings of objects (Yonelinas *et al.* 2001). We found bilateral hippocampal and parahippocampal activation under conditions in which subjects were retrieving associative information accurately about study items (i.e. the colour it appeared in during the study phase), relative to conditions under which they were making accurate item recognition memory judgements (see Figure 3.8*a*). In contrast, item recognition for previously studied drawings compared with new drawings was not associated with hippocampal or parahippocampal activation but rather was associated with activation in the left inferior temporo-occipital regions (see Figure 3.8*b*). Thus, hippocampal and parahippocampal regions were involved in the associative test, in which recollection was required, but were not involved in the old item recognition test, in which familiarity was sufficient to discriminate between studied and non-studied items. In an fMRI study examining recognition memory for words, the left hippocampus was associated with greater activation for 'remembered' old words compared with correctly rejected new words, whereas the old words that elicited 'know' responses did not lead to hippocampal activation relative to new items

(Henson *et al.* 1999). Remembering and knowing were also found to involve the frontal and parietal cortices differentially in that study, i.e. the left parietal cortex showed greater activation for 'remember' responses while the right lateral and medial frontal cortex showed greater activation for 'know' responses. In another study examining recognition memory for words, correct 'remember' responses were associated with increases in hippocampal activation while 'know' responses were not related to increases in hippocampal activation (Eldridge *et al.* 2000).

These neuroimaging studies indicate that the hippocampus is involved in recollection, and they suggest that this region is less important for familiarity. The regions found to be involved in familiarity, however, were less consistent across experiments and future studies are necessary in order to clearly delineate the anatomical substrates of this process. Nonetheless, the fMRI results are clear in showing that the two processes do not rely on identical brain regions, and thus indicate that recollection and familiarity reflect distinct memory retrieval processes.

Taken together, the behavioural, ERP and fMRI results are consistent with the assumption that recollection and familiarity reflect independent memory retrieval processes. However, it seems quite likely that there may be conditions under which these processes interact and future studies that aim to examine such interactions will be extremely useful in developing future models of episodic memory. Still, in light of the evidence supporting the independence assumption, and the dual-process model's success at accounting for the existing recognition memory data, it appears that in general the two processes operate in an independent manner.

3.8. The phenomenological and behavioural validity of recollection and familiarity

The dual-process signal-detection model can be used in conjunction with recognition memory confidence results to derive quantitative estimates for the contribution of recollection and familiarity. That is, by fitting the model equations described earlier to observed ROCs, the model can be used to derive estimates of recollection and familiarity. The method is similar to conducting a linear regression in which one fits a line to the observed data points in order to derive estimates of slope and intercept, but in this case the function is nonlinear and the estimates are of recollection and familiarity (for a detailed description of several fitting methods, see Yonelinas 1999*a*). This method has been used to examine the effects of different experimental manipulations on recollection and familiarity (e.g. Yonelinas 2001) and to determine the fate of these two processes in different patient populations (e.g. Yonelinas *et al.* 1998).

However, one concern that arises when modelling recognition ROCs in this way is that the parameter estimates that are produced may only reflect a convenient mathematical description of the ROC data and they may not capture any real psychological processes. Although it is important that models provide accurate quantitative accounts of existing data, it is equally important that the model's underlying processes are psychologically valid. The validity of these processes can be assessed by asking whether they correspond with other behaviour measures that are expected to index recollection and familiarity. For example, recollection should correspond with the ability to determine where or when an item was presented, and the estimates derived from the ROC analysis should thus parallel those derived from the process dissociation procedure in which recollection is measured as the ability to determine the study source. A related approach is to ask whether these processes have any phenomenological validity. That is, do they correspond to processes that are available to introspective conscious experience. Thus, one can ask whether the estimates derived from the ROC analysis correspond to those derived from the remember–know procedure.

To assess these questions one can examine studies that used the ROC procedure, and either the remember–know procedure or the process dissociation procedure, and plot the estimates derived from the ROC procedure against those derived from the other procedures. If the ROC method produces estimates of recollection and familiarity that converge with those derived from the other methods, it would indicate that the method is accurately characterizing the processes underlying recognition memory. Figure 3.9 presents estimates for recollection (*a*) and familiarity (*b*) derived from 20 different experimental conditions from four published studies (Yonelinas 1994; Yonelinas 2001; Yonelinas *et al.* 1996; Yonelinas & Jacoby 1995). The bottom axis on each graph represents the estimates derived from the ROC analysis. The vertical axis represents the estimates from the remember–know procedure (top panels) and process dissociation procedure (bottom panels). The top two figures indicate that the ROC and remember–know procedures produce estimates that are almost identical (i.e. the points fall along the diagonal). The bottom figures show that the estimates from the ROC and process dissociation procedure are also quite close. Thus, the estimates from the ROC method

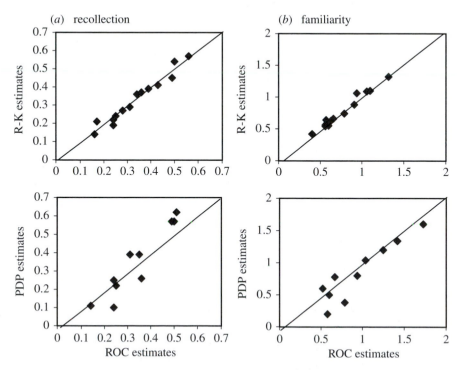

Fig. 3.9. Comparisons of (*a*) recollection and (*b*) familiarity estimates derived from ROC, remember–know and process-dissociation procedures (PDP) (Yonelinas 1994; Yonelinas 2001; Yonelinas *et al.* 1996; Yonelinas & Jacoby 1995).

converge with estimates derived using the process dissociation and remember–know procedures.

Although the three methods produce estimates that are quite close, it is useful to consider the conditions under which the procedures do differ. For example, the two points in the bottom left panel of Figure 3.9 that fall the farthest below the diagonal reflect estimates of recollection derived from a study that used the ROC and process dissociation procedures (Yonelinas & Jacoby 1995). The discrepancy in that study is probably due to the fact that the test conditions in the two tasks were not identical. Most important was that the list discrimination required in the process dissociation task was particularly difficult because the encoding conditions in the two study lists were similar. Because the process dissociation procedure used in that study measured recollection as the ability to discriminate between these two similar lists, the subsequent estimates of recollection were quite low. In contrast, in the ROC confidence procedure, because list discrimination was not required, any information that the subject remembered could be used as a basis for recollection and thus the estimates of recollection were higher. Thus, discrepancies can arise between these different methods of measuring recollection and familiarity when the processes are measured under different conditions. However, there is generally good agreement across the procedures when the conditions are held constant.

The convergence of the results from the three different methods indicates that it is not necessary to plot an entire ROC in order to determine its shape. Rather, asking a subject to make remember–know judgements or source memory judgements appears to provide the same information. Conversely, it does not appear to be necessary to ask subjects to report on the subjective experiences of recollection and familiarity in order to determine the likelihood that subjects will have these conscious experiences. Rather the ROC or process dissociation procedures can be used in conjunction with the dual-process model to predict the occurrence of these conscious states.

The utility of a memory theory is determined in part by its ability to reveal hidden order in otherwise complex datasets. The dual-process model succeeds in doing this by revealing the direct relationship between ROC, process dissociation and remember–know paradigms. It shows that there are two processes, recollection and familiarity, that underlie episodic recognition memory, and that these two processes are responsible for the complex patterns of results that we see in recognition ROCs, tests of associative or source recognition, and in subjective reports of remembering and knowing.

3.9. Model limitations

Despite the model's successes, it is quite clear that it is insufficient. Its most obvious limitation is that it is too simple. That recognition memory performance could be accounted for with two or three free memory parameters is extremely unlikely, and there will undoubtedly be cases in which additional processes and alternative assumptions will be required. Preliminary evidence that the model may be too simple comes from studies indicating that it is sometimes found to deviate slightly from the observed recognition ROC data (e.g. Ratcliff *et al.* 1995; Glanzer *et al.* 1999; Yonelinas 1999*b*, 1994). The deviation takes the form that the ROCs are sometimes slightly more curved than the dual-process model predicts. Note that the same problem arises for the unequal-variance signal-detection model as well. However, the observed deviations from the dual-process model are quite subtle: typically the observed points and the points predicted by the model deviate by about 0.01 or 0.02. Nonetheless, these deviations may be important and may indicate that a noise parameter or guessing process is needed (for a discussion of possible explanations for these deviations, see Ratcliff *et al.* 1994; Yonelinas 1999*b*).

Related issues may arise in tests of associative and source recognition. Although associative and source recognition ROCs can be linear, there are cases in which these ROCs are noticeably curved. One possible explanation for these findings is that a signal-detection process is contributing to these judgements. For example, there may be conditions under which recollection behaves in a more continuous manner, or in which familiarity supports source or associative memory judgements. Preliminary studies have already begun to investigate these issues. For example, one obvious case in which familiarity can support source memory judgements is when one list of items is presented much earlier than another. In this case, subjects may accept the more familiar items as having originated in the more recent list. As expected, source memory ROCs under these conditions tend to be curved (e.g. see Yonelinas 1999*a*).

Familiarity can also contribute to associative memory judgements under some conditions. For example, if associative information is 'unitized' during encoding then familiarity may support associative judgements. That is, if the subject treats two aspects of a study event as a whole unit, or gestalt, then that whole unit, as well as its constituent parts, may become familiar. For example, when subjects are required to discriminate between repeated faces and rearranged faces (e.g. the internal features of a studied face, such as the eyes, nose and mouth, are paired with external features, such as the hair, ears and chin, of another studied face), because each face is treated as a holistic unit (for a review, see Searcy & Bartlett 1996) a repeated face should be more familiar than a mixed face. Thus subjects may make use of familiarity to make the associative memory judgement, leading to curvilinear ROCs. As expected, the associative ROCs under these conditions are found to be curvilinear (Yonelinas *et al.* 1999). Note, however, that when the faces are studied and tested upside down, each face is no longer treated as holistic unit and the resulting associative ROCs are linear.

Familiarity can also support associative memory for word pairs as long as the two words are treated as a single unit. For example, when two words form a compound word (e.g. sea-food, off-shore, ice-cube), repeated word pairs (e.g. ice-cube) are more familiar than new word pairings (e.g. sea-shore) and the resulting ROCs are also curvilinear (J. Quamme & A. P. Yonelinas, unpublished data). The same effects are also observed when the word pairs do not form pre-existing compound words (e.g. sea-cube), as long as the subjects encode the pair as a coherent whole (e.g. at study they are instructed to generate a definition for the novel compound word sea-cube).

These studies indicate that familiarity may be more flexible than was originally thought and that there may be conditions under which it can support recognition judgements previously thought to require recollection. These results are important in reminding us that memory tests should not be treated as direct measures of underlying memory processes (for similar arguments, see Jacoby 1991) and that determining the contribution of recollection and familiarity to memory performance requires careful consideration of the task demands of each memory test.

Probably the most critical limitation of the current model is that it does not specify how memories are represented or how these processes are neurally instantiated. Although it is broadly consistent with some neuroanatomical models that postulate that recollection and familiarity processes are supported by distinct temporal lobe regions (e.g. Aggleton & Brown 1999; Eichenbaum *et al.* 1994; O'Reilly *et al.* 1997), the neural substrates of recollection and familiarity are not yet known. Careful consideration of neuroanatomy and neurophysiology will be essential in future developments of any episodic memory model.

The approach taken here is to begin with a simple quantitative model and to carefully test the model's assumptions. The idea is that once the basic assumptions are verified and the boundary conditions under which these assumption hold are determined, additional assumptions can be added or the existing assumptions can be modified. This approach differs from the two approaches that have dominated recent cognitive research in memory. One approach has been to propose complex quantitative models that require numerous assumptions about how items are represented and how the retrieval mechanisms work (e.g. the global memory models). The advantage of this approach is that the models make quantitative predictions that can be directly tested. The complexity of these models, however, has in general precluded the possibility of testing their individual assumptions. Moreover, these models have in general focused on behavioural results rather than on neurobiological findings and thus they tend to say very little about the data coming from neuropsychological and neuroimaging studies. An alternative approach that is dominant in cognitive neuroscience studies of memory is to propose general theoretical frameworks that are designed to capture the important distinctions seen in the neuropsychological and neuroimaging literatures. For example, theories proposing distinctions between episodic and semantic memory (Tulving 1983), or between declarative and procedural memory (Squire 1987), have been useful in guiding research and relating human and non-human studies of memory, but because they are generally not quantitative models their predictive power has been limited.

The dual-process model reflects a theory that lies somewhere between these two dominant approaches and I would like to believe that it builds on the strengths associated with each approach. The model is a gross oversimplification of the processes that subjects bring to bear in episodic memory tests. However, the model does provide a very simple and powerful tool for understanding memory performance in a variety of recognition memory paradigms, and it does point to a fundamental distinction between two different types of recognition retrieval processes.

3.10. Conclusions

Dissociations observed in recognition memory performance indicate that there are at least two components of episodic memory. A dual-process model that assumes that subjects can make recognition responses on the basis of independent recollection and familiarity processes is found to be consistent with behavioural, neuropsychological and neuroimaging studies of recognition memory. The results indicate that recollection is well described as a threshold process, whereby qualitative information about previous study events is retrieved, whereas familiarity is well described as a classical signal-detection process, whereby familiar items are accepted as having been studied.

The work was supported by grant MH59352 from the National Institute of Mental Health Bethesda, MD, USA.

References

Aggleton, J. P. & Brown, M. B. 1999 Episodic memory, amnesia and the hippocampal–anterior thalamic axis. *Behav. Brain Sci.* **22**, 425–490.

Atkinson, R. C. & Juola, J. F. 1974 Search and decision processes in recognition memory. In *Contemporary developments in mathematical psychology. Vol. 1. Learning, memory & thinking* (ed. D. H. Krantz, R. C. Atkinson, R. D. Luce & P. Suppes). San Francisco: Freeman.

Clark, S. E. & Gronlund, S. D. 1996 Global matching models of recognition memory: how the models match the data. *Psychon. Bull. Rev.* **5**, 37–60.

Curran, T. 2000 Brain potentials of recollection and familiarity. *Mem. Cognit.* **28**, 923–938.

Dobbins, I., Yonelinas, A. P., Kroll, N. E. A, Soltani, M. & Knight, R. T. 1998 Recognition memory in amnesia and healthy subjects. Paper presented at the *Annual Meeting of the Cognitive Neuroscience Society*, San Francisco.

Donaldson, W. & Murdock, B. B. 1968 Criterion change in continuous recognition memory. *J. Exp. Psychol.* **76**, 325–330.

Düzel, E., Yonelinas, A. P., Mangun, G. R., Heinze, H. & Tulving, E. 1997 Event-related brain potential correlates of two states of conscious awareness in memory. *Proc. Natl Acad. Sci. USA* **94**, 5973–5978.

Eichenbaum, H., Otto, T. & Cohen, N. 1994 Two functional components of the hippocampal memory system. *Behav. Brain Sci.* **17**, 449–518.

Eldridge, L. L., Knowlton, B. J. Furmanski, C. S., Bookheimer, S. Y. & Engel, S. A. 2000 Remembering episodes: a selective role of the hippocampus during retrieval. *Nature Neurosci.* **3**, 1149–1152.

Gardiner, J. M. 1988 Functional aspects of recollective experience. *Mem. Cognit.* **16**, 309–313.

Gardiner, J. M. & Java, R. I. 1990 Recollective experience in word and nonword recognition. *Mem. Cognit.* **18**, 23–30.

Glanzer, M., Kim, K., Hilford, A. & Adams, J. K. 1999 Slope of the receiver operating characteristic in recognition memory. *J. Exp. Psychol. Learn. Mem. Cogn.* **25**, 500–513.

Henson, R. N. A., Rugg, M. D., Shallice, T., Josephs, O. & Dolan, R. J. 1999 Recollection and familiarity in recognition memory: an event-related functional magnetic resonance imaging study. *J. Neurosci.* **19**, 3962–3972.

Hintzman, D. L. 1986 'Schema abstraction' in a multiple trace memory model. *Psychol. Rev.* **94**, 341–358.

Hockley, W. E. 1991 Recognition memory for item and associative information: a comparison of forgetting rates. In *Relating theory and data: essays on human memory in honor of Bennet B. Murdock* (ed. W. E. Hockley & S. Lewandowsky), pp. 227–248. Hillsdale, NJ: Erlbaum.

Huppert, F. & Piercy, M. 1976 Recognition memory in amnesic patients: effects of temporal context and familiarity of material. *Cortex* **12**, 3–20.

Jacoby, L. L. 1991 A process dissociation framework: separating automatic from intentional uses of memory. *J. Mem. Lang.* **30**, 513–541.

Jacoby, L. L. & Dallas, M. 1981 On the relationship between autobiographical memory and perceptual learning. *J. Exp. Psychol. Gen.* **110**, 306–340.

Jacoby, L. L., Yonelinas, A. P. & Jennings, J. M. 1997 The relationship between conscious and unconscious (automatic) influences: a declaration of independence. In *Scientific approaches to the question of consciousness* (ed. J. Cohen & J. W. Schooler), pp. 13–47. Hillsdale, NJ: Earlbaum.

Jennings, J. M. & Jacoby, L. L. 1993 Automatic versus intentional uses of memory: aging, attention, and control. *Psychol. Aging* **8**, 283–293.

Kelley, R. & Wixted, J. T. 2001 On the nature of associative information in recognition memory. *J. Exp. Psychol. Learn. Mem. Cogn.* **27**, 701–722.

Macmillan, N. A. & Creelman, C. D. 1991 *Detection theory: a user's guide.* Cambridge University Press.

Mandler, G. 1980 Recognizing: the judgment of previous occurrence. *Psychol. Rev.* **87**, 252–271.

Mayes, A. R. 1988 *Human organic memory disorders.* Cambridge University Press.

Murdock, B. B. 1982 A theory of storage and retrieval of item and associative information. *Psychol. Rev.* **89**, 609–666.

Murdock, B. B. & Dufty, P. O. 1972 Strength theory and recognition memory. *J. Exp. Psychol. Gen.* **94**, 284–290.

O'Reilly, R. C., Norman, K. A. & McClelland, J. L. 1997 A hippocampal model of recognition memory. *Proceedings of the Neural Information Processing Systems Meeting,* CS7, p. 73.

Rajaram, S. 1993 Remembering and knowing: two means of access to the personal past. *Mem. Cogn.* **21**, 89–102.

Ratcliff, R., Sheu, C. F. & Gronlund, S. D. 1992 Testing global memory models using ROC curves. *Psychol. Rev.* **3**, 518–535.

Ratcliff, R., McKoon, G. & Tindall, M. 1994 Empirical generality of data from recognition memory receiver-operating characteristic functions and implications for the global memory models. *J. Exp. Psychol. Learn. Mem. Cogn.* **20**, 763–785.

Ratcliff, R., Van Zandt, T. & McKoon, G. 1995 Process dissociation, single process theories, and recognition memory. *J. Exp. Psychol. Gen.* **124**, 352–374.

Rotello, C. M., Macmillan, N. A. & Van Tassel, G. 2000 Recall-to-reject in recognition: evidence from ROC curves. *J. Mem. Lang.* **43**, 68–88.

Searcy, J. H. & Bartlett, J. C. 1996 Inversion and processing of component and spatial-relation information in faces. *J. Exp. Psychol. Hum. Percept. Perform.* **22**, 904–915.

Squire, L. R. 1987 *Memory and brain.* New York: Oxford University Press.

Toth, J. P. 1996 Conceptual automaticity in recognition memory: levels-of-processing effects on familiarity. *Can. J. Exp. Psychol.* **50**, 123–138.

Tulving, E. 1983 *Elements of episodic memory.* Oxford University Press.

Tulving, E. 1985 Memory and consciousness. *Can. Psychol.* **26**, 1–12.

Yonelinas, A. P. 1994 Receiver-operating characteristics in recognition memory: evidence for a dual-process model. *J. Exp. Psychol. Learn. Mem. Cogn.* **20**, 1341–1354.

Yonelinas, A. P. 1997 Recognition memory ROCs for item and associative information: evidence for a dual-process signal-detection model. *Mem. Cogn.* **25**, 747–763.

Yonelinas, A. P. 1999*a* The contribution of recollection and familiarity to recognition and source memory judgments: a formal dual-process model and an ROC analysis. *J. Exp. Psychol. Learn. Mem. Cogn.* **25**, 1415–1434.

Yonelinas, A. P. 1999*b* Recognition memory ROCs and the dual-process signal detection model: comment on Glanzer, Kim, Hilford and Adams (1999). *J. Exp. Psychol. Learn. Mem. Cogn.* **25**, 514–521.

Yonelinas, A. P. 2001 The three Cs of recognition memory: consciousness, control and confidence. *J. Exp. Psychol. Gen.* (In the press.)

Yonelinas, A. P. & Jacoby, L. L. 1994 Dissociation of processes in recognition memory: effects of interference and of test speed. *Can. J. Exp. Psychol.* **48**, 516–534.

Yonelinas, A. P. & Jacoby, L. L. 1995 The relation between remembering and knowing as bases for recognition: effects of size congruency. *J. Mem. Lang.* **34**, 622–643.

Yonelinas, A. P. & Levy, B. 2001 Dissociating familiarity from recollection in human recognition memory. (Submitted.)

Yonelinas, A. P., Dobbins, I., Szymanski, M. D., Dhaliwal, H. S. & King, L. 1996 Signal-detection, threshold, and dual-process models of recognition memory: ROCs and conscious recollection. *Conscious. Cogn.* **5**, 418–441.

Yonelinas, A. P., Kroll, N. E. A., Dobbins, I. G., Lazzara, M. & Knight, R. T. 1998 Recollection and familiarity deficits in amnesia: convergence of remember/know, process dissociation, and ROC data. *Neuropsychology* **12**, 323–339.

Yonelinas, A. P., Kroll, N. E. A., Dobbins, I. G., Soltani, M. 1999 Recognition memory for faces: when familiarity supports associative recognition judgments. *Psychonom. Bull. Rev.* **6**, 654–661.

Yonelinas, A. P., Hopfinger, J. B., Buonocore, M. H., Kroll., N. E. A., & Baynes, K. 2001 Hippocampal, parahippocampal and occipital-temporal contributions to associative and item recognition memory: An fMRI study. *Neuroreport* **12**, 2001.

4

Sensory-perceptual episodic memory and its context: autobiographical memory

Martin A. Conway

Episodic memory is reconceived as a memory system that retains highly detailed sensory perceptual knowledge of recent experience over retention intervals measured in minutes and hours. Episodic knowledge has yet to be integrated with the autobiographical memory knowledge base and so takes as its context or referent the immediate past of the experiencing self (or the 'I'). When recalled it can be accessed independently of content and is recollectively experienced. Autobiographical memory, in contrast, retains knowledge over retention intervals measured in weeks, months, years, decades and across the life span. Autobiographical knowledge represents the experienced self (or the 'me'), is always accessed by its content and, when accessed, does not necessarily give rise to recollective experience. Instead, recollective experience occurs when autobiographical knowledge retains access to associated episodic memories. In this reworking of the 'episodic memory' concept autobiographical memory provides the instantiating context for sensory-perceptual episodic memory.

4.1. Sensory-perceptual episodic memory and its context: autobiographical memory

Over the past decade our research into autobiographical memory has led us to an account of human memory in which personal goals play a major role in the formation, access and construction of specific memories (Conway & Pleydell-Pearce 2000). A central tenet of this account is that a fundamental function of human memory is to retain knowledge on the progress of personal goals, i.e. whether they have been achieved or not. Goals are considered to be represented in complex goal hierarchies where they form a part of the 'working self'. Because goals in a hierarchy will vary in how near or distant they are from attainment, a wide range of different types of knowledge are required to make accurate assessments of goal attainment progress. For example, successful completion of the goal of 'taking a coffee break' may be part of the goal hierarchy 'to write a paper', which in turn is part of a wider hierarchy of goals that collectively aim to reduce discrepancies between parts of the self and satisfy broad sets of motives. Recalling the coffee break provides evidence that the goal was achieved and, perhaps, reminds the rememberer that a larger goal has not been achieved. Of course, once the paper has been written, recalling, for example, putting it in the mail, is itself 'evidence' of goal attainment. Episodic information, because it is frequently of actual experience (is 'experience-near') has a special status as evidence that goals have been achieved, have not been achieved, have been modified, changed or abandoned.

The term 'episodic information' refers to knowledge contained in episodic memories and this is conceived as being very largely sensory-perceptual in nature. Such experience-near sensory-perceptual knowledge, when accessed during remembering, supports 'recollective experience' and, consequently, episodic memory has a unique affinity for this type of memory awareness (Wheeler *et al.* 1997). Recollective experience is the sense or experience of the self in the past and is induced by images, feelings and other memory details that come to mind during remembering—see Gardiner & Richardson-Klavehn (1999) and Gardiner (this issue) for reviews. In our approach this memory awareness or feeling state (the sense of the self in the past) signals to a rememberer that the mental representation it is associated with is in fact a memory of an experience that actually occurred and is not a fantasy, dream, plan or some other (experience-distant) mental construction. Thus, recollective experience effectively says 'this mental representation is a memory of an event experienced by the self'. Note that it does not follow from this that recollective experience always indicates a true memory— 'true' in the sense that the recalled experienced actually occurred—but when recollection is present the probability is high that the remembered event was one that had been previously experienced (see Conway *et al.* 1996; Roediger & McDermott 1995).

These considerations lead us to a revision of the 'episodic memory' concept as this was originally proposed by Tulving (1972) and later elaborated (Tulving 1983, 1985; Wheeler *et al.* 1997). We conceive of episodic memory as a system that contains experience-near, highly event specific, sensory-perceptual details of recent experiences—experiences that lasted for comparatively short periods of time (minutes and hours). These sensory-perceptual episodic memories do not endure in memory unless they become linked to more permanent autobiographical memory knowledge structures, where they induce recollective experience in autobiographical remembering. By this view access to episodic memories (EMs) rapidly degrades and most are lost within 24 h of formation. Only those EMs integrated at the time or consolidated later, possibly during the sleep period following formation, remain accessible and can enter into the subsequent formation of autobiographical memories (AMs).

We have further concluded that EMs are represented in the brain regions most closely involved in the processing that took place during actual experience. Because of this, EM sensory-perceptual details are represented in posterior regions of the brain and especially in networks sited in the occipital lobes, posterior parts of the temporal lobes, and (conceivably) in posterior parietal lobes. Other more conceptual and abstract, experience-distant, autobiographical knowledge may be represented in networks with a more anterior location. Thus, it is proposed that EM is, in terms of neuroanatomy, a topographically separate memory system. Table 4.1 summarizes the main points of our revised conception of EM (for more detailed accounts see Conway 1992, 1996; Conway & Pleydell-Pearce 2000).

According to the present view, EMs represent knowledge of specific actions and action outcomes derived from moment-by-moment experience—the minutiae of memory. Although this is specific evidence on the progress of immediate and recent plans, it cannot on its own be used to evaluate more complex goals in working-self goal hierarchies. Instead, the organization of groups of episodic memories and abstractions drawn from them, along with attitudes and beliefs of the working self, form conceptual autobiographical knowledge. Such conceptual autobiographical knowledge is a major part of AM where it contextualizes and 'frames' EMs while simultaneously providing higher order evidence of goal completion, suspension, revision or abandonment.

Table 4.1.   Characteristics of sensory-perceptual episodic memory.

- Retains records of sensory-perceptual processing derived from working memory
- Contains organizing abstract knowledge derived from goals active during experience
- Represents short time slices, possibly determined by changes in goal-processing
- Represented roughly in the order in which they occurred
- Has a short duration (measured in hours)
- If they become integrated with AM, access becomes stable and durable
- They are recollectively experienced when accessed
- When included as part of an AM construction they provide specificity
- Neuroanatomically they may be represented in brain regions separate from other AM knowledge
- They may have a distinctive form of organization
- They may have EM-unique retrieval process in addition to more general access processes

Autobiographical memory is, then, a type of memory that persists over weeks, months, years, decades and lifetimes, and it retains knowledge (of the self) at different levels of abstraction. In what follows AM is considered first, followed by EM and contrasts between the two.

4.2. Autobiographical memory

An AM is a transitory mental representation: it is a temporary but stable pattern of activation across the indices of the AM knowledge base that encompasses knowledge at different levels of abstraction, including event-specific sensory perceptual details (EMS), very often—although by no mean always—in the form of visual mental images. This sort of memory has various functions, characteristic knowledge types, modes of access, supports certain phenomenological experiences, and is associated with certain brain areas, as will now be considered in turn.

(a) Functions

As might be expected of a complex higher order form of cognition, AM serves many functions. The particular function we have highlighted in our approach is that of grounding the self. By this we mean that memories, and autobiographical knowledge more widely, place constraints on what goals the self can realistically maintain and pursue. A corollary of this is that memory and the self strive to be congruent. The working self makes preferentially available memories and knowledge that are congruent with the goals of the self (for a review of the extensive evidence demonstrating this, see Conway & Pleydell-Pearce 2000; for an earlier account, see Greenwald 1980). Indeed, so overriding is the need for memory–self congruency that aspects of the self (attitudes and beliefs) may change to fit initially incongruent autobiographical knowledge (see Ross 1989) or memories themselves may be altered, misremembered, or inhibited in order to preserve the self from change. Memories are encoded in terms of the self (cf. Hastorf & Cantril 1952 for an early, and still one of the best, studies of this) and experiences with strong self reference may receive privileged encoding that render them highly accessible and capable of evoking intense experiences of recollection, i.e. vivid and flash bulb memories (for a review, see Conway 1995).

The importance of congruency can be seen in a variety of illnesses when the self and memory become split and no longer constrain one and other. Delusional beliefs, for example, derive their pathological status in part from the fact that they are fantastic for the individual who holds them. Thus, the deluded schizophrenics interviewed by Baddeley *et al.* (1996) all had (deluded) beliefs that were either not supported or that were contradicted by accessible autobiographical memories. On the other hand, they all also described 'memories' (usually of implausible events, e.g. having most of their brain removed by a bad angel, etc.) that in some often obscure respects were consistent with their delusions and even supported them. It seems clear that in this sample of patients at least, memory no longer grounds the self in the sense that it places constraints on what the self can be. A similar split, disruption, or attenuation may occur in neurological patients who suffer damage to the frontal lobes and subsequently confabulate. In the case of plausible confabulations the false memories are constructed from autobio-graphical knowledge but configured in ways that depict events that did not occur—they are in Moscovitch's (1989) memorable phrase 'honest lies'. Such configurations may not be random but instead reflect the operation of a damaged working self generating memories with (in most cases) an impaired goal system. Motivated confabulations may support the fabrication of a past that serves a function in the present. Thus, the confabulated memories of extensive family support by a frontal patient living through a time of illness and loneliness provide a source of support (Conway & Tacchi 1996), just as the confabulated memories of arranging business meetings by another frontal patient provided him with a sense of continuing at his former level of professional functioning (Burgess & McNeil 1999).

The integrity of the self and autobiographical knowledge is then, critical for a normally functioning system and this is because AM is the knowledge base of the self. Once the connection becomes impaired in some way, either neurologically or psychologically, then autobiographical knowledge, which may remain accessible, no longer constrains the goals of the working self and delusions and confabulations then occur. This grounding or constraining function also has another aspect in that it provides the self with continuity and stability. Knowledge of goal attainment contained in AMs and autobiographical knowledge generally can be a positive resource of the self (even if plausibly confabulated) during times of stress (Robinson 1986). On the other hand it can be negative, as a constant reminder of failure, and so may be defended against as in patients with clinical levels of depression who recall many 'over-general' memories (Williams 1996). Autobiographical knowledge then functions to ground the self in memories of actual experiences or in remembered reality (which does not always, even though it may usually, correspond to actual reality).

(b) Knowledge

We have identified three basic types of autobiographical knowledge that vary in their conceptual specificity, ranging from the abstract and generic to the sensory perceptual and event specific, as well as in their temporal specificity, denoting periods measured in decades and years to periods covering minutes and hours (see Conway & Pleydell-Pearce 2000; Conway & Fthenaki 2000). 'Lifetime periods' are the most abstract and temporally extended AM knowledge structures. They contain knowledge about others, activities locations, feelings and evaluations common to a period as a whole. A period such as 'when I was at secondary/high school' might contain generic images of teachers, classrooms, sports hall, thoughts about particular class topics, e.g. English, Maths, etc., as well as evaluations about what the person was good/bad at, their likes and dislikes, what was achieved academically and otherwise, and what changes mark the start and completion of the period. A lifetime period may also contain a more or less detailed evaluation, e.g. 'this was a good/bad time for me' and they may be chunked into higher order units to form life story schema which in turn form part of the self concept (see Bluck & Habermas 2001). Lifetime periods are thus abstract mental models of the self during a delineated period of time usually defined by a theme or common set of themes, e.g. school, work, relationships, etc.

Lifetime period knowledge can be used to access other more specific knowledge and in particular representations of what we have termed 'general events'. The level of general events is the preferred level of processing in AM and optimizes the amount of specific information available for least cognitive effort (see Rosch 1978). It is worth noting that accessing autobiographical knowledge is effortful. For instance, generating a specific memory captures attention and averages, under laboratory conditions, 5 to 7 s with few retrieval times less than 2 s. Therefore, a basic level at which cognitive effort is reduced and access maximized provides a relatively non-demanding point of entry into this complex knowledge base. General events are more experience-near than lifetime periods and contain information about others, activities, locations, feelings and evaluations relating to specific experiences. These experiences might be of repeated events, e.g. 'walks in the fields' (see Barsalou 1988), extended events, e.g. 'our holiday in Italy', or they may be more specific, e.g. 'the interview', 'day trip to London' and so on. Furthermore, there may be local organization in general events leading to the formation of 'mini-histories' (Robinson 1992) such as learning to drive a car, learning to use the library, romantic first relationship, making friends with X, etc. Mini-histories may have very direct connections (one-to-one mappings in cues) to an associated lifetime period, e.g. 'when I was at secondary/high school'. General events are, then, heterogeneous and contain information that can be used as cues to access lifetime periods or sensory perceptual EMs. It is these latter knowledge structures that form the third level of autobiographical knowledge and they are considered in detail in §4.3 below, although it might be noted here that when an EM or set of EMs are included as an active part of a constructed memory they always evoke recollective experience (the sense of the self in the past).

(c) Access

Autobiographical memories are patterns of activation over the indices of AM knowledge structures and typically consist of a general event plus one or more EMs. Lifetime period structures are not always active, as the same lifetime period may access many general events and, once a search of general events is initiated, local organization at this level may make access of the lifetime period redundant in subsequent searches of the same region of the knowledge base. Indeed, when the system is in retrieval mode, i.e. there is a conscious intention to retrieve memories, then searches at the level of general events may be preferred. Conway & Pleydell-Pearce (2000) review a large body of findings, demonstrating that two types of cue-driven retrieval processes mediate access to the data base and memory construction—direct and generative retrieval.

In general, it is proposed that the AM knowledge base is highly sensitive to cues. These can be externally presented or internally generated and their effect is to automatically cause patterns of activation to constantly arise and dissipate within the knowledge base. These endogenous patterns of activation, the result of encoding specificity (Tulving & Thompson 1973), do not usually stabilize into representations that could become memories nor do they attain a threshold that can capture attention. The reason for this is that most cues activate knowledge in general events and lifetime periods. Undirected activation spreading from lifetime period knowledge weakly activates many general events and therefore rapidly dissipates. Similarly, activation automatically spreading from a general event weakly activates a single or (rarely) multiple lifetime periods, associated general events and a pool of sensory-perceptual EMs. Again, this uncontrolled spread of activation to associated structures quickly weakens and fades. Direct access only occurs when a cue maps on to and, consequently, highly activates EM (either a single or set of EMs) and activation spreads from here to a single general event and to an associated lifetime period. Automatic activation of EM by an endogenous cue is, however, a comparatively rare occurrence because the cue would have to closely correspond to the sensory-perceptual content of an EM and the probability of processing some item in a way highly similar in content to an existing EM is low (Conway & Pleydell-Pearce 2000; see also Conway, 1992, 1996, 2001). Although the probability is low, given the constant effect of cues on the knowledge base, it must be the case that direct access leads to the formation of patterns of activation that can become memories on at least some occasions. The final step in memory formation is for the (stable) pattern of activation to become linked to the goal structure of the working self and enter consciousness. It seems that even at this stage a memory may not be formed, especially if this will disrupt current processing sequences that are prioritized. Nevertheless, recent data indicates that people experience the sort of 'spontaneous' retrieval that direct access can give rise to at a rate of two to three memories on average per day (Berntsen 1996). Moreover, in pathological conditions such as post-traumatic stress disorder intrusive involuntary recall triggered by cues that correspond to event specific knowledge (ESK) is a major symptom of the disorder (for a recent review, see Brewin 1998). In this case the intrusion or spontaneous recall rate can be at chronically high levels, especially in the early post-trauma period.

Recalling autobiographical memories is often an intentional act in which the remember enters 'retrieval mode' and actively searches for particular types of knowledge in order to construct or generate a memory. Convergent evidence points to a complex generative retrieval process in which cues are first elaborated, memory searched (an automatic part of the cycle), the outputs from memory are then evaluated and, if required, these are then elaborated further and another search undertaken. In this way a specific memory (a pattern of activation in the knowledge base) is iteratively constructed. For example, consider a participant in an AM cue-word experiment whose task is to recall specific memories to cues presented by the experimenter (a common procedure in this area) and the word 'chair' is presented. A typical initial elaboration is to map the cue onto one's current environment and perhaps the participant thinks of 'the chair in the hallway at home'. The next elaboration might be to generate a template for a specific event in which this object once featured and the cue might then be refined into 'when did we buy it'? This may lead to access of lifetime period knowledge e.g. 'that was when we lived in city X in the house at Y'. Recycling this information in a further search produces 'saw it in a sale at store W', followed by access of EMs and a flood of event-specific details in the form of visual images. This latter point in retrieval is highly characteristic of the endpoint of memory construction (at least when studied in the laboratory, cf. Conway 1996). Conway & Pleydell-Pearce (2000) describe how generative retrieval is controlled by a 'retrieval model', used to verify and elaborate memory output, that in turn is generated by the working self and derived from the currently active goal structure. Despite the slow construction times seen in the laboratory in extended intentional memory construction, in everyday life when cues in the environment, e.g. in interaction with family members, friends, colleagues, etc., are more potent and when the knowledge base has been repeatedly sampled, raising the activation levels of relevant autobiographical knowledge generally, memory construction will then be facilitated and access will occur much more rapidly—see Crovitz (1986) for a powerful demonstration of this with a post-traumatic amnesic patient, and see Conway & Bekerian (1987) for evidence that cues which map on to individual autobiographical knowledge can produce average retrieval times of about 2 s, which is nearly twice as fast as mean retrieval times in cue-word experiments.

(d) Phenomenology

Much goal-centred processing takes place outside awareness and this is especially true of the autobiographical knowledge base in which patterns of activation constantly arise and dissipate without becoming conscious. This, however, serves to sharpen the question of why memories enter into consciousness given that access to the knowledge base can be non-conscious. We believe that one function of consciousness is to facilitate decision making and plan formulation by enabling the ability to choose. Thus, conscious awareness allows intentional choice among alternative courses of action with different goals. Because memories carry information about goal attainment they are particularly useful in goal-appraisal, change and formation, which will inevitably feature conscious intentional choices (for a related view, see Schank 1982). Note that information about goal attainment does not have to be explicit in a memory. Rather autobiographical knowledge and the mental representations to which it is able to give rise can be conceived as being the output or expression of the goal system at a previous point in the past. It is the content of the knowledge—what it makes plausible and what it makes implausible for the self—and its configuration that carries the goal attainment knowledge. Goal attainment autobiographical knowledge is therefore important in these decision making processes because it carries information about the outcomes of previous choices and plans—hence, perhaps, the inter-relatedness of memory, self and consciousness.

One of the main ways that this inter-relatedness may occur in remembering is through the special mental state known as 'retrieval mode' (Tulving 1983). Little research had been specifically directed at this but nonetheless some points can be made. Retrieval mode is characterized by a turning inwards of attention, a redirecting of attention from action to mental representations and, as a consequence, can probably only be engaged in under certain circumstances, i.e. those that place a low demand on conscious decision making (Conway 2001). Retrieval mode is also a state in which the cognitive system is prepared for or expects memory construction and recollection, i.e. networks are dysfacilitated or decoupled from other processing sequences in which they currently run and reassembled into interlocked networks primed for memory generation (cf. Damasio 1989, and see Lepage *et al.* 2000 for a recent neuroimaging study). One aim of retrieval mode might be to facilitate the occurrence of recollective experience when the 'me' self (the autobiographical self) is experienced as the 'I' (the working self). Thus, recollective experience might be thought of as a feeling state that arises when the working or experiencing self initiates retrieval mode and constructs a specific memory containing, among other knowledge types, sensory perceptual ESK, and in this way 'experiences' the past. A function of recollective experience itself might be to signal that the currently attended mental representation is a representation of the self in the past, the 'me', and not some other type of representation such as a daydream, fantasy or rumination. In enabling the subjective experience of the past, the recollective feeling state indicates that potentially useful goal attainment knowledge is currently available.

Although the endpoint and, perhaps, the main aim of retrieval mode is recollective experience and the phenomenological experiences associated with it, another feeling state is also possible—that of feelings of knowing (Tulving 1985). Feelings of knowing arise when conceptual, generic or abstract knowledge is activated (Conway *et al.* 1997) and this must occur during the course of AM construction too, when generic autobiographical knowledge in lifetime periods and general events is accessed. Rememberers 'just know' they attended a specific school, had a particular job, lived with a certain person, and so on. A possibility here is that the 'knowing' or 'just knowing' feeling state is one that, in terms of cognitive effort, is less costly than recollective experience and although it may occur when the system is in retrieval mode as specific memories are constructed, it can also occur in other states that do not feature retrieval mode.

Finally, in this section very recent work is considered showing that rememberers have cognitive reactions to their memories and these reactions relate to the perceived consistency of memories. Beike & Landoll (2000) found that when a memory was recalled from a lifetime period, but the recalled event was inconsistent with the lifetime period, various reactions followed. For a memory of an event judged to be a good, or positive experience drawn from a lifetime period judged as negative, the dissonant memory might be set against the many negative memories available from the lifetime period and in this way outweighed. Alternatively, rememberers provided justifications for the remembered experience, some unique reason why it was inconsistent, i.e. 'it was a fluke', 'it happened by chance', and so on. The important point is that constructing an AM not only features characteristic forms of conscious experience but also can cause other reactions and feelings relating to current goals of the self and to the requirement that the self and memory should be congruent.

(e) Neurology

There is a large clinical literature, mainly on case studies of impairments of AM, demonstrating that this type of remembering can be disrupted by impairments to many different brain regions including networks in frontal, temporal and occipital lobes as well to midbrain structures in hippocampus, amygdala, fornix, and thalamus (for a review, see Conway & Fthenaki 2000). Given the complexity of AM and its role in the self and consciousness, wide distribution of the processes that mediate it is only to be expected. Here we will focus on a recent electroencephalography (EEG) study from our laboratory that mapped changes in slow cortical potentials (SCPs) detected from electrodes on the scalp during autobiographical remembering (Conway *et al.* 2001*a*) and which provides a good summary of the neurological complexity of autobiographical remembering. Changes in SCPs were monitored while participants: prepared to recall memories (pre-retrieval phase); recalled memories to cue words (retrieval phase); made a manual response to indicate when they had a detailed and specific memory in mind; and then held the memory in mind for several seconds (hold memory in mind phase). Head plots of patterns of activation taken from one second epochs early, middle and late, in the three phases and baselined to a point in the inter-trial interval are shown in Figure 4.1. Note that the head plots are statistical extrapolations from activity detected by individual electrodes placed in a international 10–20 system. The top of each plot represents the front part of the brain, the left and right sides of each plot correspond to left and right cortical hemispheres, red shading indicates regions in which negativity (activation) was detected and blue shading indicates areas of positivity (dysfacilitation). The leftmost plot in each row is taken from an early point in that phase, the middle plot from a midpoint, and the right-hand plot from a period close to the end of the phase.

The head plots in Figure 4.1*a* show the pattern of activation detected in the pre-retrieval phase after the start of a trial has been signalled and while participants focus on a fixation point and await the presentation of the (next) cue word. Early in this phase bilateral prefrontal activation is present but, as the phase proceeds, activation spreads and, most notably, the anterior part of the left temporal lobe becomes highly active, especially so just before presentation of the cue. One possibility is that this activation reflects pre-retrieval priming of networks in the frontal lobes and left anterior temporal lobe that will mediate generative retrieval once that is initiated by presentation of the cue. More generally, this might reflect the system entering retrieval mode in preparation for memory construction (see Lepage *et al.* 2000).

Figure 4.1*b* shows that once retrieval starts negativity rises sharply in the frontal lobes and the source of this emanates from networks in the left prefrontal cortex. As the retrieval period proceeds, activation starts to build in posterior sites (middle and right side head plots in Figure 4.1*b*), sites which had previously been strongly positive or dysfacilitated. Once a memory is formed this pattern of left frontal activation linked to mainly right posterior temporal and occipital activation is temporarily lost (left head plot of figure 4.1*c*). This period just after memory formation is particularly interesting because after participants made a (manual) response, to indicate that a memory was in mind, we detected a very strong negative wave bilaterally and centrally placed in the frontal lobes. This component was found to be unrelated to motor activity and may be what we have termed a memory engagement potential (MEP). The MEP occurs as frontal networks reconnect, following co-ordinating the motor response with the recently formed memory and, while the fully formed memory is held in mind, activation is then detected in the left frontal lobes, right posterior temporal lobes and bilaterally (stronger on the right than left) in the occipital lobes.

These neurophysiological findings fit well with other studies that have also detected posterior activation in episodic remembering (Nyberg *et al.* 2000; Wheeler *et al.* 2000; see also Markowitsch 1998) and collectively they suggest that EMs may be represented

pre-retrieval phase

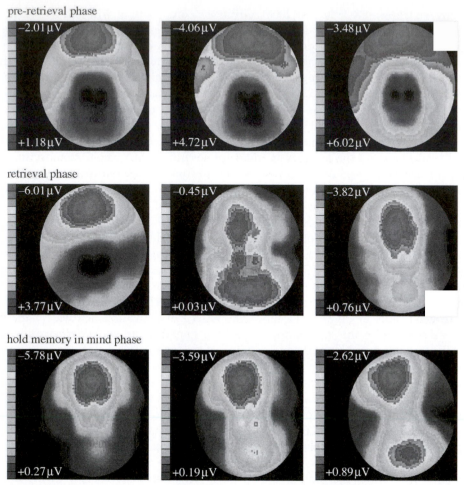

Fig. 4.1. Topographic representations of the distribution of surface negativity during (*a*) pre-retrieval, (*b*) retrieval and (*c*) the 'hold memory in mind' phase. The plots employ a separate minimum–maximum scale determined by the most negative and positive electrodes in that phase. This is in order to optimize visual comparison between electrodes within each phase.

in those sensory-perceptual regions of the brain involved in their original processing. AM is, however, more than just a record of sensory-perceptual processing, and the pattern of activation unfolding over the whole period and culminating in an interlocked pattern of frontal and posterior activation once a memory is formed shows, by the present view, conceptual autobiographical knowledge being linked to sensory-perceptual episodic memory, and in so doing provides a retrieval context for EMs.

4.3. Episodic memory

In our view EM refers to the ability to recall in considerable detail what occurred a few minutes ago and a few hours ago. Its temporal range may be defined by the individual's sleep/wake cycle and it may not extend beyond a sleep period during which, perhaps, some consolidation into AM occurs, as well as some forgetting. Because of its duration it is separate from conceptions of short-term memory (see Gathercole 1996, 1999) and working memory (Baddeley 1986). It is, however, closely related to a recent development in the working memory model that postulates a new temporary store termed the 'episodic buffer' (Baddeley 2000). The episodic buffer is a store in which knowledge from different areas of long-term memory and different modalities of input are bound into a memory representation and retained for a brief period of time (no more than a few minutes). One way in which to conceptualize EM is, then, as a type of memory that retains representations of states of the episodic buffer. According to the present approach, episodic memories are short-duration summary representations of previous states of the working memory system and it is this conception that is considered in the following sections.

(a) Functions

One of the primary functions of EM is to keep track of progress on active goals as plans are executed. Because of this, episodic memory is especially attuned to changes in the goal states of the working self which, in turn, are marked by changes in the contents of consciousness. As attention turns from one activity, e.g. making a coffee, to another, e.g. writing a paper, so the currently active working self goals change. The central idea of this conception of EM is that when the goals change an EM is formed that links together states of the episodic buffer that occurred while those goals endured (cf. Newtson 1976). Outputs of the episodic buffer may be similar to what we have previously called 'event specific knowledge' and, when linked together into an EM, approximate to what Conway (1992) called 'phenomenological records'—records of recent states of consciousness. The purpose of the retention of such records over a period of minutes and hours is to provide highly specific information on recent plan execution, e.g. while drinking coffee recalling that the milk was returned to the fridge, or while writing recalling that a particular topic has been covered. This type of memory is a constant reminder of progress on current goals.

(b) Knowledge

EMs are highly detailed and retain knowledge of sensory-perceptual information abstracted from working memory, abstract knowledge (evaluations) relating to very specific goals (goals that download into actions without further subgoal processing), sensory-perceptual summaries, and even some literal records of states of the episodic buffer (ones that carry goal attainment information). By this view, then, EMs contain both abstract–conceptual and sensory-perceptual knowledge, with the latter dominating. Conceptual knowledge in an EM might function to organize sensory-perceptual details into coherent chunks of experience. For example, schema knowledge such as 'making a cup of coffee' might index or organize images of the kitchen, the fridge, the kettle, the mug tree, etc., as these were in a recent encounter as well as records of taking the milk out of the fridge, pouring the boiling water and other goal-relevant actions. Thus, EMs contain some abstract knowledge and substantial event-specific knowledge. They do not, however, contain general event knowledge or lifetime period knowledge and this is because they have yet to be integrated with knowledge structures in the autobiographical knowledge base. Instead, their context or index is 'today' or, possibly, 'yesterday' and they act as the database of the 'I' or experiencing self. However, even though their context is the 'I' they are in a form of 'goal-related-abstract-knowledge-plus-event-specific-knowledge' that can be readily incorporated into the autobiographical knowledge base (the 'me').

Yet despite the preparedness of EMs for integration with existing AM knowledge structures, it is unlikely that many are retained. Given the heavy storage cost of the large numbers of minutely detailed EMs generated in any one day, long-term retention is unfeasible. Instead, through rehearsal, or lack of it, and associated inhibition (see Conway *et al.* 2000) most EMs may be lost (permanently) within a short period. Retention critically depends on integration with existing structures in the knowledge base, which themselves may be changing and developing into stable AM knowledge structures. Because EMs are sensory and highly goal-specific, when accessed as event-specific in autobiographical remembering they have a special status in goal attainment appraisal. Even the mundane example of recalling a coffee break taken while writing a paper carries with it a great deal of goal-relevant information about how a past self dealt with a difficult and complex task. Recalling images and feelings gives rise to recollective experience which convinces the rememberer that the event in mind did in reality occur and, consequently, inferences about the past self are based on, or grounded in (memories of) actual actions.

(c) Access

Episodic memory, like AM, is undoubtedly highly cue-sensitive. External and internal cues in the immediate environment will map directly onto recently formed EMs and in this way reminding of the recent past will be potentiated and must frequently occur. Given this high degree of cue sensitivity, direct retrieval may be one of the main ways in which EMs are accessed. However, an important difference between EM and AM is that EM (as conceived here) does not support generative retrieval. This is because EMs are not organized in terms of an elaborate conceptual structure. Instead they are conceived as being represented in a rudimentary form of temporal organization, possibly according to actual order of experience (Conway 1992). This temporal form of organization supports a type of access not possible in AM, namely cue-independent access. Cue-independent access may involve a 'mental reaching back' into the very recent past. When retrieval takes this special form, EMs of the actions of a few minutes or hours ago 'pop' into mind. In fact, there is often a cue present in the cue-independent retrieval but it is a general one and does not correspond to EM content, e.g. 'What was I doing earlier?', 'What was I doing this morning?', or even the more general 'What was I doing?'. It is also noteworthy that the focus of retrieval here is very often on what the rememberer had previously been doing, or, in other words, on memories for goal-driven actions. EMs can then be accessed by cues that map onto memory content, i.e. by the process of encoding specificity (Tulving & Thomson 1973), or alternatively they can be accessed in a way that does not depend on memory content and which, therefore, is independent of encoding specificity. This alternative way in which to retrieve EMs involves a 'mental reaching back' which is unique to episodic remembering.

(d) Phenomenology

Brown & Kulik (1977) in their original paper on 'flash bulb' memories noted the 'live' quality of these long-lasting highly vivid memories. They observed that such memories often contained the very sort of event-specific sensory-perceptual details that are typically lost from memories of other less consequential experiences. These details and the 'live' quality are, however, ubiquitous features of EM and, as a consequence, our recall of the very recent past is flash bulb-like in its clarity. All of which promotes the experience of recollection that is a characteristic, if not defining, feature of EM (Wheeler *et al.* 1997). Indeed, it is only when EMs become incorporated into an AM during memory construction that the past is recollectively experienced and a specific memory formed. Autobiographical knowledge can, however, be accessed independently of EMs and when this occurs recollective experience is absent and, instead, access is accompanied by feelings of knowing.

Another feature of the phenomenology of EMs is that they can also give rise to feelings of familiarity. That is they may trigger a feeling that some item has been recently encountered without leading to recollective recall of associated EMs. Presumably this occurs when memories are activated by a cue but the activation does not exceed a threshold leading to full memory formation. The 'feeling-of-familiarity-of-occurrence' is not the same as feelings of knowing encountered in autobiographical remembering and other types of access of long-term knowledge (cf. Conway *et al.* 1997). These latter knowing feelings are about feeling that what has been accessed is correct for a particular task or they are a type of recognition that what has been accessed is part of long-term knowledge, part of what a person knows. Thus, EM and AM are associated with different types of memory awareness. Episodic memory supports recollection and familiarity, whereas AM primarily supports feelings of knowing.

(e) Neurology

Many neuroimaging studies of human memory focus on recall of minutiae over short retention intervals and so, in effect, are studies of the type of sensory-perceptual EM considered here. Nyberg *et al.* (1996) in a meta-analysis identified several right hemisphere sites as critical in remembering minutiae from the very recent past (usually, but not always, recognition of individual words from a previously presented list). The convergent finding over many studies was that of activation of regions in the right prefrontal cortex (PFC), supporting the proposal of Tulving and colleagues (e.g. Tulving *et al.* 1994) that the right PFC was specialized for retrieval and the left for encoding. Subsequent meta-analyses have questioned this, and in their review Nolde *et al.* (1998) conclude that for simple memory tasks, such as recognition, typically only regions of the right PFC are activated, whereas for more complex memory tasks, such as cued and free recall, regions of both right and left PFC are active. The present perspective suggests that the more complex memory tasks are, the more they directly engage the goal structure of the working self—if only because they are more cognitively demanding—and left PFC activation may reflect this. In contrast, right side activation may reflect activation of networks that mediate EM. According to this reasoning the differences in laterality of activation across different memory tasks are related to the degree to which the working self becomes involved in accessing EMs (cf. Craik *et al.* 1998).

The emphasis on the role of the PFC in remembering very recent events has perhaps diverted attention from other regions that may also play an important role in episodic and autobiographical remembering. For instance, imagery is frequently present during remembering and so it might be expected that regions known to be involved in imagery (cf. Thompson & Kosslyn 2000) would become active in remembering—especially in episodic remembering where sensory perceptual knowledge of the past dominates. Regions of the occipital lobes, inferior and posterior temporal lobes have been found to be active in recognition of words (Gonsalves & Paller 2000) and in the recall of autobiographical memories (Conway *et al.* 2001*a*). Presumably these regions would be active in episodic remembering too and, indeed, Nyberg *et al.* (1996, fig. 2) present findings that this is the case. In many studies, however, activation in these regions may go undetected because it is subtracted out from control and contrast tasks, which themselves feature imagery. Interestingly, in Nyberg *et al.* (1996), Fink *et al.* (1996) and Conway *et al.* (2001*a*), strong activation of predominantly right temporal and occipital lobes was detected in both an episodic task (recognition of very recently studied materials) and in the recall of autobiographical memories, which is what might be expected if both involve the activation of sensory perceptual EMs.

Another region long known to be involved in the recall of recent memories, the hippocampus and associated structures, is also relatively rarely detected as selectively active in neuroimaging studies of EM and AM (for a recent study, see Conway *et al.* 1999). In contrast, neurological injury to this region invariably results in amnesia and other types of memory impairment. Especially interesting here is a report by Bancaud *et al.* (1994) who describe how epileptic seizures with a medial temporal lobe focus often result in a 'dreamy state' consisting of vivid memory-like hallucinations and intense feelings of *déjà vu*. Conway & Fthenaki (2000) argued that the feeling of 'pastness' that characterizes the *déjà vu* experience is similar to the feeling of pastness present in recollective experience. That is to say that *déjà vu* might be thought of as 'recollective experience for the present'. Bancaud *et al.* (1994) report the findings of a neuroimaging study, which included implantation of electrodes into various brain regions of epileptic patients with seizure foci in the temporal lobes. In this study they recorded the locus of activations occurring during the dreamy *déjà vu* state that preceded seizure onset and, also, the spread of activation. They concluded that a network distributed through medial and lateral temporal lobes mediated the experience of *déjà vu* and that the anterior hippocampus, amygdala and superior temporal gyrus had direct access to this circuit (activation of networks in these structures could spread to the medial–lateral temporal circuit and activate it). If, as we have suggested, *déjà vu* is a type of inappropriate recollective experience for the present then, possibly, the feeling of pastness present in recollection is mediated by networks in temporal and limbic sites.

Dysfunctions of recollective experience have not been extensively studied but the few studies that have examined impairments following brain damage (Curran *et al.* 1997; Levine *et al.* 1998) have found this to be associated with frontal pathology. In contrast, a recent patient we have been studying (A.K.P., Moulin *et al.* 2001) has medial temporal pathology, more prominent on the left compared with the right, with atrophied hippocampi. Note that this is not degenerative and a diagnosis of probable dementia of the Alzheimer's type has not been made. Frontal pathology has not been detected in A.K.P., he presents as intellectually intact and competent and performs well on neuropsychological tests of frontal function. He does, however, confabulate and these confabulations are largely associated with (frequent) experiences of *déjà vécu* in which he has a strong feeling of having done what he has done before. For example, when given the morning newspaper by his wife he claims to have already read it. When this is questioned he confabulates a memory of having been to the newsagents earlier in the morning and read it then. When his wife found a coin in a public place he remembered putting it there for her to find. While on a walk he was amazed to observe the same bird on the same bough of the same tree that he had seen previously. Indeed so powerful is his experience of *déjà vu* that he watches far less television than he used to because he feels he has already seen most of the programmes; he also reads far fewer books again feeling that he has already read any title presented to him. In various memory tests featuring judgements of recollective experience he systematically over-extended recollective experience to new items which he incorrectly judged as old. There was also confabulation of some autobiographical memories as well as some accurate recall.

Presumably, the temporal and hippocampal damage has led to his chronic *déjà vu* and this lends further weight to the suggestion of a recollective experience circuit in these regions. Perhaps this is normally controlled by other (frontal) systems, such as the goal structure of the working self, that acts to suppress not only awareness of task-irrelevant knowledge but also recollective experience. A further notable aspect of A.K.P.'s pathology is the linkage between recollective experience (*déjà vu*) and confabulated memories. This may occur because recollective experience signals to a rememberer that what is in mind is a memory of an actual experience and not some other type of representation such as a fantasy or dream. As a result of his brain damage this signalling occurs inappropriately in A.K.P. where normally it would have been suppressed or prevented by frontal control systems. These or other control systems then confabulate an account in response to the experience of recollection. The confabulations function to justify or make consistent the recollective experience. This may be a non-conscious process as A.K.P. has little insight into his memory problems and he is strongly resistant to surrendering his confabulations when challenged. From the present perspective with its focus on goals and memory it is particularly relevant that A.K.P., because of feelings of remembering, no longer undertakes certain goal-related habitual activities.

4.4. Sensory-perceptual episodic memory

This view of sensory-perceptual episodic memory categorizes EMs as unusual mental representations in that they are conceived as small 'packets' of experience derived from conscious states that remain intimately connected to consciousness by instigating recollective experience during remembering. It is their 'near-experience' quality that sets them apart from other types of knowledge and other, more conceptual, representations of the past (such as AM). In the present conception EMs provide a link from working memory to long-term memory and in so doing suggest ways in which momentary experience might be retained and later incorporated into consciously formed memories.

The author thanks Alan Baddeley, John Gardiner and Sue Gathercole for insightful comments on an earlier version of this paper and also Kit Pleydell-Pearce, Sharon Whitecross, & Helen Sharp for Figure 4.1 and EEG data. Writing was supported by the Department of Experimental Psychology, University of Bristol, England, and by the Biotechnology and Biological Sciences Research Council, grant 7/S10578.

References

Baddeley, A. D. 1986 *Working memory*. Oxford: Clarendon Press.

Baddeley, A. D. 2000 The episodic buffer: a new component of working memory? *Trends Cogn. Sci.* **4**, 417–423.

Baddeley, A. D., Thornton, A., Chua, S. E. & McKenna, P. 1996 Schizophrenic delusions and the construction of autobiographical memory. In *Remembering our past: studies in autobiographical memory* (ed. D. C. Rubin), pp. 384–428. Cambridge University Press.

Baddeley, A. D., Vargha-Khadem, F. & Mishkin, M. 2001 Preserved recognition in a case of developmental amnesia: implications for the acquisition of semantic memory? *J. Cogn. Neurosci.* (In the press.)

Bancaud, J., Brunet-Bourgin, F., Chauvel, P. & Halgren, E. 1994 Anatomical origin of *déjà vu* and vivid 'memories' in human temporal lobe epilepsy. *Brain* **117**, 71–90.

Barsalou, L. W. 1988 The content and organization of autobiographical memories. In *Remembering reconsidered: ecological and traditional approaches to the study of memory* (ed. U. Neisser & E. Winograd), pp. 193–243. Cambridge University Press.

Beike, D. R. & Landoll, S. L. 2000 Striving for a consistent life story: cognitive reactions to autobiographical memories. *Social Cogn.* **18**, 292–318.

Berntsen, D. 1996 Involuntary autobiographical memories. *Appl. Cogn. Psychol.* **10**, 435–454.

Bluck, S. & Habermas, T. 2001 The life story schema. *Motivation Emotion* **24**. (In the press.)

Brewin, C. R. 1998 Intrusive autobiographical memories in depression and post-traumatic stress disorder. *Appl. Cogn. Psychol.* **12**, 359–370.

Brown, R. & Kulik, J. 1977 Flashbulb memories. *Cognition* **5**, 73–99.

Burgess, P. W. & McNeil, J. E. 1999 Content-specific confabulation. *Cortex* **35**, 163–182.

Conway, M. A. 1992 A structural model of autobiographical memory. In *Theoretical perspectives on autobiographical memory* (ed. M. A. Conway, D. C. Rubin, H. Spinnler & W. A. Wagenaar), pp. 167–194. Dordrecht: Kluwer.

Conway, M. A. 1995 *Flashbulb memories*. Hove, Sussex: Lawrence Erlbaum Associates.

Conway, M. A. 1996 Autobiographical memories and autobiographical knowledge. In *Remembering our past: studies in autobiographical memory* (ed. D. C. Rubin), pp. 67–93. Cambridge University Press.

Conway, M. A. 2001 Phenomenological records and the self-memory system. In *Time and memory: issues in philosophy and psychology* (ed. C. Hoerl & T. McCormack), pp. 336–389. Oxford University Press.

Conway, M. A. & Bekerian, D. A. 1987 Organization in autobiographical memory. *Memory & Cogn.* **15**, 119–132.

Conway, M. A. & Fthenaki, A. 2000 Disruption and loss of autobiographical memory. In *Handbook of neuropsychology: memory and its disorders*, 2nd edition (ed. L. Cermak), pp. 257–288. Amsterdam: Elsevier.

Conway, M. A. & Pleydell-Pearce, C. W. 2000 The construction of autobiographical memories in the self memory system. *Psychol. Rev.* **107**, 261–288.

Conway, M. A. & Tacchi, P. C. 1996 Motivated confabulation. *Neurocase* **2**, 325–339.

Conway, M. A., Collins, A. F., Gathercole, S. E. & Anderson, S. J. 1996 Recollections of true and false autobiographical memories. *J. Exp. Psychol. Gen.* **125**, 69–95.

Conway, M. A., Gardiner, J. M., Perfect, T. J., Anderson, S. J. & Cohen G. M. 1997 Changes in memory awareness during learning: the acquisition of knowledge by psychology undergraduates. *J. Exp. Psychol. Gen.* **126**, 1–21.

Conway, M. A., Turk, J. D., Miller, S. L., Logan, J., Nebes, R. D., Meltzer, C. C. & Becker, J. T. 1999 The neuroanatomical basis of autobiographical memory. *Memory* **7**, 1–25.

Conway, M. A., Harries, K., Noyes, J., Racsma'ny, M. & Frankish, C. R. 2000 The disruption and dissolution of directed forgetting: inhibitory control of memory. *J. Mem. Lang.* **43**, 409–430.

Conway, M. A., Pleydell-Pearce, C. W. & Whitecross, S. 2001*a* The neuroanatomy of autobiographical memory: a slow cortical potential study (SCP) of autobiographical memory retrieval. *J. Mem. Lang.* **45**, 493–524.

Conway, M. A., Pleydell-Pearce, C. W. & Sharpe, H. 2001*b* Neurophysiological similarities and differences between true and false autobiographical memories. (In preparation.)

Craik, F. I. M., Moroz, T. M., Moscovitch, M., Stuss, D. T., Winocur, G., Tulving, E. & Kapur, S. 1998 In search of self: a PET investigation of self-referential information. *Psychol. Sci.* **10**, 26–34.

Crovitz, H. F. 1986 Loss and recovery of autobiographical memory after head injury. In *Autobiographical memory* (ed. D. C. Rubin), pp. 273–290. Cambridge University Press.

Curran, T., Schacter, D. L., Norman, K. A. & Galluccio, L. 1997 False recognition after a right frontal lobe infarction: memory for general and specific information. *Neuropsychologia* **35**, 1035–1049.

Damasio, A. R. 1989 Time-locked multiregional retroactivation: a systems-level proposal for the neural substrates of recall and recognition. *Cognition* **33**, 25–62.

Fink, G. R., Markowitsch, H. J., Reinkemeier, M., Bruckbauer, T., Kessler, J. & Heiss, W. 1996 Cerebral representation of one's own past: neural networks involved in autobiographical memory. *J. Neurosci.* **18**, 4275–4282.

Gardiner, J. M. & Richardson-Klavehn, A. 1999 Remembering and knowing. In *Handbook of memory* (ed. E. Tulving & F. I. M. Craik), pp. 229–244. Oxford University Press.

Gathercole, S. E. (ed.) 1996 *Models of short-term memory*. Hove, Sussex: Lawrence Erlbaum Associates.

Gathercole, S. E. 1999 Cognitive approaches to the development of short-term memory. *Trends Cogn. Sci.* **3**, 410–419.

Gonsalves, B. & Paller, K. A. 2000 Brain potentials associated with recollective processing of spoken words. *Mem. Cogn.* **28**, 321–330.

Greenwald, A. G. 1980 The totalitarian ego: fabrication and revision of personal history. *Am. Psychol.* **35**, 603–618.

Hastorf, A. H. & Cantril, H. 1952 They saw a game: a case study. *J. Abn. Social Psychol.* **49**, 129–134.

Lepage, M., Ghaffar, O, Nyberg, L. & Tulving, E. 2000 Prefrontal cortex and episodic memory retrieval mode. *Proc. Natl Acad. Sci. USA* **97**, 506–511.

Levine, B., Black, S. E., Cabeza, R., Sinden, M., Mcintosh, A. R., Toth, J. P., Tulving, E. & Stuss, D. T. 1998 Episodic memory and the self in a case of isolated retrograde amnesia. *Brain* **121**, 1951–1973.

Markowitsch, H. J. 1998 Cognitive neuroscience of memory. *Neurocase* **4**, 429–446.

Moscovitch, M. 1989 Confabulation and the frontal systems: strategic versus associative retrieval in neuropsychological theories of memory. In *Varieties of memory and consciousness: essays in honour of Endel Tulving* (ed. H. L. Roediger III & F. I. M. Craik), pp. 133–160. Hillsdale, NJ: Lawrence Erlbaum Associates.

Moulin, C. A., Conway, M. A. & Thomas, K. 2001 A case of chronic deja vu. (In preparation.)

Newtson, D. 1976 Foundations of attribution: the perception of ongoing behaviour. In *New directions in attribution research*, vol. 1 (ed. J. H. Harvey, J. W. Ickes & R. F. Kidd), pp. 41–67. Hillsdale, NJ: Lawrence Erlbaum Associates.

Nolde, S. F., Johnson, M. K. & Raye, C. L. 1998 The role of prefrontal cortex during tests of episodic memory. *Trends Cogn. Sci.* **2**, 399–406.

Nyberg, L., Cabeza, R. & Tulving, E. 1996 PET studies of encoding and retrieval: the HERA model. *Psychonomic Bull. Rev.* **3**, 135–148.

Nyberg, L., Habib, R., McIntosh, A. & Tulving, E. 2000 Reactivation of encoding-related brain activity during memory retrieval. *Proc. Natl Acad. Sci.* USA **97**, 11 120–11 124.

Robinson, J. A. 1986 Autobiographical memory: a historical prologue. In *Autobiographical memory* (ed. D. C. Rubin), pp. 19–24. Cambridge University Press.

Robinson, J. A. 1992 First experience memories: contexts and function in personal histories. In *Theoretical perspectives on autobiographical memory* (ed. M. A. Conway, D. C. Rubin, H. Spinnler & W. Wagenaar), pp. 223–239. Dordrecht: Kluwer.

Roediger, H. L. & McDermott, K. B. 1995 Creating false memories: remembering words not presented in lists. *J. Exp. Psychol. Learn. Mem. Cogn.* **21**, 803–814.

Rosch, E. 1978 Principles of categorization. In *Cognition and categorization* (ed. E. Rosch & B. B. Lloyd), pp. 25–49. Hillsdale, NJ: Lawrence Erlbaum Associates.

Ross, M. 1989 Relation of implicit theories to the construction of personal histories. *Psychol. Rev.* **96**, 341–357.

Schank, R. C. 1982 *Dynamic memory.* New York: Cambridge University Press.

Thompson, W. L. & Kosslyn, S. M. 2000 Neural systems activated during visual mental imagery. A review and meta-analyses. *Brain Mapping* (In the press.)

Tulving, E. 1972 Episodic and semantic memory. In *Organization of memory* (ed. E. Tulving & W. Donaldson), pp. 382–403. New York: Academic Press.

Tulving, E. 1983 *Elements of episodic memory.* Oxford: Clarendon Press.

Tulving, E. 1985 Memory and consciousness. *Can. Psychol.* **26**, 1–12.

Tulving, E. & Thomson, D. M. 1973 Encoding specificity and retrieval processes in episodic memory. *Psychol. Rev.* **80**, 353–373.

Tulving, E., Kapur, S., Craik, F. I. M., Moscovitch, M. & Houle, S. 1994 Hemispheric encoding/ retrieval asymmetry in episodic memory: positron emission tomography findings. *Proc. Natl Acad. Sci.* USA **91**, 2016–2020.

Wheeler, M. A., Stuss, D. T. & Tulving, E. 1997 Towards a theory of episodic memory: the frontal lobes and autonoetic consciousness. *Psychol. Bull.* **121**, 351–354.

Wheeler, M. E., Petersen, S. E. & Buckner, R. L. 2000 Memory's echo: vivid remembering reactivates sensory-specific cortex. *Proc. Natl Acad. Sci.* USA **97**, 11 125–11 129.

Williams, J. M. G. 1996 Depression and the specificity of autobiographical memory. In *Remembering our past: studies in autobiographical memory* (ed. D. C. Rubin), pp. 244–267. Cambridge University Press.

5

Misattribution, false recognition and the sins of memory

Daniel L. Schacter and Chad S. Dodson

Memory is sometimes a troublemaker. Schacter has classified memory's transgressions into seven fundamental 'sins': transience, absent-mindedness, blocking, misattribution, suggestibility, bias and persistence. This paper focuses on one memory sin, misattribution, that is implicated in false or illusory recognition of episodes that never occurred. We present data from cognitive, neuropsychological and neuroimaging studies that illuminate aspects of misattribution and false recognition. We first discuss cognitive research examining possible mechanisms of misattribution associated with false recognition. We also consider ways in which false recognition can be reduced or avoided, focusing in particular on the role of distinctive information. We next turn to neuropsychological research concerning patients with amnesia and Alzheimer's disease that reveals conditions under which such patients are less susceptible to false recognition than are healthy controls, thus providing clues about the brain mechanisms that drive false recognition. We then consider neuroimaging studies concerned with the neural correlates of true and false recognition, examining when the two forms of recognition can and cannot be distinguished on the basis of brain activity. Finally, we argue that even though misattribution and other memory sins are annoying and even dangerous, they can also be viewed as by-products of adaptive features of memory.

5.1. Introduction

Memory plays an important role in numerous aspects of everyday life, allowing us to recollect past experiences and learn new facts, navigate our environments, and remember what we need to do in the future. But memory can also fail us and sometimes fool us: we may forget or distort past experiences, and even claim to remember events that never occurred. These imperfections can provide insights into how memory works, and are therefore studied intensively by many researchers. But they can also have serious consequences for many people in our society. Forgetfulness that turns into Alzheimer's disease (AD), for instance, has profound effects on patients and their families (Pierce 2000). During the 1990s, issues concerning the accuracy of memories of childhood trauma recovered during psychotherapy led to a bitter controversy that divided professionals and destroyed families (e.g. Conway 1997; Lindsay & Read 1994; Loftus 1993; Pendergrast 1995; Schacter 1996). Similar concerns arose in cases of preschool children who, as a result of suggestive questioning, 'remembered' abusive events at the hands of teachers and others—despite an absence of objective evidence that such events ever occurred (Bjorklund 2000; Ceci & Bruck 1995; Ceci & Friedman 2000). And cases in which DNA testing has documented wrongful imprisonment almost always involve some type of faulty eyewitness memory (e.g. Wells *et al.* 1998).

Schacter (1999, 2001) recently classified the misdeeds of memory into seven basic 'sins': transience, absent-mindedness, blocking, misattribution, suggestibility, bias and persistence. The first three sins involve types of forgetting. Transience involves decreasing accessibility of information over time; absent-mindedness entails inattentive or shallow processing that contributes to weak memories of ongoing events or forgetting to do things in the future; and blocking refers to the temporary inaccessibility of information that is stored in memory. The next three sins all involve distortion or inaccuracy. Misattribution involves attributing a recollection or idea to the wrong source; suggestibility refers to memories that are implanted at the time of retrieval; and bias involves retrospective distortions and unconscious influences that are related to current knowledge and beliefs. The seventh and final sin, persistence, refers to intrusive memories that we cannot forget, even though we wish that we could.

The seven sins of memory resemble in some respects the ancient seven deadly sins (pride, anger, envy, greed, gluttony, lust and sloth). Both types of sins occur often in our daily lives. Moreover, we can view the ancient sins as exaggerations of adaptive human traits that may be necessary for survival. Similarly, memory's sins can be conceptualized as by-products of adaptive features of memory, rather than as flaws in system design or errors made by Mother Nature during evolution (Schacter 1999, 2001; see also Anderson & Schooler 1991; Bjork & Bjork 1988).

Given the focus of this issue on episodic memory, it is perhaps worth noting that all of the sins described by Schacter (1999, 2001) involve episodic memory, although they may involve other forms of memory as well. For instance, a prominent example of the sin of blocking is the 'tip-of-the tongue' state, where people cannot produce a word or name even though they feel that they are on the verge of recovering it (for reviews, see Brown 1991; Schwartz 1999). Although tip-of-the-tongue states primarily involve semantic memory, blocking can also occur in episodic memory (Roediger & Neely 1982; Schacter 1999, 2001).

In this paper we consider evidence and ideas pertaining to one of the major sins of episodic memory: the sin of misattribution. Misattribution of memories to the wrong source is a common form of memory distortion, both in the laboratory (Dodson & Schacter 2001a; Jacoby et al. 1989; Johnson et al. 1993; Schacter et al. 1998a), and in everyday life. For instance, after the tragic 1995 bombing of an office building in Oklahoma City, law enforcement officers quickly apprehended a suspect called 'John Doe 1', Timothy McVeigh, who was eventually convicted of the crime. But the officers also conducted a failed search for a second suspect called 'John Doe 2' who, they believed, had accompanied McVeigh when he rented a van two days before the bombing. An artist's sketch of John Doe 2 depicted a young square-faced man with dark hair and a stocky build wearing a blue-and-white cap. A witness who had seen McVeigh rent his van also recalled seeing John Doe 2 with him. But it was later discovered that the witness had actually seen a man who fit the description of John Doe 2 at the body shop the day after he saw McVeigh there. The witness misattributed his memory of John Doe 2 to the wrong episode, leading to needless confusion and wasted effort (for more details, see Schacter 2001).

We will discuss cognitive, neuropsychological and neuroimaging evidence that has bearing on a form of misattribution known as false recognition, where individuals mistakenly claim that a novel item or episode is familiar (e.g. Underwood 1965). During the past several years, false recognition has been studied extensively, and we are beginning to understand some of its cognitive and neural underpinnings. After summarizing relevant evidence from some of our own and others' research, we will argue that misattribution can be viewed as a by-product of otherwise adaptive memory processes.

5.2. False recognition: cognitive perspectives

Cognitive psychologists have studied false recognition for decades, using a variety of experimental procedures and paradigms (for reviews, see Alba & Hasher 1983; Johnson *et al.* 1993; Roediger 1996; Schacter 1995). During the past few years, however, interest in the phenomenon has intensified, in large part because of demonstrations of conditions under which extremely high levels of false recognition can be obtained (Hintzman 1988; Roediger & McDermott 1995; Shiffrin *et al.* 1995). In particular, Roediger & McDermott (1995) demonstrated exceptionally high levels of false recognition in experiments using a modified version of a paradigm initially developed by Deese (1959). In what has come to be known as the Deese–Roediger–McDermott (DRM) paradigm, participants study lists of words (e.g. tired, bed, awake, rest, dream, night, blanket, doze, slumber, snore, pillow, peace, yawn and drowsy) that are related to a non-presented lure word (e.g. sleep). On a subsequent old–new recognition test containing studied words (e.g. tired, dream), new words that are unrelated to the study list items (e.g. butter) and new words that are related to the study list items (e.g. sleep), participants frequently claim that they previously studied the related lure words. In many instances, false recognition of the related lure words is indistinguishable from the true recognition rate of studied words (e.g. Dodson & Schacter 2000; Mather *et al.* 1997; Norman & Schacter 1997; Payne *et al.* 1996; Roediger & McDermott 1995; Schacter *et al.* 1996a; cf. Miller & Wolford 1999; Roediger & McDermott 1999).

   Although the mechanisms underlying this robust false recognition effect are not yet fully understood, two main sources of the effect have been considered. First, false recognition could be the result of 'implicit associative responses' (Underwood 1965) that occur when participants are exposed to lists of semantic associates during the study phase of the experiment: studying associated words (e.g. bed, tired, doze, and so forth) might lead participants to generate on their own the non-presented lure word (i.e. sleep). On a later memory test, participants may experience source confusion (Johnson *et al.* 1993): they may mistakenly recollect that they heard or saw the related lure word on the study list when in fact they had generated it on their own (Roediger & McDermott 1995; Roediger *et al.* 2001). A second possibility is that studying numerous related words results in high levels of semantic overlap among the corresponding memory representations (Schacter *et al.* 1998a). This failure to keep representations of each item separate will produce robust memory for semantic similarities among the items, together with poor memory for the unique or distinctive aspects of each item. Because subjects have difficulty recollecting the distinctive characteristics of the specific studied items, they tend to make recognition responses on the basis of overall similarity of the lure item to the studied items—that is, participants will respond on the basis of semantic gist (Brainerd & Reyna 1998; Payne *et al.* 1996; Schacter *et al.* 1996a) rather than on the basis of specific recollections.

   It seems likely that both implicit associative responses and memory for semantic gist play some role in the robust false recognition that occurs in the DRM paradigm (e.g. Roediger *et al.* 2001). Evidence that false recognition can be driven mainly by gist-based processes, rather than implicit associative responses, comes from a categorized pictures paradigm developed by Koutstaal & Schacter (1997). In their paradigm, younger and older adults studied large numbers of pictures from a variety of different categories (e.g. cars, shoes, and so forth). On a subsequent recognition test, participants were shown previously studied pictures, related new pictures from previously studied categories, and unrelated new pictures. Koutstaal & Schacter reasoned that it is highly unlikely that participants would generate the related new pictures during the study phase of the experiment, in the same way that they might generate the word 'sleep' as an implicit associative response when studying related words in the DRM procedure. Koutstaal & Schacter found that participants often falsely recognized related new pictures from the same categories as the studied pictures. Rates of false recognition for young adults were considerably lower than in the DRM procedure, whereas older adults showed high levels of false recognition that, in some conditions, approached the levels observed in the DRM procedure. Overall, these data indicate that similarity or gist-based false recognition can occur even when implicit associative responses are an unlikely source of misattribution.

Whether driven by implicit associative responses or gist-based similarity, false recognition of related lures reflects some form of memory for semantic or associative information acquired during list presentation that is misattributed to a specific past sensory encounter with the item.

One implication of this line of reasoning is that false recognition can be reduced by encouraging subjects to focus on distinctive characteristics of individual items, rather than on semantic or associative properties that are common to all items. Israel & Schacter (1997) and Schacter *et al.* (1999) tested this idea by examining whether false recognition of semantic associates is reduced when subjects encode DRM lists along with detailed pictures corresponding to each item. They reasoned that presenting study-list items as pictures should increase encoding of distinctive, specific details of each item (Hunt & McDaniel 1993), which in turn should make them easier to discriminate from non-studied semantic associates. The experiments involved two key study conditions. In the word-encoding condition, participants both heard and saw lists of DRM semantic associates, whereas in the picture-encoding condition, participants heard the same lists of semantic associates and also saw line-drawings corresponding to each word. After the word- or picture-encoding conditions, previously studied words, related lures and unrelated lures were tested on an old–new recognition task (test items presented as pictures or as words). Consistent with the reasoning outlined earlier, false recognition of related lures was significantly reduced after pictorial encoding compared with word encoding. Dodson & Schacter (2000) reported a similar pattern of results using a different manipulation of distinctive encoding (saying words aloud compared with hearing them).

We (Dodson & Schacter 2000; Israel & Schacter 1997; Schacter *et al.* 1999, experiment 1) have argued that reduced false recognition after encoding distinctive information depends on a shift in responding based on participants' metamemorial assessments of the kinds of information they believe they should remember. For instance, having encountered pictures with each of the presented words, participants in the picture-encoding condition may have used a rule of thumb where they demanded access to detailed pictorial information in order to support a positive recognition decision (cf. Rotello 1999; Strack & Bless 1994). Thus, reduced false recognition appears to result from a general expectation that a test item would elicit a vivid perceptual recollection if it had in fact been presented previously. Participants in standard word-encoding conditions, by contrast, did not expect to retrieve distinctive representations of previously studied items. By our account, they were much less likely to demand access to detailed recollections. Schacter *et al.* (1999) referred to the hypothesized 'rule of thumb' in the picture-encoding condition as a distinctiveness heuristic.

Related evidence indicates that the distinctiveness heuristic has some generality across subject populations and experimental paradigms. For instance, Schacter *et al.* (1999) examined false recognition in the DRM paradigm after word and picture encoding in a group of elderly adults. Replicating previous studies (Norman & Schacter 1997; Tun *et al.* 1998), in the word-encoding condition older adults showed relatively higher levels of false recognition than younger adults. But in the picture-encoding condition, older adults reduced their levels of false recognition just as much as the younger adults did, indicating an intact ability to use the distinctiveness heuristic.

We have also found that participants can use the distinctiveness heuristic to reduce false recognition in paradigms other than the DRM procedure. Dodson & Schacter (2001*b,c*) used a repetition lag procedure adapted from Jennings & Jacoby (1997). In this paradigm, subjects study a list of unrelated words, and later make old–new recognition judgements about previously studied words and new words. The critical manipulation is that some new words on the recognition tests are repeated after varying lags. Even though participants are specifically instructed to say 'old' only to words from the study list, and not to new words that are repeated, after sufficiently long lags participants make false alarms to some repeated new words. Participants misattribute their familiarity with the repeated new words to a prior appearance in the study list. Jennings & Jacoby (1997) demonstrated that the effect is especially pronounced in older adults. In recent experiments by Dodson & Schacter (2001*b*), younger and older adults studied words, pictures, or a mixture of both, and then completed a recognition test in which studied items appeared once and new items appeared twice. Several experiments demonstrated that, compared with the word-encoding condition, studying pictures produced a significant reduction in false recognition rates to repeated new words for both older and younger adults. The reduction in false recognition was particularly dramatic for older adults, who showed high false recognition rates in the word-encoding condition, replicating the earlier results of Jennings & Jacoby (1997). Dodson & Schacter (2001*b*) attributed the reductions in false recognition to the use of a distinctiveness heuristic.

5.3. Neuropsychology of false recognition: evidence from amnesia and Alzheimer's Disease

Cognitive studies have provided important information about the properties of misattribution and false recognition, but they are mute about relevant underlying brain systems. Studies of brain-damaged patients have begun to provide some insights into the brain regions that are implicated in false recognition. For example, a number of studies have revealed that patients with damage to various sectors of the frontal lobes show increased levels of false recognition compared with age-matched control subjects

(Curran *et al.* 1997; Delbecq-Derouesné *et al.* 1990; Parkin *et al.* 1996, 1999; Ward *et al.* 1999; Rapcsak *et al.* 1999; Schacter *et al.* 1996*b*). Explanations for this increased false recognition have varied across patients, depending on particular features of their performance. Some investigators have focused on inadequate encoding of item-specific details (e.g. Parkin *et al.* 1999), whereas others have emphasized defective retrieval monitoring processes (e.g. Delbecq-Derouesné *et al.* 1990; Rapcsak *et al.* 1999; Schacter *et al.* 1996*b*, 1998*a*; for more detailed discussion, see Dodson & Schacter 2001*a*).

Studies of false recognition in amnesic patients with memory disorders resulting from damage to the medial temporal lobes (MTLs) and related structures in the diencephalon have provided important additional insights. Such patients have great difficulty remembering recent experiences and acquiring new information, despite relatively intact perception, language and general intellectual function (e.g. Parkin 2001; Squire 1992).

Schacter *et al.* (1996*a*) used the DRM paradigm to investigate false recognition in amnesic patients. Amnesiacs and matched control subjects studied lists of semantic associates, and then made old–new recognition judgements about studied words, new related words (e.g. sleep after studying tired, bed, awake, rest, and so forth), and new unrelated words (e.g. point). They found that, as expected, amnesiacs recognized fewer studied items than did the matched controls, and also made more false alarms to unrelated new words. More importantly, amnesiacs showed reduced false recognition of the related lure words (for replication and extension, see Melo *et al.* 1999). Schacter *et al.* (1997*a*) demonstrated that amnesiacs' reduced false recognition of related lure items extends to perceptual materials. After studying perceptually related words (e.g. fade, fame, face, fake, mate, hate, late, date and rate), amnesiacs were less likely than controls both to correctly recognize studied words and to falsely recognize perceptually related lure words (e.g. fate). The results thus indicate that in amnesic patients, the same processes that support accurate recognition of studied words also contribute to the false recognition of semantically or perceptually related lures.

The same general pattern of results has been observed in experiments involving pictorial materials. Using Koutstaal & Schacter's (1997) categorized pictures paradigm described earlier, Koutstaal *et al.* (2001) found that amnesic patients were less likely than controls to falsely recognize new pictures after studying numerous similar items from the same category. Koutstaal *et al.* (1999) reported a similar pattern in an experiment that examined true and false recognition of pictures of abstract objects. Each picture belonged to a particular perceptual category and was similar to a prototype that defined the category. The categories included either one, three, six or nine pictures. All participants then completed a recognition test containing studied pictures and new pictures that were either related or unrelated to studied items. They (Koutstaal *et al.* 1999) found that, for control subjects, both true and false recognition of the abstract pictures increased with category size, whereas category size had only a slight effect on true and false recognition in amnesic patients. With larger categories, amnesic patients showed less true and false recognition than did control subjects.

Recent work by Budson *et al.* (2000) has revealed the same general pattern of results in studies of patients with memory disorders resulting from AD. AD patients showed reduced false recognition of semantic associates in the DRM word recognition paradigm. Further, Budson *et al.* (2001) have found that AD patients show reduced false recognition of pictures of abstract objects from large categories in the paradigm developed by Koutstaal *et al.* (1999).

Interestingly, studies of both amnesic patients and AD patients have identified conditions within the DRM paradigm in which patients can show as much or more false recognition of related lures compared with controls. Schacter *et al.* (1998*b*) presented amnesiacs and controls with DRM lists of semantic associates, and then gave a standard old–new recognition test. This study–test procedure was repeated five times. On the first trial, amnesiacs showed reduced true and false recognition of semantic associates compared with controls, replicating the previous results discussed (Schacter *et al.* 1996*a*, 1997*a*). Across the five study–test trials, control subjects showed increased true recognition of studied words together with reduced false recognition of semantic associates. As they remembered more detailed information about specific words that actually appeared on the study list, control subjects were able to use this information to reduce or suppress their tendency to make false recognition responses based on semantic similarity or gist information. Amnesic patients, in contrast, showed no reduction in false recognition across study–test trials. In fact, they showed an opposite tendency for increased false recognition across study trials. This latter result was mainly attributable to patients with amnesia that resulted from Korsakoff's disease, who are characterized by damage to diencephalic structures and often show signs of frontal lobe damage. Patients with amnesia that resulted from MTL damage tended to show a flat or fluctuating pattern of false recognition across trials. Budson *et al.* (2000) used the same paradigm, and found that AD patients who exhibited reduced false recognition of semantic associates on the first trial, showed steadily increasing levels of false recognition across trials. By the fifth and final trial, AD patients showed higher levels of false recognition than did controls.

Both Schacter *et al.* (1998*b*) and Budson *et al.* (2000) argued that with repeated study and testing of semantic associates, patients strengthened their initially degraded representation of the semantic features or gist of the studied items, leading them to false alarm more frequently to related lure words. Unlike control subjects, however, amnesic and AD patients do not develop increasingly detailed representations of the specific words they studied. Whereas controls can use such specific representations to counter or oppose the increasing influence of semantic gist, amnesic and AD patients do not. In this paradigm, then, misattribution occurs when participants rely on representations of semantic gist that are unchecked by specific episodic memories of the actual list words. For control subjects, this pattern of influences is maximal on the first trial and reduced by the final trial. For amnesic and AD patients, it takes several trials to build up the semantic gist information that is responsible for the misattribution error.

5.4. Neuroimaging of true and false recognition

Several neuroimaging studies using positron emission tomography (PET), functional magnetic resonance imaging (fMRI) and event-related potentials (ERPs) have begun to explore misattributions associated with false recognition. Two studies from our laboratory made use of the DRM false recognition paradigm.

Schacter *et al.* (1996*c*) investigated true and false recognition with PET, and Schacter *et al.* (1997*b*) carried out a similar study with fMRI. In both studies, participants heard lists of semantic associates prior to entering the scanner; scanning was performed later as participants made old–new judgements about previously studied words, critical lures that were semantically related to the studied items, and unrelated lure words. The main finding from the two studies is that patterns of brain activity were highly similar during true and false recognition. Differences in brain activity during true and false recognition were relatively small and depended on specific characteristics of recognition testing procedures (for discussion, see Schacter *et al.* 1997*b*; also see Johnson *et al.* 1997).

Frontal lobe activation was quite prominent in each of the PET and fMRI studies of false recognition. Consistent with other imaging evidence concerning episodic memory (e.g. Henson *et al.* 1999), both studies reported evidence that regions within the frontal lobes may be involved in strategic monitoring processes that are invoked as participants struggle to determine whether a related lure word was actually presented earlier in a study list (for further relevant evidence, see Johnson *et al.* 1997). These findings fit well with the neuropsychological data discussed earlier (§ 5.3) that damage to areas within the frontal lobe can be associated with heightened false recognition.

Consistent with the studies discussed earlier (§ 5.3), showing reduced false recognition of semantic associates in amnesic patients, both the PET and fMRI studies revealed some evidence of MTL activity during false and true recognition. However, there were no detectable differences in MTL activity during true and false recognition.

In a more recent fMRI experiment, Cabeza *et al.* (2001) attempted to create conditions that would increase the likelihood of finding differences in brain activity during true and false recognition. Recall the behavioural evidence discussed earlier (§ 5.2) that differences between true and false recognition can be increased when study lists are presented in a perceptually distinct manner (e.g. presenting pictures with words in the DRM paradigm; Israel & Schacter (1997) and Schacter *et al.* (1999)). In the previous neuroimaging studies that used the DRM procedure, words were presented auditorily to participants. In an attempt to increase the perceptual encoding of study list words, Cabeza *et al.* (2001) had a male and female speaker present lists of semantically related words. Participants were specifically instructed to try to remember which speaker said each word. Thus, studied words should be associated with a specific source or perceptual input in a way that related lure words would not.

The most relevant imaging findings from the Cabeza *et al.* (2001) experiment concern the MTL. They found that a region of posterior MTL, in the parahippocampal gyrus, showed increased activity (relative to an unrelated lure baseline) for previously studied words but not for semantically related lure words. By contrast, a more anterior MTL region within the hippocampus showed significantly increased activity for both studied words and related lures compared with unrelated lures. The posterior MTL region may have been sensitive to perceptual differences between studied words and non-studied semantic associates. Consistent with this suggestion, an earlier study by Schacter *et al.* (1997*c*) revealed that this same posterior MTL region responded more strongly to previously studied visual objects that were tested in the same perceptual format than in a different perceptual format (i.e. when the size or orientation of the object was altered between study and test). In contrast, the anterior MTL region appeared to be responding on the basis of semantic information common to both studied words and related lures. Cabeza *et al.* (2001) thus suggested that anterior MTL is involved primarily in the recovery of semantic information, whereas posterior MTL is involved primarily in the recovery of sensory information (for further evidence of different brain responses during true and false recognition, see Fabiani *et al.* 2000).

Studies concerned with the neural correlates of misattribution have also examined false recognition errors within the context of source confusions (e.g. Johnson *et al.* 1993, 1996; Nolde *et al.* 1998). As discussed earlier (§ 5.2), one explanation for the robust false recognition effect in the DRM paradigm involves source confusion: when individuals fail to distinguish between what they generate as an implicit associative response (e.g. sleep) and what was actually presented during the study phase (e.g. bed, tired, dream, etc., cf. Mather *et al.* 1997; Roediger *et al.* 2001). This source confusion error, also known as an error in reality monitoring, can also refer to instances in which an individual confuses test items that were earlier imagined with items that were earlier perceived (Johnson & Raye 1981). Recently, Gonsalves & Paller (2000) used ERPs to investigate brain potentials at encoding and at retrieval that are associated with reality monitoring errors (see also Johnson *et al.* 1996; Nolde *et al.* 1998). During the study phase of their experiment, participants saw words and imagined the corresponding object, such as seeing the word 'cat' and then imagining a picture of a cat. However, half of the words were followed by a corresponding picture (the 'word plus picture' trials), whereas no picture was presented for the remaining study words (the 'word only' trials). On a later memory test, participants indicated whether or not each test item had been seen earlier as a picture.

As expected on the basis of previous work (e.g. Durso & Johnson 1980), participants made reality monitoring errors and claimed that some items in the 'word only' study condition had been presented with a picture. Because ERPs were recorded during the study phase, it was possible to examine whether there were different patterns of brain activity at encoding that were later associated with true and false recognition, as has been done previously in ERP and fMRI studies of true recognition (for review, see Wagner *et al.* 1999). In other words, are there differences in brain potentials when participants initially see the study words that predict whether or not that word will be falsely recognized on the test as having been seen as a picture? Interestingly, Gonsalves & Paller (2000) found that ERPs recorded during the study phase in posterior cortical regions (i.e. occipital and parietal locations) were more positive for items in the 'word only' condition that were later falsely remembered as pictures than for those items that were correctly rejected as not accompanied with a picture. These positive ERPs may be providing an index of brain activity related to words that elicit strong visual imagery at encoding, which in turn enhances their likelihood of being falsely remembered as pictures on a later test.

5.5. Misattribution and false recognition: vices or virtues?

Misattribution and false recognition are sins of memory in the sense that they are associated with inaccurate reports about the past: people make claims about previous experiences that are, at least in some respects, incorrect. Similar sentiments apply to the other memory sins, which involve errors of omission or commission. These observations could easily lead one to conclude that evolution burdened us with an extremely inefficient, even defective, memory system—a system so prone to error that it may even jeopardize our well-being.

In contrast to this rather dark view of memory, Schacter (1999, 2001) argued that each of the sins is a by-product of adaptive features of memory, and in that sense they do not represent flaws or defects in the system (cf. Anderson & Schooler 1991; Bjork & Bjork 1988). Instead, the memory sins can be thought of as costs associated with benefits that make memory work as well as it does most of the time. Here we consider the case for the adaptive value of misattribution.

Consider that many instances of misattribution reflect poor memory for the source of an experience, such as the precise details of who said a particular fact, when and where a familiar face was encountered, or whether an object was perceived or only imagined. When source details are not initially well encoded, or become inaccessible with the passing of time, conditions are ripe for the kinds of misattributions associated with false recognition. But consider the consequences and costs of retaining each and every contextual detail that defines our numerous daily experiences. Anderson & Schooler (1991) (see also Schooler & Anderson 1997) have argued persuasively that memory is adapted to retain information that is most likely to be needed in the environment in which it operates. Because we do not frequently need to remember all the precise, source-specifying details of our experiences, an adapted system should not routinely record all such details as a default option. Instead, the system would record such details only when circumstances warn that they will be needed—and this is what human memory tends to do.

A second and related factor that contributes to misattributions involving false recognition concerns the distinction between memory for gist and specific information discussed earlier (§ 5.2) (Brainerd & Reyna 1998; Reyna & Brainerd 1995). False recognition often occurs when people remember the semantic or perceptual gist of an experience but do not recollect specific details. However, memory for gist may also be fundamental to such abilities as categorization and comprehension, and may facilitate the development of transfer and generalization across tasks. McClelland (1995, p. 84) has argued along these lines and noted that generalization often results from gist-like, accumulated effects of prior experiences. While depicting such generalization as central to intelligent behaviour and cognitive development, McClelland also noted that 'such generalization gives rise to distortions as an inherent by-product'.

We have already considered evidence that fits well with such a position, namely the consistent finding that amnesic patients show reduced false recognition of semantically and perceptually related words (Schacter et al. 1996a, 1997a, 1998b). Further, amnesiacs also show reduced false recognition of categorized pictures and novel objects that depend on retaining gist information (Koutstaal et al. 1999). These observations suggest that false recognition and misattribution based on gist reflect the workings of a normally functioning, healthy memory system. A damaged system such as that in amnesic patients does not either encode, retain or retrieve the information that leads healthy people to show high levels of gist-based false recognition.

Beversdorf et al. (2000) have recently provided striking evidence that supports this point. They studied adults with a condition known as autistic spectrum disorder. Such individuals are in many respects similar to autistic children, except that they tend to function at a higher level. Autistic children rely on a relatively literal style of processing information, and do not take advantage of semantic context to the same extent as normal children. Beversdorf *et al.* (2000) used the DRM semantic associates paradigm to assess whether adults with autistic spectrum disorder also show impaired sensitivity to semantic context. After studying lists of semantic associates, the autistic spectrum disorder group showed significantly less false recognition of semantically related lure words than did the healthy controls. However, the autistic spectrum disorder group showed normal hit rates for previously studied words, resulting in greater discrimination between true and false memories than in the control group. The autistic spectrum disorder group appeared to be relying on a highly literal form of memory, missing out on the semantic gist that supports false recognition responses. Once again, misattributions resulting in false recognition appear to reflect the operation of a healthy memory system.

These findings support the idea that misattribution can reflect adaptive aspects of memory function. Buss *et al.* (1998) (see Schacter 1999, 2001) have distinguished between two senses of the term 'adaptive' in evolutionary discussions. One is based in evolutionary theory: it rests on a technical definition of an adaptation as a feature of a species that came into existence through the operation of natural selection because it in some way increased reproductive fitness. The other is a non-technical, everyday sense of the term that refers to features of organisms that have positive functional consequences, regardless of whether they arose directly from natural selection. Some generally useful or 'adaptive' features of organisms are not adaptations in the strict sense. Sometimes termed 'exaptations' (Gould & Vrba 1982), these useful functions arise as a consequence of other related features that are adaptations in the technical sense. Such adaptations are sometimes coopted to perform functions other than the one for which they were originally selected.

With respect to the memory sins, it is difficult to determine definitively which (if any) are genuine adaptations and which are exaptations (for detailed discussion, see Schacter 2001). One strong candidate for an adaptation is the sin of persistence—intrusive, unwanted recollection of disturbing experiences—which usually results from the encoding and retrieval of enduring memories for highly emotional or arousing events. If persistence arose in response to life-threatening situations that endangered an organism's survival, animals and people who could remember those experiences persistently would probably be favoured by natural selection. If persistence is indeed an adaptation, many species should have neural mechanisms dedicated to preserving life-threatening experiences across lengthy time-periods. And, indeed, LeDoux (1996) has argued forcefully that the amygdala and related structures are implicated in long-lasting fear learning across diverse species, including humans, monkeys, cats and rats.

In contrast to this view of persistence, misattributions involved in false recognition are unlikely to be adaptations: it is difficult to see how or why remembering an experience inaccurately would result in increased survival and hence reflect the operation of natural selection. Instead, misattribution is more probably a by-product of adaptations and exaptations that have yielded a memory system that does not routinely preserve all the source-specifying details of an experience. Misattribution could also be a by-product of gist-based memory processes, which could have arisen as either adaptations or exaptations.

This sort of by-product fits what Gould & Lewontin (1979) called a 'spandrel': a type of exaptation that is a side consequence of a particular function. The term spandrel is used in architecture to refer to left-over spaces between structural elements in a building. Gould & Lewontin described the example of the four spandrels in the central dome of Venice's Cathedral of San Marco, which are left-over spaces between arches and walls that were later decorated with four evangelists and four Biblical rivers. The spandrels were not built in order to house these paintings, but they do the job quite well (for further discussion of spandrels, see Buss *et al.* 1998; Gould 1991).

If we think of misattribution and false recognition as psychological spandrels, they differ in at least one important way from the architectural spandrels discussed by Gould & Lewontin (1979). The latter generally have benign consequences, whereas misattribution and false recognition can cause serious problems, as illustrated by the consequences of faulty eyewitness identifications (Wells *et al.* 1998) and problems created by false memories recovered in psychotherapy (e.g. Bjorklund 2000; Loftus 1993; Lindsay & Read 1994; Pendergrast 1995; Schacter 1996). We thus might think of misattribution and false recognition as spandrels gone awry (Schacter 2001): consequences of adaptive features of memory sometimes turn the system's virtues into vices.

The authors are supported by grants from the US National Institute on Aging (AGO8441) and the National Institute of Mental Health (MH60941). We thank Steven Prince (Department of Psychology, Duke University, Durham, NC, USA) for assistance in manuscript preparation.

References

Alba, J. W. & Hasher, L. 1983 Is memory schematic? *Psychol. Bull.* **93**, 203–231.

Anderson, J. R. & Schooler, L. J. 1991 Reflections of the environment in memory. *Psychol. Sci.* **2**, 396–408.

Beversdorf, D. Q. (and 10 others) 2000 Increased discrimination of 'false memories' in autistic spectrum disorder. *Proc. Natl Acad. Sci. USA* **97**, 8734–8737.

Bjork, R. A. & Bjork, E. L. 1988 On the adaptive aspects of retrieval failure in autobiographical memory. In *Practical aspects of memory: current research and issues* (ed. M. M. Gruneberg, P. E. Morris & R. N. Sykes), pp. 283–288. Chichester: Wiley.

Bjorklund, D. F. (ed.) 2000 *False-memory creation in children and adults: theory, research, and implications*. Mahwah, NJ: Lawrence Erlbaum.

Brainerd, C. J. & Reyna, C. F. 1998 When things that were never experienced are easier to 'remember' than things that were. *Psychol. Sci.* **9**, 484–489.

Brown, A. S. 1991 A review of the tip-of-the-tongue experience. *Psychol. Bull.* **109**, 204–223.

Budson, A. E., Daffner, K. R., Desikan, R. & Schacter, D. L. 2000 When false recognition is unopposed by true recognition: gist-based memory distortion in Alzheimer's disease. *Neuropsychology* **14**, 277–287.

Budson, A. E., Desikan, R., Daffner, K. R. & Schacter, D. L. 2001 Perceptual false recognition in Alzheimer's disease. *Neuropsychology* **15**, 230–245.

Buss, D. M., Haselton, M. G., Shackelford, T. K., Bleske, A. L. & Wakefield, J. C. 1998 Adaptations, exapations, and spandrels. *Am. Psychol.* **53**, 533–548.

Cabeza, R., Rao, S., Wagner, A. D., Mayer, A. & Schacter, D. L. 2001 Can the hippocampal memory system distinguish true from false? (Submitted.)

Ceci, S. J. & Bruck, M. 1995 *Jeopardy in the courtroom*. Washington DC: APA Books.

Ceci, S. J. & Friedman, R. D. 2000 The suggestibility of children: scientific research and legal implications. *Cornell Law Rev.* **86**, 33–108.

Conway, M. A. (ed.) 1997 *Recovered memories and false memories*. Oxford University Press.

Curran, T., Schacter, D. L., Norman, K. A. & Galluccio, L. 1997 False recognition after a right frontal lobe infarction: memory for general and specific information. *Neuropsychologia* **35**, 1035–1049.

Deese, J. 1959 On the prediction of occurrence of particular verbal intrusions in immediate recall. *J. Exp. Psychol.* **58**, 17–22.

Delbecq-Derouesné, J., Beauvois, M. F. & Shallice, T. 1990 Preserved recall versus impaired recognition. *Brain* **113**, 1045–1074.

Dodson, C. S. & Schacter, D. L. 2000 'If I had said it I would have remembered it': reducing false memories with a distinctiveness heuristic. *Psychonomic Bull. Rev.* **8**, 155–161.

Dodson, C. S. & Schacter, D. L. 2001*a* Memory distortion. In *The handbook of cognitive neuropsychology: what deficits reveal about the human mind* (ed. B. Rapp), pp. 445–463. Philadelphia, PA: Psychology Press.

Dodson, C. S. & Schacter, D. L. 2001*b* Aging, strategic retrieval processes and false recognition: reducing false memories with a distinctiveness heuristic. (Submitted.)

Dodson, C. S. & Schacter, D. L. 2001*c* When false recognition meets metacognition: the distinctiveness heuristic. *J. Memory Language.* (In the press.)

Durso, F. T. & Johnson, M. K. 1980 The effects of orienting tasks on recognition, recall, and modality confusion of pictures and words. *J. Verb. Learn. Verb. Behav.* **19**, 416–429.

Fabiani, M., Stadler, M. A. & Wessels, P. M. 2000 True but not false memories produce a sensory signature in human lateralized brain potentials. *J. Cogn. Neurosci.* **12**, 941–949.

Gonsalves, B. & Paller, K. A. 2000 Neural events that underlie remembering something that never happened. *Nature Neurosci.* **3**, 1316–1321.

Gould, S. J. 1991 Exaptation: a crucial tool for evolutionary psychology. *J. Social Issues* **47**, 43–65.

Gould, S. J. & Lewontin, R. C. 1979 The spandrels of San Marco and the Panglossian paradigm: a critique of the adaptationist programme. *Proc. R. Soc. Lond.* B **205**, 581–598.

Gould, S. J. & Vrba, E. S. 1982 Exaptation: a missing term in the science of form. *Paleobiology* **8**, 4–15.

Henson, R. N. A., Rugg, M. D., Shallice, T., Josephs, O. & Dolan, R. J. 1999 Recollection and familiarity in recognition memory: an event-related functional magnetic resonance imaging study. *J. Neurosci.* **19**, 3962–3972.

Hintzman, D. L. 1988 Judgements of frequency and recognition memory in a multiple-trace memory model. *Psychol. Rev.* **95**, 528–551.

Hunt, R. R. & McDaniel, M. A. 1993 The enigma of organization and distinctiveness. *J. Mem. Lang.* **32**, 421–445.

Israel, L. & Schacter, D. L. 1997 Pictorial encoding reduces false recognition of semantic associates. *Psychonomic Bull. Rev.* **4**, 577–581.

Jacoby, L. L., Kelley, C. M. & Dywan, J. 1989 Memory attributions. In *Varieties of memory and consciousness: essays in honor of Endel Tulving* (ed. H. L. Roediger III & F. I. M. Craik), pp. 391–422. Hillsdale, NJ: Lawrence Erlbaum Associates.

Jennings, J. M. & Jacoby, L. L. 1997 An opposition procedure for detecting age-related deficits in recollection: telling effects of repetition. *Psychol. Aging* **12**, 352–361.

Johnson, M. K. & Raye, C. L. 1981 Reality monitoring. *Psychol. Rev.* **88**, 67–85.

Johnson, M. K., Hashtroudi, S. & Lindsay, D. S. 1993 Source monitoring. *Psychol. Bull.* **114**, 3–28.

Johnson, M. K., Kounios, J. & Nolde, S. F. 1996 Electrophysiological brain activity and memory source monitoring. *NeuroReport* **8**, 1317–1320.

Johnson, M. K., Nolde, S. F., Mather, M., Kounios, J., Schacter, D. L. & Curran, T. 1997 The similarity of brain activity associated with true and false recognition memory depends on test format. *Psychol. Sci.* **8**, 250–257.

Koutstaal, W. & Schacter, D. L. 1997 Gist-based false recognition of pictures in older and younger adults. *J. Mem. Lang.* **37**, 555–583.

Koutstaal, W., Schacter, D. L., Verfaellie, M., Brenner, C. J. & Jackson, E. M. 1999 Perceptually based false recognition of novel objects in amnesia: effects of category size and similarity to category prototypes. *Cogn. Neuropsychol.* **16**, 317–341.

Koutstaal, W., Verfaellie, M. & Schacter, D. L. 2001 Recognizing identical vs. similar categorically related common objects: further evidence for degraded gist-representations in amnesia. *Neuropsychology* **15**, 269–290.

LeDoux, J. E. 1996 *The emotional brain.* New York: Simon & Schuster.

Lindsay, D. S. & Read, J. D. 1994 Psychotherapy and memories of childhood sexual abuse: a cognitive perspective. *Appl. Cogn. Psychol.* **8**, 281–338.

Loftus, E. F. 1993 The reality of repressed memories. *Am. Psychol.* **48**, 518–537.

McClelland, J. L. 1995 Constructive memory and memory distortions: a parallel-distributed processing approach. In *Memory distortion: how minds, brains and societies reconstruct the past* (ed. D. L. Schacter), pp. 69–90. Cambridge, MA: Harvard University Press.

Mather, M., Henkel, L. A. & Johnson, M. K. 1997 Evaluating characteristics of false memories: remember/know judgments and memory characteristics questionnaire compared. *Mem. Cogn.* **25**, 826–837.

Melo, B., Winocur, G. & Moscovitch, M. 1999 False recall and false recognition: an examination of the effects of selective and combined lesions to the medial temporal lobe/diencephalon and frontal lobe structures. *Cogn. Neuropsychol.* **16**, 343–359.

Miller, M. B. & Wolford, G. L. 1999 Theoretical commentary: the role of criterion shift in false memory. *Psychol. Rev.* **106**, 398–405.

Nolde, S. F., Johnson, M. K. & D'Esposito, M. 1998 Left prefrontal activation during episodic remembering: an event-related fMRI study. *NeuroReport* **9**, 3509–3514.

Norman, K. A. & Schacter, D. L. 1997 False recognition in young and older adults: exploring the characteristics of illusory memories. *Mem. Cogn.* **25**, 838–848.

Parkin, A. J. 2001 The structure and mechanisms of memory. In *The handbook of cognitive neuropsychology: what deficits reveal about the human mind* (ed. B. Rapp), pp. 399–422. Philadelphia, PA: Psychology Press.

Parkin, A. J., Bindschaedler, C., Harsent, L. & Metzler, C. 1996 Pathological false alarm rates following damage to the left frontal cortex. *Brain Cogn.* **32**, 14–27.

Parkin, A. J., Ward, J., Bindschaedler, C., Squires, E. J. & Powell, G. 1999 False recognition following frontal lobe damage: the role of encoding factors. *Cogn. Neuropsychol.* **16**, 243–265.

Payne, D. G., Elie, C. J., Blackwell, J. M. & Neuschatz, J. S. 1996 Memory illusions: recalling, recognizing, and recollecting events that never occurred. *J. Mem. Lang.* **35**, 261–285.

Pendergrast, M. 1995 *Victims of memory: incest accusations and shattered lives.* Hinesburg, VT: Upper Access.

Pierce, C. P. 2000 *Hard to forget: an Alzheimer's story.* New York: Random House.

Rapcsak, S. Z., Reminger, S. L., Glisky, E. L., Kasniak, A. W. & Comer, J. F. 1999 Neuropsychological mechanisms of false facial recognition following frontal lobe damage. *Cogn. Neuropsychol.* **16**, 267–292.

Reyna, V. F. & Brainerd, C. J. 1995 Fuzzy-trace theory: an interim synthesis. *Learn. Individ. Differences* **7**, 1–75.

Roediger III, H. L. 1996 Memory illusions. *J. Mem. Lang.* **35**, 76–100.

Roediger III, H. L. & McDermott, K. B. 1995 Creating false memories: remembering words not presented in lists. *J. Exp. Psychol. Learn. Mem. Cogn.* **21**, 803–814.

Roediger III, H. L. & McDermott, K. B. 1999 False alarms about false memories. *Psychol. Rev.* **106**, 406–410.

Roediger III, H. L. & Neely, J. H. 1982 Retrieval blocks in episodic and semantic memory. *Can. J. Psychol.* **36**, 213–242.

Roediger III, H. L., Balota, D. A. & Watson, J. M. 2001 Spreading activation and the arousal of false memories. In *The nature of remembering: essays in honor of Robert G. Crowder* (ed. H. L. Roediger III, J. S. Nairne, I. Neath & A. M. Surprenant). Washington, DC: American Psychological Association.

Rotello, C. M. 1999 Metacognition and memory for nonoccurrence. *Memory* **7**, 43–63.

Schacter, D. L. 1995 Memory distortion: history and current status. In *Memory distortion: how minds, brains and societies reconstruct the past* (ed. D. L. Schacter), pp. 1–43. Cambridge, MA: Harvard University Press.

Schacter, D. L. 1996 *Searching for memory: the brain, the mind, and the past*. New York: Basic Books.

Schacter, D. L. 1999 The seven sins of memory: insights from psychology and cognitive neuroscience. *Am. Psychol.* **54**, 182–203.

Schacter, D. L. 2001 *The seven sins of memory: how the mind forgets and remembers*. Boston, MA: Houghton Mifflin.

Schacter, D. L., Verfaellie, M. & Pradere, D. 1996a The neuropsychology of memory illusions: false recall and recognition in amnesic patients. *J. Mem. Lang.* **35**, 319–334.

Schacter, D. L., Curran, T., Galluccio, L., Milberg, W. & Bates, J. 1996b False recognition and the right frontal lobe: a case study. *Neuropsychologia* **34**, 793–808.

Schacter, D. L., Reiman, E., Curran, T., Yun, L. S., Bandy, D., McDermott, K. B. & Roediger III, H. L. 1996c Neuroanatomical correlates of veridical and illusory recognition memory: evidence from positron emission tomography. *Neuron* **17**, 267–274.

Schacter, D. L., Verfaellie, M. & Anes, M. D. 1997a Illusory memories in amnesic patients: conceptual and perceptual false recognition. *Neuropsychology* **11**, 331–342.

Schacter, D. L., Buckner, R. L., Koutstaal, W., Dale, A. M. & Rosen, B. R. 1997b Late onset of anterior prefrontal activity during retrieval of veridical and illusory memories: an event-related fMRI study. *NeuroImage* **6**, 259–269.

Schacter, D. L., Uecker, A., Reiman, E., Yun, L. S., Bandy, D., Chen, K., Cooper, L. A. & Curran, T. 1997c Effects of size and orientation change on hippocampal activation during episodic recognition: a PET study. *NeuroReport* **8**, 3993–3998.

Schacter, D. L., Norman, K. A. & Koutstaal, W. 1998a The cognitive neuroscience of constructive memory. *A. Rev. Psychol.* **49**, 289–318.

Schacter, D. L., Verfaellie, M., Anes, M. D. & Racine, C. 1998b When true recognition suppresses false recognition: evidence from amnesic patients. *J. Cogn. Neurosci.* **10**, 668–679.

Schacter, D. L., Israel, L. & Racine, C. A. 1999 Suppressing false recognition in younger and older adults: the distinctiveness heuristic. *J. Mem. Lang.* **40**, 1–24.

Schooler, L. J. & Anderson, J. R. 1997 The role of process in the rational analysis of memory. *Cogn. Psychol.* **32**, 219–250.

Schwartz, B. L. 1999 Sparkling at the end of the tongue: the etiology of tip-of-the-tongue phenomenology. *Psychonomic Bull. Rev.* **6**, 379–393.

Shiffrin, R. M., Huber, D. E. & Marinelli, K. 1995 Effects of category length and strength on familiarity in recognition. *J. Exp. Psychol. Learn. Mem. Cogn.* **21**, 267–287.

Squire, L. R. 1992 Memory and the hippocampus: a synthesis from findings with rats, monkeys, and humans. *Psychol. Rev.* **99**, 195–231.

Strack, F. & Bless, H. 1994 Memory for nonoccurrences: metacognitive and presuppositional strategies. *J. Mem. Lang.* **33**, 203–217.

Tun, P. A., Wingfield, A., Rosen, M. J. & Blanchard, L. 1998 Response latencies for false memories—gist-based processes in normal aging. *Psychol. Aging* **13**, 230–241.

Underwood, B. J. 1965 False recognition produced by implicit verbal responses. *J. Exp. Psychol.* **70**, 122–129.

Wagner, A. D., Koutstaal, W. & Schacter, D. L. 1999 When encoding yields remembering: insights from event-related neuroimaging. *Proc. R. Soc. Lond.* B **354**, 1307–1324.

Ward, J., Parkin, A. J., Powell, G., Squires, E. J., Townshend, J. & Bradley, V. 1999 False recognition of unfamiliar people: 'seeing film stars everywhere'. *Cogn. Neuropsychol.* **16**, 293–315.

Wells, G. L., Small, M., Penrod, S., Malpass, R. S., Fulero, S. M. & Brimacombe, C. A. E. 1998 Eyewitness identification procedures: recommendations for lineups and photospreads. *Law Hum. Behav.* **22**, 603–647.

6

Theories of episodic memory

Andrew R. Mayes and Neil Roberts

Theories of episodic memory need to specify the encoding (representing), storage, and retrieval processes that underlie this form of memory and indicate the brain regions that mediate these processes and how they do so. Representation and re-representation (retrieval) of the spatiotemporally linked series of scenes, which constitute an episode, are probably mediated primarily by those parts of the posterior neocortex that process perceptual and semantic information. However, some role of the frontal neocortex and medial temporal lobes in representing aspects of context and high-level visual object information at encoding and retrieval cannot currently be excluded. Nevertheless, it is widely believed that the frontal neocortex is mainly involved in coordinating episodic encoding and retrieval and that the medial temporal lobes store aspects of episodic information. Establishing where storage is located is very difficult and disagreement remains about the role of the posterior neocortex in episodic memory storage. One view is that this region stores all aspects of episodic memory *ab initio* for as long as memory lasts. This is compatible with evidence that the amygdala, basal forebrain, and midbrain modulate neocortical storage. Another view is that the posterior neocortex only gradually develops the ability to store some aspects of episodic information as a function of rehearsal over time and that this information is initially stored by the medial temporal lobes. A third view is that the posterior neocortex never stores these aspects of episodic information because the medial temporal lobes store them for as long as memory lasts in an increasingly redundant fashion. The last two views both postulate that the medial temporal lobes initially store contextual markers that serve to cohere featural information stored in the neocortex. Lesion and functional neuroimaging evidence still does not clearly distinguish between these views. Whether the feeling that an episodic memory is familiar depends on retrieving an association between a retrieved episode and this feeling, or by an attribution triggered by a priming process, is unclear. Evidence about whether the hippocampus and medial temporal lobe cortices play different roles in episodic memory is conflicting. Identifying similarities and differences between episodic memory and both semantic memory and priming will require careful componential analysis of episodic memory.

6.1. Introduction

Episodic memory is memory for personally experienced events. The person who later remembers these events always consciously experiences them as an observer and also often as an actor. Most typically, events comprise interactions (including the experiencer's actions) over limited periods of time between various animate and inanimate objects in a specific context. They are experienced as a continuous series of linked scenes, each made up of several objects (which include the experiencer), located in particular spatial positions. The original experience may involve emotional arousal (e.g. fear) that was associated with the event and this emotion may be remembered when the linked scenes, constituting the episode, are later retrieved. The experiencer may also be vaguely aware during the episode itself of the more general spatio-temporal context in which the event is set and how it fits into his or her life story. Nearly always, events are automatically interpreted in a meaningful way through the use of available semantic knowledge. Events that are later remembered are, therefore, initially consciously experienced, either in association with emotion or not, as a series of perceptual and semantic representations of objects, including the experiencer, that interact in space and time within a larger spatio-temporal context.

The rememberer is not only aware of the scenes that constituted an experienced event, but is usually also aware that s/he experienced these scenes at an earlier date, i.e. s/he has the conscious feeling that the scenes are being remembered. Rememberers will often know where an event fits into their life story by inference rather than by directly remembering their awareness of the event's general context at the time when it was originally experienced (there may have been no such awareness). Although episodic memory usually involves recall of a previously experienced event, it can sometimes involve recognition that something was personally experienced even when nothing extra is recalled. Thus, one can recognize that one experienced a particular event from a photograph or video of the occasion even though one may not recall anything else about it.

The boundaries of what counts as remembering an episode are, however, blurred. For example, one can recollect in detail the experience of learning each component of a recently heard news story or word list. Such recollection clearly involves episodic memory. However, when specifically asked to recall recently encountered news stories or word lists, then it seems possible that just these things are remembered with very little, if any, reference to the episode in which the information was learned. Such remembering seems to be at least mainly of semantic, rather than episodic, information. Most people seem to assume that word-list or story recall are obviously examples of episodic memory. Their assumption is probably based on the belief that in order to know which word list or story to retrieve, one needs to retrieve some contextual (episodic) information. However, even if no specific cue is given (e.g. what was the story you just heard or what words were in the word list you just heard?), people may find that the recently encountered factual information just pops into their minds without the need to retrieve associated information about the learning context. The issue is an empirical one although it is difficult to resolve. Two related questions need to be answered. What proportion of the retrieved information is semantic and what proportion is episodic? How much, if at all, does retrieval of semantic information critically depend on cueing provided by retrieved and associated episodic information? Although the proportion of specifically episodic information that is retrieved, and how much it increases the retrieval of semantic information, should be influenced by instructions and the kind of cueing given, its role in story and word-list recall may be considerably less than is commonly assumed.

Any theory of episodic memory should characterize: (i) the encoding, storage, and retrieval processes that mediate this complex form of memory; (ii) the brain regions that perform each of these processes and how these regions interact with each other so that the processes work in an integrated manner; (iii) how the neurons within each relevant brain region interact so as to perform specific processes, and how the neurons in different regions interact so as to integrate the various processes that mediate episodic memory; (iv) how these episodic memory processes are similar to and/or differ from the processes that mediate other putative forms of memory, and to what extent the same brain regions mediate memory for episodes and other kinds of information.

This paper focuses on theoretical characteristics (i), (ii) and (iv) and has the following structure. First, the processes and information involved in making episodic representations at encoding will be outlined and the underlying brain regions considered. Second, major views about the psychological and physiological processes underlying consolidation and long-term storage of episodic representations will be outlined and differing views concerning where these processes are located in the brain are discussed. Third, views about how retrieval is achieved and the feeling that retrieved episodes are being remembered is produced. Which brain structures mediate these processes will be discussed. Where relevant, the similarities and differences between episodic memory and both semantic memory and priming will be discussed whilst assessing these theories. Each section will highlight where there are theoretical disagreements, or processes and their neural bases that have been poorly specified, and will consider how lesion and functional neuroimaging research is helping with theory development in these problem areas.

6.2. Representing episodes at encoding: processes, information and brain regions

Encoding episodes typically involves representing a sequence of linked scenes that occur over a short period of time. As such, it requires the representation of objects perceived from the observer's perspective in different positions that change across time. In episodes experienced by humans, visual information is usually most salient. However, information from other senses often plays a key role and all this sensory information is likely to be interpreted automatically by the observer in terms of available semantic knowledge, and may be coloured by emotion. These experiences are usually meaningfully interpreted. The major feature of episodic representations, therefore, is that they associate together very different kinds of information, which include perceptual and semantic aspects of objects and how these are located in space and time relative both to each other and the self. The experiencer deploys attention so that only some components of the episode will reach consciousness. How attention is deployed will determine how well aspects of the episode get into memory. It seems likely that spatial and temporal information will be represented in more than one kind of way when episodes are experienced. Spatial locations will, of course, be experienced from the observer/actor's perspective, i.e. egocentrically, but there may also be an allocentric awareness of objects' positions in each scene. A temporally ordered sequence of scenes will be experienced, but the observer/actor will also be aware of the duration of the different scenes constituting an episode.

Tulving (1995) has argued that episodic encoding depends on information being processed successfully through semantic memory. So if semantic memory is deficient, as in semantic dementia, episodic memory will be impaired. However, although it is trivially true that subjects will not remember semantic features of episodes that were not represented in the first place, there is good evidence that memory for perceptual aspects of episodes is relatively normal even when much of the episode cannot be meaningfully represented. Thus, patients with semantic dementia, who cannot meaningfully interpret episodes, can encode and later recognize the perceptual features of experienced objects relatively normally (e.g. Graham *et al.* 1997). It seems likely that spatio-temporal contextual features of experienced episodes can also be encoded and later remembered relatively normally in patients with semantic memory deficits, although this remains to be shown. Adequate representations of perceptual features and spatio-temporal context can probably be made without semantic processing. However, meaningfully interpreting an episode should help to link its components in an integrated representation, which may facilitate later recall more than recognition.

Functional neuroimaging evidence is consistent with the widely held view that the representations of episodes and their components, made during encoding, are based on complex patterns of neural activity that are primarily located in distributed sites within those parts of the posterior neocortex that represent both meaningfully interpreted and relatively uninterpreted sensory information (e.g. Montaldi *et al.* 1998*a*). Episodes are, however, not only complex but highly variable in their information content, so which posterior neocortical regions are activated at encoding depends on the nature of the experience (see Mayes & Montaldi 1999). The precuneus has often been found to activate during episodic retrieval (e.g. Fletcher *et al.* 1995) so it is interesting that it has also been found to activate during the encoding of complex scene pictures and that its level of activation correlates with subsequent memory for the pictures (Montaldi *et al.* 1998*b*). This study's findings suggest that: (i) episodic retrieval may reactivate the posterior neocortical structures that were activated during the episode's initial representation, and (ii) the richer the initial representation as indicated by the level of precuneus activation the better the memory. What information precuneus activation represents is unresolved, but the activation was relative to that produced by the matching of similar pictures—so it may involve an association between visual images and their verbal semantic interpretation. Future work needs to identify more precisely where different episodic components are represented in the posterior neocortex, and how inter-component associations are represented. Also, the degree to which encoding activations are regenerated at retrieval needs to be determined.

It is unknown how awareness of scenes and their components is generated by the brain. It also seems likely, however, that neocortical activity is vital for such awareness even if subcortical activity is also essential. Emotional arousal, which may be experienced during an episode, is believed to depend on activity not only in neocortical sites but also in limbic system regions such as the amygdala (e.g. Gloor *et al.* 1982).

The frontal neocortex is also known to be active when episodes are represented (e.g. Kapur *et al.* 1994). It is widely believed that this activity controls executive functions, such as how attention is directed, which through 'top-down' influences on the more posterior sensory cortices coordinates which components of an episode are represented. It has been suggested that these 'top-down' influences play a key role in integrating the sensory and contextual components of the episodic representation (see Squire & Kandel 1999). Whether the frontal neocortex also plays a more direct role in representing some aspects of episodes, notably certain contextual components such as their temporal features, is uncertain. Although the neural mechanisms of spatial representation are quite well understood (see Burgess *et al.* 1997), those underlying the perception of temporal order and duration are much less so. It remains an interesting possibility that components of complex episodic representations are represented together through their spatiotemporal relationships within the frontal neocortex.

The medial temporal lobes have also been related to processing that leads to contextual memory (see Mayes 1988). However, although this region is often activated when episodic information is encoded (e.g. Montaldi *et al*. 1998*a*,*b*), it is unclear whether this activation reflects the processes involved in representing context and other kinds of episodic information or the early consolidation processes that put this information into long-term memory. Even if the activation does reflect representational processes, this does not prove that either the hippocampus or the medial temporal lobe cortex plays a critical role in making episodic representations. Nevertheless, Murray & Bussey (1999) have argued exactly this in their proposal that the perirhinal cortex plays an essential role in the making of high-level visual object representations. According to this proposal, without a perirhinal cortex this information cannot be represented at all and there will be a high-level visual agnosia. This cortex certainly receives an appropriate convergence of high-level visual object information from the ventral stream (as well as inputs from other sensory modalities) to enable it to perform the postulated integrative operations efficiently. As indicated above, this does not establish that the perirhinal cortex plays a critical role in high-level visual perception. To do this, one needs to show that high-level object information does not converge at neocortical sites as well because these structures may be able to perform the appropriate integrative operations in a sufficiently similar way. This has not been shown convincingly. Also, at least in humans, there is some preliminary evidence that patients with extensive bilateral lesions to the medial temporal lobe cortices show normal short-term memory, let alone preserved matching abilities, for complex non-meaningful visual stimuli despite having very severe recognition deficits at longer delays (Buffalo *et al*. 1998). Murray & Bussey (1999) have questioned whether this task tapped the high-level integrative functions that they believe are performed by the perirhinal cortex alone, so further work with human patients is needed to ensure that these functions are tapped in an unequivocal way.

An argument similar to that of Murray & Bussey (1999) could be made about the hippocampus and entorhinal cortex. This region receives a convergence of spatial and object-related information, which may remain separate in the perirhinal and parahippocampal cortices, so it might be argued that associations, such as those necessary for representing scenes, can only be made in the hippocampus and entorhinal cortex. Information represented in different neocortical regions may particularly converge in the hippocampus–entorhinal cortex complex. If so, hippocampal–entorhinal cortex lesions should cause an inability to perceive associations between these kinds of information unless the reciprocal connections which exist between the perirhinal and parahippocampal cortices are sufficient to integrate spatial and object information outside the hippocampus–entorhinal cortex complex (Suzuki & Amaral 1994). However, even amnesics with lesions that include the perirhinal and parahippocampal cortices as well as the hippocampus–entorhinal cortex complex often show preserved intelligence and can answer questions about the locations of object pictures, following brief presentations, as accurately as control subjects when tested immediately (Mayes *et al*. 1993). This suggests that neocortical regions may also be able to perform basically similar object-location integrative operations. Nevertheless, as with the perirhinal cortex encoding hypothesis, it may prove difficult to detect subtle encoding deficits because subjects may use compensatory strategies based on slightly less appropriate neocortical representations.

6.3. Consolidation and storage of episodic representations

(a) Psychological and physiological storage processes

Only a tiny fraction of experienced episodes are put into long-term memory storage and, even with those that are, only a small proportion of the experienced episode is later retrievable. As already discussed, the extent to which one retrieves episodic (contextual) information when trying to remember a recently heard story, and how memory of the story is improved by the availability of episodic information, is uncertain. However, if given appropriate instructions and cues (e.g. 'tell me about the story involving the woman who was robbed'), very little, if any, episodic information may need to be recalled, so the rememberer may be showing relatively pure semantic memory. The extent to which story memory is affected by context-dependent forgetting may provide one indication of how much, if at all, retrieval of semantic story information is being influenced by the availability of episodic information. The boundaries of episodic memory are, therefore, vague and hard to identify, but one must surely show some remembering of the original experience, i.e. perceptions, their temporal and spatial features, and usually their interpretations. In other words, however feebly, episodic memory must involve re-experiencing or reliving the original episode. The degree to which long-term episodic memory is typically attenuated requires further exploration. Although one can later recall that certain sensations and emotions were felt in a remembered episode, and that this episode occurred in a specific context within one's life story, it is unclear how much this ability derives directly from being able to retrieve the contents of the earlier episodic experience and how much it derives from inferences partially based on personal semantic knowledge.

Episodic memories, however fragmentary, can be formed without deliberate intent on the basis of the single experience of the episode, although memories are often strengthened by subsequent rehearsals. Part of an experienced episode may be retained in memory for life and memory is present from immediately after the occurrence of the episode. It is, therefore, of interest that Baddeley (2000) has recently proposed that working memory probably includes an episodic buffer that can hold episodic information for a few seconds or perhaps minutes. It is plausible to postulate that working memory buffers may be mediated by a continuation of the pattern of neural activity that originally represented the experience of the speech pattern, visual pattern or episode. Unless one believes, as some do (e.g. Miller & Matzel 2000), that a relatively stable memory store can be largely created in less than a second, one must postulate a short-term storage mechanism like continued neural activity, which can come into existence immediately, and maintains the memory until a more stable store is produced. The postulate is supported by single unit recording studies in monkeys which indicate that activity in sensory neocortical regions such as the TE and certain frontal regions continues for some seconds following stimulus presentation. Whereas continued activity in the TE was found to be disrupted by presenting further visual stimuli during the delay, this was not found with frontal cortex activity (see Squire & Kandel 1999). The frontal region may play a 'top-down' controlling role that enables the sensory representations produced in the TE and other posterior neocortical sensory regions to be sustained across filled delays for a short period, the duration of which cannot yet be specified. With an episodic buffer, frontal regions might also integrate the representation, particularly the linked sequence of scenes.

Evidence from extensive animal research suggests that long-term episodic memory depends on the growth of new synapses, a process which is mediated by the synthesis of new proteins (Bailey *et al.* 1996). This consolidation process will take some time to complete, but there is evidence that memories can be maintained for intermediate durations by subtler changes in synaptic efficacy (such as shifts in the location of vesicles in relation to the active zone), which do not depend on new protein synthesis and can be achieved relatively rapidly (see Squire & Kandel 1999). The strength of episodic memories varies greatly. Some of this variation will relate to the richness and coherence of the original representation, but it will also depend to a large extent on the strength of the consolidation changes that lead to the growth of new synapses where the memory is stored. Emotional arousal and arousal generally is known to strengthen episodic memory (McGaugh 2000). There is evidence that such arousal slows forgetting in the first hour or so following learning (e.g. Kleinsmith & Kaplan 1963), which is consistent with the arousal enhancing the protein-synthesis-dependent consolidation process.

(b) Neuroanatomy of storage processes

Where do the storage changes that underlie long-term episodic memory occur in the brain? There is a widely held view that information is stored where it was originally represented in the brain (e.g. Gaffan & Hornak 1997) so that there should be a heavy overlap between the neural array that represents an episodic experience as it occurs and the array that is reactivated during later remembering of the episode. A corollary of this view is that basically the same array will be reactivated whether an episode is remembered immediately, after a short delay, or after a delay of days or even years, provided that the same information is retrieved. There is some direct support from functional neuroimaging studies that the arrays that represent and re-represent experienced episodes lie primarily in the posterior neocortex (e.g. Conway *et al.* 1999). However, there is no agreement about whether the storage changes are confined to these representing regions and whether storage locations change over time. Three broad views can be identified.

The first view is that the storage changes that enable episodic memory to be shown at any stage following experience primarily lie within neural arrays located in the posterior neocortex. This view is the least popular of the three broad positions because most researchers believe that organic amnesia is caused by a storage deficit. Amnesia is caused by brain lesions in any of a number of regions: the medial temporal lobes, the midline diencephalon, the basal forebrain, and possibly the ventromedial frontal cortex (see Mayes 1988). One possibility is that although episodic information is not stored in the regions damaged in organic amnesia, these regions (perhaps particularly the hippocampus and the medial temporal lobes) are involved in orienting produced by the novelty that episodes usually involve (e.g. Gray 1982). Such orienting could lead to the arousal without which the key consolidation processes, which are critical for long-term episodic memory, do not occur. In other words, the regions implicated in organic amnesia, and perhaps particularly the hippocampus and the medial temporal lobes, modulate the consolidation that primarily occurs in the posterior neocortex.

If this view is correct, then damage to a structure such as the hippocampus should not impair memory storage. Hippocampal damage impairs the acquisition of episodic memory and also the retrieval of episodic memories acquired normally before the damage occurred, so it is hard to know whether the damage disrupts the representation of episodic information at encoding, its consolidation into long-term memory, its maintenance in long-term storage, its retrieval, or some combination of these processes. In particular, it is hard to establish from lesion studies whether the hippocampus is a site where at least some kinds of episodic information are stored (e.g. contextual information). One attempt to address this question has been developed by Riedel *et al.* (1999). These workers used a water-soluble antagonist of AMPA/kainate receptors to inactivate the dorsal hippocampus of rats in a reversible fashion. They were able to show that temporary inactivation during training in a water maze or later, during testing for memory of the maze, disrupted memory for the location of the hidden platform. This implies that the hippocampus plays a critical role in both the acquisition and retrieval of spatial memory. More strikingly, they showed that inactivating the dorsal hippocampus for seven days, beginning either 1 or 5 days after the end of training, disrupted memory even though this was tested when the hippocampus seemed to working normally. Riedel *et al.* (1999) concluded that prolonged hippocampal inactivation was either disrupting a slow consolidation process that was stabilizing the spatial memory or it was degrading the already present synaptic changes underlying long-term spatial memory. However, it remains uncertain whether these slow consolidation or long-term storage maintenance processes occur in the hippocampus itself or in a connected brain region where they may be disrupted if the hippocampus is inactive for a prolonged time. Although the reversible inactivation method is excellent for identifying when the hippocampus is involved in memory processing, it alone cannot identify with confidence whether the hippocampus is a storage site for aspects of episodic information.

There is one way in which this uncertainty about where long-term storage is located can be addressed. This depends on the use of more effective brain transplant procedures involving the use of stem cells, which enable the lost neuronal architecture of damaged structures to be restored to a good approximation. If (i) lesioning the hippocampus causes loss of memory for a component of episodic memory, and (ii) transplanting tissue restores the lost hippocampal neuronal architecture and restores the lost memory, then that memory could not have been stored within the hippocampus. This is because storage would involve altered synaptic connections in the storage site, and these could not be replaced by transplanting new tissue. An effect precisely of this kind has been found in monkeys. Thus, Virley *et al.* (1999) found that excitotoxic CA1 lesions impaired already learned conditional discriminations in which two different pairs of identical objects signalled reward in either a left or right food well. Foetal CA1 transplants as well as stem cell transplants were found to restore memory of these previously learned discriminations to apparently normal levels. More precisely, the animals in whom lost hippocampal CA1 tissue had been replaced by transplanted tissue relearned the preoperatively trained discriminations to criterion as fast as unlesioned control animals. Assuming that the transplant recipients and their controls relearned at the same rate, the former animals had recovered their memories to normal levels even if memory for the discrimination was not present on initial re-testing.

This result strongly suggests that the discrimination memory was not stored in the CA1 field of the hippocampus of these monkeys. It could, however, have been stored in another hippocampal field, e.g. CA3, and the memory not been expressible initially because the CA1 lesion disrupted the hippocampal circuitry. The conclusion that the memory was not stored in CA1 would not only apply if all of the following conditions obtained. First, the memory was earlier stored in CA1 and possibly other sites as well as in CA3 in a distributed fashion, but could not be expressed when storage in CA1 was removed by a lesion. Second, following the transplantation, all the continuously intact brain sites that contained the remaining distributed memory were somehow able to restore the missing memory to the virgin transplanted CA1 tissue so that the whole distributed memory could be fully expressed. Nevertheless, with this one possible exception, the principle is clear. Provided stem cell transplantation does enable lesioned neuronal architecture to be reasonably restored, then the procedure provides the first powerful means of determining whether storage rather than merely processing and representation are mediated by a specific structure. If transplantation fails to restore pre-lesion memories, but enables similar ones to be acquired normally, then the damaged structure is very likely to be the site of storage.

Despite the shortage of direct supporting evidence, it seems probable that the hippocampus and medial temporal lobes do play a role in storing certain kinds of episodic information. The region's possible role in upregulating episodic storage processes in the neocortex does not mean that it cannot also store other kinds of episodic information. It therefore seems likely that the medial temporal lobes do play a role in storing episodic representations but the possible storage role of the posterior neocortex has been insufficiently appreciated. The two regions may store different components of episodic information.

The second view, which is perhaps the most widely believed, is that long-term episodic memories, dependent on new protein synthesis and storage changes at synapses, initially occur in the medial temporal lobes and hippocampus but that, as a result of voluntary and involuntary rehearsal over long periods of time, storage changes gradually occur primarily in the posterior neocortex so that retrieval ceases to depend on the medial temporal lobes (see Squire & Alvarez 1995). The view presupposes that whereas the medial temporal lobes are very plastic, at least some sites in the neocortex are much less so. Most frequently, it is interpreted as proposing that the medial temporal lobes initially store a kind of index. This index enables the different neocortical regions that represent the distinct components of a remembered episode to be activated together despite the fact that there are no direct links between them initially. Gradually, the associative links provided by the medial temporal lobes cease to be necessary because direct links develop slowly through the neocortical plastic process. There is no agreement about whether the medial temporal lobes cease to be involved in storage altogether and, if so, whether this is because the stored memory is overwritten by later memories or whether it fades rapidly even without such interference (e.g. Squire & Alvarez 1995). The time scale of this transfer in which memory storage gradually develops in the posterior neocortex is only loosely specified, as is whether the key factor is the number of rehearsals rather than the passage of time *per se*.

The third view states that some aspects of episodic information (e.g. spatial context) depend on the medial temporal lobes for their storage and retrieval for as long as they are in memory, whereas other aspects of episodic information (e.g. feature information) depend on the neocortex for their storage and retrieval for as long as they are in memory (see Nadel & Moscovitch 1997). According to this view, those aspects of episodic information which are initially stored in the medial temporal lobes are not transferred to neocortical storage as a function of rehearsal and time. Instead, it is proposed that rehearsal causes these kinds of episodic information to be stored within the medial temporal lobes in an increasingly redundant fashion so that episodic memory becomes less vulnerable to damage in this region as time passes. Transfer of storage does not occur with rehearsal and the passage of time presumably because the relevant components of episodic representations only converge in the hippocampus and, to a lesser extent, the parahippocampal and perirhinal cortices and so can only be stored in these structures. Although the view postulates that the medial temporal lobes store marker information (e.g. about spatial context), which coheres the feature information that is stored in the neocortex, it does not specify whether the medial temporal lobes are critical for the initial representation of spatial context. In other words, although the region is critical for encoding spatial context into long-term memory (i.e. consolidation), it is not clear whether it is critical for experiencing and representing spatial context normally during episodic experience (encoding *per se*).

The three views about where episodic memories are stored do not specify in much detail where and how the components of episodic representations are stored and associated together, although this is beginning to be done by neural network models (e.g. O'Reilly *et al.* 1998). It has also been argued that the perirhinal cortex mainly receives high-level sensory object-related inputs from the posterior association neocortex and plays an important role in object memory, whereas the parahippocampal cortex mainly receives spatial information inputs and plays an important role in spatial memory (Zola-Morgan & Squire 1993). Spatial and object information may be linked together in memory in the hippocampus and perhaps in the entorhinal cortex (see Mayes *et al.* 2001; Vargha-Khadem *et al.* 1997). However, much more needs to be specified about not only where, but also how the components of episodic memory are put into memory storage.

Most researchers believe that the hippocampus and medial temporal lobes are involved in storing episodic information and that long-term potentiation may indicate the mechanism of storage (e.g. Morris & Frey 1997) although proving these two proposals is very difficult. If the storage view is correct, determining whether episodic memories remain stored in the medial temporal lobes for as long as they last, or whether in time they transfer to the neocortex, is also likely to prove difficult. The Squire & Alvarez (1995) view predicts that amnesics with selective medial temporal lobe lesions, and particularly hippocampal lesions, should show relatively normal recall and recognition of pre-morbid episodic memories that were acquired sufficiently long before their trauma. Tests of this prediction have yielded conflicting results and although most studies find evidence of relative sparing of older memories, the time-scale is typically one of decades (see Mayes 1988). For example, on the one hand, Teng & Squire (1999) found that a 70-year-old amnesic with nearly total bilateral destruction of his medial temporal lobes was able to recall routes normally that had been learnt 50 years before, although his more recent route memories were grossly impaired. In contrast, Cipolotti *et al.* (2001) reported that a patient with damage apparently mainly confined to the hippocampus showed no relative sparing of episodic memories that were decades old. Conflicting results like this might arise because:

(i) Subtle, but important, brain damage to neocortical structures is being missed. Such damage can cause retrograde amnesia with no sparing of older episodic memories and could do so because it disrupts representation and also possibly the storage of episodic information (see Nadel & Moscovitch 1997).

(ii) Some patients have an atypical and perhaps reorganized neocortically based storage system for older episodic memories.

(iii) Only some features of episodic memory show transfer whereas others do not. For example, it has been argued that older premorbid memories are not spared in amnesics when detailed episodic recall or memory for less prominent landmarks on routes is the measure, but sparing can occur for gist (e.g. Rosenbaum *et al.* 2000).

The time-scale of transfer suggested by the majority of studies of retrograde amnesia that do find sparing of older episodic memories is of the order of decades (see Nadel & Moscovitch 1997). If the transfer process were as slow as this, transfer would have taken longer than the typical human lifetime in prehistoric times. Other interpretations for very long temporal gradients with retrograde amnesia have therefore to be considered. If transfer does occur, it is surely likely to operate over a shorter period of between months and a few years rather than a few decades. Such shorter transfer times are supported by some animal studies. For example, rats were found to show more hippocampal and less temporal and frontal neocortex activation when they retrieved five-day-old memories than when they retrieved 25-day-old memories (Bontempi *et al.* 1999). There is evidence for a subgroup of amnesics who show basically normal episodic and factual memory at delays of around one day and possibly longer, but then over a period of weeks show accelerated forgetting (e.g. Kapur *et al.* 1996). In unpublished work, the author and his colleagues found that one such patient, who had hippocampal sparing and major damage to her anterior temporal cortex, showed basically normal memory at delays of one day but severely impaired memory after delays of three weeks. She also showed impaired recall of information to which she had been repeatedly exposed over periods of several years. One interpretation of this memory impairment is that affected patients are unable to transfer episodic and factual memories to their posterior neocortices although initial storage in the medial temporal lobes is preserved.

Neuroimaging studies of retrieval of recent and remote episodic memories in humans have, however, typically looked at comparisons between memories years and decades old, respectively. An exception was a study which found that recognizing items studied immediately before testing produced no more medial temporal lobe activation than recognizing items studied one week before (Stark & Squire 2000*a*). If transfer occurs, it is unlikely that it could be completed in one week even if rehearsal is intense. Two other studies have found no difference in medial temporal lobe activation even when the older memories that subjects recalled were years older than the more recent memories. In the first study, young subjects recalled autobiographical incident memories formed roughly 20 years and just under a year earlier, respectively (Conway *et al.* 1999). In the second case, recall of similar memories formed between about one and four years earlier and over 30 years earlier, respectively, was compared (Ryan *et al.* 2001).

Mayes *et al.* (2000) found a similar lack of difference in the hippocampal and parahippocampal cortex activation produced when subjects recalled personally relevant routes learned about 30 years earlier and routes learned in the past few months. Although the results of this last study seem to conflict with evidence that remote spatial route recall may be relatively normal following extensive medial temporal lobe lesions (Teng & Squire 1999), there may be no conflict. The subjects in the neuroimaging study visualized following the remembered routes. Rosenbaum *et al.* (2000) have reported that patient K.C., who has extensive brain damage including severe bilateral atrophy of the hippocampus, showed relatively normal memory for the allocentric spatial features of the locality which had been his neighbourhood for almost 40 years. He was unable to remember details about local routes, however, which would probably have prevented him from visualizing remembered routes. If visualization does involve retrieval of aspects of spatial memory that are critically dependent on the medial temporal lobes for their storage, then the neuroimaging and lesion studies are not in conflict. However, the neuroimaging study did find that activity in a region that may have included the retro-splenial and posterior cingulate cortex was greater when more recent spatial routes were recalled.

In an unpublished neuroimaging study of episodic and semantic retrieval, however, the author and his colleagues have found that recalling recently acquired (weeks to a few months) episodic incident memories produced slightly, but significantly, more left hippocampal activation than recalling remote (5–10 years) episodic incident memories. Bilateral parahippocampal cortex activation relative to baseline remained unchanged, but activation in the retrosplenial–posterior cingulate cortex and precuneus also reduced. Although these results seem to support the view that episodic memory storage transfers to the posterior neocortex, interpretation is difficult. A potential problem with all neuroimaging studies of recent and remote memory retrieval is that retrieval is accompanied by re-encoding which may obscure retrieval-related changes in activation. There would be no problem if re-encoding and retrieval were physiologically identical in the hippocampus, and resolution may still be possible if Lepage *et al.* (1998) are correct to suggest that encoding occurs slightly more anteriorly in the hippocampus than retrieval. Nevertheless, it is safest to conclude that the case is still not proved that episodic storage transfers to the posterior neocortex with time and rehearsal.

There are several further areas of disagreement about how and where episodic storage is achieved, and key processes are not characterized in sufficient detail. First, it is unclear where and how episodic storage is modulated. Is episodic storage in both the posterior neocortex and medial temporal lobes modulated, and, if so, what structures mediate this modulation? It is also unclear what structures, as well as what psychological triggers (other than orienting to novel information), are involved in the modulation of episodic storage.

There is good evidence from lesion and functional neuroimaging studies that the amygdala modulates the activity of the hippocampus (as well as of other structures) in response to the presence of emotionally arousing stimuli during encoding so as to enhance later episodic memory. For example, Phelps *et al.* (1998) have found that a patient with bilateral amygdala damage, unlike control subjects, showed no slowing of forgetting for emotionally arousing words, although she showed a normal improvement of episodic memory when emotion provided an organizing principle at encoding. Relatedly, in a positron emission tomography (PET) study, Cahill *et al.* (1996) found that subjects who later showed better memory for emotionally arousing stimuli, but not neutral ones, showed more amygdala activation during encoding. Similarly, Hamann *et al.* (1999) found that the amygdala activation found during encoding of emotionally arousing stimuli correlated with the subsequent memory advantage shown for these stimuli relative to neutral, non-arousing stimuli. This correlation was not found with arousing but non-emotional stimuli. Amygdala activation was also found to correlate with hippocampal activation during encoding.

The amygdala may, therefore, modulate storage of episodic information by the hippocampus specifically in response to emotionally arousing stimuli. However, as already discussed, it is disputed whether or not the hippocampus itself modulates posterior neocortical storage sites, and whether the basal forebrain, midbrain and possibly the frontal neocortex (in a controlling role) are involved with modulating posterior neocortical storage sites in response to different kinds of arousal. This latter possibility is supported by the finding that transection of the fornix, amygdala and anterior temporal stem, which disconnected the temporal cortex from the potentially modulating influence of the basal forebrain and midbrain, caused profound impairment in monkeys on several memory tests, including one that involved scene-related object memory (Gaffan *et al.* 2001). A companion study found that crossed unilateral lesions of the basal forebrain and either the inferior temporal or frontal cortex caused an impairment in memory for object–reward associations as severe as that produced by the fornix, amygdala, temporal stem transection (Easton & Gaffan 2001).

One interpretation of these results is that the frontal cortex controls the basal forebrain, which in turn upregulates the inferior temporal cortex's ability to store episodic memories. This claim, which is consistent with the view that initial storage of different components of episodes depends on both medial temporal cortex and temporal neocortex (see Mayes *et al.* 1985), warrants careful examination. It leaves open the possibility that the components initially stored by the medial temporal lobes are slowly transferred to the posterior neocortex.

Second, it is unclear to what extent the storage of semantic and episodic information differ from each other, both in terms of where storage occurs and how it is mediated. There are two issues here: (i) are there differences which relate to the kinds of information being stored and (ii) are there differences which relate to the amount of rehearsal which that information typically receives over long periods of time? Implicit in the view that storage and encoding sites for the same information are very similar is the universal belief that different information is processed and represented by different neural arrays. Semantic information comprises many kinds of knowledge, such as word meanings and knowledge about famous paintings, which are presumably stored in different brain regions. Therefore some kinds of semantic information are much more similar than others to episodic information (which also varies considerably), and so presumably show greater overlap of storage sites. Most typically, episodic memory involves retrieval of perceptual information in spatio-temporal settings, whereas semantic memory, albeit with important exceptions, does not. Episodic memory may also be coloured by emotion and some degree of self-awareness. It is unclear to what extent these two features will require storage in regions not involved in storing factual information. Also, although semantic memory cannot include self-awareness, it can surely be coloured by emotion without becoming episodic memory. For example, one's knowledge of certain historical characters, such as Hitler or Stalin, may be associated with disgust and hatred. The nature of this emotional colouring is, however, different from that involved with episodic memory because no specific emotional experience is being remembered.

Semantic information typically receives far more rehearsal than does episodic information over long periods of time, although episodic memories of great personal significance also typically receive a large amount of rehearsal over the years. Nadel & Moscovitch (1997) have argued that whereas episodic information depends on hippocampal storage for as long as episodic memory lasts and regardless of how much rehearsal occurs, the storage of factual information may be reorganized over time until it depends only on the neocortex. In other words, they agree with Squire & Alvarez (1995) that semantic memory becomes independent of the medial temporal lobes with rehearsal over relatively long time periods because neocortical storage is gradually strengthened until it alone can effectively support semantic retrieval.

Vargha-Khadem *et al.* (1997) have reported that three young people, who suffered early and relatively selective hippocampal damage, showed impaired acquisition and retention of episodic memories. Despite this clear episodic memory deficit, these subjects developed relatively normal long-term semantic memories for facts to which they would have been repeatedly exposed over long time periods, as indicated by their relatively normal language, reading, writing and general knowledge. The subjects were impaired at recalling stories to which they had been exposed once only a short while earlier. Unless one cannot recall such stories except by recalling some of the experiential context in which they were learned, their recall is likely to depend on semantic memory. The findings, therefore, suggest that although semantic memory initially depends on the hippocampus, the slow repetition-rehearsal-dependent transfer process works normally without the hippocampus.

Two unpublished studies by the author and his colleagues, however, point to the need for caution in interpreting the findings. In the first study, a patient, who had suffered a relatively selective hippocampal lesion in her adult years, was, like the patients of Vargha-Khadem and her colleagues, impaired at recalling stories after a brief delay following study. This patient was further impaired at recalling new word meanings after a brief delay even when given up to ten learning trials. But the patient was also mildly impaired at recalling word meanings (e.g. MIR) to which she had been repeatedly exposed over a period of several years. That semantic memory in the patient should have been impaired for factual information repeatedly encountered in this way is plausible because the hippocampus is critical for recall, and hence rehearsal, and so should play a role in 'teaching' the neocortex.

In the second study, which used a block design functional magnetic resonance imaging (fMRI) procedure, it was found that even after healthy young male subjects had been given one week's intensive practice in learning new word definitions, their recall still produced a larger blood-oxygen-level-dependent (BOLD) response than a baseline condition on both sides of the hippocampus. Recall of equivalently practised and slightly older episodic memories also activated the hippocampus bilaterally and significantly more so on the right than did the verbal semantic retrieval. As with episodic memory, recall of these recently acquired semantic memories produced slightly more hippocampal activation (on the right) than did recall of remotely and heavily over-learned word meanings. Again resembling episodic memory, recall of the recent semantic memories activated the retrosplenial–posterior cingulate cortex and precuneus regions more than did recall of remote but similar semantic memories. Activation of all these regions was less with semantic recall and it also reduced more over time in the retrosplenial–posterior cingulate cortex and precuneus regions. Interestingly, recall of

recently acquired memories for geographical maps also activated the right hippocampus slightly more than recall of remote over-learned map memories. This neuroimaging
study, therefore, suggests that both verbal and geographical semantic memory is
similar to episodic memory in several ways. However, the study also found
differences between the two kinds of memory, regardless of whether episodic
memory involved recalling standard episodes or experiences in following specific
routes and semantic memory involved recalling word meanings or maps. Episodic
recall produced more activation than semantic recall in the hippocampus,
parahippocampal cortex, inferior temporal neocortex, precuneus, posterior cingulate
and medial frontal neocortex bilaterally and the ventrolateral frontal neocortex on
the right. Whether these effects indicate qualitative or quantitative differences in
what is stored requires further investigation.

Third, there is disagreement about whether primed information is stored in similar
sites to episodic information. Humans show priming of semantic as well as perceptual
information, so this form of memory involves retrieval of kinds of information that
may sometimes form components of an episodic memory. However, in priming,
memory is revealed by the efficiency with which previously experienced information is
processed when re-encoded without the rememberer needing to be aware that this
information has been encountered before. Retrieval of episodic memories, in contrast,
is usually accompanied by the feeling that the episode has been experienced before.
Both lesion and functional neuroimaging evidence has been used to argue that
perceptual priming at least involves the posterior neocortex but not the structures
damaged in organic amnesia (e.g. Moscovitch 2000). For example, it has been claimed
that lesions in the right posterior neocortex disrupt certain kinds of perceptual priming
but not explicit memory for the same nominal stimuli, and that a reverse pattern of
deficit is found in amnesics (Gabrieli *et al.* 1995). However, it has also been argued that
all forms of priming, whether for information that was familiar prior to the priming
experience or novel, are disrupted in organic amnesia (Ostergaard 1999). This suggests
that primed memories may at least be partially stored in structures, such as the
hippocampus, which are implicated in amnesia. An intermediate position was
supported by a recent meta-analysis (Gooding *et al.* 2000), which found that amnesics
showed normal perceptual and semantic priming of information that was familiar prior
to study, but impaired priming of items and associations that were novel at the time of
study.

This meta-analysis suggests that storing new representations critically involves
structures such as the medial temporal lobes regardless of whether the stored
representation later supports priming or episodic memory. If this position is wrong
and the priming of novel information does not need to involve the structures damaged
in amnesia, as Moscovitch (2000) argues, then it must be possible for new memory
representations of perceptual information to become established in the neocortex after
one learning trial. One possibility is that priming of certain kinds of intra-item
association depends on neocortical storage, which is achieved rapidly and can be very
long lasting. The storage of episodic experiences may depend on this rapid storage of
at least some intra-component associations in the posterior neocortex. However, these
episodic components, which are set up in the neocortex, may initially (and perhaps for
as long as episodic memory lasts) only be associated together in memory in the
hippocampus and medial temporal lobes. The inter-component linkage could be

achieved by using some kind of index that perhaps uses spatio-temporal relations between the components.

6.4. Episodic retrieval: processes and brain regions

Recall of episodic information is usually intentional and effortful, but it can occur unintentionally and automatically when a particular thought or perception directly triggers the recollection of an associated experience. Both recall and recognition of an earlier experience are accompanied by the feeling that one is remembering, pathology of which is displayed in *déjà vu* and *jamais vu* experiences. This feeling is not explained simply by the reactivation of previously stored information. It has been argued that priming, which does not involve this feeling, depends on storage changes within the representing neural array such that primed information is represented more efficiently possibly by fewer neurons so that the information can later be more efficiently processed (i.e. primed) (e.g. Wiggs & Martin 1998). This process, which presumably involves rapid strengthening of synaptic connections between a subset of the neurons in the encoding array, does not, however, explain why a feeling of remembering should be produced when this array is next activated as a result of recall or recognition. By itself, reactivation of the representation does not give any information about whether the representation has been encountered before or is new (e.g. imagined). The problem also applies to semantic memories because these often carry the feeling that they are true.

Moscovitch (2000) reviews different theoretical accounts of 'consciousness and memory'. However, most of the theories do not address the above problem. Moscovitch's own theory proposes that the memory trace comprises not just the information features of the episode but also components that constitute the consciousness of it, so that at retrieval not only the episode but the consciousness of it is reactivated. But it is hard to see how being conscious of the episodic information will produce the feeling that the episode has been previously experienced rather than imagined unless 'consciousness' is being used in an unusual sense. Moscovitch, however, does liken his theory to Milner's (1999) view. According to this view, episodic memory involves a trace in which a representation of the information that constitutes an episode is associated with a representation of a feeling of familiarity such that when the episodic representation is reactivated it feels familiar. If Moscovitch's theory is equivalent to Milner's, then it does address the problem of how a feeling of remembering is produced. Milner's theory also implies that priming and episodic memory may be relatively independent of each other. This is because priming of previously new information depends entirely on a memory trace that links the information; episodic memory depends at least as much on the strength of the association between this representation and a representation of a feeling of familiarity. Milner proposed that this feeling is generated by the hippocampus (and perhaps also by the medial temporal lobe cortices) as the inverse of its function of triggering a feeling of novelty. Whether the medial temporal lobes are critical for episodic memory for this reason only, or because they also store, at least for a while, an index which interconnects the episode's components, is not specified by Milner. He also does not specify whether the representation of the familiarity feeling is stored in the medial temporal lobes or merely generated there and stored elsewhere.

Although Milner's theory is attractive it fails to give a convincing mechanism for how the association between the representations of the episode and the familiarity feeling is acquired in one trial. This is because when the episode is first experienced it is usually accompanied by a feeling of novelty rather than familiarity. If the theory is incorrect, the only other theory that provides a plausible mechanism for how the feeling that an episodic memory is familiar is generated is an elaboration of the attribution view (see Jacoby *et al.* 1989). According to this theory, when information is processed more fluently as a result of priming, subjects may be aware of the enhanced fluency and attribute it to the fact that the primed information has been previously encountered. In other words, the awareness of the enhanced fluency with which the information has been encoded automatically triggers a feeling that the information has been remembered. This theory has been used primarily to give an attributionist account of item familiarity, but it can be extended to cover all processes underlying episodic retrieval. The dual process theory of recognition (e.g. Mandler 1980) postulates that recognition depends not only on how familiar encoded item information feels but also on whether anything else can be recalled about the item and/or the episode in which it appeared. This latter process of recollection is a form of recall and, therefore, shares recall's defining feature, which is that non-encoded information is retrieved from memory. Extension of the attributionist theory to recall postulates that recall involves an organized search process in which the rememberer tries to retrieve appropriate cues, which when encoded will automatically and fluently elicit the target memory. The rememberer is aware of this fluency and automatically attributes it to the retrieved information coming from memory. The theory applies not just to item memory but to aware memory of the complex associations that constitute episodes (Mayes 2001).

Even the version of this theory that applies merely to item familiarity is controversial for two reasons. First, priming may be preserved in dense amnesics even when they show no item recognition (Hamann & Squire 1997; Stark & Squire 2000*b*). This observation is not fatal for the theory because extra conditions, which are not met in dense amnesia, may have to be present before memory attributions are made. For example, there may need to be a general memory of the context in which the item occurred, which dense amnesics lack. Second, it is unclear whether subjects can detect that studied items have been more fluently processed than equivalent unstudied items would have been (see Mayes 2001). This is a serious problem for the theory, but it may be that the measure of enhanced fluency provided by behavioural priming is indirect and poor, or even that the kind of enhanced fluency relevant to memory attribution is distinct from what is measured in behavioural priming. It is clear, therefore, that there are currently no strongly supported theories of the mechanism that generates the aware feeling of memory for an episode.

Recall and, to a lesser extent, recognition of episodes typically involves a directed search for a target memory. This may involve several stages in which the rememberer retrieves cues, which then reactivate further memories until eventually it is judged that a retrieved memory corresponds to the correct episode. A good illustration of the operation of these monitoring processes is when someone experiencing *déjà vu* is quickly able to identify that the feeling of familiarity is false because other memories are all inconsistent with this one being true. The search and monitoring processes are widely believed to depend on activity in a number of frontal neocortical regions that control different executive processes. The belief is supported by extensive evidence from lesion and functional neuroimaging studies (see Mayes 1988; Nyberg 1999; Rugg & Wilding 2000). However, although variations in retrieval tasks have been shown to activate somewhat different regions of the frontal pole, dorsolateral frontal, ventrolateral frontal, as well as other frontal regions (e.g. orbitofrontal cortex), identification of the control functions of these regions is only just beginning (Fletcher & Henson 2001).

Although there is surprisingly little evidence that the processes of recall and recognition produce different patterns of brain activation (Cabeza *et al.* 1997), lesion evidence suggests that these two forms of retrieval are based on different processes that are mediated by different brain regions. For example, in a factor analysis of 50 memory impaired patients, Hunkin *et al.* (2000) found independent factors that loaded heavily on recall and recognition test scores, respectively. If the recollection that occurs in recognition is regarded as a kind of recall, then familiarity in which no additional information beyond that which is already encoded is retrieved may be regarded as the only true form of recognition. There is a widely held view, developed in its most complete form by Aggleton & Brown (1999), that recollection/recall depends critically on the hippocampus and the fornix, mammillary bodies and anterior thalamus that are linked to it (Aggleton & Brown 1999). Familiarity depends on a different neural array, which includes the perirhinal cortex, the dorsomedial thalamus and parts of the frontal neocortex. The neural network model of O'Reilly & Rudy (1999) postulates that this separation of recall/recollection and familiarity occurs because of the different way in which the hippocampus and neocortex/medial temporal cortices represent information in memory. The hippocampus rapidly makes memory representations that differentiate similar kinds of input (pattern separation), a process which facilitates the completion of memories from their encoded components (pattern completion). In contrast, the cortical structures make memory representations that emphasize the common features of different inputs, although representations which do allow pattern completion to be achieved may develop through a slow process of learning.

The above view indicates that the hippocampus plays only a minor role in item recognition because although it plays a critical role in recollection, it is not involved in familiarity judgements. The view is supported by a recent fMRI study, which found that although recollection (as indicated by remember responding with the remember–know procedure) activated the hippocampus, familiarity (as indicated by know responding using this procedure) did not (Eldridge *et al.* 2000). However, findings with patients reported to have selective hippocampal lesions are conflicting. Vargha-Khadem *et al.* (1997) and Mayes *et al.* (2001) have found that four people with fairly focal hippocampal lesions showed relatively intact recognition not only for items but also for associations between similar kinds of items such as words or faces. In contrast, Reed & Squire (1997) have found clear item recognition impairments in patients with apparently similarly restricted lesions.

These differences are unlikely to relate to test differences because the patients with clear item recognition deficits differed from the relatively intact patients even when the same test was used. Nor are reorganizational changes likely to be the explanation for the relatively preserved item recognition of the patient of Mayes *et al.* (2001) because, like the patients of Reed & Squire (1997), this patient suffered adult onset damage (this explanation cannot be ruled out for the patients of Vargha-Khadem and her colleagues, however, because these patients suffered damage very early). Although the patients of

Reed & Squire had generally more severe memory deficits than those of Vargha-Khadem, Mayes and their colleagues, the overall mildness of their memory deficits is also unlikely to be the explanation of the relatively preserved item recognition of the latter patients. This is because some of the patients, reported by Hunkin *et al.* (2000), who had equivalently mild overall memory deficits, showed item recognition deficits of similar severity to those of Reed & Squire (1997). Therefore, patients with mild overall memory deficits can have either clearly impaired or relatively intact item recognition depending on the nature of their neural dysfunction.

It is more likely that the differences between the patients with clearly impaired and relatively intact item recognition relate to variation in the extent of subtle, but functionally significant, damage or dysfunction outside of the hippocampus, which current imaging techniques have not detected. Interestingly, Baxter & Murray (2001) have reported a meta-analysis of three monkey studies of the effects of hippocampal lesions on object recognition. Although object recognition was significantly impaired, a negative correlation was found between the extent of hippocampal damage and the size of the object recognition deficit. Although one should be cautious in accepting this conclusion before it is checked further, it suggests that the greater the extent of residual hippocampus the more it disrupts neighbouring and perhaps intact structures, such as the perirhinal cortex, that mediate item familiarity memory. This interpretation is weakly supported because several of the patients of Reed & Squire (1997) had smaller hippocampal volume reductions than did the patients of Vargha-Khadem, Mayes and their colleagues. If this interpretation is correct, then a negative correlation between severity of item recognition impairment and extent of hippocampal volume reduction should be found in larger groups of human patients with relatively selective hippocampal lesions, and patients with clearly impaired recognition should show abnormal functional activity in structures, like the perirhinal cortex, which are believed to be critical for familiarity memory.

Even when patients show relatively preserved item recognition, it has been found that they are clearly impaired at some forms of associative recognition. Thus, both Vargha-Khadem, and Mayes and their colleagues, have found that their patients had clear recognition deficits for associations between different kinds of information (such as location and objects, or words and temporal order), which are likely to be represented in distinct neocortical regions. This suggests that the hippocampus is most concerned with memory for associations between components that are likely to be represented in distinct neocortical regions. These associations notably involve spatial and temporal relationships, which play a critical role in the kinds of context memory that is central to recollecting episodes.

Although the brain regions supporting recall/recollection and familiarity, and the different memory representation systems on which they may be based, could well be partially distinct, they have still only been given a preliminary rough characterization. It is also still poorly understood how much overlap there is between the processes underlying retrieval and encoding and hence how much the brain regions underlying both will be the same. Although both retrieval and encoding have been shown to activate common anterior cingulate, frontal and insular regions bilaterally (Nyberg *et al.* 1996), it has been found repeatedly that they also activate different frontal regions (Tulving *et al.* 1994) and it has been argued that encoding episodes activates more anterior regions of the medial temporal lobes than does retrieval (Lepage *et al.* 1998), although this is disputed (Schacter & Wagner 1999). One would expect retrieval to reactivate only some of the neocortical regions that represented the original episodic experience, the amount depending on how much was retrieved. One would also expect that some of the search and monitoring processes may be specific to retrieval and, if the retrieved episode feels familiar, this may involve brain regions not involved in encoding.

6.5. Conclusion

Although it is agreed that the posterior neocortex, frontal neocortex and brain regions damaged in amnesics all play a role in encoding, storing and retrieval episodes, there is far less agreement about what the precise processing roles of these regions are. In particular, there is disagreement or uncertainty about several important issues. First, it is uncertain which regions represent the different components of an episode at encoding and retrieval. For example, although there is lesion and functional neuroimaging evidence that right-sided posterior neocortical regions are critical for retrieval (e.g. Markowitsch *et al.* 2001), some studies indicate the importance of left-sided or bilateral activation (e.g. Conway *et al.* 1999). These differences probably relate to the kind of information being retrieved. Second, it remains unclear what regions are involved in storing the different components of episodes and how this changes across time. Third, there is disagreement about the extent of the processing differences in the medial temporal lobes, although it has been agreed since O'Keefe and Nadel's (1978) suggestion that the hippocampus plays an important role in episodic memory. For example, are the hippocampus and perirhinal cortex critical for encoding different kinds of association and/or do they store different kinds of association? Fourth, it is unclear how the feeling of episodic familiarity is produced by the brain. Fifth, the relationship of episodic memory to priming of complex associations is still unresolved, although there is some direct evidence that medial temporal lobe lesions can disrupt certain kinds of associative priming (Chun & Phelps 1999). Sixth, it is not agreed to what extent dissimilarities in the brain regions mediating semantic and episodic memory depend on rehearsal/repetition differences and to what extent they depend on differences in the information retrieved. Finally, even less is known about how the involved brain regions actually perform their functions.

Resolution of some of these issues will be helped by the use of animal models of amnesia, and also by the use of neuroanatomically constrained neural network models of episodic memory. The use of new techniques, such as the lesion followed by hippocampal transplant procedure adopted by Virley *et al.* (1999), will be valuable in providing more convincing evidence about whether specific regions are involved in storing components of episodic memory. Above all, it will be important to focus more on the components of episodic memory such as emotional feeling, perceptual representations, representations of oneself, representations of spatial location and temporal order and duration, different kinds of association, and how feelings of familiarity for an episode are produced.

This work was supported by a Programme Grant from the UK Medical Research Council. I am grateful to John Downes, Juliet Holdstock, Nikki Hunkin, Daniela Montaldi, QiYong Gong and Tom Spencer for their collaboration on some of the experimental work described.

References

Aggleton, J. P. & Brown, M. W. 1999 Episodic memory, amnesia, and the hippocampal-anterior thalamic axis. *Behav. Brain Sci.* **22**, 425–489.

Baddeley, A. D. 2000 The episodic buffer: a new component of working memory? *Trends Cogn. Sci.* **4**, 417–422.

Bailey, C. H., Bartsch, D. & Kandel, E. R. 1996 Toward a molecular definition of long-term memory. *Proc. Natl Acad. Sci. USA* **93**, 13445–13452.

Baxter, M. G. & Murray, E. A. 2001 Opposite relationship of hippocampal and rhinal cortex damage to delayed nonmatching-to-sample deficits in monkeys. *Hippocampus* **11**, 61–71.

Bontempi, B., Laurent-Demir, C., Destrade, C. & Jaffard, R. 1999 Time-dependent reorganization of brain circuitry underlying long-term memory storage. *Nature* **400**, 671–675.

Buffalo, E. A., Reber, P. J. & Squire, L. R. 1998 The human perirhinal cortex and recognition memory. *Hippocampus* **8**, 330–339.

Burgess, N., Jeffery, K. J. & O'Keefe, J. O. 1997 What are the parietal and hippocampal contributions to spatial cognition? *Phil. Trans. R. Soc. Lond.* B **352**, 1395–1543.

Cabeza, R., Kapur, S., Craik, F. I. M., McIntosh, A. R., Houle, S. & Tulving, E. 1997 Functional neuroanatomy of recall and recognition: A PET study of episodic memory. *J. Cogn. Neurosci.* **9**, 254–269.

Cahill, L., Haier, R. J., Alkire, M. T., Tang, C., Keator, D., Wu, J. & McGaugh, J. L. 1996 Amygdala activity at encoding correlated with long-term free-recall of emotional information. *Proc. Natl Acad. Sci. USA* **93**, 8016–8021.

Chun, M. M. & Phelps, E. A. 1999 Memory deficits for implicit contextual information in amnesic subjects with hippocampal damage. *Nature Neurosci.* **2**, 844–847.

Cipolotti, L., Shallice, T., Chan, D., Fox, N., Scahill, R., Harrison, G., Stevens, J. & Rudge, P. 2001 Long-term retrograde amnesia: the crucial role of the hippocampus. *Neuropsychologia* **39**, 151–172.

Conway, M. A., Turk, D. J., Miller, S. L., Logan, J., Nebes, R. D., Metzler, C. C. & Becker, J. T. 1999 A positron emission tomography (PET) study of autobiographical memory retrieval. *Memory* **7**, 679–702.

Easton, A. & Gaffan, D. 2001 Crossed unilateral lesions of the medial forebrain bundle and either inferior temporal or frontal cortex impair object-reward association learning in Rhesus monkeys. *Neuropsychologia* **39**, 71–82.

Eldridge, L. L., Knowlton, B. J., Furmanski, C. S., Bookheimer, S. Y. & Engel, S. A. 2000 Remembering episodes: a selective role for the hippocampus during retrieval. *Nature Neurosci.* **3**, 1149–1152.

Fletcher, P. C. & Henson, R. N. A. 2001 Frontal lobes and human memory-insights from functional neuroimaging. *Brain* **124**, 849–881.

Fletcher, P. C., Frith, C. D., Baker, S. C., Shallice, T., Frackowiak, R. S. & Dolan, R. J. 1995 The mind's eye-precuneus activation in memory-related imagery. *Neuroimage* **2**, 195–200.

Gaffan, D. & Hornak, J. 1997 Amnesia and neglect: beyond the Delay-Brion system and the Hebb synapse. *Phil. Trans. R. Soc. Lond.* B **352**, 1481–1488.

Gaffan, D., Parker, A. & Easton, A. 2001 Dense amnesia in the monkey after transection of fornix, amygdala and anterior temporal stem. *Neuropsychologia* **39**, 51–70.

Gabrieli, J. D. E., Fleischman, D. A., Keane, M. M., Reminger, S. L. & Morrell, F. 1995 Double dissociation between memory systems underlying explicit and implicit memory in the human brain. *Psychol. Sci.* 6, 76–82.

Gloor, P., Olivier, A., Quesney, L. E., Andermann, F. & Horowitz, S. 1982 The role of the limbic system in experiential phenomena of temporal lobe epilepsy. *Ann. Neurol.* **12**, 129–144.

Gooding, P. A., Mayes, A. R. & Van Eijk, R. 2000 A meta-analysis of indirect memory tests for novel material in organic amnesics. *Neuropsychologia* **38**, 666–676.

Graham, K. S., Becker, J. T. & Hodges, J. R. 1997 On the relationship between knowledge and memory for pictures: evidence from the study of patients with semantic dementia and Alzheimer's disease. *J. Internat. Neuropsychol. Soc.* **3**, 534–544.

Gray, J. A. 1982 *The neuropsychology of anxiety.* Oxford University Press.

Hamann, S. B. & Squire, L. R. 1997 Intact perceptual memory in the absence of conscious memory. *Behav. Neurosci.* **111**, 850–854.

Hamann, S. B., Ely, T. D., Grafton, S. T. & Kilts, C. D. 1999 Amygdala activity related to enhanced memory for pleasant and aversive stimuli. *Nature Neurosci.* **2**, 289–293.

Hunkin, N. M., Stone, J. V., Isaac, C. L., Holdstock, J. S., Butterfield, R., Wallis, L. I. & Mayes, A. R. 2000 Factor analysis of three standardized tests of memory in a clinical population. *Br. J. Clin. Psychol.* **39**, 169–180.

Jacoby, L. L., Kelley, C. M. & Dywan, J. 1989 Memory attributions. In *Varieties of memory and consciousness: essays in honour of Endel Tulving* (ed. H. L. Roediger & F. I. M. Craik), pp. 391–422. Hillsdale, NJ: Lawrence Erlbaum Associates.

Kapur, S., Craik, F. I. M., Tulving, E., Wilson, A. A., Houle, S. & Brown, M. 1994 Neuroanatomical correlates of encoding in episodic memory: levels of processing effect. *Proc. Natl Acad. Sci. USA* **91**, 2012–2015.

Kapur, N., Scholey, K., Moore, E., Barker, S., Brice, S., Thompson, S., Shiel, A., Carn, R., Abbott, P. & Fleming, J. 1996 Long-term retention deficits in two cases of disproportionate retrograde amnesia. *J. Cogn. Neurosci.* **8**, 416–434.

Kleinsmith, L. J. & Kaplan, S. 1963 Paired-associate learning as a function of arousal and interpolated interval. *J. Exp. Psychol.* **67**, 124–126.

Lepage, M., Habib, R. & Tulving, E. 1998 Hippocampal PET activations of memory encoding and retrieval: the HIPER model. *Hippocampus* **8**, 313–322.

McGaugh, J. L. 2000 Memory: a century of consolidation. *Science* **287**, 248–251.

Mandler, G. 1980 Recognizing: the judgment of previous occurrence. *Psychol. Rev.* **87**, 252–271.

Markowitsch, H. J., Thiel, A., Reinkemeier, M., Kessler, J., Koyuncu, A. & Heiss, W.-D. 2001 Right amygdalar and temporofrontal activation during autobiographic, but not during fictitious memory retrieval. *Behav. Neurol.* (In the press.)

Mayes, A. R. 1988 *Human organic memory disorders.* Cambridge University Press.

Mayes, A. R. 2001 Aware and unaware memory. Does unaware memory underlie aware memory? In *Time and memory: issues in philosophy and psychology* (ed. D. McCormack & C. Hoerl), pp. 187–211. Oxford University Press.

Mayes, A. R. & Montaldi, M. 1999 The neuroimaging of long-term memory encoding processes. *Memory* **7**, 613–660.

Mayes, A. R., Meudell, P. R. & Pickering, A. D. 1985 Is organic amnesia caused by a selective deficit in remembering contextual information? *Cortex* **21**, 167–204.

Mayes, A. R., Downes, J. J., Shoqeirat, M., Hall, C. & Sagar, H. J. 1993 Encoding ability is preserved in amnesia: evidence from a direct test of encoding. *Neuropsychologia* **31**, 745–759.

Mayes, A. R., Mackay, C. E., Montaldi, D., Downes, J. J., Singh, K. D. & Roberts, N. 2000 Does retrieving decades-old spatial memories activate the medial temporal lobes less than retrieving recently acquired spatial memories? *Neuroimage* **11**, S421.

Mayes, A. R., Isaac, C. L., Downes, J. J., Holdstock, J. S., Hunkin, N. M., Montaldi, D., MacDonald, C., Cezayirli, E. & Roberts, J. N. 2001 Memory for single items, word pairs, and temporal order of different kinds in a patient with selective hippocampal lesions. *Cogn. Neuropsychol.* **18**, 97–123.

Miller, R. R. & Matzel, L. D. 2000 Memory involves far more than 'consolidation'. *Nature Rev. Neurosci.* **1**, 214–216.

Milner, P. 1999 *The autonomous brain.* Mahwah, NJ: Lawrence Erlbaum Associates.

Montaldi, D., Mayes, A. R., Barnes, A., Pirie, H., Hadley, D. M., Patterson, J. & Wyper, D. J. 1998a Associative encoding of pictures activates the medial temporal lobes. *Hum. Brain Mapp.* **6**, 85–104.

Montaldi, D., Mayes, A. R., Pirie, H., Barnes, A., Hadley, D. M., Patterson, J. & Wyper, D.
    1998*b* Dissociating novelty detection and associative encoding in the processing of complex
    scenes. *Neuroimage* **7**, S816.

Morris, R. G. M. & Frey, U. 1997 Hippocampal synaptic plasticity: role in spatial learning or the
    automatic recording of attended experience? *Phil. Trans. R. Soc. Lond.* B **352**, 1489–1503.

Moscovitch, M. 2000 Theories of memory and consciousness. In *The Oxford handbook of memory*
    (ed. E. Tulving & F. I. M. Craik), pp. 609–626. New York: Oxford University Press.

Murray, E. A. & Bussey, T. J. 1999 Perceptual-mnemonic functions of the perirhinal cortex.
    Trends Cogn. Sci. **3**, 142–151.

Nadel, L. & Moscovitch, M. 1997 Memory consolidation, retrograde amnesia and the
    hippocampal complex. *Curr. Opin. Neurobiol.* **7**, 217–227.

Nyberg, L. 1999 Imaging episodic memory: Implications for cognitive theories and phenomena.
    Memory **7**, 585–597.

Nyberg, L., McIntosh, A. R., Cabeza, R., Habib, R., Houle, S. & Tulving, E. 1996 General and
    specific brain regions involved in encoding and retrieval of events: what, where and when.
    Proc. Natl Acad. Sci. USA **93**, 11 280–11 285.

O'Keefe, J. & Nadel, L. 1978 *The hippocampus as a cognitive map.* Oxford University Press.

O'Reilly, R. C. & Rudy, J. W. 1999 *Conjunctive representations in learning and memory: principles
    of cortical and hippocampal function.* University of Colorado, Institute of Cognitive Sciences
    Technical Report, 99-01.

O'Reilly, R. C., Norman, K. A. & McClellan, J. L. 1998 A hippocampal model of recognition
    memory. In *Advances in neural information processing systems*, 10 (ed. M. I. Jordan,
    M. J. Kearns & J. L. McClelland). Cambridge, MA: MIT Press.

Ostergaard, A. L. 1999 Priming deficits in amnesia: now you see them, now you don't. *J.
    Internat. Neuropsychol. Soc.* **5**, 175–190.

Phelps, E. A., LaBar, K. S., Anderson, A. K., O'Connor, K. J., Fulbright, R. K. & Spencer, D. D.
    1998 Specifying the contributions of the human amygdala to emotional memory: a case study.
    Neurocase **4**, 527–540.

Reed, J. M. & Squire, L. R. 1997 Impaired recognition memory in patients with lesions limited to
    the hippocampal formation. *Behav. Neurosci.* **111**, 667–675.

Riedel, G., Micheau, J., Lam, A. G. M., Roloff, E. v. L., Martin, S. J., Bridge, H., de Hoz, L.,
    Poeschel, B., McCulloch, J. & Morris, R. G. M. 1999 Reversible neural inactivation reveals
    hippocampal participation in several memory processes. *Nature Neurosci.* **2**, 898–905.

Rosenbaum, R. S., Priselac, S., Kohler, S., Black, S. E., Gao, F., Nadel, L. & Moscovitch, M.
    2000 Remote spatial memory in an amnesic person with extensive bilateral hippocampal
    lesions. *Nature Neurosci.* **3**, 1044–1048.

Rugg, M. D. & Wilding, E. L. 2000 Retrieval processing and episodic memory. *Trends Cogn. Sci.*
    4, 108–115.

Ryan, L., Nadel, L., Keil, K., Putnam, K., Schnyer, D., Troward, T. & Moscovitch, M. 2001 The
    hippocampal complex and retrieval of recent and very remote autobiographical memories:
    evidence from functional magnetic resonance imaging in neurologically intact people.
    Hippocampus (In the press.)

Schacter, D. L. & Wagner, A. D. 1999 Medial temporal lobe activations in fMRI and PET studies
    of encoding and retrieval. *Hippocampus* **9**, 7–24.

Squire, L. R. & Alvarez, P. 1995 Retrograde amnesia and memory consolidation: a
    neurobiological perspective. *Curr. Opin. Neurobiol.* **5**, 169–177.

Squire, L. R. & Kandel, E. R. 1999 *Memory: from mind to molecules.* New York: W. H. Freeman
    and Company.

Stark, C. E. L. & Squire, L. R. 2000*a* fMRI activity in the medial temporal lobe during
    recognition memory as a function of study-test interval. *Hippocampus* **10**, 329–337.

Stark, C. E. L. & Squire, L. R. 2000*b* Chance recognition memory performance in severe amnesia:
    no evidence for the use of priming in familiarity judgments. *Behav. Neurosci.* **114**, 459–467.

Suzuki, W. A. & Amaral, D. G. 1994 Topographical organization of the reciprocal connections between the monkey entorhinal cortex and the perirhinal and parahippocampal cortices. *J. Neurosci.* **14**, 1856–1877.

Teng, E. & Squire, L. R. 1999 Memory for places learned long ago is intact after hippocampal damage. *Nature* **400**, 675–677.

Tulving, E. 1995 Organization of memory. *Quo vadis?* In *The cognitive neurosciences* (ed. M. S. Gazzaniga), pp. 11–42. Cambridge, MA: MIT Press.

Tulving, E., Kapur, S., Craik, F. I. M., Moscovitch, M. & Houle, S. 1994 Hemispheric encoding/ retrieval asymmetry in episodic memory: Positron emission tomography findings. *Proc. Natl Acad. Sci. USA* **91**, 2016–2020.

Vargha-Khadem, F., Gadian, D. G., Watkins, K. E., Connelly, A., Van Paesschen, W. & Mishkin, M. 1997 Differential effects of early hippocampal pathology on episodic and semantic memory. *Science* **277**, 376–380.

Virley, D. (and 10 others) 1999 Primary CA1 and conditionally immortal MHP36 cell grafts restore conditional discrimination learning and recall in marmosets after excitotoxic lesions of the hippocampal CA1 field. *Brain* **122**, 2321–2335.

Wiggs, C. L. & Martin, A. 1998 Properties and mechanisms of perceptual priming. *Curr. Opin. Neurobiol.* **8**, 227–233.

Zola-Morgan, S. & Squire, L. R. 1993 Neuroanatomy of memory. *A. Rev. Neurosci.* **16**, 547–563.

7

The loss of episodic memories in retrograde amnesia: single-case and group studies

Michael D. Kopelman and Narinder Kapur

Retrograde amnesia in neurological disorders is a perplexing and fascinating research topic. The severity of retrograde amnesia is not well correlated with that of anterograde amnesia, and there can be disproportionate impairments of either. Within retrograde amnesia, there are various dissociations which have been claimed—for example, between the more autobiographical (episodic) and more semantic components of memory. However, the associations of different types of retrograde amnesia are also important, and clarification of these issues is confounded by the fact that retrograde amnesia seems to be particularly vulnerable to psychogenic factors. Large frontal and temporal lobe lesions have been postulated as critical in producing retrograde amnesia. Theories of retrograde amnesia have encompassed storage versus access disruption, physiological processes of 'consolidation', the progressive transformation of episodic memories into a more 'semantic' form, and multiple-trace theory. Single-case investigations, group studies and various forms of neuroimaging can all contribute to the resolution of these controversies.

7.1. Introduction

The nature of retrograde amnesia (RA) in brain disease is a particularly intriguing problem. Recent research has emphasized differing patterns (dissociations) of memory loss in RA. Less emphasis has been placed upon important associations (correlates) of retrograde memory loss, which may contribute to or explain these differing patterns. There can also be differential patterns of deficit in the retention of 'old' memories (RA), on the one hand, and the acquisition of 'new' memories (anterograde amnesia (AA)), on the other. One obvious factor which may putatively influence these varying patterns of deficit is the site or sites of focal brain pathology. However, psychological factors are increasingly recognized to have an important influence on the retrieval of 'old' memories; RA seems to be particularly vulnerable to psychogenic phenomena. In this article, these various factors will be reviewed, and current theories of RA will be considered in the light of them.

7.2. Dissociations within RA

(a) Autobiographical versus semantic remote memory

The most common distinction employed in this literature is that between episodic or autobiographical memory and semantic memory. Autobiographical memory refers, characteristically, to a person's recollection of past incidents and events, which occurred at a specific time and place. Episodic memory is a somewhat broader term, encompassing autobiographical memories as well as performance on certain learning tasks such as recall of a word-list. However, the terms 'autobiographical' and 'episodic' are often used interchangeably. Semantic memory is commonly defined as referring to knowledge of language, concepts, and facts, which do not have a specific time or location. ('Paris is the capital of France' may once have been learned at a particular time and place, but these contextual aspects are seldom retained.) Many authors have postulated dissociations between the autobiographical and semantic aspects of remote memory, and these will be reviewed below. However, it is possible that there is simply a continuum of knowledge across these domains: for example, autobiographical 'facts', often known as 'personal semantic memory' (e.g. knowledge of the names of school teachers, addresses where someone has lived, etc.), fall midway between the two. Moreover, performance on many existing retrograde memory tasks—e.g. recognizing and identifying pictures of famous faces or famous news events (such as Margaret Thatcher leaving office)—may involve both autobioraphical ('I was on business in Edinburgh when Thatcher lost office') as well as more purely semantic knowledge. It is difficult to develop equivalent tests of autobiographical and semantic remote memory for comparative purposes.

De Renzi *et al.* (1987) reported the case of a 44-year-old woman who, following an episode of herpes encephalitis, displayed a severe impairment of semantic knowledge, contrasting with normal memory for autobiographical events. She was impaired at tasks demanding the retrieval of words or of their meaning, such as (i) a confrontation naming test, (ii) a sentence verification test, and (iii) a task requiring classification of items to categories. More particularly, she was impaired at knowledge of famous people (including Hitler, Mussolini and Stalin) and on knowledge of public events. For example, she was unable to provide any information about either the Second World War or the assassination of the Italian Prime Minister, Moro, a recent event at the time she was tested. Cueing helped her in some instances, but she was never able to achieve precise recollection. By contrast, it was apparent that not only did she remember personal incidents that had occurred before and after the acute stage of her disease, but she was well informed on current issues in her family, and she could recall the bulk of what had been done from testing session to testing session. A 20-item questionnaire was constructed about autobiographical memories, and her performance was generally very satisfactory. A magnetic resonance imaging (MRI) scan showed a wide irregular area of increased signal density extending over the inferior and anterior part of the left temporal lobe, above and lateral to the temporal horn (which was enlarged), involving the amygdala, the uncus, the hippocampus and the parahippocampal gyrus. The frontal lobes and the language areas of the temporal and parietal lobes were spared. In the right hemisphere, there were minimal signs of increased signal density in the white matter of the inferior temporal lobe.

Grossi *et al.* (1988) reported similar losses of remote semantic knowledge in a patient who had a large left parietal lesion evident on computed tomography (CT) scan, following a head trauma. This patient was also impaired on logical memory and failed to learn a word-list to criterion. Semantic memory deficits extended to vocabulary, arithmetic and geographical knowledge, and appreciation of concepts such as geometrical forms; but recollection of personally experienced events from the age of 6 to 18 years was excellent. Disproportionate impairment of public knowledge compared with autobiographical memories has also been noted in patients with left temporal lobe epilepsy or temporal lobectomy (Barr *et al.* 1990; Kapur *et al.* 1989). This has also been noted in two cases of irradiation necrosis to anterior and inferior temporal lobe structures (Kapur *et al.* 1994; Yasuda *et al.* 1997). A particular group in whom there may be disproportionate semantic memory loss is patients with semantic dementia, usually resulting from left temporal lobe atrophy. However, the interpretation of their remote memory loss is controversial: some studies report preservation for 'recent' but not distant autobiographical memories (Snowden *et al.* 1996; Graham & Hodges 1997), whereas others find a more uniform loss, largely secondary to their semantic memory deficit (Moss *et al.* 2000).

Other patients have shown the opposite pattern of performance. Dalla Barba *et al.* (1990) described a female Korsakoff syndrome patient, who manifested a severe impairment of autobiographical memory but preserved semantic memory. Despite her episodic memory problems, she was intact in detecting semantic anomalies, defining words, identifying inanimate from animate objects, and category naming. She also performed well when asked questions about famous people or events. It is of interest that she had a lower intelligence quotient (IQ) than the De Renzi *et al.* (1987) patient (92 versus 108), but much better semantic memory.

O'Connor *et al.* (1992) described a patient who had extensive damage to right temporal lobe structures, which resulted in a disproportionately severe impairment in the recall of autobiographical incidents, relative to remote semantic information. This patient also exhibited severe visuoperceptual deficits, and the authors argued that she may have had a particular difficulty in conjuring up the visual images necessary for the retrieval of past autobiographical experiences. There was only moderate impairment in memory for public events which had occurred in the 5-year period before the encephalitis, and knowledge of earlier public events was preserved, whereas the loss of autobiographical incidents was extensive and showed little evidence of earlier memories being spared. Similarly, Ogden (1993) reported severe autobiographical memory loss, prosopagnosia and visual agnosia in a head injury patient, who had relative preservation of remote semantic knowledge. In this case, the pathology was more posterior, but projections from the right occipital to the right temporal lobe were disrupted. Ogden also suggested that a failure in visual imagery might be contributing to the autobiographical memory loss. Both patients (O'Connor *et al.* 1992; Ogden 1993) also had a severe impairment of visual, anterograde memory. Rubin & Greenberg (1998) reviewed a series of similar cases, in whom 'visual memory-deficit amnesia' gave rise to disproportionate impairments in autobiographical memory.

Partial dissociations of autobiographical and semantic memory have also been claimed. For example, Hodges & McCarthy (1993) reported a case of amnesia following bilateral thalamic infarction, in which there was dense autobiographical memory loss, together with memory loss for public events, but in whom knowledge of famous personalities was relatively intact. Mackenzie Ross & Hodges (1997) reported a patient who was severely impaired at autobiographical memory and knowledge of public events, but whose ability was surprisingly preserved at a famous faces task. As the patient had presumed cerebral hypoxia following a cardiac arrest with a normal CT scan, it is difficult to relate this finding to focal pathology.

Moreover, group studies have indicated that this simple left–semantic versus right–autobiographical distinction, postulated in single-case reports, does not necessarily hold good. Kopelman *et al.* (1999) did indeed find particularly severe autobiographical

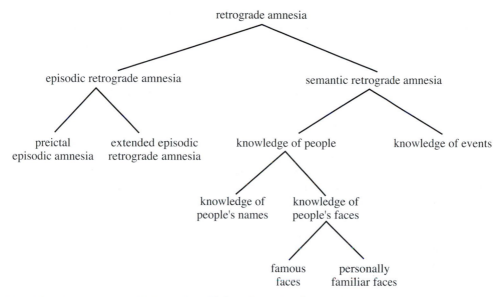

Fig. 7.1. A provisional framework outlining the major forms of neurological RA, taken from Kapur (1999). Episodic RA refers to loss of memory for personally experienced events. Semantic RA refers to loss of specific forms of acquired knowledge. The framework is not meant to represent a comprehensive taxonomic classification—for example, more general forms of loss of knowledge (dysphasia, apraxia, etc.), psychogenic RA, and loss of personal semantic verbal knowledge, are not included.

memory loss in patients with right-sided temporal lobe damage from herpes encephalitis, relative to patients with left-sided pathology, consistent with several studies cited above (O'Connor *et al.* 1992; Ogden 1993; Rubin & Greenberg 1998). However, the right-sided patients were also particularly impaired on a measure of famous news events, particularly when these images involved perception of famous faces, perhaps reflecting both 'episodic' and face recognition components to the task. Left-sided patients were particularly impaired when they had to 'complete' the names of famous people from the past from word-stems: this was interpreted as reflecting a deficit in the lexical–semantic labelling of remote memories. This double dissociation was statistically significant. By contrast, Eslinger (1998) also examined patients with left or right temporal lobe pathology, finding that left medial temporal lobe lesions caused time-limited retrograde autobiographical memory changes. More extensive left temporal lobe pathology impaired personal semantic memory, but did not affect recollection of autobiographical incidents. However, right temporal lobe lesions did not appear to affect either personal semantic or autobiographical incident recall. Bilateral temporal lobe lesions seemed to be required to cause extensive autobiographical memory deficits, and Eslinger (1998) postulated that interactions between prefrontal cortex and diverse temporal lobe regions were involved in autobiographical memory retrieval.

In summary, there is evidence that the more semantic remote memories are dependent upon left temporal lobe function, that the retrieval of autobiographical incidents is more dependent upon the integrity of right temporal lobe structures, and that bilateral damage is probably more harmful than unilateral. Figure 7.1 is taken from Kapur (1999) and illustrates further proposed dissociations within autobiographical and semantic remote memory. However, the autobiographical–semantic distinction is by no means clear-cut, perhaps reflecting the fact that performance on many remote memory tasks involves aspects of both types of memory.

(b) Explicit versus implicit remote memory

There have been several attempts to identify an implicit component in RA, although this is much more difficult and vulnerable to criticism than in AA.

A novel dissociation in remote memory was reported by Warrington & McCarthy (1988) and McCarthy & Warrington (1992). They described a 54-year-old man who had suffered herpes encephalitis, resulting in bitemporal damage that was worse on the right. He showed extensive retrograde memory loss for autobiographical episodes and also for knowledge of public events, famous faces and famous names. Despite this, he performed within normal limits at a word-completion task (completing a name when given a stem cue) for famous names and at familiarity judgements for famous faces. The authors proposed a dual system for the semantic representation of names and faces: a vocabulary-like fact memory which was preserved in this patient, and a cognitive mediational memory system, which was impaired. The implication seemed to be that the former was analogous to so-called 'implicit' memory, which is preserved in AA.

Eslinger et al. (1996) compared the performance of two post-encephalitic patients on several tests, similar to those employed by Warrington and McCarthy (1988). A patient who had sustained left inferior and anterior medial temporal lobe pathology, together with a small right temporal polar lesion, was substantially impaired at a name-completion task when the cue was paired with a famous face. By contrast, a patient with right inferior and anterior medial temporal lobe pathology showed only very mild impairment at this task.

In a group study, Kopelman et al. (1999) obtained results consistent with those of Eslinger et al. (1996). Two patients with unilateral left temporal lobe pathology following herpes encephalitis were severely impaired at a name-completion task, whereas herpes patients with predominantly right temporal lobe pathology were virtually intact at this test, consistent with the Warrington & McCarthy (1988) findings. Taken together, these results suggest that the 'vocabulary-like fact memory' is sensitive only to certain types of left temporal lobe damage. However, Reed & Squire (1998) found impairment in patients with temporal lobe lesions at a more difficult task, in which only the names were presented for completion (in the absence of the associated famous faces), indicating that task difficulty needs to be taken into account in evaluating such findings.

Two further studies (Tulving et al. 1988; Lhermitte & Serdaru 1993) have shown that progressive priming or prompting in training sessions over a number of days or weeks can help to restore a number of personal semantic memories, but that this procedure fails to alter loss of memory for autobiographical incidents.

In addition, at least three studies of psychogenic amnesia (see § 7.6) have addressed this issue. Kopelman et al. (1994) described a patient with psychogenic amnesia, who failed to show word-completion priming of the names of people and places known to her preceding the onset of her amnesia, whereas she showed normal priming of the names of people and places that she had learned only since the onset of her disorder. However, this patient may have been simulating by the time she was tested on this task. Markowitsch *et al.* (1997) used a word-stem completion task involving the names of people and companies that a psychogenic amnesic patient had worked with in the past. This patient performed very badly at this task. Again, there were issues of possible simulation, and incidental statements by this patient suggested that the task was not, in fact, measuring implicit memory in this case. Campodonico & Rediess (1996) examined this issue using tests of semantic knowledge in a patient with 'profound psychogenic RA'. On a measure of indirect remote memory, their patient showed more rapid learning of famous identities relative to novel ones, compared with control subjects, despite having been unable to name the famous faces at baseline. She also learned the names and occupations of famous people better than she did those of unknown people. The authors interpreted their findings as evidence for preserved 'implicit' remote semantic knowledge, despite impaired 'explicit' recall of the same material.

In summary, the idea that there might be a preserved 'implicit' component in RA, as many studies have found in AA, is indeed attractive. Such a finding might also be valuable in differentiating authentic or 'hysterical' psychogenic amnesia from simulated or factitious amnesia. However, it is much harder to demonstrate unequivocally an implicit component in RA than it is in AA. There have been few studies to date, and the findings so far remain vulnerable to alternative interpretations.

(c) Brief versus extensive episodic RA

Various authors have argued for qualitatively different types of RA, broadly related to the time-span (temporal extensiveness) that it covers (e.g. Williams & Zangwill 1952; Symonds 1966; Squire *et al.* 1984; Kapur 1999). The nature of RA may vary according to whether it covers a matter of (i) seconds, minutes or hours; (ii) days, weeks or months up to a period of 2 to 3 years; or (iii) an extensive retrograde memory loss covering years or decades.

Kapur (1999) distinguished two classes of RA, which he called 'pre-ictal amnesia' and 'extended episodic RA', respectively. Kapur (1999) put forward four arguments in favour of this distinction:

(i) The delayed onset of certain types of brief RA. Lynch & Yarnell (1973) studied American footballers who had incurred a mild head injury. These footballers were initially able to describe what had happened just before the blow, but, when reinterviewed some minutes later, they were unable to recall these events. This has usually been interpreted as a failure of memory consolidation following the blow, resulting in a brief period of RA lasting a matter of minutes. Consistent with this, Russell & Nathan (1946) also noted that in some patients pretraumatic events were briefly recalled in the first few minutes following a head injury, but then were rapidly forgotten.

(ii) Following a closed head injury, an extensive RA characteristically shrinks to a much briefer period, which may be a matter of minutes, hours or days, depending upon severity of the injury (Russell & Nathan 1946; Williams & Zangwill 1952; Wasterlain 1971). Kapur (1999) also noted that, following episodes of transient global amnesia (TGA), there is commonly some residual 'pre-ictal RA', lasting a matter of minutes or (exceptionally) hours (Fisher 1982; Hodges 1991; Kapur *et al.* 1998).

(iii) There are qualitative discontinuities in the density of pre-injury memory loss reported by patients. For example, following head injury, there is commonly a short, virtually complete RA lasting a matter of minutes or hours. In some cases, there is also a far less dense loss of memories for incidents or events over the preceding few weeks (Russell & Nathan 1946; Williams & Zangwill 1952).

(iv) Some experimental studies also support this distinction. Electrical stimulation (under local anaesthetic) of temporal lobe regions in epileptic patients with complex partial seizures produces a period of pre-ictal RA, ranging from a few minutes to a few days or weeks (Bickford *et al.* 1958). Bickford *et al.* (1958) also found that the longer the duration of electrical stimulation, the more extensive was this brief or pre-ictal RA. Electroconvulsive therapy (ECT) also gives rise to a brief RA lasting a matter of days (Squire *et al.* 1981) and complaints of memory loss which may go back to 2–3 years (Squire & Slater 1983).

A fifth argument is that there is at least some evidence that patients with lesions confined to the diencephalic or medial temporal structures have an RA which may extend back 2–3 years but no further (Milner 1966; Zola-Morgan *et al.* 1986; Dusoir *et al.* 1990; Graff-Radford *et al.* 1990; Snowden *et al.* 1996; Graham & Hodges 1997; Guinan *et al.* 1998). As will be discussed below (§ 7.5), cortical damage seems to be required for a more extensive RA, going back years or decades as is seen in (for example) the Korsakoff syndrome, herpes encephalitis, or Alzheimer dementia (e.g. Albert *et al.* 1981; Kopelman 1989; Wilson *et al.* 1995; Kopelman *et al.* 1999). This distinction between a brief or short RA (2–3 years) and much longer RA (years or decades) has also been made in connection with the literature on focal RA (Kopelman 2000*a*).

In brief, there are several reasons for attempting to distinguish the mechanisms which underlie these different components of RA. The precise boundaries of these different types of RA, and whether they should be differentiated into two, three, or more subtypes, remain unclear. To date, most neuropsychological literature has concentrated on understanding the nature of an extensive RA.

7.3. Associations of RA

Important factors to consider in assessing and interpreting the 'temporal gradient' of RA, i.e. the relative sparing of early memories, are the duration (time since onset) of the amnesia and the age of the subject. Surprisingly, the duration of amnesia was seldom reported in the earlier quantitative studies from the 1970s and 1980s. The age of the subject is obviously important in reviewing the items in any given remote memory task. Furthermore, there is some evidence that older amnesic patients (aged 40 or over) are more likely to show a steep temporal gradient than patients under 40, particularly in recalling facts about themselves (Kopelman *et al.* 1989). This finding does not appear to be related to the severity, rate of onset or duration of amnesia, but suggests that older subjects may encode new memories in a way which makes them more vulnerable to the effects of brain damage than are new memories in younger subjects.

Second, other factors which determine performance on remote memory tasks include intelligence, education and media exposure. Kopelman (1989) found significant correlations between full-scale IQ and measures of 'semantic' remote memory—tests of famous news event recall and recognition, and a test involving famous personalities. However, correlations with IQ were not significant for measures of autobiographical incidents and 'personal semantic' facts. Likewise, Kapur *et al.* (1999) found a trend in the same direction in healthy subjects between estimated premorbid IQ and a public events remote memory measure. Moreover, Kapur *et al.* (1999) also found that this fairly typical test of retrograde memory correlated even more closely with an estimate of media exposure, based on how often a subject watched the television news, read newspapers, etc.

Third, a subject's ability at executive or 'frontal' tests may also be an important predictor of remote memory performance. This may be particularly the case for autobiographical recall, where active reconstruction or recollection is required, but significant correlations with executive test scores are not confined to episodic RA tests. Kopelman (1991) found that six out of eight executive or frontal tests correlated significantly with retrograde memory performance, but only one out of eight tests correlated significantly with a 'composite' measure of anterograde memory performance. Whereas anterograde test scores predicted only 21% of the variance in retrograde memory scores, a regression equation based on three of the executive or frontal tests predicted 64% of the variance. There were significant correlations with news event recall and recognition scores as well as with memory for autobiographical incidents and facts. Similarly, Verfaellie *et al.* (1995*b*) obtained a significant correlation between a measure of more purely semantic memory (words which had come into the vocabulary at different times) and a 'composite' measure of frontal function. Moreover, D'Esposito *et al.* (1996) contrasted subarachnoid haemorrhage patients who performed well or badly on executive tests, finding that only patients with severe executive impairment showed RA on a famous faces test, and that improvement in executive scores was correlated with improvement in RA.

Fourth, the extent of cortical pathology is probably also important, as will be discussed further below (§ 7.5). Schmidtke & Vollmer (1997) developed a 'new' test of semantic memory, requiring subjects to retrieve 81 items of well-rehearsed semantic knowledge across various domains: scores on this test were interpreted as an index of neocortical-dependent memory representation. Scores on the Wechsler Memory Scale (WMS) were assumed to reflect hippocampal-dependent memory. On the basis of regression analyses, remote autobiographical memory scores and performance on a test of memory for famous people were found to be predicted by the measure of 'neocortical' function, according to these criteria. Other potentially important correlates of remote memory performance include direct, quantitative measures of brain volume on MRI, brain metabolism on positron emission tomography (PET), and cerebral perfusion on single-photon emission computed tomography, as will be considered below (§ 7.5).

In summary, there are a number of important correlates of performance on measures of retrograde memory, which are apparent in larger-scale group studies. Understandably, these factors tend to be ignored in single-case reports, but they may help to account for some of the dissociations which are reported. Amongst patients with memory disorders, the combination of low IQ, poor education, limited media exposure and relatively mild amnesia may give the impression of disproportionate impairment on the 'more semantic' remote memory tests (Kapur *et al.* 1999; Kopelman 2000*a*). The opposite pattern—severe autobiographical memory loss in someone with good background semantic knowledge (high IQ and education)—will give a pattern of performance the other way round. Before dissociations are claimed in particular patients and attributed to differing sites of pathology, it is always necessary to control for such factors.

7.4. RA versus AA

As already mentioned (§ 7.3), there is generally a poor correlation between scores on retrograde and anterograde memory tests. This has been shown in Korsakoff syndrome patients by Shimamura & Squire (1986), Kopelman (1989, 1991) and Parkin (1991), in a mixed group of amnesic patients by Mayes *et al.* (1994), and in Alzheimer dementia patients by Kopelman (1989, 1991) and Greene & Hodges (1996). In the Kopelman (1989) study, only one out of five measures of RA showed a significant correlation with a composite measure of AA, and shared variance between RA and AA was only 21%. Somewhat similar findings were obtained by Mayes *et al.* (1997), although these authors also observed that higher correlations were found between anterograde and retrograde tests where the tasks were similar in format and in the kind of information tapped.

It is widely accepted that AA can occur with minimal or no RA—for example, in some cases of TGA (Hodges & Ward 1989), head injury (particularly if mild or penetrating) (Russell & Nathan 1946; Dusoir *et al.* 1990), some cases of thalamic infarction (Dall'Ora *et al.* 1989; Graff-Radford *et al.* 1990; Parkin *et al.* 1994; Winocur *et al.* 1984), and in certain deep midline tumours (Kapur *et al.* 1996; Guinan *et al.* 1998). In particular, penetrating lesions to the brain often arise in the absence of any RA, despite the presence of moderate or severe post-traumatic amnesia (Russell 1948; Lishman 1968; Teuber 1969, 1975; Teuber *et al.* 1968; Grafman *et al.* 1985).

Much more contentious is the nature of disproportionate RA, sometimes known as 'focal' or 'isolated' RA. Kapur *et al.* (1992) described a 26-year-old woman who had fallen from a horse, sustaining left and right frontal contusions, evident on CT scan, and subsequent signal alteration on MRI at the left and right temporal poles. The patient was impaired across all remote memory tests employed, with normal or only moderate impairment at various anterograde tests. Similarly, Levine *et al.* (1998) described a patient who was involved in a road traffic accident, resulting in a right frontal lesion involving the uncinate fasciculus as well as prefrontal haemorrhages. The patient had an initially severe AA, but this resolved leaving a (Wechsler Memory Scale—Revised) verbal memory index of 128 and a severe RA.

The present authors have debated the underlying nature of focal RA elsewhere (Kopelman 2000*a,b*; Kapur 2000). Patients with disproportionate RA often have an initially severe or moderately severe AA, which subsequently subsides, and the importance of this is disputed. Second, they may have some degree of residual AA, which begs the question of whether measures of retrograde and anterograde memory are strictly comparable. Third, patients with specific deficits in autobiographical memory, or public semantic knowledge, or both, are commonly labelled as instances of 'focal RA', and it is important to remember that they differ. More specifically, patients with transient epileptic amnesia—TGA with an epileptic aetiology—commonly complain of 'gaps' in their autobiographical memory. The explanation for these gaps could be either that current epileptic activity has caused impaired retrieval of much earlier encoded memories, or that previously undetected 'subclinical' ictal activity resulted in faulty (anterograde) encoding of specific memories. Likewise, patients with semantic dementia have been reported to show a 'reversed' temporal gradient, analogous to that seen in focal RA (Snowden *et al.* 1996; Graham & Hodges 1997), but there are a number of alternative explanations for this, including the fact that difficulty in retrieving 'old' memories may reflect these patients' linguistic or semantic disorder. Finally, it is important to remember that psychogenic amnesia can produce temporal gradients which resemble those in focal RA (Kopelman *et al.* 1994; Kritchevsky *et al.* 1997). Psychiatric and psychogenic factors may be important, even in the presence of brain pathology (see §7.6).

In summary, the severity and extent of RA is poorly correlated with the severity of AA, although most investigations of this topic have looked at the more extensive forms of RA rather than the briefer forms mentioned in §7.2. While AA can exist alongside little or no RA, the interpretation of disproportionate retrograde impairments remains controversial and several different types of factor may produce this phenomenon.

7.5. Structural brain pathology and RA

There is little doubt that a variety of sites of pathology can give rise to RA, as has been reviewed in detail elsewhere (Kopelman 1993, 2000c).

Large temporal lobe lesions can produce an extensive RA. As already considered, there is a differing pattern of deficit across left- and right-sided lesions. Left-sided lesions tend to produce damage to semantic remote memory (De Renzi *et al.* 1987), right-sided lesions to autobiographical memory (O'Connor *et al.* 1992), and bilateral lesions affect both (Wilson *et al.* 1995). Cermak & O'Connor (1983), studied a patient S.S., who had suffered herpes encephalitis resulting in bitemporal pathology and a severe AA. On a test of famous faces (Albert *et al.* 1979), he showed a marked impairment with a temporal gradient, i.e. relative sparing of early memories. During follow-up over a number of years, there was substantial improvement. Asked about events from his past life (from the 1930s to the 1970s) on a questionnaire, he showed impairment for the two most recent decades only. Given cue-words, and asked to describe specific episodes from his past relating to these words, S.S. seemed to display only a 'personal pool of generalized knowledge about himself, i.e. his own semantic memory'. On the other hand, his past knowledge about physics and laser technology (his profession) appeared to be intact, although he was not able to retain information encountered in a new article about the subject. A further study showed that he was impaired in recalling and recognizing the meaning of words which had come into the language only since the onset of his amnesia (Verfaellie *et al.* 1995a).

Large frontal lobe lesions can also produce retrograde memory loss, particularly if bilateral. Baddeley & Wilson (1986) described impaired retrieval of autobiographical memories in two such patients, and florid confabulation in autobiographical memory retrieval in two others. Larger group studies in patients with neuroradiologically delineated frontal lesions have also demonstrated severe impairments in autobiographical memory retrieval (Della Sala *et al.* 1993; Kopelman *et al.* 1999), public or news event knowledge (D'Esposito *et al.* 1996; Mangels *et al.* 1996; Kopelman *et al.* 1999), and famous faces (Mangels *et al.* 1996).

Findings in patients with diencephalic lesions are variable. There is little doubt that Korsakoff syndrome patients generally show an extensive RA with a relatively steep temporal gradient (Zola-Morgan *et al.* 1983; Butters & Cermak 1986; Kopelman 1989; Kopelman *et al.* 1999). Squire *et al.* (1989) compared the performance of seven patients with the alcoholic Korsakoff syndrome with that of five patients of more acute onset on six tests of remote memory. In both groups, there was a temporal gradient to the RA extending across a period of about 15 years, and the gradient was closely similar between the two groups. Verfaellie *et al.* (1995*b*) examined remote memory for semantic information in Korsakoff syndrome and other amnesic patients, using a test of vocabulary for words which had come into the language between 1955 and 1989. They found an impairment in the Korsakoff syndrome group in the recall of these words, and that there was a temporal gradient such that their knowledge of recent words was more impaired than that of remote words. However, it seems to be the concomitant presence of some degree of frontal lobe pathology which contributes to this. This was first postulated on the basis of correlations between RA scores and frontal or executive test performance by Kopelman (1991), and it appears to be corroborated by subsequent studies (e.g. Hodges & McCarthy 1993; Kopelman *et al.* 1999). Hodges & McCarthy (1993) found severe impairment of autobiographical memory in a patient with bilateral paramedian thalamic infarction, whereas other studies of patients with thalamic infarction have found preserved remote memory (e.g. Winocur *et al.* 1984; Graff-Radford *et al.* 1990): it seems likely that the extent of involvement of frontal projections from the thalamus may determine the severity and extent of RA. Similarly, Kopelman *et al.* (1999) compared Korsakoff syndrome patients with a degree of frontal atrophy and patients who had focal diencephalic pathology, resulting from pituitary tumours and their treatment: only the former group showed an extensive retrograde memory loss.

Most controversial is the issue of whether damage confined to the medial temporal lobes produces an extensive RA. Following a bitemporal lobectomy, patient H.M. appeared in initial studies to have an RA of only 2–3 years (Milner 1966, 1972), and this appeared to be confirmed on tests of famous faces and famous news events (Marslen-Wilson & Teuber 1975; Gabrieli *et al.* 1988). Similarly, Zola-Morgan *et al.* (1986) found a 2-year RA in a patient with moderately severe AA following hypoxic brain damage to the CA1 regions of the hippocampi bilaterally. In contrast, Nadel & Moscovitch (1997) have reviewed the literature, and have suggested that hippocampal pathology alone can produce an extensive RA. Unfortunately, many of the studies which they reviewed involved patients with extensive temporal lobe pathology, confounding the interpretation of the findings. Two of the better studies were by Victor & Agamanolis (1990) and Kartsounis *et al.* (1995). These authors described single cases who showed either a relatively specific loss of neurons in the hippocampi bilaterally (Victor & Agamanolis 1990) or signal alteration on MRI in the hippocampi bilaterally in the CA1 and CA2 fields (Kartsounis *et al.* 1995), respectively. (Quantified MRI evidence of severe hippocampal atrophy in the latter patient has recently been provided by Cipolotti *et al.* (2001).) However, it is of interest that both patients had a history of heavy drinking, although the authors stated that this had not been true in recent years.

Kopelman *et al.* (1999) carried out the first study comparing groups of patients with temporal lobe, frontal or diencephalic lesions across several RA tasks, including recall of autobiographical incidents, personal semantic facts, and famous news events. As already stated, Korsakoff syndrome patients (with combined diencephalic and frontal pathology) showed severe RA across all tasks with a relatively steep temporal gradient, whereas patients who had been treated for pituitary tumours extending into the diencephalon showed severe AA but no evidence of RA. Patients with temporal lobe pathology also showed a severe RA, although their temporal gradients appeared to be 'flatter' than those of Korsakoff syndrome patients. Patients with frontal lobe lesions showed severe impairment in the recall of autobiographical incidents and famous news events, but were relatively intact in the retrieval of well-rehearsed personal semantic facts—i.e. this latter group seemed to be particularly impaired where 'effortful' or organized retrieval processes were required for reconstructing 'old' memories. In general, patients with bilateral frontal lesions performed worse than did patients with unilateral frontal lesions. Subsequent analysis has shown significant correlations with quantitative MRI measures of the volume of specific brain structures in these patients, such that 60–68% of variance on autobiographical memory tasks could be accounted for by these brain volume measures.

In summary, large temporal lobe or frontal lesions can produce an extensive RA. Diencephalic lesions appear to contribute to an extensive RA where there is concomitant frontal pathology. The contribution of medial temporal lobe pathology in isolation remains controversial. Somewhat different patterns of RA are found between left and right temporal lobe lesions, and between frontal and temporal lobe pathology.

7.6. Psychogenic influences on RA

Psychological forms of RA can be relatively 'pure', in that there is no known evidence of cerebral pathology, or they can occur in the context of either minor or major brain disorder (Kapur 1999). However, even in 'pure' cases, which are the ones usually referred to as 'psychogenic amnesia', there is commonly a past history of a transient organic memory loss (Stengel 1941; Berrington *et al.* 1956; Kopelman 1987, 2000*a,c*; Markowitsch 1996). Psychogenic amnesia can be situation-specific, e.g. loss of memory for an offence (including child sexual abuse) by either the perpetrator or the victim: in these cases, there is a brief gap in memory for the episode, presumably as a result of compromised anterograde memory encoding (Kopelman 1987, 2000*c*). Alternatively, psychogenic amnesia can be 'global', encompassing the whole of a person's past, as occurs in a so-called 'fugue' episode, also known as 'functional RA'.

Schacter *et al.* (1982) described a young man who developed 'functional RA' after attending the funeral of his grandfather, to whom he had been very close. When asked to retrieve autobiographical memories to cue-words, the median age of his retrieved memories was very short (i.e. recent), relative to both healthy controls and his own subsequent (post-recovery) performance. However, there were some preserved 'islands' of autobiographical memory from the happiest period of his life. He recovered his memories after seeing a television programme in which a funeral was shown.

Kopelman *et al.* (1994) reported a 'reverse' temporal gradient on autobiographical and public event remote memory tasks in a patient with psychogenic amnesia. Anterograde memory test scores were normal. Following a marital crisis, this woman disappeared from her home, flew across the Atlantic, and 'came round' in the London Underground. There was a persistent amnesic gap for a 1-week period, which was thought to reflect an authentic fugue state, although this lady was shown to be at least partially simulating some 3 months after first being seen.

Kapur & Abbott (1996) described a 19-year-old male university student, who was found in a city park a few days before his university examinations were due to start. In addition to the likely stress resulting from his pending examinations, the patient's grandmother had died 8 months earlier, and the patient had been quite close to her. Witness accounts were obtained from people who had observed the episode from the onset, and the authors monitored the acute stages of recovery of memory function over the next 4 weeks. The memory loss was characterized by impaired performance on both autobiographical and public events memory tests, in the context of normal anterograde memory scores. Shrinkage of RA took place over a 4-week period, with the autobiographical and public events components of retrograde memory recovering at the same rate.

Kritchevsky *et al.* (1997) obtained a pronounced recency effect on a cued autobiographical memory task in nine patients with functional RA, similar to that obtained in the Kopelman *et al.* (1994) patient. This gradient was in stark contrast to a conventional 'Ribot' temporal gradient (i.e. sparing of early memories) obtained in patients during a TGA episode.

Markowitsch *et al.* (1997) described a 37-year-old man, who experienced a 'fugue' episode lasting 5 days when out bicycling, and who then had a persistent loss of autobiographical memory, lasting 8 months or more. During this period, the patient was required to listen to sentences containing information about his past, either preceding or following the onset of amnesia, while undergoing an oxygen-15 PET scan. The authors found reduced right hemisphere activation, relative to healthy controls performing a similar task.

Costello *et al.* (1998) described a man in his 40s who, following a left superior dorsolateral prefrontal haemorrhage, developed a dense RA for the 19 years preceding his stroke. However, the authors considered that 'a purely organic account of the condition does not seem very plausible'. They also carried out PET activation study, in which the subject attempted to recall events using family photographs as stimuli in three conditions—events for which he was amnesic but at which he had been present, events from the amnesic period at which he was not present, and events outside the amnesic period. In the 'amnesic–present' condition, activation was diminished in both the right ventrolateral frontal cortex and a region close to the site of the haemorrhage. The finding of reduced right frontal activation is broadly consistent with the finding of Markowitsch *et al.* (1997) of diminished right hemisphere activation.

These last two studies suggest that there may be common pathways which are affected in both neurological and psychogenic forms of RA (cf. Markowitsch 1996). However, Kapur (1999) has pointed out that there may be differences in the influences that psychosocial variables can have on functional anatomy in these cases. Furthermore, much more common than cases of 'pure' psychogenic amnesia are patients in whom psychosocial factors are combined with mild or moderate degrees of brain pathology to produce an RA which is very much disproportionate to what would be expected on the basis of the cerebral pathology alone. Kopelman (2000*a*) described several such cases, including 'Patient E' who experienced a minor cerebral ischaemic episode, but whose autobiographical memory loss was quite disproportionate to this: it was probably related to the severe employment and marital problems that he was undergoing at the time. The effect of psychogenic factors can also be seen in patients with more severe brain pathology, as described by Stuss & Guzman (1988) and Binder (1994).

Kopelman (2000*a*) argued that even patients with clear-cut brain pathology can 'use' that pathology to differing ends, and that there may be variable degrees of awareness in psychological forms of amnesia. Taking account of various known associates of psychogenic amnesia—a severe precipitating stress, depression or extreme arousal, and a past history of a transient organic amnesia—Kopelman (2000*a*) proposed a model to suggest how psychosocial factors interact with brain systems known to be involved in memory. Figure 7.2 illustrates this model. The relevant social and psychological factors are indicated in the ovals, and the brain systems in rectangular boxes. The model postulated that stress can affect frontal control or executive systems such that there is inhibition in the retrieval of autobiographical and episodic memories. This inhibition is

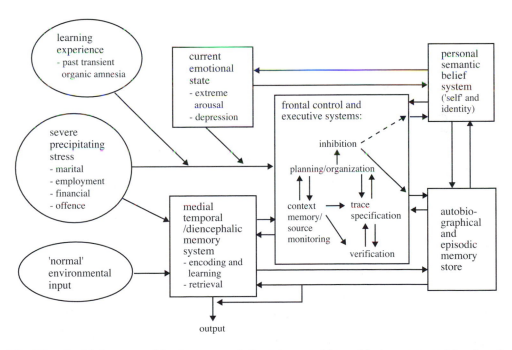

Fig. 7.2. Social factors and brain systems influencing autobiographical memory retrieval and personal identity. The relevant social and psychological factors are indicated in the ovals. The brain systems are indicated in the rectangular boxes. Severe stress affects frontal control and executive systems, thereby inhibiting the retrieval of autobiographical or episodic memories. This is more likely if the subject is extremely aroused, very depressed, or if there is a past experience of a transient organic amnesia. If the stress is severe, there may even be a transient loss of knowledge of self and identity (dashed arrow). From Kopelman (2000*a*).

exacerbated, or made more likely, when a subject is extremely aroused, very depressed, or when there has been a past 'learning experience' of transient amnesia. When such stresses are severe, the inhibition may even affect a 'personal semantic belief system', resulting in a transient loss of knowledge of self and identity (see dotted arrow)—as is characteristic of 'fugue' states. If this occurs, there is negative feedback to the emotional state, such that the subject is commonly described as appearing 'flat' or perplexed. Despite this suppression of autobiographical memory retrieval by these frontal inhibitory mechanisms, anterograde learning (and 'new' episodic memory retrieval) can occur from 'normal' environmental stimuli via the intact medial temporal or diencephalic system, as illustrated in Figure 7.2.

7.7. Theories of RA

Theories of RA have traditionally focused on three issues. The first is whether the problem is essentially a failure of access or retrieval or a loss of storage. The second concerns the nature of the temporal gradient which characterizes RA in most forms of organic amnesia. The third concerns the respective roles of specific brain structures in storing and accessing remote memories, and how these structures interact.

There are several reasons for supposing that the RA in amnesic or dementing patients might result, at least in part, from a retrieval deficit—or from a disruption in the organization of retrieval processes—rather than from a destruction of memory storage itself. Various studies have shown that amnesic or dementing patients manifest a remarkably good response to recognition or contextual cues, compared with their very poor recall memory performance (Kopelman 1989; Parkin et al. 1990; Verfaellie et al. 1995b; Kopelman et al. 1999). Weiskrantz (1985) pointed out that a marked response to recognition testing or cueing for memories long preceding the onset of an illness must be indicative of a retrieval component to the RA, whatever the slope of the remote memory curve. A deficit in retrieving remote memories, superimposed upon an anterograde learning deficit, is consistent with the finding that there are generally low and non-significant correlations between the severity of AA and performance on various tests of RA (Shimamura & Squire 1986; Kopelman 1989, 1991; Parkin 1991; Mayes et al. 1994, Greene & Hodges 1996). In addition, there are sometimes inconsistencies in the retrieval of past memories by individual patients (Cermak & O'Connor 1983; Sagar et al. 1988). Obviously, where RA shrinks (as in head injury, following ECT, and in TGA), there must have been an important retrieval component to the deficit (Kapur 1999). However, this does not exclude the possibility that loss of actual storage might occur in certain forms of focal brain atrophy or dementia. Moreover, as Kapur (1999) pointed out, it may be more important to identify at which point in a network of associations a breakdown has occurred than simply to pursue dichotomies, such as retrieval versus storage.

Various theories have been postulated to account for the temporal gradient in RA. One view is that there is a prolonged process of physiological consolidation of memories, during which memories are initially dependent upon the medial temporal lobe system but gradually become established in other areas of the brain ('structural reallocation'). According to this view, there is a gradual reorganization of memory storage, whereby memories that are initially dependent upon the medial temporal lobes eventually do not require this system. A more permanent memory, independent of the medial temporal lobes, gradually develops, presumably in neocortex (Alvarez & Squire 1994; Murre 1997). However, very extensive temporal gradients, extending over 20–30 years, provide a problem for this theory, as they imply that this process of physiological consolidation must continue for a very long time indeed.

A second approach emphasizes that, as episodic memories are rehearsed through time, they adopt a more semantic form, which protects them against the effects of brain disorder (e.g. Cermak 1984; Weiskrantz 1985; Sagar *et al.* 1988). In other words, the contextual components of these memories become attenuated or lost, making the memories feel much less immediate and vivid, but they are better preserved. This hypothesis is not incompatible with the notion of structural reallocation, proposed in consolidation theory. Although an attractive idea, the problem with this view is that the notion of 'semanticization' is poorly specified and therefore somewhat unsatisfactory. Moreover, it does not explain why knowledge which is semantic virtually from the outset, such as knowledge of the meaning of new words, also shows a temporal gradient (Verfaellie *et al.* 1995b).

A third approach is multiple-trace theory, proposed by Nadel & Moscovitch (1997). These authors accept that the hippocampi and related structures in the medial temporal lobes and diencephalon are involved in a short-term consolidation process, that they call 'cohesion', which is critical to memory formation. However, they argued against a notion of long-term consolidation, lasting years or even decades. They postulated that the hippocampi or medial temporal lobe structures are continuously involved in the storage and retrieval of memories, both new and old, in interaction with neocortex. They argued that an ensemble of hippocampal neurons acts as a pointer or index to those neocortical neurons that represent information, and this ensemble serves as a mechanism for binding information into a coherent memory trace. The entire hippocampus–neocortical ensemble constitutes the memory trace for an episode. Each reactivation of this memory trace occurs in an altered neuronal and experiential context, resulting in the creation of a newly encoded trace. The creation of multiple, related traces facilitates the 'extraction' of factual information from an episode and its integration with pre-existing semantic memory stores. Hence, facts about the world are separated from an episode and ultimately stored independently of it. However, the spatial and temporal contextual information that conveys the episodic quality to a memory depends, according to Nadel & Moscovitch (1997), upon the continuing involvement of the hippocampi (for spatial context) and the frontal cortex (for temporal context). Consequently, autobiographical memory always depends upon the hippocampal complex and its provision of contextual information.

According to Nadel & Moscovitch (1997), as memories age, they are either forgotten or they benefit from the formation of multiple traces in the hippocampal complex and neocortex. Thus, older episodic memories will be associated with a greater number of traces, and retrieval will become easier as the number of traces proliferates, in parallel with the number of access routes to them. However, because neural connections in the hippocampi are sparse, even minimal damage in the hippocampal formation will affect the retention and recovery of memory traces. Newly acquired traces will be particularly vulnerable, whereas older memories, which are multiply represented, will be able to withstand the loss of more hippocampal tissue. This gives rise to the temporal gradient.

The extent of the RA and the slope of the gradient will depend upon the size of the hippocampal lesion.

This theory, which has resemblances to Morton's 'headed records' model (Morton *et al.* 1985), makes the prediction that temporal gradients will be steeper in semantic memory, where some structural reallocation can occur, than in episodic memory. Support for this is provided in a study by Viskontas *et al.* (2000), who showed steeper gradients for personal semantic facts, compared with the recall of autobiographical incidents, in a study of patients with temporal lobe epilepsy. However, the theory cannot account for the finding that some patients with medial temporal lobe or diencephalic pathology and severe AA have only a brief (2–3 year) RA, and many of the studies reviewed by Nadel & Moscovitch (1997) involved patients whose pathology extended far beyond the medial temporal lobes.

The third theoretical issue mentioned above—namely, the relative contribution of specific brain structures to RA and their interaction—is closely tied to the first two theoretical topics. Controversies concern whether structural reallocation occurs or whether the hippocampi are continuously involved in memory, whether that structural reallocation applies more to semantic than autobiographical memory, whether damage to the hippocampal system alone can produce an extensive RA, and whether there are distinct functional roles of the frontal lobes and of the left and right temporal lobes in maintaining and retrieving 'old' memories. Kapur (1999) concluded that, although the representation of old memories may be widely distributed as multiple neural networks, this does not exclude the possibility that some regional specialization of function can occur. Similarly, Kopelman (2000c) concluded that, while there is evidence that widespread networks underlie the storage of old memories, there is also evidence of functional specialization.

7.8. Conclusions

There is a need for both single-case and group studies in investigating RA. Single-case investigations permit the identification of dissociations in RA, but group studies are required to corroborate and quantify these differing patterns of performance and also to establish the correlates (associations) of performance at different tasks. There is much evidence that there is a broad distinction between the autobiographical and semantic aspects of RA, but this distinction is not always clear-cut and its relationship to specific sites of damage (e.g. right versus left temporal lobe) is not entirely consistent across different studies. Large lesions in the temporal or frontal lobes produce RA, but precise delineation in terms of specific structures has not proved possible: it is most likely that the storage and retrieval of old memories depend on a widespread network of neural connections. Similarly, the specific role of the hippocampi and other medial temporal lobe structures remains highly controversial. This latter point relates to controversies concerning the nature of the temporal gradient in RA—whether it results from physiological consolidation and structural reallocation, memories acquiring a more semantic form, or the acquisition of multiple traces within the hippocampal system. Moreover, investigation of all these issues is confounded by psychological factors, which frequently contribute to, bias, or exaggerate patterns of RA in particular patients. Nevertheless, advances in our understanding of RA in the last 30 years have been considerable.

The work of M.D.K and N.K. was supported by the Wellcome Trust.

References

Albert, M. S., Butters, N. & Levin, J. 1979 Temporal gradients in the retrograde amnesia of patients with alcoholic Korsakoff's disease. *Archiv. Neurol.* **36**, 211–216.

Albert, M. S., Butters, N. & Brandt, J. 1981 Patterns of remote memory in amnesic and demented patients. *Archiv. Neurol.* **38**, 495–500.

Alvarez, P. & Squire, L. R. 1994 Memory consolidation and the medial temporal lobe: a simple network model. *Proc. Natl Acad. Sci. USA* **91**, 7041–7045.

Baddeley, A. D. & Wilson, B. 1986 Amnesia, autobiographical memory, and confabulation. In *Autobiographical memory* (ed. D. C. Rubin), pp. 225–252. Cambridge University Press.

Barr, W. B., Goldberg, E., Wasserstein, J. & Novelly, R. 1990 Retrograde amnesia following unilateral temporal lobectomy. *Neuropsychologia* **28**, 243–255.

Berrington, W. P., Liddell, D. W. & Foulds, G. A. 1956 A re-evaluation of the fugue. *J. Ment. Sci.* **102**, 281–286.

Bickford, R. G., Mulder, D. W., Dodge, H., Svien, H. & Rome, H. P. 1958 Changes in memory function produced by electrical stimulation of the temporal lobe in man. *Res. Publ. Assoc. Res. Nerv. Ment. Dis.* **36**, 227–243.

Binder, L. M. 1994 Psychogenic mechanisms of prolonged autobiographical amnesia. *Clin. Neuropsychol.* **8**, 439–450.

Butters, N. & Cermak, L. S. 1986 A case study of the forgetting of autobiographical knowledge: implications for the study of retrograde amnesia. In *Autobiographical memory* (ed. D. C. Rubin), pp. 253–271. Cambridge University Press.

Campodonico, J. R. & Rediess, S. 1996 Dissociation of implicit and explicit knowledge in a case of psychogenic retrograde amnesia. *J. Int. Neuropsychol. Soc.* **2**, 146–158.

Cermak, L. S. 1984 The episodic-semantic distinction in amnesia. In *The neuropsychology of memory*, 1st edn (ed. L. R. Squire & N. Butters), pp. 55–62. New York and London: Guilford Press.

Cermak, L. S. & O'Connor, M. 1983 The anterograde and retrograde retrieval ability of a patient with amnesia due to encephalitis. *Neuropsychologia* **21**, 213–234.

Cipolotti, L., Shallice, T., Chan, D., Fox, N., Scahill, R., Harrison, G., Stevens, J. & Rudge, P. 2001 Long-term retrograde amnesia—the crucial role of the hippocampus. *Neuropsychologia* **39**, 151–172.

Costello, A., Fletcher, P. C., Dolan, R. J., Frith, C. D. & Shallice, T. 1998 The origins of forgetting in a case of isolated retrograde amnesia following a haemorrhage: evidence from functional imaging. *NeuroCase* **4**, 437–446.

Dalla Barba, G., Cipolotti, L. & Denes, G. 1990 Autobiographical memory loss and confabulation in Korsakoff's syndrome: a case report. *Cortex* **26**, 525–534.

Dall'Ora, P., Della Sala, S. & Spinnler, H. 1989 Autobiographical memory: its impairment in amnesic syndromes. *Cortex* **25**, 197–217.

Della Sala, S., Laiacona, M., Spinnler, H. & Trivelli, C. 1993 Impaired autobiographical recollection in some frontal patients. *Neuropsychologia* **31**, 823–840.

De Renzi, E., Liotti, M. & Nichelli, P. 1987 Semantic amnesia with preservation of autobiographical memory: a case report. *Cortex* **23**, 575–597.

D'Esposito, M., Alexander, M. P., Fischer, R., McGlinchey-Berroth, R. & O'Connor M. 1996 Recovery of memory and executive function following anterior communicating artery aneurysm rupture. *J. Int. Neuropsychol. Soc.* **2**, 1–6.

Dusoir, H., Kapur, N., Byrnes, D. P., McKinstry, S. & Hoare, R. D. 1990 The role of diencephalic pathology in human memory disorder: evidence from a penetrating paranasal injury. *Brain* **113**, 1695–1706.

Eslinger, P. J. 1998 Autobiographical memory after temporal lobe lesions. *NeuroCase* **4**, 481–496.

Eslinger, P. J., Easton, A., Grattan, L. M. & Van Hoesen, G. W. 1996 Distinctive forms of partial retrograde amnesia after asymmetric temporal lobe lesions: possible role of the occipitotemporal gyri in memory. *Cereb. Cortex* **6**, 530–539.

Fisher, C. M. 1982 Transient global amnesia. *Archiv. Neurol.* **39**, 605–608.

Gabrieli, J. D. E., Cohen, N. J. & Corkin, S. 1988 The impaired learning of semantic knowledge following bilateral medial temporal lobe resection. *Brain Cogn.* **7**, 157–177.

Graff-Radford, N. R., Tranel, D., Van Hoesen, G. & Brandt, J. P. 1990 Diencephalic amnesia. *Brain* **113**, 1–25.

Grafman, J., Salazar, A. M., Weingartner, H., Vance. & Ludlow, C. 1985 Isolated impairment of memory following a penetrating lesion of the fornix. *Archiv. Neurol.* **42**, 1162–1168.

Graham, K. S. & Hodges, J. R. 1997 Differentiating the roles of the hippocampal complex and neocortex in long-term memory storage. Evidence from the study of semantic dementia and Alzheimer's disease. *Neuropsychology* **11**, 77–89.

Greene, J. & Hodges, J. 1996 Identification of famous faces and famous names in early Alzheimer's disease. Relationship to anterograde episodic and general semantic memory. *Brain* **119**, 111–128.

Grossi, D., Trojano, L., Grasso, A. & Orsini, A. 1988 Selective 'semantic amnesia' after closed-head injury. A case report. *Cortex* **24**, 457–464.

Guinan, E. M., Lowy, C., Stanhope, C., Lewis, P. D. R. & Kopelman, M. D. 1998 Cognitive effects of pituitary tumours and their treatments: two case studies and an investigation of 90 patients. *J. Neurol. Neurosurg. Psychiatry* **65**, 870–876.

Hodges, J. R. 1991 *Transient amnesia*. New York: Saunders.

Hodges, J. R. & McCarthy, R. A. 1993 Autobiographical amnesia resulting from bilateral paramedian thalamic infarction. A case study in cognitive neurobiology. *Brain* **116**, 921–940.

Hodges, J. R. & Ward, C. D. 1989 Observations during transient global amnesia: a behavioural and neuropsychological study of five cases. *Brain* **112**, 595–620.

Kapur, N. 1999 Syndromes of retrograde amnesia. A conceptual and empirical synthesis. *Psychol. Bull.* **125**, 800–825.

Kapur, N. 2000 Focal retrograde amnesia and the attribution of causality: an exceptionally benign commentary. *Cogn. Neuropsychol.* **17**, 623–637.

Kapur, N. & Abbot, P. 1996 A study of recovery of memory function in a case of witnessed functional retrograde amnesia. *Cogn. Neuropsychiatry* **1**, 247–258.

Kapur, N., Young, A., Bateman, D. & Kennedy, P. 1989 Focal retrograde amnesia: a long-term clinical and neuropsychological follow-up. *Cortex* **25**, 387–402.

Kapur, N., Ellison, D., Smith, M., McLellan, L. & Burrows, E. H. 1992 Focal retrograde amnesia following bilateral temporal lobe pathology: a neuropsychological and magnetic resonance study. *Brain* **116**, 73–86.

Kapur, N., Ellison, D., Parkin, A. J., Hunkin, N., Burrows, E., Simpson, S. & Morrison, E. 1994 Bilateral temporal lobe pathology with sparing of medial temporal lobe structures: lesion profile and pattern of memory disorder. *Neuropsychologia* **23**, 23–38.

Kapur, N., Thompson, S., Cook, P., Lang, D. & Brice, J. 1996 Anterograde but not retrograde memory loss following combined mammillary body and medial thalamic lesions. *Neuropsychologia* **34**, 1–8.

Kapur, N., Miller, J., Abbott, P. & Carter, M. 1998 Recovery of function processes in human amnesia: evidence from transient global amnesia. *Neuropsychologia* **36**, 99–107.

Kapur, N., Thompson, P., Kartsounis. L. & Abbott, P. 1999 Retrograde amnesia: clinical and methodological caveats. *Neuropsychologia* **37**, 27–30.

Kartsounis, L. D., Rudge, P. & Stevens, J. M. 1995 Bilateral lesions of CA1 and CA1 fields of the hippocampus are sufficient to cause a severe amnesic syndrome in humans. *J. Neurol. Neurosurg. Psychiatry* **59**, 95–98.

Kopelman, M. D. 1987 Amnesia: organic and psychogenic. *Br. J. Psychiatry* **150**, 428–442.

Kopelman, M. D. 1989 Remote and autobiographical memory, temporal context memory, and frontal atrophy in Korsakoff and Alzheimer patients. *Neuropsychologia* **27**, 437–460.

Kopelman, M. D. 1991 Frontal lobe dysfunction and memory deficits in the alcoholic Korsakoff syndrome and Alzheimer-type dementia. *Brain* **114**, 117–137.

Kopelman, M. D. 1993 The neuropsychology of remote memory. In *Handbook of neuropsychology*, vol. 8 (ed. F. Boller & H. Spinnler), pp. 215–238. Amsterdam: Elsevier.

Kopelman, M. D. 2000*a* Focal retrograde amnesia and the attribution of causality: an exceptionally critical review. *Cogn. Neuropsychol.* **17**, 585–621.

Kopelman, M. D. 2000*b* Comments on focal retrograde amnesia and the attribution of causality: an exceptionally benign commentary by Narinder Kapur. *Cogn. Neuropsychol.* **17**, 639–640.

Kopelman, M. D. 2000*c* The neuropsychology of remote memory. In *Handbook of neuropsychology*, vol. 2, 2nd edn (ed. L. Cermak), pp. 251–280. Amsterdam: Elsevier.

Kopelman, M. D., Wilson, B. A. & Baddeley, A. D. 1989 The Autobiographical Memory Interview: a new assessment of autobiographical and personal semantic memory in amnesic patients. *J. Clin. Exp. Neuropsychol.* **11**, 724–744.

Kopelman, M. D., Christensen, H., Puffett, A. & Stanhope, N. 1994 The Great Escape: a neuropsychological study of psychogenic amnesia. *Neuropsychologia* **32**, 675–691.

Kopelman, M. D., Stanhope, N. & Kingsley, D. 1999 Retrograde amnesia in patients with diencephalic, temporal lobe or frontal lesions. *Neuropsychologia* **37**, 939–958.

Kritchevsky, M., Zouzounis, J. & Squire, L. 1997 Transient global amnesia and functional retrograde amnesia: contrasting examples of episodic memory loss. *Phil. Trans. R. Soc. Lond.* B **352**, 1747–1754.

Levine, B., Black, S., Cabeza, R., Sinden, M., Macintosh, A., Toth, J., Tulving, E. & Stuss, D. 1998 Episodic memory and the self in a case of isolated retrograde amnesia. *Brain* **121**, 1951–1973.

Lhermitte, F. & Serdaru, M. 1993 Unconscious processing in memory recall: a study of three amnesic patients. *Cortex* **29**, 25–43.

Lishman, W. A. 1968 Brain damage in relation to psychiatric disability after head injury. *Br. J. Psychiatry* **114**, 373–410.

Lynch, S. & Yarnell, P. R. 1973 Retrograde amnesia: delayed forgetting after concussion. *Am. J. Psychol.* **86**, 643–645.

McCarthy, R. A. & Warrington, E. K. 1992 Actors but not scripts: the dissociation of people and events in retrograde amnesia. *Neuropsychologia* **30**, 633–644.

Mackenzie Ross, S. J. & Hodges, J. R. 1997 Preservation of famous person knowledge in a patient with severe post anoxic amnesia. *Cortex* **33**, 733–742.

Mangels, J. A., Gershberg, F. B., Shimamura, A. P. & Knight, R. T. 1996 Impaired retrieval from remote memory in patients with frontal lobe damage. *Neuropsychology* **10**, 32–41.

Markowitsch, H. J. 1996 Organic and psychogenic retrograde amnesia: two sides of the same coin? *NeuroCase* **2**, 357–371.

Markowitsch, H. J., Fink, G., Thone, A., Kessler, J. & Heiss, W. D. 1997 A PET study of persistent psychogenic amnesia covering the whole life span. *Cogn. Neuropsychiatry* **2**, 135–158.

Marslen-Wilson, W. & Teuber, H. L. 1975 Memory for remote events in anterograde amnesia. *Neuropsychologia* **13**, 353–364.

Mayes, A. R., Downes, J. J., McDonald, C., Poole, V., Rooke, S., Sagar, H. & Meudell, P. R. 1994 Two tests for assessing remote public knowledge: a tool for assessing retrograde amnesia. *Memory* **2**, 183–210.

Mayes, A. R., Daum, I., Markowitsch, H. J. & Sauter, B. 1997 The relationship between retrograde and anterograde amnesia in patients with typical global amnesia. *Cortex* **33**, 197–217.

Milner, B. 1966 Amnesia following operation on the temporal lobes. In *Amnesia*, 1st edn (ed. C. W. M. Whitty & O. Zangwill), pp. 109–133. London: Butterworth.

Milner, B. 1972 Disorders of learning and memory after temporal lobe lesions in man. *Clin. Neurosurg.* **19**, 421–426.

Morton, J., Hammersley, R. H. & Bekerian, D. 1985 Headed records: a model for memory and its failures. *Cognition* **20**, 1–23.

Moss, H., Capelletti, M., De Mornay Davis, P., Jaldow, E. & Kopelman, M. D. 2000 Lost for words or loss of memories? Autobiographical memory in semantic dementia. *Brain Lang.* **32**, 350–354.

Murre, J. M. J. 1997 Implicit and explicit memory in amnesia: some explanations and predictions by the TraceLink model. *Memory* **5**, 213–232.

Nadel, L. & Moscovitch, M. 1997 Memory consolidation, retrograde amnesia and the hippocampal complex. *Curr. Opin. Neurobiol.* **7**, 217–227.

O'Connor, M., Butters, N., Miliotis, P., Eslinger, P. & Cermak, L. S. 1992 The dissociation of anterograde and retrograde amnesia in a patient with herpes encephalitis. *J. Clin. Exp. Neuropsychol.* **14**, 159–178.

Ogden, J. A. 1993 Visual object agnosia, prosopagnosia, achromatopsia, loss of visual imagery, and autobiographical amnesia following recovery from cortical blindness: case M.H. *Neuropsychologia* **31**, 571–589.

Parkin, A. J. 1991 Recent advances in the neuropsychology of memory. In *Memory: neurochemical and abnormal perspectives* (ed. J. Weinman & J. Hunter), pp. 141–162. London: Harwood.

Parkin, A. J., Montaldi, D., Leng, N. R. C. & Hunkin, N. M. 1990 Contextual cueing effects in the remote memory of alcoholic Korsakoff patients and normal subjects. *Q. J. Exp. Psychol.* **42A**, 585–596.

Parkin, A. J., Rees, J. E., Hunkin, N. M. & Rose, P. E. 1994 Impairment of memory following discrete thalamic infarction. *Neuropsychologia* **32**, 39–52.

Reed, J. M. & Squire, L. 1998 Retrograde amnesia for facts and events: findings from four new cases. *J. Neurosci.* **18**, 3943–3954.

Rubin, D. & Greenberg, D. 1998 Visual memory-deficit amnesia: a distinct amnesic presentation and etiology. *Proc. Natl Acad. Sci. USA* **95**, 5413–5416.

Russell, W. R. 1948 Studies in amnesia. *Edinburgh Med. J.* **55**, 92–99.

Russell, W. R. & Nathan, P. 1946 Traumatic amnesia. *Brain* **69**, 280–300.

Sagar, H., Cohen, N., Sullivan, E., Corkin, S. & Growdon, J. 1988 Remote memory function in Alzheimer's disease and Parkinson's disease. *Brain* **111**, 185–206.

Schacter, D. L., Wang, P. L., Tulving, E. & Freedman, M. 1982 Functional retrograde amnesia: a quantitative case study. *Neuropsychologia* **20**, 523–532.

Schmidtke, K. & Vollmer, H. 1997 Retrograde amnesia. A study of its relation to anterograde amnesia and semantic memory deficits. *Neuropsychologia* **35**, 505–518.

Shimamura, A. P. & Squire, L. R. 1986 Korsakoff's syndrome: a study of the relation between anterograde amnesia and remote memory impairment. *Behav. Neurosci.* **100**, 165–170.

Snowden, J., Griffiths, H. & Neary, D. 1996 Semantic-episodic memory interaction in semantic dementia: implications for retrograde memory function. *Cogn. Neuropsychol.* **13**, 1101–1137.

Squire, L. R. & Slater, P. C. 1983 ECT and complaints of memory dysfunction: a prospective three-year follow-up study. *Br. J. Psychiatry* **142**, 1–8.

Squire, L. R., Slater, P. C. & Miller, P. L. 1981 Retrograde amnesia and bilateral electroconvulsive therapy. *Archiv. Gen. Psychiatry* **38**, 89–95.

Squire, L. R., Cohen, N. J. & Nadel, L. 1984 The medial temporal region and memory consolidation: a new hypothesis. In *Memory consolidation* (ed. H. Weingartner & E. Parker), pp. 185–210. Hillsdale, NJ: Lawrence Erlbaum Associates.

Squire, L. R., Haist, F. & Shimamura, A. P. 1989 The neurology of memory: quantitative assessment of retrograde amnesia in two types of amnesic patients. *J. Neurosci.* **9**, 828–839.

Stengel, E. 1941 On the aetiology of the fugue states. *J. Ment. Sci.* **87**, 572–599.

Stuss, D. & Guzman, D. 1988 Severe remote memory loss with minimal anterograde amnesia: a clinical note. *Brain Cogn.* **8**, 21–30.

Symonds, C. 1966 Disorders of memory. *Brain* **89**, 625–644.

Teuber, H. L. 1969 Neglected aspects of the post-traumatic syndrome. In *The late effects of head injury* (ed. A. E. Walker, W. F. Caveness & M. Critchley), pp. 13–34. Springfield, IL: Thomas.

Teuber, H. L. 1975 Recovery of function after brain injury in man. In *Outcome of severe damage to the central nervous system* (ed. R. Porter), pp. 159–190. Amsterdam: Elsevier.

Teuber, H. L, Milner, B. & Vaughan, H. G. 1968 Persistent anterograde amnesia after stab wound of the basal brain. *Neuropsychologia* **6**, 267–282.

Tulving, E., Schacter, D. L., McLachlan, D. R. & Moscovitch, M. 1988 Priming of semantic autobiographical knowledge: a case study of retrograde amnesia. *Brain Cogn.* **8**, 3–20.

Verfaellie, M., Croce, P. & Milberg, W. P. 1995*a* The role of episodic memory in semantic learning: an examination of vocabulary acquisition in a patient with amnesia due to encephalitis. *NeuroCase* **1**, 291–304.

Verfaellie, M., Reiss, L. & Roth, H. L. 1995*b* Knowledge of new English vocabulary in amnesia: an examination of premorbidly acquired semantic memory. *J. Int. Neuropsychol. Soc.* **1**, 443–453.

Victor, M. & Agamanolis, D. 1990 Amnesia due to lesions confined to the hippocampus: a clinical-pathologic study. *J. Cogn. Neurosci.* **2**, 246–257.

Viskontas, I. V., McAndrews, M. P. & Moscovitch, M. 2000 Remote episodic memory deficits in patients with unilateral temporal lobe epilepsy and excisions. *J. Neurosci.* **20**, 5853–5857.

Warrington, E. K. & McCarthy, R. A. 1988 The fractionation of retrograde amnesia. *Brain Cogn.* **7**, 184–200.

Wasterlain, C. 1971 Are there two types of post-traumatic retrograde amnesia? *Eur. Neurol.* **5**, 225–228.

Weiskrantz, L. 1985 On issues and theories of the human amnesia syndrome. In *Memory systems of the brain* (ed. N. M. Weinberger, J. L. McGaugh & G. Lynch), pp. 380–418. New York: Guilford Press.

Williams, M. & Zangwill, O. L. 1952 Memory defects after head injury. *J. Neurol. Neurosurg. Psychiatry* **13**, 30–35.

Wilson, B. A., Baddeley, A. D. & Kapur, N. 1995 Dense amnesia in a professional musician following herpes simplex virus encephalitis. *J. Clin. Exp. Neuropsychol.* **17**, 668–681.

Winocur, G., Oxbury, S., Roberts, R., Agnetti, V. & Davis, C. 1984 Amnesia in a patient with bilateral lesions to the thalamus. *Neuropsychologia* **22**, 123–143.

Yasuda, K., Watababe, O. & Ono, Y. 1997 Dissociation between semantic and autobiographic memory: a case report. *Cortex* **33**, 623–638.

Zola-Morgan, S., Cohen, N. J. & Squire, L. R. 1983 Recall of remote episodic memory in amnesia. *Neuropsychologia* **21**, 487–500.

Zola-Morgan, S., Squire, L. R. & Amaral, D. G. 1986 Human amnesia and the medial temporal region: enduring memory impairment following a bilateral lesion limited to field CA1 of the hippocampus. *J. Neurosci.* **6**, 2950–2967.

8

Episodic memory:
insights from semantic dementia

John R. Hodges and Kim S. Graham

Semantic dementia, also known as the temporal lobe variant of fronto-temporal dementia, results in a progressive yet relatively pure loss of semantic knowledge about words, objects and people, and is associated with asymmetric, focal atrophy of the antero-lateral temporal lobes. Semantic dementia provides a unique opportunity to study the organization of long-term memory particularly since initial observations suggested sparing of episodic memory. Recent studies reveal, however, a more complex but theoretically revealing pattern. On tests of autobiographical memory, patients with semantic dementia show a 'reverse step function' with sparing of recall of events from the most recent 2 to 5 years but impairment on more distant life periods. Anterograde recognition memory for visual materials is extremely well preserved, except in the most deteriorated cases, although performance is heavily reliant upon perceptual information about the studied stimuli, particularly for items that are no longer known by the subjects. On tests of verbal anterograde memory such as word learning, performance is typically poor even for words which are 'known' to the patients. A source discrimination experiment, designed to evaluate familiarity and recollection-based anterograde memory processes, found that patients with semantic dementia showed good item detection, although recollection of source was sometimes impaired. Semantic knowledge about studied items and measures of item detection and source discrimination were largely independent. The implications of these findings for models of long-term memory are discussed. The results support the concept that episodic memory, or at least the recall of temporally specific autobiographical experiences, draws upon a number of separable memory processes, some of which can function independently of semantic knowledge.

8.1. Introduction

Memory, in its broadest sense, refers to the storage and retrieval of any form of information but, when considered as an aspect of human cognition, it clearly does not describe a unitary function. Memorizing a new telephone number, recalling the details of a past holiday, acquiring the facts necessary to practise medicine, learning a new language or knowing how to drive a car are all tasks that depend on memory, but proficiency in one does not guarantee competence in the other. More importantly, these abilities may break down differentially in patients with brain disease.

There is, as yet, no universally accepted classification of subcomponents of memory, but virtually all contemporary cognitive models distinguish between working (immediate) and longer-term memory—and within the latter recognize both explicit and implicit types. Within explicit long-term memory an influential distinction is that between episodic and semantic memory. The former refers to our personal store of temporally-specific experiences (or episodes), the retrieval of which has been likened to 'mental time travel' in which the person doing the remembering experiences the conscious sensation of travelling back in time to relive the original event (Tulving 1985, 1999). In contrast, semantic memory refers to our database of knowledge about things in the world and their inter-relationships, which includes words, objects, places and people (Garrard *et al.* 1997; Patterson & Hodges 2000). Semantic memory is, therefore, the most central of all cognitive processes and is fundamental to language production and comprehension, reading and writing, object and face perception.

Despite the central role of semantic memory, its study is relatively recent and in the modern era begins in 1975 with the description by Elizabeth Warrington of three patients with selective loss of semantic memory (Warrington 1975). Such patients had been described in the neurological literature for over 100 years, under the rubric of Pick's disease and, in the neuropsychological literature, as cases of associative agnosia or amnesic aphasia (Hodges 2000). Warrington, drawing on the work of Tulving, recognized the cross-modal nature of their cognitive deficit and the fundamental loss of the conceptual knowledge that underlay the patients' various symptoms. The term 'semantic dementia' was coined for this syndrome by Snowden *et al.* (1989) and has now been widely accepted in the cognitive literature. Readers should also be aware that patients with semantic dementia may be described clinically as having the temporal variant of fronto-temporal dementia (FTD) (Edwards Lee *et al.* 1997; Hodges & Miller 2001*a,b*). Criteria for the diagnosis of semantic dementia have been proposed by an international consensus study group (Neary *et al.* 1998).

Semantic memory breakdown also occurs in a number of other conditions, most notably after herpes simplex encephalitis (for a review, see Garrard *et al.* 1997) and Alzheimer's disease (Hodges & Patterson 1995). In these conditions, the semantic deficit is almost always accompanied by other major cognitive deficits. For this reason, the study of patients with semantic dementia, who have progressive, yet selective and often profound, breakdown of semantic memory, provides unparalleled insights into the organization of semantic memory and the impact of semantic disintegration on other cognitive processes. Following the description of a typical case, the rest of this review deals with our work on episodic memory in semantic dementia and attempts to answer four key questions:

(i) what is the impact of semantic memory loss on episodic memory? and, more specifically,

(ii) is autobiographical memory spared in semantic dementia?

(iii) does loss of semantic knowledge result in impaired new learning?, and finally,

(iv) what does this tell us about the nature of episodic memory?

8.2. Case report

The following case-history, of a patient who was studied longitudinally over 5 years, illustrates the pattern of cognitive deficits commonly seen in the disorder (see also Graham & Hodges 1997; Hodges & Patterson 1996; Knott *et al.* 1997).

A.M. (b. 1930) presented in April 1994 with a history of 'loss of memory for words', which had progressed slowly over the previous two years. His wife has also noted a decline in his comprehension ability initially affecting less common words. Despite these problems he still played golf (to a high standard) and tennis. He was still driving and able to find his way to various golf clubs alone and without difficulty. Day-to-day memory was also good and when seen in the clinic he was able to relate—albeit with prominent word finding difficulties—the details of their recent holiday in Australia and his latest golfing achievements. There had been only a slight change in personality at that time with mild disinhibition and a tendency to stick to fixed routines.

The following transcription illustrates that A.M.'s speech was fluent and without phonological or syntactic errors but strikingly devoid of content. It also shows his recall of undergoing a brain scan some six months previously.

E: Can you tell me about a last time you were in hospital?

AM: That was January, February, March, April, yes April last year, that was the first time, and eh, on the Monday, for example, they were checking all my whatsit, and that was the first time when my brain was, eh, shown, you know, you know that bit of the brain (indicates left), not that one, the other one was okay, but that was lousy, so they did that, and then like this (indicates scanning by moving his hands over his head) and probably I was a bit better than I am just now.

Formal neuropsychological testing in April 1994 revealed that A.M. was severely impaired on tests of picture naming. On the category fluency test, in which subjects are asked to generate exemplars from a range of semantic categories, within a set time, he was able to generate a few high-frequency animal names (cat, dog, horse) but no exemplars from more restricted categories such as birds or breeds of dog. He was only able to name three out of 48 black and white line drawings of highly familiar objects and animals from the Hodges and Patterson semantic battery (Hodges & Patterson 1995). Most responses were vague circumlocutions such as 'thing you use' but he also produced some category coordinate errors, such as horse for elephant. On a word–picture matching test, based on the same 48 items, in which A.M. had to point out a picture from eight other exemplars (e.g. zebra from eight other foreign animals), he scored 36 out of 48 (25 age-matched controls scored on average 47.4 ± 1.1). When asked to provide descriptions of the 48 items in the battery from their names, he produced very few details, most were vague or generic responses containing the superordinate category only ('a musical instrument', 'in the sea' etc.). On the picture version of the Pyramid and Palm Trees Test, a measure of associative semantic knowledge in which the subject has to decide which of two pictures (a fir tree or a palm tree) goes best with a target picture (pyramid) (Howard & Patterson 1992), A.M. scored 39 out of 52 when he first presented. Control subjects typically score close to ceiling on this test.

On tests of reading A.M. showed the typical pattern of surface dyslexia (Patterson & Hodges 1992): normal ability to read aloud words with regular spelling to sound correspondence, but errors when reading aloud irregular words (pint, island, leopard, etc.).

By contrast, on non-semantic tasks (such as copying the Rey Complex Figure) A.M.'s performance was faultless. When asked to reproduce the Rey Complex Figure after a 45-minute delay, A.M. scored well within the normal range. On non-verbal tests of problem-solving, such as Raven's Coloured Matrices, a multiple-choice test of visual pattern matching that requires the subject to conceptualize spatial relationships, A.M.

was also remarkably unimpaired. Auditory–verbal short-term memory was spared as judged by a digit span of six forwards and four backwards.

A.M. was tested approximately every 6 months over the next 3 years. A.M. was so profoundly anomic when he first presented that there was little room for further decline. On tests of comprehension, by contrast, there was a relentless drop; for instance, on the word–picture matching test, A.M.'s score fell from 36 to 5 out of 48 in November 1996 (controls = 47.4 ± 1.1). Likewise on the pictorial version of the Pyramid and Palm Trees Test his score fell progressively from 39 out of 52 to chance.

Despite this rapid loss of semantic knowledge, A.M. showed no significant decline on tests of non-verbal problem-solving or visuo-spatial ability over the same time period. For instance, on Raven's Coloured Matrices he still scored perfectly in November 1996.

A.M.'s impairment in semantic knowledge had a considerable impact on his everyday activities. On various occasions he misused objects (e.g. he placed a closed umbrella horizontally over his head during a rainstorm), selected an inappropriate item (e.g. bringing his wife, who was cleaning in the upstairs bathroom, the lawnmower instead of a ladder) and mistook various food items (e.g. on different occasions, A.M. put sugar into a glass of wine, orange juice into his lasagne and ate a raw defrosting salmon steak with yoghurt). Activities that used to be commonplace acquired a new and frightening quality to him: on an aeroplane trip early in 1996 he became clearly distressed at his suitcase being X-rayed and refused to wear a seat belt in the aeroplane.

After 1996, behavioural changes became more prominent with increasing social withdrawal, apathy and disinhibition. Like another patient described by Hodges *et al.* (1995), A.M. showed a fascinating mixture of 'preserved and disturbed cognition'. Hodges *et al.*'s patient, J.L., would set the house clocks and his watch forward in his impatience to get to a favourite restaurant, not realizing the relationship between clock and world time. A.M. made similar apparently 'insightful' attempts to get his own way. For example, his wife reported an incident in which she secretly removed his car keys from his key-ring to stop him taking the car for a drive. At this point, A.M. was obsessed with driving and very quickly noticed the missing keys. He solved the problem by taking his wife's car keys off her key-ring without her knowledge and going to the locksmiths, successfully, to get a new set cut. At no point did A.M. realize his wife had taken the keys from his key-ring. Despite virtually no language output and profound comprehension difficulties he still retained some skills, e.g. he continued to play sport (particularly golf) regularly each week, remembering correctly when he was to be picked up by his friends, until 1998 when he entered permanent nursing care.

Serial brain imaging using magnetic resonance imaging (MRI) images showed the pattern typical of semantic dementia, namely striking asymmetrical atrophy of the anterior temporal lobes involving the temporal pole, fusiform gyrus and infero-lateral region, but with relative sparing of the hippocampus. Figure 8.1 shows an illustrative coronal T1 weighted MRI image from another more recently studied patient with semantic dementia and a comparative normal brain from a control subject of the same age.

In summary, A.M.'s case-history illustrates a number of the characteristic neuropsychological features of semantic dementia: (i) selective impairment of semantic memory causing severe anomia, impaired single-word comprehension, reduced generation of exemplars on category fluency tests, and an impoverished fund of general knowledge; (ii) surface dyslexia; (iii) relative sparing of syntactic and phonological aspects of language; (iv) normal perceptual skills and non-verbal

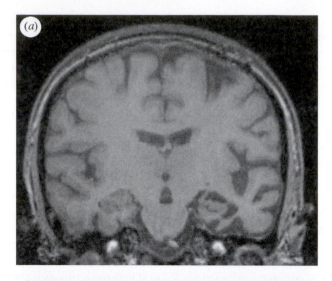

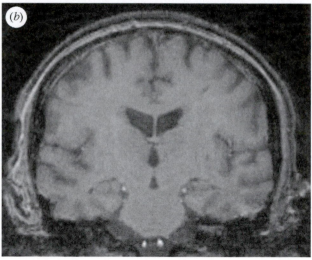

Fig. 8.1. An illustrative coronal T1 weighted magnetic resonance imaging (MRI) image from a patient in the early stages of semantic dementia (*a*) and a comparative normal brain from a control subject of the same age (*b*). The scan from the patient with semantic dementia reveals moderate to severe atrophy of the left temporal lobe, including the parahippocampal gyrus, fusiform and inferior temporal gyrus. The left hippocampus is mildly atrophied.

problem-solving abilities; and (v) relatively preserved recent autobiographical and day-to-day (episodic) memory.

8.3. Autobiographical memory in semantic dementia

Initial clinical descriptions of patients with semantic dementia suggested that this syndrome provided compelling evidence for a dissociation between preserved autobiographical and impaired semantic memory. Patients are typically well orientated and can relate the details and incidents—albeit anomically—about their life. They also retain broad facts about their own life, such as past occupation, whether they are married, numbers of children and grandchildren, etc. (Hodges *et al.* 1992). Clinically, therefore, the neuropsychological profile of semantic dementia is quite unlike that seen in patients with classic amnesia.

More detailed empirical investigation of episodic memory (in particular, autobiographical memory) has revealed, however, a more complex, and theoretically interesting pattern with a major confound of memory age. While patients with the amnesic syndrome, as a result of hippocampal damage (following anoxic brain damage or in the early stages of Alzheimer's disease), typically show preservation of autobiographical memory for their early life compared with the more recent past (Greene & Hodges 1996; for a review, see Hodges 1995), patients with semantic dementia show the opposite pattern, i.e. a reversal of the usual temporal gradient effect, with memory for remote events most vulnerable (Graham & Hodges 1997; Hodges & Graham 1998; Snowden *et al.* 1996).

The first clear evidence of this unusual pattern came from Snowden *et al.* (1996) who tested autobiographical memory using the Autobiographical Memory Interview (AMI) (Kopelman *et al.* 1990): patients with semantic dementia were significantly better at retrieving both personal semantic and autobiographical memories from the recent time period compared with two earlier life periods (childhood and early adulthood). A similar study by Graham & Hodges (1997) replicated this pattern in six patients with semantic dementia, as well as demonstrating that a group of severely amnesic patients, with presumed early Alzheimer's disease, showed the more typical pattern where current memories were more impaired than memories from the past.

Graham & Hodges (1997) also reported a more detailed single case-study in which they investigated the ability of a patient with semantic dementia, A.M. (described in §8.2 above), to retrieve event-based memories from cue words (e.g. party, animal, etc.) across the whole of his lifetime. A.M. was much better at retrieving autobiographical episodes from the last five years of his life compared with the 60 years which encompassed the rest of his life (see Figure 8.2). By contrast, a group of age- and education-matched control subjects showed no significant difference between their performance on any of the time-periods tested. Other patients with semantic dementia, such as patient J.H., have been shown to demonstrate a similar pattern (Figure 8.2).

'1TThe use of the term 'gradient' is slightly confusing when considered in connection with semantic dementia. On the AMI (Kopelman *et al.* 1990) patients seem to show a reverse temporal gradient because the test taps only three time-periods: childhood, early adulthood and recent life. When more detailed autobiographical memory tasks are used, however, patients were found to show preservation of autobiographical memories for only a short period of time (in most cases, two to three years prior to testing)—more of a 'step' effect rather than a gradient (Nestor *et al.* 2001). It appears then that autobiographical memory, at least for more remote time-periods, is deficient in semantic dementia.

(a) Theoretical explanations for the reverse step function of autobiographical memory found in semantic dementia

There is a number of possible explanations for the pattern seen in semantic dementia. One view is that semantic and autobiographical memory may represent independent

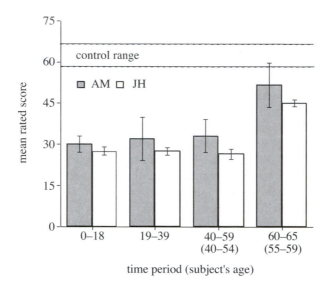

Fig. 8.2. The performance of two patients with semantic dementia (A.M. and J.H.) and three age- and education-matched control subjects on a modified version of the Galton–Crovitz autobiographical memory test (Crovitz 1986). The subjects were asked to produce 15 autobiographical memories from each of four different time-periods spanning the whole of their life (A.M.: 0–18, 19–39, 40–59 and J.H.: 0–18, 19–39, 40–54 and 55–59). These memories were scored from 0–5 for detail and episodic specificity (for details, see Graham & Hodges 1997). A.M.'s and J.H.'s ability to produce detailed memories from the past was strongly affected by time: virtually all their specific events were recalled in the most recent five years.

'stores' within the brain, and that both of these memory repositories are damaged in semantic dementia. Within long-term memory there is now overwhelming evidence for the separation of knowledge according to a number of dimensions, including: natural kinds versus artefacts, and nouns versus verbs or actions (Caramazza 1998). It is possible, therefore, that autobiographical memory is also neurally segregated from our semantic knowledge about the world, to the extent that knowledge about objects and animals, such as a dog, is stored separately from any personal experiences related to dogs. This multiple stores hypothesis cannot be entirely dismissed but seems implausible given that there is little in the way of neuropsychological evidence to support such a model (see Kitchener & Hodges 1999). In particular, although there are now numerous case reports of patients with isolated autobiographical amnesia (Kopelman & Kapur 2001) there are practically no descriptions in the literature of patients with loss of semantic memory in the context of spared autobiographical memory (for an exception, see De Renzi *et al.* 1987). This finding suggests that autobiographical memory may actually be dependent, to some extent, on the normal functioning of semantic memory. By contrast, loss of autobiographical episodes does not necessarily have a direct impact on access and retrieval of previously learned semantic facts.

The reason for this may be as follows. Autobiographical memories tend to be composed of different pieces of information typically involving different modalities (e.g.

vision, sound). For example, remembering a particular episode that occurred during a visit to the zoo may necessitate the retrieval of visual and sound information, plus spatial knowledge about the location of participants and how they interacted (see Conway 2001). At least two different types of pathological process could lead, therefore, to extensive autobiographical memory loss in the context of preserved semantic memory: (i) diffuse but patchy neocortical damage, which is insufficient to cause loss of semantic memory but impairs cortico–cortical interconnectivity (Evans *et al.* 1996); and (ii) severe damage to a vital component of autobiographical memory, such as visual imagery (Rubin & Greenberg 1998) or semantic knowledge (Kitchener & Hodges 1999). Rubin & Greenberg (1998) observed that loss of visual imagery is almost invariably associated with severe impairment of autobiographical memory. They argued that loss of a critical component of memory recollection, such as the capability to evoke visual memories, could result in an inability to activate other aspects of the memory experience thereby producing an extensive and non-temporally graded deficit in episodic memory retrieval. Moscovitch & Nadel (1999) have extended this view by suggesting that semantic memory, like visual imagery, is a critical component of autobiographical memories, and that loss of this type of information might result in a similar pattern of autobiographical memory loss to that seen in Rubin and Greenberg's patients. In support of this proposal, it is notable that the pattern seen in semantic dementia seems to correspond closely to that seen in Rubin and Greenberg's patients.

In addition to the effects of cortical damage and loss of memory representations or their interconnections, a number of authors have emphasized the role of frontal lobe based processes in strategic search, verification and cross-checking, and have pointed out that autobiographical recall typically involves these processes to a greater degree than does retrieval of semantic knowledge (Burgess & Shallice 1996; Moscovitch 1994; Hodges & McCarthy 1993). At present, it seems unlikely that poor strategic retrieval is the cause of the long-term memory deficit seen in semantic dementia, although further studies are required to address this issue (Nestor *et al.* 2001).

(b) Preservation of recent memories in semantic dementia and the role of the hippocampal complex

Having discussed the possible reasons for the loss of old autobiographical memory in semantic dementia, it is still necessary to explain the preservation of recent memories. Our initial explanation for this effect was in terms of what has become known as the standard model of long-term memory consolidation (Graham & Hodges 1997). According to this view, the neocortex and hippocampus play distinct, but complementary, roles in long-term memory storage. While initially the retrieval of a recently experienced event is reliant upon the hippocampal system, repeated reinstatement of the hippocampal–neocortical ensemble over time results in the formation of a more permanent, hippocampally independent, memory representation in the neocortex (for a review, see Murre *et al.* 2001; Mayes & Roberts 2001). We suggested, therefore, that the better recall of recent memories in semantic dementia might be due to relative preservation of the hippocampal complex, thereby allowing the encoding of new experiences. Loss of more distant personal events could be attributed neuroanatomically to the significant atrophy seen in the temporal neocortex and to the progressive loss of semantic memory caused by this type of pathology.

Our view that the hippocampus is spared in semantic dementia was based on a number of lines of evidence. Clinical scanning experience in semantic dementia, including more than 30 patients studied in Cambridge, suggested that the most consistent finding in the disease is marked focal atrophy of the polar and infero-lateral aspect of the temporal lobe, which is typically most marked on the left but may be bilateral (Garrard & Hodges 2000). Our first quantitative analysis using the technique of voxel-based morphometry of the MRI scans of six patients with semantic dementia confirmed that the most significant and consistent locus of atrophy was the left polar and inferior temporal lobe (Brodmann area 38/20) but suggested that the hippocampus was spared (Mummery et al. 2000). A detailed quantitative neuropathological study by Harasty et al. (1996) also found significant bilateral atrophy to the inferior and middle temporal gyri but sparing of the hippocampal formation. Given these studies, it seems plausible that the better recall of recent episodic memories is attributable to the relative preservation of the hippocampus.

Two more recent MRI based studies have, however, cast doubt on these earlier findings. In Cambridge, we have now measured the volume of the hippocampus, parahippocampal region and multiple temporal lobe regions in a much larger series of semantic dementia cases ($n = 18$), as well as in a similar-sized set of patients with Alzheimer's disease (AD) matched for disease severity and a group of normal controls (Galton et al. 2001a,b). The major findings from this study were: (i) patients with AD typically had moderate to severe bilateral and symmetrical hippocampal atrophy compared with the control subjects, but little involvement of other temporal lobe structures; (ii) patients with semantic dementia had severe but asymmetric atrophy of the temporal pole, fusiform and inferolateral gyri and parahippocampal regions, but in addition the degree of involvement of the left hippocampus was largely indistinguishable from that seen in AD. The majority of cases had preservation of the right hippocampus and, as a group, the volume of the right hippocampus was not significantly different from controls (see Figure 8.3). In summary, there was little difference in hippocampal volumes, at least on the left side, between the two patient groups, although it should be noted that there was considerable variability in the semantic dementia population. In terms of other medial temporal lobe structures, the entorhinal cortex, which constitutes a major component of the parahippocampal gyrus, is also severely affected in semantic dementia. The rostral part of the perirhinal cortex, which has a complex anatomy in man, occupying the banks of the collateral sulcus and medial aspect of the temporal lobe, is almost certainly affected, although the caudate part might be partially spared (Simons et al. 1999).

Almost identical findings emerged from a recent study by the London Dementia Research Group (Chan et al. 2001), which obtained volumetric measures of temporal atrophy in patients with AD and semantic dementia. Taken together, these studies confirm that atrophy of the polar and infero-lateral temporal regions differentiates patients with AD and semantic dementia, but that atrophy to hippocampal and parahippocampal regions can be present in both diseases, with bilateral involvement in AD and predominantly left-sided atrophy in semantic dementia.

Comparisons of the degree of atrophy of temporal regions in the AD patients with that in the group with semantic dementia provide some explanation for our initial assumptions about the relative preservation of the hippocampus and other medial temporal lobe structures. In the patients with semantic dementia, there was profound

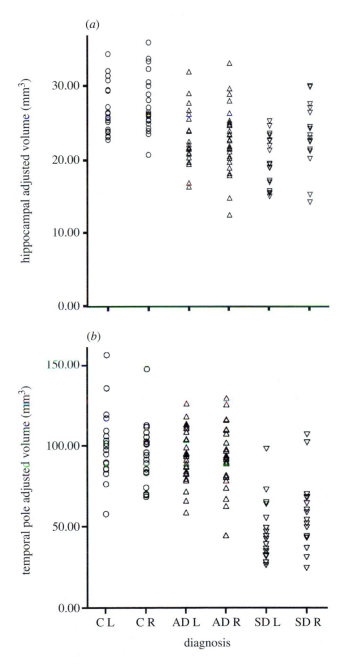

Fig. 8.3. Scatterplots of adjusted hippocampal (*a*) and temporal pole volumes (*b*) in mm² by group (CL, control left; CR, control right; ADL and ADR, Alzheimer's disease left and right; SDL and SDR, semantic dementia left and right). Volumetric analysis was conducted by tracing round the components of the temporal lobes and correcting for head size (Galton *et al.* 2001*b*). There was little difference in hippocampal volume, except on the right, across the AD and SD groups. The temporal pole volumes were, by contrast, normal in the AD group and significantly reduced bilaterally in the SD group.

atrophy of surrounding structures compared with the hippocampus: the average volume loss of the temporal pole, fusiform and infero-lateral gyri was 50% and in some cases up to 80% compared with an average of 20% loss of hippocampal volume. This dramatic difference in extent of atrophy may result in one incorrectly assuming that the hippocampus is 'relatively' preserved. In contrast, the 20% loss of hippocampus in AD stands out against the normal polar and infero-lateral structures (Galton *et al.* 2001*b*).

These findings clearly cast some doubt on an explanation of the autobiographical memory data, in particular the relatively better recall of recent events, simply in terms of hippocampal preservation. Future work may well reveal that the asymmetric nature of the pathology in semantic dementia is critical to under-standing the pattern of autobiographical memory loss, and the variability seen across patients needs to be taken into account. Moreover, equivalent volume loss in patients with AD and semantic dementia should not be taken as evidence of equivalent pathology. It is quite likely that the pathological processes that cause the two dementias affect different cell populations within the hippocampus.

(c) Multiple-trace theory of memory consolidation

Another important recent development that needs to be considered with respect to the findings in semantic dementia is the recent development of the multiple-trace model of long-term memory by Nadel & Moscovitch (Nadel & Moscovitch 1997; Moscovitch & Nadel 1999). Contrary to the accepted model discussed above, these authors have argued that the neuropsychological literature is more in keeping with the view that the hippocampus is necessary for the retrieval of all episodic memories regardless of the age of the memory. Nadel & Moscovitch (1997) hypothesize that, just as in the standard model, geographically separate neural components of a recently experienced memory are bound together by the hippocampal complex, creating a medial temporal–neocortical ensemble. The hippocampal constituent acts as an indexer pinpointing the different neocortical areas that need to be activated to produce the full content of the event. Unlike the standard model, however, whereby repeated reinstatement of memories results in the formation of a permanent, hippocampally-independent, neocortical representation of the episodic memory, repeated retrieval of personal experiences in the multiple trace model creates re-coded traces of the experience within the hippocampal complex. These traces are distributed throughout the medial temporal lobe and the number of traces is positively correlated with how often an event has been retrieved.

To explain the reverse step function found in semantic dementia, Nadel and Moscovitch (Moscovitch & Nadel 1999; Nadel & Moscovitch 1997) proposed a number of alternative explanations: (i) that there was only one patient (A.M., reported in Graham & Hodges 1997) who showed preservation of very recently experienced memories (1–2 years prior to testing); (ii) the pattern may be due to strategic retrieval deficits caused by concomitant frontal pathology; and (iii) verbally-based testing of autobiographical memory may have exacerbated the patient's remote memory deficit. We have now shown that the pattern seen in semantic dementia on tests of autobiographical memory is unlikely to be due to any one or a combination of these factors (see Nestor *et al.* 2001). As shown in Figure 8.2, other patients with semantic dementia show the same effect of time on the detailed autobiographical tests as A.M. In

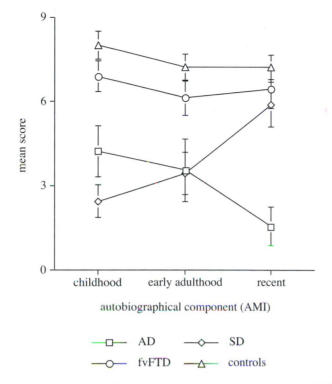

Fig. 8.4. Performance of control subjects, patients with semantic dementia (SD), frontal variant fronto-temporal dementia (fvFTD) and early Alzheimer's disease (AD) on the incidents component of the Autobiographical Memory Interview (AMI) (Kopelman *et al.* 1990). Subjects are asked to relate three specific life events from each of three life periods: childhood, early adulthood and the most recent five years. Each memory is then scored for richness of detail and specificity on a 0–3 scale.

a recent study, we compared the performance of groups of patients with early AD, semantic dementia and the frontal variant of fronto-temporal dementia (fvFTD) on the AMI (Nestor *et al.* 2001). Patients with fvFTD have profound behavioural changes with frontal executive dysfunction and evidence of frontal lobe atrophy in the absence of significant semantic memory impairment. Only those patients with semantic dementia demonstrated the reverse step function. Patients with AD had a classic temporally graded impairment, while the group with fvFTD performed within the normal range (see Figure 8.4). In addition, the use of family photographs to prompt recall of episodes appeared not to benefit one of our patients (for contrary results, see Westmacott *et al.* 2001).

8.4. New learning in semantic dementia

Until very recently, there had been few formal investigations of the integrity of anterograde episodic memory in semantic dementia. Anecdotal evidence supports the view that patients show preservation of new learning, despite their loss of semantic knowledge. For example, in November 1996, when A.M. was scoring at chance on tests of semantic memory, he was still able to tell his wife that someone had rung while she was out. He showed no problems finding his way around his town and remembered golfing appointments, etc. A.M.'s performance on non-verbal tests of new learning at that time also pointed to some preservation of episodic memory (e.g. delayed recall of the Rey Complex Figure). Warrington (1975), however, noted that her three cases showed poor episodic memory as measured by story recall, reproduction of visual designs and recognition memory for words and faces; by contrast, recognition memory for paintings was preserved.

(a) Recognition memory for non-verbal stimuli

Recently, more experimentally driven studies of new learning in patients with semantic dementia have begun to confirm the anecdotal reports but, as with the findings on autobiographical memory discussed above, a more complex picture is emerging. In our first study, we found evidence of completely normal recognition memory for real and non-real animals in a group of patients with semantic dementia (Graham *et al.* 1997). Compared with both control subjects and patients in the early stages of AD, by contrast, the patients were significantly impaired on the study task in which they had to say whether the animals were real or not real. These data provided compelling evidence for the separation of semantic knowledge and new learning (at least as judged by tests of recognition memory).

Two further experiments have provided additional insights into our understanding of the processes involved in new learning in semantic dementia. Graham *et al.* (2000) found that a group of eight patients with semantic dementia showed normal recognition memory when the target item in the recognition memory task was identical to the item that had been seen at study. By contrast, when the target item was changed between study and test (e.g. a round dial telephone was replaced with a push button telephone), the patients were significantly impaired (compared with control subjects) on items that they were unable to name from a picture. This result suggests that loss of semantic knowledge only affects recognition memory when the target item is perceptually different from the studied item. Graham and colleagues suggested that the striking difference between the perceptually identical and perceptually different conditions reflected the differential involvement of higher-order perceptual areas and semantic knowledge in new learning. This hypothesis was further supported by a case study in which recognition memory for 'known' and previously familiar 'unknown' items was investigated. The only circumstances under which the patient showed poor recognition memory was for perceptually different items that were no longer known. Recognition memory for all perceptually identical items and for 'known' perceptually different items was not significantly impaired (see Figure 8.5).

We have since extended this technique to studying face recognition memory. Simons *et al.* (2001) investigated face recognition in a series of patients with semantic dementia and showed that: (i) patients with selective left temporal lobe atrophy were not significantly impaired on the faces component of the Warrington Recognition Memory Test; (ii) a group of patients with predominantly right temporal lobe atrophy performed poorly on the test; (iii) within this group, the status of the parahippocampal gyrus (which includes the perirhinal cortex) was most important; and (iv) that, like the object data described above, face recognition memory was affected by a change of picture (e.g. the Queen without a head-scarf and the Queen with a head-scarf), but only for items which were no longer familiar to the patients.

These results are illuminating with regard to current cognitive models of long-term memory as they suggest that the ability to form an episodic memory is not critically dependent upon the integrity of semantic knowledge (as proposed by Tulving 1985, 1995). The replication by Simons *et al.* (2001) of the Graham *et al.* (2000) study using different stimuli (faces compared with objects) provides strong support for the view that new learning in semantic dementia is based largely on good perceptual processing as input to the episodic memory system. A wider implication is that the medial temporal-based episodic system receives multiple sensory inputs from many disparate areas of the brain only some of which are damaged in semantic dementia.

(b) Verbal learning in semantic dementia

In contrast to their good performance on different forms of non-verbal anterograde memory tests, semantic dementia patients typically perform very poorly on classic clinical tests of verbal memory such as story recall and word list learning. Even their performance on more simple recognition memory tests is often impaired. The experiments discussed above help to understand this finding. If new learning in semantic dementia relies heavily upon intact perceptual processes, than one would expect performance on word-based tests to be particularly poor since words, unlike pictures and faces, are perceptually impoverished. The ability to recall words is, therefore, almost entirely dependent on semantic encoding. Furthermore, unlike pictures, there is an arbitrary relationship between phonological (and orthographic) forms and semantic representations. In other words, there is nothing about the word 'horse' which gives any clue to its meaning, and in fact the phonological form is ambiguous out of context. Another fact to take into consideration is that the pathology in semantic dementia almost always involves the left temporal lobe to a greater degree than the right. We predict, therefore, that experiments based on the learning of known and unknown words would produce the same advantage for known items as in the experiments described above but, unlike pictures, we also expect patients to be impaired on the apparently 'known' items since it is very likely that the underlying semantic representations for these items are not totally intact.

Very recently we have gone some way to testing these predictions using a word list learning paradigm with delayed recall and recognition, based on the shortened version of the Rey Auditory Verbal Learning Test described by Greene *et al.* (1996). A group of semantic dementia patients were pretested on the entire Snodgrass & Vanderwart (1980) corpus of 260 pictures to determine sets of known and unknown words (based on naming and word–picture matching) matched for word frequency and length. Compared with controls, semantic dementia patients showed very poor recall of both known and unknown words but with an advantage for known stimuli. Delayed recall for both categories was very poor. Even in the recognition format, there was a significant impairment of item recognition when analysed using signal detection methods, particularly for items that were no longer known to the patients. Analysis of the performance of individual cases showed a very marked effect of disease severity:

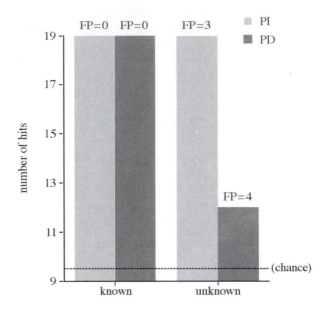

study

perceptually identical

perceptually different

those with mild semantic breakdown showed good item detection for all items, those with moderate semantic loss for known items only, and more demented cases showed marked impairment in both conditions (Graham *et al.* 2001). We have also shown that a patient with semantic dementia can relearn 'forgotten' vocabulary through frequent practice but the benefit of this rote learning is quickly lost once practice ceases (Graham *et al.* 1999). These two studies suggest that verbal learning can occur with practice in semantic dementia but that recall, and to a lesser extent recognition memory, is strongly affected by semantic knowledge and the delay between study and test.

(c) Source memory in semantic dementia: recollection and familiarity

It has recently been proposed that two functionally and neurally separate processes contribute to recognition memory: 'recollection', subserved by the hippocampal memory system—the hippocampus, fornix, mammillary bodies and anterior thalamic nuclei—and 'familiarity', supported by the perirhinal cortex–dorsomedial thalamic nuclei system (Aggleton & Brown 1999; Aggleton 2001). According to this view, the hippocampal system supports the recollection of stored memories with their associated temporal, spatial and semantic context (remembering) as measured by tests of recall, associative memory, memory for spatial location and temporal source memory. By contrast, the perirhinal system underlies familiarity-based recognition of prior occurrence ('knowing'), as indexed primarily by recognition memory. There is fairly good evidence to support the separation of recollection- and familiarity-based memory systems from lesion studies in animals, including rats and non-human primates (for a review, see Aggleton & Brown 1999; Murray & Bussey 1999). The evidence from human studies is more controversial but is strongest in the case of patients with fornix lesions and development amnesia secondary to hypoxic hippocampal damage early in life (Vargha-Khadem *et al.* 1997; Vargha-Khadem 2001).

The experiments described so far have demonstrated consistently that recognition memory for pictorial stimuli (pictures of objects, animals and faces) is preserved in many patients with semantic dementia although patients are heavily dependent on perceptual features. Given the proposed dichotomy between recollection- and familiarity-based memory systems it is important to establish whether there is evidence for the preservation of recollective memory in semantic dementia or alternatively whether patients are performing well on recognition memory tests purely on the basis of familiarity judgments. We have already shown that autobiographical memory, at least for recent life events, is fairly well preserved in semantic dementia which would lead to the prediction that patients should show good performance on recollective tests which might be dependent upon the hippocampus.

Fig. 8.5. (*opposite*) Examples of the stimuli used in the semantic naming task (top), the perceptually identical condition (middle) and the perceptually different (bottom) conditions of a forced choice episodic recognition memory test (see experiment 1, Graham *et al.* 2000). The graph shows the performance of a patient with semantic dementia (J.H.) on the perceptually identical (PI) and perceptually different (PD) conditions of the recognition memory test for 'known' and 'unknown' but previously familiar objects (see experiment 2, Graham *et al.* 2000). The only significant impairment shown by J.H. was on the perceptually different condition for 'unknown' items.

To examine this hypothesis we recently used a standard source monitoring paradigm (Mitchell & Johnson 2000) in 10 patients with semantic dementia, ranging in severity of semantic impairment from mild to severe, and 12 matched controls. All subjects were given two sets of 30 line drawings at study, in which they were asked to name the pictures. After a short delay, memory for the pictures and in which set they had been presented was examined using a three-choice alternative forced-choice test. The results were analysed using a multinomial model to produce separable estimates of familiarity- and recollection-based memory. Volumetric analysis of the hippo-campus and parahippocampal gyrus was also available (Galton *et al.* 2001*b*). Item detection (akin to familiarity) was normal in seven out of the 10 semantic dementia patients. This finding is in keeping with prior studies and confirms that even in a difficult test, on which normal subjects perform below ceiling, most patients with semantic dementia showed normal ability to detect items that have been seen previously from those which had not. The three patients who showed deficits were the three most semantically impaired cases. A more complicated picture emerged from the analysis of the source discrimination parameter. Seven out of the 10 patients performed no differently from the control group. The three patients showing impairment of source discrimination were not, however, the most semantically impaired; indeed, two were among the five mildest cases. An analysis of the correspondence between naming and both item detection and source discrimination on an item-by-item basis in four of the patients revealed no relationship between semantic status and test performance.

If source discrimination is hippocampally dependent then perhaps the variability seen in semantic dementia reflects differences in the status of the hippocampal formation, which we now know is involved in at least some cases with semantic dementia (see above). Analyses in our group, however, failed to confirm this hypothesis: there was no significant relationship between performance on the source monitoring tests and volumetric measures of the hippocampus and parahippocampal gyrus. Instead, a further experiment in seven patients found that the variability in source discrimination was significantly related to performance on a battery of frontal executive tasks (Simons 2000).

8.5. Implications for models of long-term memory

The results of studies of different aspects of long-term memory in patients with semantic dementia reveal a complex picture but two principal conclusions can be drawn. First, although semantic breakdown has an impact on some aspects of episodic memory (notably remote autobiographical memory and anterograde verbal recall), other aspects (recognition of pictures of objects, animals and faces, and even source discrimination) can function independently of semantic memory. Particularly critical were the recognition memory test analyses that consistently showed no evidence, at least on an item-by-item level, that degraded knowledge about a particular stimulus necessarily leads to failure of recognition of that item in a memory test. These findings are clearly contrary to the view that the acquisition of 'episodic memory depends upon an intact semantic system' as proposed by Tulving in his serial processing model of long-term memory (Tulving 1995). The explanation we prefer is that successful recognition memory in semantic dementia is supported by information from perceptual processing systems. Rather than recognition memory proceeding in a strictly serial fashion, with perceptual information about a stimulus feeding only into the semantic system, which subsequently transmits information about the meaning of the stimulus to the episodic memory system, we have proposed an alternative multiple input hypothesis. According to this view, information from the perceptual system can feed directly into episodic memory: in healthy individuals, therefore, recognition memory typically draws upon multiple inputs from perceptual and semantic systems (Graham *et al.* 2000; Simons *et al.* 2001).

The second conclusion concerns the nature of episodic memory. This term has been applied to a broad range of memory processes, including anterograde and remote autobiographical memory, recall of stories and non-verbal materials, recognition memory for a range of different stimuli and source discrimination. Yet, as shown above, these processes disassociate and it is increasingly apparent that they do not have a single neural substrate. It is meaningless, therefore, to argue about which type of memory is truly 'episodic'. Although the term 'episodic memory' is an extremely useful heuristic, particularly in clinical practice, the work in semantic dementia, and in patients with classic amnesia, suggests that it describes a family of processes rather than a single definable entity. In recent formulations, Tulving and colleagues (Tulving & Markowitsch 1998; Tulving 1995) have stressed the uniquely human aspects of episodic memory, which involves the ability to engage in 'mental time travel' when retrieving the temporal and spatial elements of a prior experience. In terms of the neuropsychological literature, this equates most closely to autobiographical memory. Yet, compared with the vast literature on other aspects of memory we really know very little about autobiographical memory in brain injured patients and particularly the relationship between performance on tests of autobiographical memory and other types of new learning (Conway 2001). Our studies of semantic dementia patients suggest that autobiographical memory depends in turn on a range of different memory processes some of which can function in the absence of semantic knowledge. The ability to store and retrieve personally-based memories from the distant and very recent past requires the interaction of a number of different cognitive processes which must be subserved by different neural substrates.

Finally, the investigations of long-term memory in semantic dementia described here have also provided a new challenge to memory researchers. This task is to understand how patients with equivalent, albeit asymmetric, medial temporal lobe damage, as seen in semantic dementia and AD, can show such disparate patterns of performance on tests of human long-term memory.

References

Aggleton, J. P. & Brown, M. W. 1999 Episodic memory, amnesia and the hippocampal-anterior thalamic axis. *Behav. Brain Sci.* **22**, 425–444.
Aggleton, J. P. & Pearce, J. M. 2001 Neural systems underlying episodic memory: insights from animal research. *Phil. Trans. R. Soc. Lond.* B **356**, 1467–1482.
Burgess, P. W. & Shallice, T. 1996 Confabulation and the control of recollection. *Memory* **4**, 359–411.

Caramazza, A. 1998 The interpretation of semantic category-specific deficits: what do they reveal about the organization of conceptual knowledge in the brain? Introduction. *Neurocase* **4**, 265–272.

Chan, D., Fox, N. C., Scahill, R. I., Crum, W. R., Whitwell, J. L., Leschziner, G., Rossor, A. M., Stevens, J. M., Cipolotti, L. & Rossor, M. N. 2001 Patterns of temporal lobe atrophy in semantic dementia and Alzheimer's disease. *Ann. Neurol.* **49**, 433–442.

Conway, M. A. 2001 Sensory-perceptual episodic memory and its context: autobiographical memory. *Phil. Trans. R. Soc. Lond.* B **356**, 1375–1384.

Crovitz, H. F. 1986 Loss and recovery of autobiographical memory after head injury. In *Autobiographical memory* (ed. D. Rubin), pp. 273–290. New York: Cambridge University Press.

De Renzi, E., Liotti, M. & Nichelli, P. 1987 Semantic amnesia with preservation of autobiographic memory: a case report. *Cortex* **23**, 575–597.

Edwards Lee, T., Miller, B., Benson, F., Cummings, J. L., Russell, G. L., Boone, K. & Mena, I. 1997 The temporal variant of frontotemporal dementia. *Brain,* **120**, 1027–1040.

Evans, J. J., Breen, E. K., Antoun, N. & Hodges, J. R. 1996 Focal retrograde amnesia for autobiographical events following cerebral vasculitis: a connectionist account. *Neurocase* **2**, 1–11.

Galton, C. J., Gomez-Anson, B., Antoun, N., Scheltens, P., Patterson, K., Graves, M., Sahakian, B. J. & Hodges, J. R. 2001*a* The temporal lobe rating scale: application to Alzheimer's disease and frontotemporal dementia. *J. Neurol. Neurosurg. Psychiatry* **70**, 165–173.

Galton, C. J., Patterson, K., Graham, K. S., Lambon-Ralph, M. A., Williams, G., Antoun, N., Sahakian, B. J. & Hodges, J. R. 2001*b* Differing patterns of temporal lobe atrophy in Alzheimer's disease and semantic dementia. *Neurology* **57**, 216–225.

Garrard, P. & Hodges, J. R. 2000 Semantic dementia: clinical, radiological and pathological perspectives. *J. Neurol.* **247**, 409–422.

Garrard, P., Perry, R. & Hodges, J. R. 1997 Disorders of semantic memory. *J. Neurol. Neurosurg. Psychiatry* **62**, 431–435.

Graham, K. S. & Hodges, J. R. 1997 Differentiating the roles of the hippocampal complex and the neocortex in long-term memory storage: evidence from the study of semantic dementia and Alzheimer's disease. *Neuropsychology* **11**, 77–89.

Graham, K. S., Becker, J. T. & Hodges, J. R. 1997 On the relationship between knowledge and memory for pictures: evidence from the study of patients with semantic dementia and Alzheimer's disease. *J. Int. Neuropsychol. Soc.* **3**, 534–544.

Graham, K. S., Patterson, K., Pratt, K. H. & Hodges, J. R. 1999 Relearning and subsequent forgetting of semantic category exemplars in a case of semantic dementia. *Neuropsychology* **13**, 359–380.

Graham, K. S., Simons, J. S., Pratt, K. H., Patterson, K. & Hodges, J. R. 2000 Insights from semantic dementia on the relationship between episodic and semantic memory. *Neuropsychologia* **38**, 313–324.

Graham, K. S., Patterson, K., Powis, J., Drake, J. & Hodges, J. R. 2001 (In preparation.)

Greene, J. D. W. & Hodges, J. R. 1996 Identification of famous faces and names in early Alzheimer's disease: relationship to anterograde episodic and semantic memory impairment. *Brain* **119**, 111–128.

Greene, J. D. W., Baddeley, A. D. & Hodges, J. R. 1996 Analysis of the episodic memory deficit in early Alzheimer's disease: evidence from the Doors and People Test. *Neuropsychologia* **34**, 537–551.

Harasty, J. A., Halliday, G. M., Code, C. & Brooks, W. S. 1996 Quantification of cortical atrophy in a case of progressive fluent aphasia. *Brain* **119**, 181–190.

Hodges, J. R. 1995 Retrograde amnesia. In *Handbook of memory disorders* (ed. A. D. Baddeley, B. A. Wilson & F. N. Watts). Chichester: John Wiley.

Hodges, J. R. 2000 Pick's disease: its relationship to semantic dementia, progressive aphasia and frontotemporal dementia. In *Dementia*, 2nd edn (ed. J. O'Brien, D. Ames & A. Burns), ch. 57, pp. 747–758. London: Hodder Headline.

Hodges, J. R. & Graham, K. S. 1998 A reversal of the temporal gradient for famous person knowledge in semantic dementia: implications for the neural organisation of long-term memory. *Neuropsychologia* **36**, 803–825.

Hodges, J. R. & McCarthy, R. A. 1993 Autobiographical amnesia resulting from bilateral paramedian thalamic infarction: a case study in cognitive neurobiology. *Brain* **116**, 921–940.

Hodges, J. R. & Miller, B. L. 2001*a* The classification, genetics and neuropathology of frontotemporal dementia (FTD). Introduction to the special topic papers: Part I. *Neurocase* **7**, 113–121.

Hodges, J. R. & Miller, B. L. 2001*b* The neuropsychology of frontal variant FTD and semantic dementia. Introduction to the special topic papers: Part II. *Neurocase* **7**. (In the press.)

Hodges, J. R. & Patterson, K. 1995 Is semantic memory consistently impaired early in the course of Alzheimer's disease? Neuroanatomical and diagnostic implications. *Neuropsychologia* **33**, 441–459.

Hodges, J. R. & Patterson, K. 1996 Nonfluent progressive aphasia and semantic dementia: a comparative neuropsychological study. *J. Clin. Exp. Neuropsychol.* **2**, 511–524.

Hodges, J. R., Patterson, K., Oxbury, S. & Funnell, E. 1992 Semantic dementia: progressive fluent aphasia with temporal lobe atrophy. *Brain* **115**, 1783–1806.

Hodges, J. R., Graham, N. & Patterson, K. 1995 Charting the progression in semantic dementia: implications for the organisation of semantic memory. *Memory* **3**, 463–495.

Howard, D. & Patterson, K. 1992 *Pyramids and palm trees: a test of semantic access from pictures and words*. Bury St Edmunds, Suffolk, UK: Thames Valley Test Company.

Kitchener, E. & Hodges, J. R. 1999 Impaired knowledge of famous people and events and intact autobiographical knowledge in a case of progressive right temporal lobe degeneration: implications for the organization of remote memory. *Cogn. Neuropsychol.* **16**, 589–607.

Knott, R., Patterson, K. & Hodges, J. R. 1997 Lexical and semantic binding effects in short-term memory: evidence from semantic memory. *Cogn. Neuropsychol.* **14**, 1165–1218.

Kopelman, M. D. & Kapur, N. 2001 The loss of episodic memories in retrograde amnesia: single-case and group studies. *Phil. Trans. R. Soc. Lond.* B **356**, 1409–1421.

Kopelman, M. D., Wilson, B. A. & Baddeley, A. D. 1990 *The autobiographical memory interview*. Bury St Edmunds, Suffolk, UK: Thames Valley Test Company.

Mayes, A. R. & Roberts, N. 2001 Theories of episodic memory. *Phil. Trans. R. Soc. Lond.* B **356**, 1395–1408.

Mitchell, K. J. & Johnson, M. K. 2000 Source monitoring: attributing mental experiences. In *Oxford handbook of memory* (ed. E. Tulving & F. I. M. Craik), pp. 179–196. New York: Oxford University Press.

Moscovitch, M. 1994 Cognitive resources and dual-task interference effects at retrieval in normal people: the role of the frontal lobes and medial temporal cortex. *Neuropsychology* **8**, 524–534.

Moscovitch, M. & Nadel, L. 1999 Multiple-trace theory and semantic dementia: response to K.S. Graham. *Trends Cogn. Sci.* **3**, 87–89.

Mummery, C. J., Patterson, K., Price, C. J., Ashburner, J., Frackowiak, R. S. J. & Hodges, J. R. 2000 A voxel based morphometry study of semantic dementia: the relationship between temporal lobe atrophy and semantic memory. *Ann. Neurol.* **47**, 36–45.

Murray, E. A. & Bussey, T. J. 1999 Perceptual–mnemonic functions of the perirhinal cortex. *Trends Cogn. Sci.* **3**, 142–151.

Murre, J. M. J., Graham, K. S. & Hodges, J. R. 2001 Semantic dementia: new constraints on connectionist models of long-term memory. *Brain* **124**, 647–675.

Nadel, L. & Moscovitch, M. 1997 Memory consolidation, retrograde amnesia and the hippocampal complex. *Curr. Opin. Neurobiol.* **7**, 217–227.

Neary, D. (and 13 others) 1998 Frontotemporal lobar degeneration: a consensus on clinical diagnostic criteria. *Neurology* **51**, 1546–1554.

Nestor, P. J., Graham, K. S., Bozeat, S., Simons, J. S. & Hodges, J. R. 2001 Memory consolidation and the hippocampus: Further evidence from the study of autobiographical memory in semantic dementia and the frontal variant of frontotemporal dementia. *Neuropsychologia* (Submitted.)

Patterson, K. & Hodges, J. R. 1992 Deterioration of word meaning: implications for reading. *Neuropsychologia* **30**, 1025–1040.

Patterson, K. & Hodges, J. R. 2000 Semantic dementia: one window on the structure and organisation of semantic memory. In *Revised handbook of neuropsychology: memory and its disorders* (ed. L. Cermak), pp. 313–333. Amsterdam: Elsevier Science.

Rubin, D. C. & Greenberg, D. L. 1998 Visual memory deficit amnesia: a distinct amnesic presentation and etiology. *Proc. Natl Acad. Sci. USA* **95**, 5413–5416.

Simons, J. S. 2000 Episodic learning in semantic dementia. PhD thesis, University of Cambridge, UK.

Simons, J. S., Graham, K. S. & Hodges, J. R. 1999 What does semantic dementia reveal about the functional role of the perirhinal cortex? *Trends Cogn. Sci.* **3**, 248–249.

Simons, J. S., Graham, K. S., Galton, C. J., Patterson, K. & Hodges, J. R. 2001 Semantic knowledge and episodic memory for faces in semantic dementia. *Neuropsychology* **15**, 101–114.

Snodgrass, J. G. & Vanderwart, M. 1980 A standardized set of 260 pictures: norms for name agreement, image agreement, familiarity, and visual complexity. *J. Exp. Psychol. Hum. Learn. Memory* **6**, 174–215.

Snowden, J. S., Goulding, P. J. & Neary, D. 1989 Semantic dementia: a form of circumscribed cerebral atrophy. *Behav. Neurol.* **2**, 167–182.

Snowden, J. S., Griffiths, H. L. & Neary, D. 1996 Semantic-episodic memory interactions in semantic dementia: implications for retrograde memory function. *Cogn. Neuropsychol.* **13**, 1101–1137.

Tulving, E. 1985 Memory and consciousness. *Can. J. Psychol.* **26**, 1–12.

Tulving, E. 1995 Organization of memory: quo vadis. In *The cognitive neurosciences* (ed. M. S. Gazzaniga), pp. 839–847. Cambridge, MA: MIT Press.

Tulving, E. 1999 On the uniqueness of episodic memory. In *Cognitive neuroscience of memory* (ed. L.-S. Nilsson & M. J. Markowitsch), pp. 11–42. Hogrefe & Huber.

Tulving, E. & Markowitsch, H. J. 1998 Episodic and declarative memory: the role of the hippocampus. *Hippocampus* **8**, 198–204.

Vargha-Khadem, F., Gadian, D. G., Watkins, K. E., Connelly, A., Van Paesschen, W. & Mishkin, M. 1997 Differential effects of early hippocampal pathology on episodic and semantic memory. *Science* **277**, 376–380.

Vargha-Khadem, F., Gadian, D. & Mishkin, M. 2001 Dissociations in cognitive memory: the syndrome of developmental amnesia. *Phil. Trans. R. Soc. Lond.* B **356**, 1435–1440.

Warrington, E. K. 1975 Selective impairment of semantic memory. *Q. J. Exp. Psychol.* **27**, 635–657.

Westmacott, R., Moscovitch, M. & Leach, L. 2001 Different patterns of autobiographical memory loss in semantic dementia and medial temporal lobe amnesia: a challenge to consolidation theory. *Neurocase* **7**, 37–57.

9

Dissociations in cognitive memory:
the syndrome of developmental amnesia

Faraneh Vargha-Khadem, David G. Gadian
and Mortimer Mishkin

The dearth of studies on amnesia in children has led to the assumption that when damage to the medial temporal lobe system occurs early in life, the compensatory capacity of the immature brain rescues memory functions. An alternative view is that such damage so interferes with the development of learning and memory that it results not in selective cognitive impairments but in general mental retardation. Data will be presented to counter both of these arguments. Results obtained from a series of 11 amnesic patients with a history of hypoxic ischaemic damage sustained perinatally or during childhood indicate that regardless of age at onset of hippocampal pathology, there is a pronounced dissociation between episodic memory, which is severely impaired, and semantic memory, which is relatively preserved. A second dissociation is characterized by markedly impaired recall and relatively spared recognition leading to a distinction between recollection-based versus familiarity-based judgements. These findings are discussed in terms of the locus and extent of neuropathology associated with hypoxic ischaemic damage, the neural basis of 'remembering' versus 'knowing', and a hierarchical model of cognitive memory.

9.1. Introduction

Until recently, there were few reports of amnesia occurring in children at any age, and none of an amnesic syndrome resulting from brain damage incurred in infancy. The cases that had been reported were of patients who had sustained medial temporal lobe damage between the ages of 8 and 10 years (Wood *et al.* 1982; Ostergaard 1987; Broman *et al.* 1997), and of these, only the patient of Broman and colleagues was examined with modern neuroimaging techniques. That study of a young man who had suffered from an anoxic encephalopathic illness and respiratory arrest at the age of 8 years, and who subsequently showed severe and chronic memory impairment, demonstrated clearly that anterograde amnesia could result from bilateral hippocampal pathology incurred in childhood.

Yet in the absence of any reports of amnesic cases with hippocampal injuries sustained still earlier in life, it was possible to suppose that there was an age below which such injury would not lead to amnesia. There were two plausible explanations why this might occur. One was that very early damage to the memory system would so compromise cognitive development that the resulting syndrome would be one not of a selective memory disorder but rather of profound mental delay and global learning disability. At the other extreme was the possibility that such damage would fail to produce any memory disorder, because the plasticity and reorganizational capacity of the immature brain would lead to rescue of memory function. Neither of these notions proved to be correct, for we have since described a group of patients with onset of bilateral hippocampal pathology that can be dated within the first year of life and with atrophy in this structure averaging *ca.* 40%, each of whom is suffering from a very clear amnesic syndrome (Vargha-Khadem *et al.* 1997; Gadian *et al.* 2000). Theirs is a limited form of amnesia, however, for although they commonly forget the events of everyday life, signifying a marked impairment in episodic memory, they have acquired an impressive amount of factual knowledge about the world, indicating relative sparing of semantic memory. To distinguish this limited form of memory impairment from adult-onset amnesia, which typically encompasses both episodic and semantic memory (Scoville & Milner 1957; Stefanacci *et al.* 2000), we have termed the new syndrome 'developmental amnesia' (DA) (Gadian *et al.* 2000).

The hippocampal damage found in the five young patients (Gadian *et al.* 2000) is likely to be due to hypoxic ischaemia, inasmuch as each of them had one or more early hypoxic episodes (perinatally in four patients, and at 1 year of age in the fifth), and voxel-based morphometry of their magnetic resonance (MR) scans showed bilaterally reduced grey-matter density not only in the hippocampus but also in the putamen and ventral parts of the thalamus, a pattern consistent with atrophy of hypoxic-ischaemic origin (Rutherford *et al.* 1994, 1995; Barkovich & Hallam 1997; Mercuri *et al.* 1999).

Unlike cases with more severe hypoxia and the more extensive neuropathology associated with it, these patients have no motor or other neurological signs, although early in life some were said to have shown clumsiness from which they have recovered. Furthermore, their spared semantic memory ability has enabled them to develop average to low-average levels of intelligence, language, literacy and social skills. On the other hand, their impairment in episodic memory is a striking one and is evident on such everyday tasks as remembering routes, belongings, appointments, messages and other daily events. These memory difficulties, first reported by parents and teachers about the time the children entered school, and which are easily confirmed with objective laboratory measures of everyday memory and delayed recall, are so severe and chronic as to preclude independence and employment later in life.

Here we review some recent studies in which we have gathered additional information concerning the syndrome of DA. In the first part, we describe two group studies that address the questions of whether the memory profile seen after bilateral hippocampal injury in childhood differs depending on age at injury (Salmond *et al.* 2000) and extent of damage (Isaacs *et al.* 2000*a*). In the second part, we review two additional investigations carried out on one of the patients, 'Jon', who was selected for these follow-up studies because of his age (20 years) and well-preserved intelligence quotient (IQ) (114). Regarding the latter investigations, we had obtained evidence in our initial report (Vargha-Khadem *et al.* 1997) that patients with DA may show a dissociation not only between episodic and semantic memory but also between recall and recognition. Thus, on neuropsychological tests, recall (like episodic memory) was markedly impaired, whereas recognition (like semantic memory) seemed to be relatively preserved. We explored this issue further with Jon, using both neuropsychological (Baddeley *et al.* 2001) and electroencephalographic techniques (Düzel *et al.* 1999, 2001).

9.2. Effects of age at hippocampal injury

Unlike adult-onset cases with profound amnesia affecting both episodic and semantic memory, a disorder most often associated with extensive bilateral damage to the medial temporal lobe, the patients with DA have a seemingly selective pattern of medial temporal neuropathology. Thus, whereas bilateral hippocampal atrophy is clearly visible on their MR scans, there is no obvious pathology on visual inspection of the underlying parahippocampal region, consisting of the entorhinal, perirhinal and parahippocampal cortices. This seemingly isolated hippocampal damage, supported by the results of the quantitative MR techniques that have been applied thus far (Vargha-Khadem *et al.* 1997; Gadian *et al.* 2000), has led us to speculate that whereas the DA patients' episodic memory impairment is presumably due to their hippocampal pathology, their relatively preserved semantic memory could be related to the integrity of the underlying cortices (Mishkin *et al.* 1997, 1998). There are of course alternative possibilities, namely, that the limited form of amnesia in our young patients is due instead to either (i) partial sparing of the hippocampal formation or (ii) a degree of functional reorganization and compensation after very early injury that is not possible after damage acquired later in life.

Recently, as we uncovered more cases with memory disorders of childhood onset, most often directly attributable as in the original cases to hypoxic ischaemia, we had the opportunity to conduct a limited test of the early-injury proposal. Several of the new cases we saw had acquired hippocampal pathology in later childhood, and consequently we were able to compare memory outcome during adolescence in two distinct groups, one whose age at injury ranged from birth to 1 year (Early Group, $n = 6$), and the other, from 6 to 14 years (Late Group, $n = 5$). We reasoned that if the timing of the hippocampal injury was the critical factor accounting for the preservation of the Early Group's semantic memory, then the Late Group should show a profile of impairment resembling more closely the global amnesia commonly seen in adult-onset cases.

Quantitative MR techniques indicated that the hypoxic episodes in the Late Group had yielded a pattern of neuropathology that was very similar to the pattern described above (§ 9.1) for the Early Group. Interestingly, despite the later onset of their damage, the patients in the Late Group showed no signs of motor impairment in association with the putamen and thalamic damage. By contrast, their memory impairment, associated with about the same degree and apparent selectivity of medial temporal lobe pathology as those found in the Early Group, was apparent immediately after they had incurred the injury.

The neuropsychological comparison of the two groups revealed few significant differences between them. Both groups were equally impaired on tests that are considered to be measures of episodic memory, such as the Rivermead Behavioural Memory Test of everyday events (Wilson *et al.* 1985) (Figure 9.1*a*) and delayed recall of verbal and non-verbal material in both the visual and auditory modalities. Most importantly from the standpoint of the study's aims, both groups showed equivalent sparing on tests of semantic memory, as indicated by their composite scores on (i) the Information, Vocabulary, and Comprehension subtests of the Wechsler Intelligence Scale (WISC) (Bracken 1992) (Figure 9.1*b*) and (ii) single word reading, spelling and

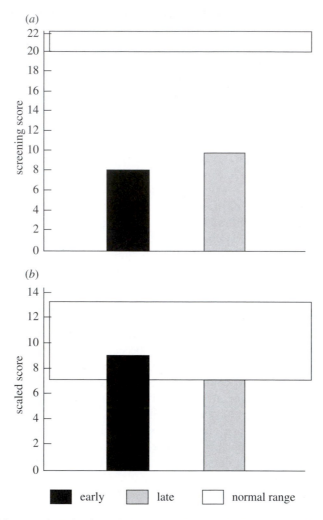

Fig. 9.1. (*a*) Rivermead Behavioural Memory Test. (*b*) Composite of the Vocabulary, Information, and Comprehension subtests of the Verbal IQ Scale of the WISC-III. Scores are means for the Early and Late Groups compared with the range for normals. The two groups of patients with DA show statistically indistinguishable degrees of deficit in (*a*) and of preservation in (*b*).

reading comprehension subtests of the Wechsler Objective Reading Dimensions Scale (Rust *et al.* 1993).

Among the many measures on which the two groups were compared, the only ones that differentiated the two groups were those of immediate memory. For example, in both immediate recall of stories and first-trial learning of verbal paired associates of the Wechsler Memory Scale, unlike the delayed recall measures on these same two subtests, the Late Group was significantly inferior to the Early Group. It is unclear whether these relative impairments in the Late Group reflect poorer episodic memory or a reduced sensory processing capacity and working memory ability. In either case, the semantic memory ability of the two groups does not appear to differ. The findings thus lead to the tentative conclusion that if DA is indeed a special syndrome related to the early occurrence of hypoxia-induced hippocampal damage, then the effective age at injury could extend from birth to puberty.

Yet these results do not rule out the broader notion that DA is a syndrome restricted to childhood-onset injury. Examining this possibility will require direct comparison with patients who have had still later onsets of the same amount and apparent selectivity of medial temporal pathology as those described here. Recently, at least three patients have been reported whose anterograde amnesia was incurred in adulthood and whose damage appears to be restricted to the hippocampus (Kitchener *et al.* 1998; Holdstock *et al.* 2000; Verfaellie *et al.* 2000). It is of interest that, despite the presence of a severe episodic memory impairment in each of these patients, each has also shown at least some degree of new semantic learning, although the extent of the newly acquired information is minimal compared with the level acquired by our patients with DA. Moreover, several other case studies of patients with adult-onset injury seemingly limited to the hippocampus have failed to uncover any evidence of preserved semantic memory ability (Kartsounis *et al.* 1995; Reed & Squire 1998). Whether this difference in semantic memory outcome is due in fact to the different ages at injury is still uncertain, however, inasmuch as there could still be undetermined differences between the adult- and childhood-onset cases in the extent of the neuropathology. Indeed, further quantitative study of the neuropathology in the hippocampus and parahippocampal region in both the childhood and adult forms of amnesia is needed to help decide among the possible explanations for the specific memory profile seen in DA.

9.3. Effects of extent of hippocampal injury

Having determined that hippocampal injury at any time during childhood yields the characteristic profile of DA, we next sought to determine whether this syndrome appears only if the hippocampal damage reaches a certain minimal extent (Isaacs *et al.* 2000*a*). We addressed this question by comparing the group of patients described above (Group DA, $n = 11$) with a group of children born extremely preterm (Group PT, $n = 11$), who were found to have sustained hippocampal damage possibly as a result of lung immaturity, for which they had required intubation and artificial ventilation (Isaacs *et al.* 2000*b*). A control group consisted of normal children born full term (Group C, $n = 8$). Each of these three groups was examined at a mean age of *ca.* 14 years.

Relative to hippocampal volumes in their age-matched normal controls, the reduction in hippocampal volume for each hemisphere in Group DA averaged 40% (range, 29–55%), whereas in Group PT it averaged 10% (ranging up to 25%). None of the children in Group PT is amnesic, and although the group did show deficits on a few items of the Rivermead Test of everyday memory, this group had no deficits on any of the other tests considered to be measures of episodic memory, such as delayed recall of verbal and non-verbal material. As a result, on every episodic memory measure in which Group DA was impaired relative to Group C, it was also impaired relative to Group PT. By contrast, there were no differences between the DA and PT Groups on any of the tests considered to be measures of semantic memory, such as the

Information, Vocabulary and Comprehension subtests of the Wechsler Intelligence Scale or the subtests of the Wechsler Objective Reading Dimensions Scale.

The results suggest that hippocampal volume must undergo a reduction of at least 25–30% on each side before DA is likely to result. The relationship between degree of memory deficit and amount of hippocampal atrophy (and possibly subhippocampal atrophy, see § 9.2) could of course be continuously graded rather than all-or-none, but resolving this issue will require study of larger numbers of patients with early hippocampal injury than have been identified so far.

9.4. Recall versus recognition after hippocampal injury

As already noted, evidence obtained in our first report on DA suggested that, like semantic memory, recognition memory may also show a surprising degree of preservation. Among the tests given to the three patients and normal controls of that study were ones that assessed one-trial recognition for lists of items, one-trial associative recognition for lists of paired items, and multi-trial associative recognition for lists of paired items within and across modalities. Of these, all but the cross-modal tests were performed by the patients at normal or near-normal levels, a finding strikingly different from their poor performance on the numerous tests of delayed recall. Yet, we could not be confident of a recall–recognition dissociation in our patients because the two measures differ so greatly in difficulty.

To address this problem, we turned to the Doors and People Test (Baddeley *et al.* 1994) in which recall and recognition of both visual and verbal stimuli were deliberately designed to be of equal difficulty through the incorporation of 'easy' recall and 'hard' recognition tests plus the use of scaled scores derived from performance of a large population of normal young adults. We gave this and other recognition tests that have normative data for young adults to Jon, one of the patients with neonatal injury. As already noted, Jon was 20 years old at the time of testing and had a full scale IQ of 114 (Verbal IQ (VIQ), 108; Performance IQ (PIQ), 120). We compared Jon's scores on these several measures with those of two normal control subjects who were matched to Jon for age and IQ, as well as to those of less well matched but larger groups from the published literature. The results (Baddeley *et al.* 2001) confirmed the initial findings; in particular, on the Doors and People Test, Jon scored below the fifth percentile on both visual and verbal recall, while scoring between the 50th and 75th percentile on both visual and verbal recognition (Figure 9.2). His two control subjects, by contrast, obtained scores between the 50th and 75th percentile on visual and verbal recall as well as recognition. On each of the other measures of recognition, whether immediate or delayed, Jon's performance likewise fell solidly within the normal range.

It is important to note here that the case of adult-onset amnesia reported by Holdstock *et al.* (2000) also showed a remarkable degree of sparing of recognition memory, and several amnesic cases cited by Aggleton & Shaw (1996) had less but still substantial sparing of this ability.

The above findings on recognition memory are of special interest in connection with evidence that has accumulated recently regarding the neural substrate of recognition in animals. The results of these lesion studies show clearly that, within the medial temporal lobe, the tissue most critical for recognition memory is the group of cortical

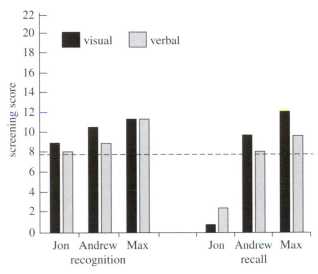

Fig. 9.2. Doors and People Test. Scores of Jon, the patient with DA, and his two age- and IQ-matched controls (normal mean, 10; standard deviation, 1.5). Jon shows preserved recognition ability, but markedly impaired recall, for both visual and verbal material.

areas that comprise the parahippocampal region. The long list of severe deficits that have been observed in rats and monkeys after selective damage to these cortical areas (i.e. the entorhinal, perirhinal and parahippocampal cortices) includes item recognition in the visual, tactile and olfactory modalities, as well as the recognition of visual–visual, visual–tactile, object–reward and object–place associations (reviewed in Mishkin *et al.* 1997, 1998). By contrast, selective damage to the hippocampus yields comparatively mild impairment or, in the majority of instances, no impairment at all on these same tasks. Importantly, neonatal damage in monkeys to the perirhinal cortex, the subhippocampal area that is most important for non-spatial recognition, produces an impairment in this ability later in life that is as severe as that produced by similar lesions in adulthood (Malkova *et al.* 1998). The findings in animals thus suggest that spared recognition ability in patients with DA, like the proposal regarding the preserved semantic memory ability in these cases, is due to the apparent preservation of the parahippocampal region.

The neuropsychological study conducted with Jon (Baddeley *et al.* 2001) also helped clarify how children with DA might acquire factual information, which is of course not limited simply to its recognition. Jon, for example, has no difficulty recalling the definitions of words, naming and describing historical figures and events, or discussing at length such subjects as current politics and computer games, both of which are his hobbies. To track his acquisition of new material, we presented Jon with a series of videos based on two newsreels of events that pre-dated his birth by many years. One reel was shown only once, while the other was shown four times over 2 days. Tested for recognition after either one or four viewings, Jon's recognition scores were generally comparable with those of his two age- and IQ-matched controls, whereas his recall score after one viewing was markedly impaired. After four viewings, however, Jon's recall score rose substantially, nearly matching those of his controls, demonstrating that his recall deficits can be minimized, given sufficient practice. A possible interpretation of this finding is provided by the episodic memory theory of Tulving (1985), namely, that through repetition Jon can recall information because he is now familiar with or 'knows' it, a characteristic of semantic memory, although he is not able to 'remember' or recollect it, i.e. bring it back to mind, the hallmark of episodic memory.

9.5. Event-related potentials (ERPs) during recognition after hippocampal injury

We recently obtained support for the foregoing interpretation from the results of an ERP study in Jon (Düzel *et al.* 1999, 2001). Word recognition experiments have shown that normal subjects can correctly recognize some words that they recollect studying, being able to report something that happened or that they had thought about when they had studied those particular words, and others on the study list that they do not recollect but nevertheless judge as familiar (e.g. Gardiner *et al.* 1996). These two types of memory can be differentially enhanced by manipulating depth of processing during study. For example, asking the subject to judge whether the word's referent is living or non-living or is abstract or concrete (deep encoding) enhances the likelihood that the word will be recollected later, whereas asking the subject whether the word's letters are printed in small or capital letters or whether its first and last letters are in alphabetical order (shallow encoding) generally leads to familiarity judgements. Importantly, these two memory types were later found to be associated with qualitatively different ERP patterns (Paller *et al.* 1995; Rugg *et al.* 1998). Thus, during familiarity-based recognition, correctly recognized old words (hits) evoke significantly more positive waves than correctly rejected new words from fronto-central electrodes in the 300–500 ms time-window, a modulation that is often referred to as the N400 effect. By contrast, during recollection-based recognition, hits evoke significantly more positive waves than correct rejections from left parietal electrodes in the 500–700 ms time-window, sometimes referred to as the late positive component (LPC) effect. The temporal and topographical dissociation of these two ERP effects suggests that they are generated by different neuronal populations.

Based on this evidence, we investigated the recognition memory of Jon during ERP recording, using a deep encoding paradigm that reliably elicits both the N400 and LPC effects in normal subjects. Thus, as illustrated in Figure 9.3, hits normally elicit more positive ERPs than correct rejections in both the N400 and LPC time-windows. In Jon, however, the ERPs showed a prominent N400 effect only, the LPC effect being entirely absent. Interestingly, in this deep encoding paradigm, Jon's recognition was not as good that of his controls, although he performed at a satisfactory level. The results are thus consistent with the notions that (i) the process of recollection is critically dependent on the hippocampus, (ii) recollection normally enhances recognition, but (iii) recognition can proceed fairly accurately without recollection, even after deep encoding, on the basis of the familiarity process alone.

9.6. Summary and conclusions

Investigation of DA is still in its early stages, and therefore many questions surrounding the memory dissociations that seem to characterize this syndrome remain unanswered.

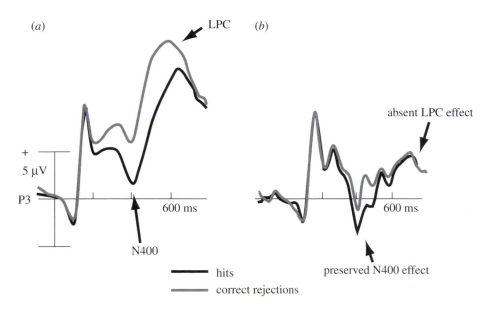

Fig. 9.3. ERPs recorded from the left parietal electrode (P3) to visual word recognition after deep encoding of the words. In normal subjects, hits (i.e. correct recognition of old words) elicit greater positivity than correct rejections of new words in both the N400 and LPC time-windows. In Jon, hits elicit greater positivity than correct rejections in the N400 time-window only. (Adapted from Düzel *et al.* 1999.)

Although the DA patients' impairments in episodic memory and recollection are very likely the result of the substantial hippocampal damage they have incurred, it is still unclear whether the relative sparing of their semantic memory and familiarity-based recognition are attributable to integrity of the subhippocampal cortices, to the partial sparing of the hippocampus, to the functional reorganization within these structures, or to some combination of these several factors. Reasons for favouring the possibility listed first come from the experimental studies in animals referred to earlier (§ 9.4) demonstrating the critical role of the subhippocampal cortices in recognition memory, even in cases of neonatal damage. The support provided by this experimental evidence for the subhippocampal proposal is only indirect, however. Further, this proposal leaves unexplained the differential outcome after childhood-onset and adult-onset hippocampal pathology, with the latter resulting in little if any preservation of semantic memory, and relatively few cases of preserved recognition memory. In sum, determining the precise neuropathological and neuropsychological explanation for the syndrome of DA remains a challenge for future research.

We are grateful to the individuals with DA, those born extremely prematurely, and the normal controls, for their participation in this research. In particular, we extend a special thanks to Jon and his family for their unfailing cooperation. We thank Claire Salmond and Elizabeth Isaacs (Institute of Child Health, University College London) for making available unpublished results from the two group studies (Salmond *et al.* 2000; Isaacs *et al.* 2000a) cited in this chapter.

References

Aggleton, J. P. & Shaw, C. 1996 Amnesia and recognition memory: a re-analysis of psychometric data. *Neuropsychologia* **34**, 51–62.

Baddeley, A. D., Emslie, H. & Nimmo-Smith, I. 1994 *Doors and People Test of visual and verbal recall and recognition*. Bury St Edmunds: Thames Valley Test Co.

Baddeley, A. D., Vargha-Khadem, F. & Mishkin, M. 2001 Preserved recognition in a case of developmental amnesia: implications for the acquisition of semantic memory. *J. Cogn. Neurosci.* **13**, 357–369.

Barkovich, A. J. & Hallam, D. 1997 Neuroimaging in perinatal hypoxic-ischaemic injury. *Ment. Retard. Devel. Disabil. Res. Rev.* **3**, 28–41.

Bracken, B. A. (ed.) 1992 *Wechsler Intelligence Scale for children*, 3rd edn. Sidcup: The Psychological Corporation.

Broman, M., Rose, A. L., Hotson, G. & Casey, C. M. 1997 Severe anterograde amnesia with onset in childhood as a result of anoxic encephalopathy. *Brain* **120**, 417–434.

Düzel, E., Vargha-Khadem, F., Heinze, H. J. & Mishkin, M. 1999 ERP evidence for recognition without episodic recollection in a patient with early hippocampal pathology. *Soc. Neurosci. Abstr.* **25**, 649.

Düzel, E., Vargha-Khadem, F., Heinze, H. J. & Mishkin, M. 2001 Hippocampal damage affects brain indices of episodic but not semantic memory. *Proc. Natl Acad. Sci. USA* **98**, 8101–8106.

Gadian, D. G., Aicardi, J., Watkins, K., Porter, D., Mishkin, M. & Vargha-Khadem, F. 2000 Developmental amnesia associated with early hypoxic-ischaemic injury. *Brain* **123**, 499–507.

Gardiner, J. M., Java, R. I. & Richardson-Klavehn, A. 1996 How level of processing really influences awareness in recognition memory. *Can. J. Exp. Psychol.* **50**, 114–122.

Holdstock, J. S., Mayes, A. R., Cezayirli, E., Isaac, C. L., Aggleton, J. P. & Roberts, N. 2000 A comparison of egocentric and allocentric spatial memory in a patient with selective hippocampal damage. *Neuropsychologia* **38**, 410–425.

Isaacs, E., Gadian, D. G., Watkins, K. E., Lucas, A., Mishkin, M. & Vargha-Khadem, F. 2000*a* Effects of early hippocampal damage: relationship between memory impairment and extent of pathology. *Soc. Neurosci. Abstr.* **26**, 1242.

Isaacs, E. B., Lucas, A., Chong, W. K., Wood, S. J., Johnson, C. L., Marshall, C., Vargha-Khadem, F. & Gadian, D. G. 2000*b* Hippocampal volume and everyday memory in children of very low birth weight. *Pediatr. Res.* **47**, 713–720.

Kartsounis, L. D., Rudge, P. & Stevens, J. M. 1995 Bilateral lesions of CA1 and CA2 fields of the hippocampus are sufficient to cause a severe amnesic syndrome in humans. *J. Neurol. Neurosurg. Psychiatry* **59**, 95–98.

Kitchener, E. G., Hodges, J. R. & McCarthy, R. 1998 Acquisition of post-morbid vocabulary and semantic facts in the absence of episodic memory. *Brain* **121**, 1313–1327.

Malkova, L., Pixley, G. L., Webster, M. J., Mishkin, M. & Bachevalier, J. 1998 The effects of early rhinal cortex lesions on visual recognition memory in rhesus monkeys. *Soc. Neurosci. Abstr.* **24**, 1906.

Mercuri, E., Guzzetta, A., Haataja, L., Cowan, F., Rutherford, M., Counsell, S., Papadimitrou, M., Cioni, G. & Dubowitz, L. 1999 Neonatal neurological examination in infants with hypoxic ischaemic encephalopathy: correlation with MRI findings. *Neuropediatrics* **30**, 83–89.

Mishkin, M., Suzuki, W., Gadian, D. G. & Vargha-Khadem, F. 1997 Hierarchical organization of cognitive memory. *Phil. Trans. R. Soc. Lond.* B **352**, 1461–1467.

Mishkin, M., Vargha-Khadem, F. & Gadian, D. G. 1998 Amnesia and the organisation of the hippocampal system. *Hippocampus* **8**, 212–216.

Ostergaard, A. L. 1987 Episodic, semantic and procedural memory in a case of amnesia at an early age. *Neuropsychologia* **25**, 341–357.

Paller, K. A., Kutas, M. & McIsaac, H. K. 1995 Monitoring conscious recollection via the electrical activity of the brain. *Psychol. Sci.* **6**, 107–111.

Reed, J. M. & Squire, L. R. 1998 Retrograde amnesia for facts and events: findings from four new cases. *J. Neurosci.* **18**, 3943–3954.

Rugg, M. D., Mark, R. E., Walla, P., Schloerscheidt, A. M., Birch, C. S. & Allan, K. 1998 Dissociation of the neural correlates of implicit and explicit memory. *Nature* **392**, 595–598.

Rust, J., Golombrok, S. & Trickey, G. 1993 *Wechsler Objective Reading Dimensions (WORD) manual.* London: The Psychological Corporation.

Rutherford, M. A., Pennock, J. M. & Dubowitz, L. M. 1994 Cranial ultrasound and magnetic resonance imaging in hypoxic-ischaemic encephalopathy: a comparison with outcome. *Devl. Med. Child Neurol.* **36**, 813–825.

Rutherford, M. A., Pennock, J. M., Schwieso, J. E., Cowan, F. M. & Dubowitz, L. M. 1995 Hypoxic ischaemic encephalopathy: early magnetic resonance imaging findings and their evolution. *Neuropediatrics* **26**, 183–191.

Salmond, C. H., Vargha-Khadem, F., Friston, K. J., Mishkin, M. & Gadian, D. G. 2000 Age at hypoxia and neuropathology in children with developmental amnesia. *Soc. Neurosci. Abstr.* **26**, 1242.

Scoville, W. B. & Milner, B. 1957 Loss of recent memory after bilateral hippocampal lesions. *J. Neurol. Neurosurg. Psychiatry* **20**, 11–21.

Stefanacci, L., Buffalo, E. A., Schmolck, H. & Squire, L. R. 2000 Profound amnesia after damage to the medial temporal lobe: a neuroanatomical and neuropsychological profile of patient E.P. *J. Neurosci.* **20**, 7024–7036.

Tulving, E. 1985 Memory and consciousness. *Can. Psychologist* **26**, 1–12.

Vargha-Khadem, F., Gadian, D. G., Watkins, K. E., Connelly, A. & Van Paesschen, W. 1997 Differential effects of early hippocampal pathology on episodic and semantic memory. *Science* **277**, 376–380.

Verfaellie, M., Koseff, P. & Alexander, M. P. 2000 Acquisition of novel semantic information in amnesia: effects of lesion location. *Neuropsychologia* **38**, 484–492.

Wilson, B., Cockburn, J. & Baddeley, A. 1985 *Rivermead Behavioural Memory Test.* Bury St Edmunds: Thames Valley Test Co.

Wood, F., Ebert, V. & Kinsbourne, M. 1982 The episodic-semantic memory distinction in memory and amnesia: clinical and experimental observations. In *Human memory and amnesia* (ed. L. S. Cermak), pp. 167–193. Hillsdale, NJ: Lawrence Erlbaum Associates.

10

Neuroimaging studies of autobiographical event memory

Eleanor A. Maguire

Commonalities and differences in findings across neuroimaging studies of autobiographical event memory are reviewed. In general terms, the overall pattern across studies is of medial and left-lateralized activations associated with retrieval of autobiographical event memories. It seems that the medial frontal cortex and left hippocampus in particular are responsive to such memories. However, there are also inconsistencies across studies, for example in the activation of the hippocampus and dorsolateral prefrontal cortex. It is likely that methodological differences between studies contribute to the disparate findings. Quantifying and assessing autobiographical event memories presents a challenge in many domains, including neuroimaging. Methodological factors that may be pertinent to the interpretation of the neuroimaging data and the design of future experiments are discussed. Consideration is also given to aspects of memory that functional neuroimaging might be uniquely disposed to examine. These include assessing the functionality of damaged tissue in patients and the estimation of inter-regional communication (effective connectivity) between relevant brain regions.

10.1. Introduction

There are a number of approaches to neuroimaging episodic memory. In many studies, subjects are scanned as they learn and/or remember stimuli such as words or word-pairs. Using paradigms such as this we continue to learn much about, for example, frontal lobe contributions to memory operations (for a review, see Fletcher & Henson 2001). The focus here, however, is the retrieval of autobiographical event memories, those personally relevant episodes with a specific spatio-temporal context, the storehouse of our life's experiences ranging from the recent to the very remote. Although neuroimaging embraces techniques such as electroencephalography (EEG) and event related potentials (ERPs), only positron emission tomography (PET) and functional magnetic resonance imaging (fMRI) will be considered in this instance, and the relevant literature briefly reviewed. While one might consider the data to raise more questions about the nature of autobiographical event memory than they answer, my aim here is to highlight issues pertinent to the interpretation of the neuroimaging findings. I will then focus on further questions about autobiographical event memory that functional neuroimaging might be uniquely disposed to address.

The background to any discussion of real world autobiographical event memory is the widely acknowledged difficulty of quantifying personal memories and assessing their retrieval (Hodges 1995; Warrington 1996). When asking someone to recall past events, they re-orient to the past, they recall abstract semantic (people, general knowledge) as well as specific information, in revisiting an event they may re-encode it, and events will naturally differ in their salience and significance to the subject. Kapur (1999) summarizes many of the variables that are likely to affect autobiographical event memory: 'encoding variables'—novelty of an event, its distinctiveness, its predictability, the number and type of sensory modalities involved, cognitive and emotional significance of events, the exposure duration and repetition profile; 'retention testing variables'—time from event to test, sensitivity of the testing measure, response modality, strategies used by the subject; in the case of patients, 'lesion variables'—site, pathology, severity, acuteness of onset, other pathology, plasticity.

It is unsurprising, given the many influencing factors, that no current method of assessment is completely satisfactory, although a wide variety of tests have been employed. One commonly used method involves variations on the Crovitz & Schiffman (1974) technique, where subjects remember specific, personally experienced events in response to cue words. However, there are problems with this technique (Hodges 1995), e.g. subjects are typically not constrained to produce memories from specific time periods. There may also be considerable variation between subjects in the time taken to produce a memory and also in factors such as emotional valence of memories. The Autobiographical Memory Interview (AMI) (Kopelman *et al*. 1990) is a test designed for use in the clinical context where subjects are questioned about memories from specific time periods, as well as personally relevant factual or semantic memories. However, there are problems here also (Oxbury *et al*. 1997), e.g. in younger subjects there is more overlap between time periods than in older subjects and personal semantic questions can often be easier than those for event memory. The AMI and most similar tests assess the recall of autobiographical event memories. Autobiographical event recognition memory is generally not assessed, but may provide additional information about preserved memories in amnesia (N. Kapur, personal communication). Despite the limitations of current tests, we continue to learn much from their use and, as is apparent in the next section, they have also been adapted for use in several PET and fMRI studies.

10.2. Neuroimaging autobiographical event memory: a review

Studying memory using neuroimaging has many acknowledged advantages—healthy brains can be scanned *in vivo*, one can achieve good spatial resolution, in the case of fMRI one can study discrete cognitive events as brief as 1–2 s, and one can examine neural activity during encoding based on whether stimuli were subsequently remembered or not (Brewer *et al*. 1998; Wagner *et al*. 1998). Neuroimaging studies of autobiographical event memory, however, are subject to all of the issues outlined in §10.1 and some more besides. For example, in fMRI, avoiding speech-related movement artefacts makes free recall difficult to operationalize. In PET (not a problem for fMRI), given that blood flow is averaged across approximately 90 s, one cannot examine discrete events. Because of these technical issues and the time and resource demands of examining autobiographical event memory *per se* (i.e. the requirement for subject-specific stimuli), functional neuroimaging studies involving the retrieval of autobiographical event memories are not numerous.

All known (eleven) studies are listed in Table 10.1. For each study, the scanning modality, general pre-scan context, scanning conditions and stimulus presentations are

Table 10.1. Functional neuroimaging studies (PET/fMRI) involving retrieval of real-world autobiographical event memories.

study[a]	modality	pre-scan context	scanning context	examples of relevant contrasts[b]	areas active[c]
Andreasen et al. (1995)	PET	15 min prior to scan, recalled one specific event from their past; no information on whether recent/remote; no rating of the memories.	One scan per task; 3 conditions: 1, recalling aloud the personal event; 2, verbal fluency (letter C) aloud; 3, rest—but here interpreted as random free associations—no verbal output	1–2	Med frontal; retrosplen; L DLPFC.
Fink et al. (1996)	PET	1 h prior to scan, presented with autobiographical information on a previously unknown person. Weeks prior to scan, semi-structured interview to obtain information on personal events from childhood to early adulthood—emphasis on affect-laden events; subjects unaware of purpose of the interview.	Auditory presentation of stimuli as sentences: no overt response; 3 conditions: 1, hear sentences from unknown person's autobiography, imagining what happened to them in the situation; 2, hear sentences about own past, imagining what happened to themselves; 3, rest—eyes closed no auditory input.	2–1	R: sup temp gyrus/insula; post cing; HC; PHG; amygdala; TPJ; prefrontal.
Markowitsch et al. (1997)	PET	Patient 59 RH female; history of child abuse; produced drawings depicting scenes from childhood: some of vivid consciously remembered events, others where she did not know specific meaning of the scene.	15 s prior to scan, shown: one of the drawings. During scan, eyes closed, had to imagine what kind of past event the scene represented. 3 conditions: 1, rest; 2, 'conscious' memories; 3, where specific meaning not known.	only 2 reported: 2–1 3–1	R temp pole R temp pole; R PHG; L HC.
Maguire & Mummery (1999)	PET	Several weeks prior to scan, subjects interviewed and questionnaire completed but not aware of specific purpose of either; memories sampled from across 20 or more years, up to very recent memories. Rated across parameters such as: amount of details recalled, emotional salience, vividness, how often rehearsed. All consciously recollected, not merely told to them by a third party.	Heard sentences during scan and responded by keypress if what they heard was true/false; ratio = 3:1; if sentences were obviously altered actual memories (pilot data showed subjects recalled original event in this context—no. of false matched across scans/tasks). For episodic events, sampled across lifetime during each scan. 6 conditions: 1, autobiographical events; 2, public events; 3, autobiographical facts; 4, general facts; 5, control—sets of function words/prepositions, decide if last word had one or more syllables; 6, as in 5, but included self-reference words such as 'you'. 8 s per stimulus (3–4 s per sentence, the remainder to respond).	1–2/3 or 4–5 1–2/3 or 4	Network of medial and L areas: temp pole, med frontal; lat temp; HC; PHG; retrosplen; TPJ and R TPJ L HC; med frontal; temp pole.

continued

Table 10.1. *continued*

Conway et al. (1999)	PET	Subjects trained prior to scan on recalling an event from their past in response to a cue word so could report the specific memory in detail. Taught a set of 15 verbal paired associates for later recall during scanning. For cues, common emotion words were excluded; frequency, imagability of words not controlled.	Stimuli presented visually (for 200 ms; ISI[d] 4800 ms); respond aloud. 3 conditions: 1, visual baseline—look at box of random intensity pixels; 2, saw first word of pairs and had to speak aloud the second word; 3, retrieved memory in response to cue word, had to respond with a word of their own. For some cues, had to respond with a recent memory (last 12 months), for others remote memories (when aged 15 years old or younger).	3–2 remote recent recent-remote	L prefrontal; L post parietal; L occipital; L lat temp. no diffs occipital lobe brain stem
Andreasen et al. (1999)	PET	Nothing specific mentioned.	2 tasks: 1, told to lie quietly with eyes closed and think about a specific event experienced in the past; 2, think about anything that occurred to them.	1–2	R cerebellum; L lat cerebellum; L med dors thal; L orbito-frontal cortex; ant cing; L parietal; med frontal.
Maguire et al. (2000)	fMRI	Same as Maguire & Mummery (1999) above.	Similar to Maguire & Mummery (1999) above except control conditions 5 and 6 amalgamated (here called 5); 6 was a rest condition.	1–2/3 or 4–5 1–2/3 or 4 effective connectivity	Network of L and medial areas: temp pole; and R temp pole; med frontal; lat temp; HC; PHG; retrosplen, TPJ; R post cerebellum L HC; med frontal PHG-HC increased for 1 as was PHG-temp pole; lat temp-temp pole increased for 2 and 4.
Maguire et al. (2001a)	e-fMRI	Same as Maguire & Mummery (1999) above.	Similar to Maguire et al. (2000) above but used an event-related analysis to model the parametric effect of memory age for autobiographical events and public events over 20 or more years.	Parametric effect Recent autobiographical events — autobiographical facts. Remote autobiographical events—autobiographical facts.	R VLPFC decrease the more remote the autobiographical event memory. L HC; med frontal. L HC; med frontal.

continued

Table 10.1. *continued*

study[a]	modality	pre-scan context	scanning context	examples of relevant contrasts[b]	areas active[c]
Ryan et al. (2001)	fMRI	Immediately prior to scan, shown a list of general life event categories, noting if had happened to them, when, if positive/negative. 10 recent (less than 4 years ago) and 10 remote (over 20 years ago) events gathered, equal numbers of positive and negative events. In 3 extra subjects, cues collected from spouses and presented to subjects for first time during scanning.	Visual cues during scanning; 3 conditions: 1, recall past event for 20 s on viewing the relevant category label from pre-scan list; 2, visual cue to relax for 16 s; 3, shown sentences with last word missing, had to covertly complete sentence with an appropriate word.	recent-remote recent-remote—2/3 (similar results for the 3 extra subjects)	No diffs L,R prefrontal; L,R precentral gyrus; L sup temp sulcus; L mid temp gyrus; L,R HC; R pulvinar; post cing; L,R precuneus; L fusiform; L inf parietal; R lat cerebellum.
Maguire et al. (2001a)	fMRI	Patient 22 RH male; selective bilateral hippocampal damage of perinatal origin. Preserved semantic but impaired episodic memory. Same procedure as Maguire & Mummery (1999), enough events recalled for viable scanning; accuracy checked with parents. Jon made a distinction the controls did not: for some events he had conscious recollection, for others, although he knew as much about, did not remember the event occurring.	Same as in Maguire et al. (2000) except two extra conditions, as well as 1, and 2, also autobiographical events he knew about but not remember the context (no. 7) and similarly for public (no. 7) events (no. 8).	1/2/3/ 4/7 or 8-5 1-2/3/4/7 or 8 effective connectivity	Same as controls in Maguire et al. (2000) but bilateral. Also L,R HC; L,R prefrontal regions. L,R HC; med frontal needed extra cons; PHG-temp pole increased for 1 as was retrosplen-HC; retrosplen-HC and retrosplen med. frontal increased in Jon versus controls for autobiographical events.
Burgess et al. (2001)	e-fMRI	VR complex town adapted from Maguire et al. (1998). The town was used as the real world context where events were experienced by subjects prior to scanning—certain people giving them objects in certain places.	Subjects scanned during retrieval of aspects of the events: 1, place; 2, person; 3, object; 4, visual control task.	1-4	L HC; retrosplen; R precuneus; L,R VLPFC; L,R PHG; L,R DLPFC; L,R post parietal; mid and ant cing; L fusiform.

[a] Liotti et al. (2000) was not included because autobiographical events, while used to elicit emotions prior to scanning, during scanning subjects had to focus only on the emotions and not specific events.
[b] The numbers refer to the conditions as described in the adjacent left column.
[c] /, or; ant, anterior; cing, cingulate; DLPFC, dorsolateral prefrontal cortex; dors, dorsal; e-fMRI, event-related fMRI; HC, hippocampus; inf, inferior; L, left; lat, lateral; med, medial; mid, middle; PHG, parahippocampal gyrus; post, posterior; R, right; retrosplen, retrosplenial; RH, right-handed; sup, superior; temp, temporal; thal, thalamus; TPJ, temporoparietal junction; VLPFC, ventrolateral prefrontal cortex; VR, virtual reality.
[d] ISI, inter-stimulus interval.

given. Also included are examples of the main contrasts relating to autobiographical event memory, and a summary of brain areas active in these contrasts. I will briefly highlight some of the findings, considering commonalities and differences across studies.

In general terms, the overall pattern across studies is of medial and left-lateralized activations associated with retrieval of autobiographical event memories. In the one study where the emphasis was on affect-laden memories, activations are described as right-sided (Fink *et al.* 1996). Areas active in many of the studies include retrosplenial cortex, parahippocampal gyrus, temporo-parietal junction, medial frontal cortex, temporal pole, cerebellum and the hippocampus. These areas clearly form the basis of a memory retrieval network but it is not clear from many of the studies (given the control tasks and comparisons, see further on in this section) whether some areas are preferentially active for the retrieval of autobiographical events as opposed to memory retrieval *per se*. Where this was specifically investigated (Maguire & Mummery 1999; Maguire *et al.* 2000, 2001*a,b*) it seems that the medial frontal cortex and left hippocampus are particularly responsive to retrieval of autobiographical event memories. Given the acknowledged role of the hippocampus in episodic memory (Scoville & Milner 1957; O'Keefe & Nadel 1978; Tulving 1983), it is perhaps surprising that some of the studies do not report hippocampal activations (Conway *et al.* 1999; Andreasen *et al.* 1995, 1999). Dorsolateral prefrontal cortex (DLPFC) is another area that is present in the results of some studies but not in others. It is likely that differences in methodological factors between studies contribute to the disparate findings. Several of these factors will now be considered; the intention is not to criticize what are difficult studies to design and execute, but rather to understand better the data collected so far.

In the first instance, it is clear that interaction with subjects prior to scanning differs widely across studies. In some studies, there was very little interaction, or subjects were given general instructions about the task just prior to scanning using variations on the Crovitz & Schiffman (1974) technique (e.g. Conway *et al.* 1999; Ryan *et al.* 2001), or the memories being tested were recently encoded (Burgess *et al.* 2001). In other studies, information was elicited from subjects weeks prior to the experiment, where subjects were naive to the specific purpose of the interviewing (e.g. Fink *et al.* 1996; Maguire & Mummery 1999; Maguire *et al.* 2000, 2001*a,b*). The issue of how to elicit stimuli for presentation during scanning is closely related to that of testing retrograde memories in general (see § 10.1 above). Does questioning subjects, even briefly, before scanning, change the essential nature of the memory one wishes to examine? Is the memory now recent as opposed to what might have been a remote memory? Has the event been re-encoded and is that what one is scanning and not recall of the original event? But if one scans subjects 'cold', so to speak, with no prior interaction, then there is less control over the time-scale of memories recalled and one is less able to control for the Kapur (1999) factors. One could, as did Ryan *et al.* (2001), glean the necessary information from spouses and/or family members, although there is no guarantee that the subject will recall the specific events or in a similar manner to the spouse.

Further cross-study differences emerge during scanning itself. Although the goal in all studies was for subjects to think about the original autobiographical events, the manner in which they are cued, the time they have to think about each personal event, the degree of retrieval effort and the requirement for a response, differed across studies. In some studies (e.g. Conway *et al.* 1999) there may not have been enough time for each event to be fully retrieved and hence the lack of hippocampal activation (although see below). Perhaps the DLPFC was not apparent in some studies (e.g. Maguire & Mummery 1999) because the amount of retrieval effort *per se* was minimized, or monitoring and response selection requirements (Fletcher & Henson 2001) were similar across all tasks and so DLPFC activations were subtracted out.

One of the principal methodological differences across studies is in the conditions used for comparison with autobiographical event memory. In terms of baseline or control conditions, various tasks have been employed which include looking at a box of pixels (Conway *et al.* 1999), or making syllable judgements (the Maguire studies). In many experiments 'rest', either interpreted as relaxation or freely associating thoughts (Andreasen *et al.* 1995, 1999), was the main baseline task. While accepting that the design of control tasks is a difficult issue in scanning experiments such as these where real-world memories are involved, rest is not an optimal choice for a control or comparison task. Its unconstrained nature is particularly unsuitable given the richly stimulating nature of the autobiographical memory task and key activations might be subtracted out if there is overspill from the active memory task (see McGuire *et al.* 1996). In some studies, memory tasks were included to compare with autobiographical event memory, such as the retrieval of paired associates learned just prior to scanning (Conway *et al.* 1999) or exposure to biographical information about an unfamiliar person, initially heard just prior to scanning (Fink *et al.* 1996). While interesting to compare with a low level non-memory task, one should be cautious in making direct comparisons of either of these tasks with autobiographical event memory as they differ in recency (autobiographical events maybe decades old compared with the newly learned material) and in the degree of personal relevance of the material.

The sentence completion task used by Ryan *et al.* (2001) raises another point in relation to these experiments—the need to compare encoding with retrieval of autobiographical event memory. Although not intended as an encoding task, they found that subjects did recall the information post-scanning, and activation of the hippocampus in relation to this presumed learning was less than that during the recall of autobiographical events. This may speak to the issue alluded to above of whether we are merely imaging re-encoding of information in these experiments. The Ryan *et al.* (2001) data suggest not, although clearly further studies are required, and a task involving encoding of autobiographical information would be particularly useful.

Other than in the Maguire experiments, none of the studies included memory comparison tasks to control for orientating towards the past and recalling specific events or personal information that evokes the same sorts of imagery, people, places, etc. as autobiographical event memory. If such memory control tasks are not included, then specific claims cannot be made about the neural basis of autobiographical memory retrieval—rather the results could be true for remembering any type of material. Hence the inclusion in our (Maguire & Mummery, 1999; Maguire *et al.* 2001, 2001*a,b*) studies of public events (also specific events but not personally relevant) and autobiographical facts (personal but not event-specific).

As is clear from Table 10.1 and the above discussion, the tasks we have used in our various studies have given consistent results across scanning modalities and even within single subjects. The approach we have taken (summarized in Table 10.1), however, has a number of potential disadvantages. First, it is time consuming in terms of subject-specific stimulus preparation. Second, in its current form there is no encoding condition, so potentially the activations observed may be due to re-encoding and not retrieval of memories. However, this re-encoding is true for all of the memory types and does not explain differential activations found for autobiographical event memory retrieval. Third, it may be that subjects remember the prior interview during scanning and not the actual events themselves. However, all subjects reported that the hearing of a statement evoked a sense of the original event in the case of both autobiographical event and public event memories. When directly probed about the prior interview, none of the subjects reported recalling this during scanning. Even if the interview had been recalled during scanning, again it is unlikely that this would have caused the differential effects across the memory types that were in fact found. Furthermore, in their study Ryan *et al.* (2001) scanned subjects where the memory information was elicited from spouses and not the subjects themselves and the same results pertained as when the information was gathered from subjects directly. Also, when we used our paradigm with a memory-impaired patient who was able to perform the tasks during scanning, similar activation patterns to control subjects were found, although the patient was amnesic for the prior interview (Maguire *et al.* 2001*b*).

There are several advantages to the approach we have used: as well as having a range of memory types controlling for personal and context factors, we know the precise timings of events, we have information about salience and emotional aspects associated with the events, the task is easy to operationalize in the scanner, there is a record of subjects' responses (and reaction times) and patients as well as healthy controls are able to perform the task in the scanning environment. While the tasks could be described as involving recognition memory, the memories were originally elicited via recall, and subjects report the statements to elicit the memory of the original events. In cases of real-world complex stimuli such as these, the tasks probably reflect a mixture of recognition and recall, so we refer to the task in generic terms as tapping memory 'retrieval'.

Using this approach we recently investigated the time-scale of neocortical and hippocampal involvement in memory, as well as the type of memories of particular interest to the hippocampus (Maguire *et al.* 2001*a*). Two prominent positions present divergent views on these issues. The oft-termed 'traditional' view (e.g. Squire 1992) is of a hippocampus which has a brief involvement in memory formation and consolidation before neocortical areas assume responsibility for storage and retrieval independent of the hippocampus. The principles of the traditional position are disputed, however, and an alternative view (Nadel & Moscovitch 1997; Nadel *et al.* 2000) holds that the hippocampus is involved during retrieval of both recent and remote memories. In functional neuroimaging terms, the traditional view would predict decreasing hippocampal activity and increasing possibly posterior neocortical activity the more remote the memories. The contrasting view would predict similar levels of hippocampal activation for both recent and remote memories. Rather than make arbitrary categorical decisions about what was recent or remote, we modelled the parametric modulation of responses to autobiographical events and public events by the age of the memories, ranging from the very recent to those dating back to 20 years or more ago. Each event—be it autobiographical or public—constituted an event in an event-related fMRI analysis.

While our design was sensitive enough to detect modulation of left hippocampal activity in relation to memory type (autobiographical events in particular), we failed to

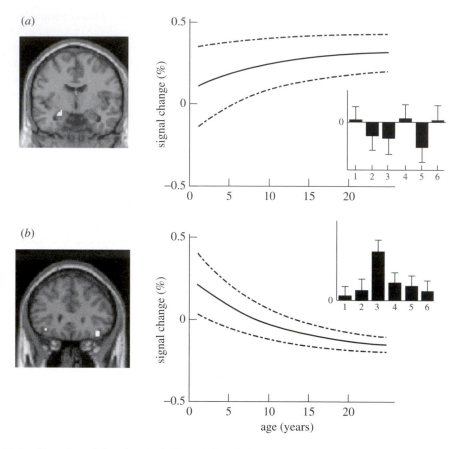

Fig. 10.1. Data from Maguire *et al.* (2001*a*) showing the parametric modulation of brain activity by memory age (see §10.2). The plots show the mean fitted response (full lines) across subjects ± one standard error (dashed lines). The bars inset into each panel depict the parameter estimate for the age effect change for each subject ± one standard error for that subject. N.B. a positive parameter estimate = a decrease with age effect. (*a*) No consistent effect in the hippocampus although there was activation associated with memory type (autobiographical event memory in particular). (*b*) Significant parametric decrease in right ventrolateral prefrontal cortex the more remote the memories; the effect is apparent in all subjects.

find any evidence for sensitivity of this region to the age of memories (Figure 10.1*a*). Half the subjects show no effect for age of memory and half actually show a trend for the opposite effect to the classic theory—actually more hippocampal activation the more remote the memory. Similarly, no consistent pattern was found for public event memories. Categorical comparison of recent (last two years) or remote memory versus the control task both showed activation of the left hippocampus for autobiographical events (as did Ryan *et al.* (2001) bilaterally in their block design study). This result is contrary to the classic view of a time-limited role for the hippocampus but concordant with the view of hippocampal involvement in autobiographical memory retrieval throughout the lifetime, whether memories be very recent or very remote.

We did observe a brain region whose activity was responsive to the age of memories. A right ventrolateral prefrontal region (BA 47) showed increased activation during retrieval of recent autobiographical events and subsequent parametric decrease in activity the more remote the memories became over 20 years or more. From Figure 10.1*b* one can see this effect was apparent for all subjects. Activation of this region has been reported in numerous previous neuroimaging studies of episodic memory retrieval (e.g. Lepage *et al.* 2000) and has been associated with specification of retrieval cues (Fletcher *et al.* 1998). We believe the present findings in ventrolateral prefrontal cortex reflect the degree of integration of the memory trace with relevant contextual information, such as temporal information—more active integration occurring the more recently acquired the memory.

Thus, in our event-related study, we see increased activity in the left hippocampus associated with the retrieval of autobiographical events but not public events. In an fMRI block design analysis, when any of the memory types described in Table 10.1 (autobiographical events, autobiographical facts, public events, general knowledge) was compared with the syllable judgement control task, we observed activation of the left hippocampus as well as a network of other mostly medial and left-lateralized areas (see Maguire *et al.* 2000, and Table 10.1). However, when autobiographical events were compared with any of the other memory types, there was increased activation of the left hippocampus and medial frontal cortex specifically for autobiographical events.

10.3. Functional neuroimaging of a patient

Having outlined in control subjects the basic memory retrieval network and differential responses of certain regions therein, one might consider using functional neuroimaging to examine patients with lesions to specific parts of this network. We recently had the opportunity to study such a patient using fMRI: Jon, a 22 year old man with selective bilateral hippocampal pathology induced by hypoxic–ischaemic episodes of perinatal origin (Vargha-Khadem *et al.* 1997; Gadian *et al.* 2000). When tested, Jon had a striking episodic memory impairment in the context of excellent general knowledge. A great many of the personal events from his life Jon could not remember but he recollected just enough episodic events in detail for viable functional scanning (Maguire *et al.* 2001*b*).

Interestingly, Jon spontaneously made an extra distinction between events that control subjects did not make, namely that some of the autobiographical and public events he clearly remembered, while others he found he knew about but did not truly remember the events occurring. To the interviewer, there was no difference in the amount or sorts of information he recalled between the two memory types. 'Remember' judgements are generally associated with the evocation of a specific, previously experienced episode, while 'knowing' is typically thought to entail a sense of familiarity, but no information about the source of familiarity (Tulving 1985; Gardiner & Java 1991; Knowlton & Squire 1995). In the case of Jon, he makes a kind of remember–know distinction, but he remembers the contexts both for the events he remembers and those that he knows, although he clearly has autonoetic conscious awareness only for the former.

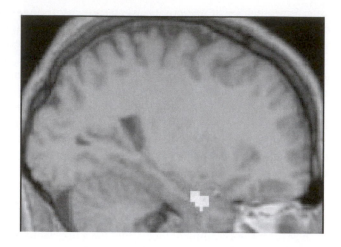

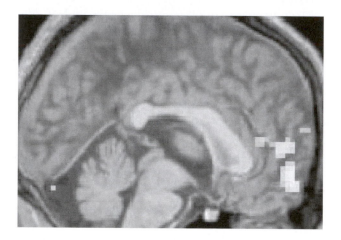

Fig. 10.2. Data from Maguire *et al.* (2001*b*) showing increased activation of patient Jon's hippocampus and medial frontal cortex during retrieval of autobiographical events he remembers (lower scan). Activations are superimposed onto a structural MRI scan of his brain.

Jon's behavioural performance during scanning was comparable with control subjects. Comparison of any of the individual memory tasks with the control task in Jon showed activation of the same network in each case, namely, a similar set of brain regions as in the control subjects (including the hippocampus) but active bilaterally in Jon (see Table 10.1).

A key comparison between autobiographical events that Jon remembered, compared with autobiographical events he merely knew about, showed that the hippocampus bilaterally was more active for personal events that he remembered experiencing. The control subjects also activated the medial frontal region for autobiographical events and indeed so did Jon (see Figure 10.2). Thus, when Jon successfully remembered something, the same set of regions active in control subjects during memory retrieval were active in Jon, albeit bilaterally. The bilateral picture might be a reflection of the early nature of Jon's damage. Of particular interest here, the hippocampi of Jon, despite being damaged, were nevertheless functional. This finding has implications for the study of patients in the clinical context, demonstrating the possibility and importance of assessing the functionality of damaged brain tissue and its contribution to partially or completely retained functions—and functional neuroimaging is well disposed to do this. Findings from Jon enable us to refine further the contribution of the hippocampus in memory retrieval beyond that discernible from control subjects. In controls, autobiographical events were always accompanied by conscious recollection of the episodes. Jon's data show that it is not enough for a memory to be an autobiographical event about which one can recall rich details—there must also be recollection of the experience in order to be of particular interest to the hippocampus. A related issue for future research concerns whether a similar functional anatomical distinction could be observed for remember–know memories in control subjects, where amount and type of details about events are matched, as, for example, in the case of real versus false memories (Dodson *et al.* 2000).

10.4. Functional integration

So far, I have outlined the anatomy of memory retrieval and the response patterns of specific regions in control subjects and also in a patient with selective bilateral hippocampal damage. However, memory is not the property of brain regions operating in isolation but rather of brain networks; thus, functional integration within this network must also be considered. In this regard, structural equation modelling has now been applied to functional neuroimaging data in several studies to estimate effective connectivity (e.g. Büchel *et al.* 1999; Horwitz *et al.* 1999), i.e. the influence one neural system exerts on another (Friston *et al.* 1993). This approach looks at the coupling between the time courses of activity in the relevant brain regions, estimating their connectivity based on putative connections between them.

I will briefly describe analyses examining regional interactions between the main limbic and cortical left-sided areas we observed to be involved in memory retrieval (Maguire *et al.* 2000, 2001*b*). Regions were: medial frontal cortex, temporal pole, hippocampus, anterior middle temporal gyrus, parahippocampal gyrus, retrosplenial cortex, temporo-parietal junction. Although activations in the patient Jon are more bilateral than in control subjects, analysis of effective connectivity was also performed for the left hemisphere in Jon to afford direct comparison with the control subjects. Firstly, in the control subjects, increased connectivity was found in two of the connections during retrieval of autobiographical event memory compared with the other memory tasks, between parahippocampal gyrus and the hippocampus, and between parahippocampal gyrus and temporal pole (Figure 10.3*a*). In contrast, the connection that showed increased connectivity during the retrieval of public events and facts was between lateral temporal cortex and the temporal pole (Figure 10.3*a*).

Extra connections were required in Jon to make the model stable (shown in blue in Figure 10.3*b*), these being between retrosplenial–medial frontal cortices, retrosplenial cortex–hippocampus, and lateral temporal cortex–temporo-parietal junction. For Jon, the only changes in the estimation of effective connectivity were in two connections

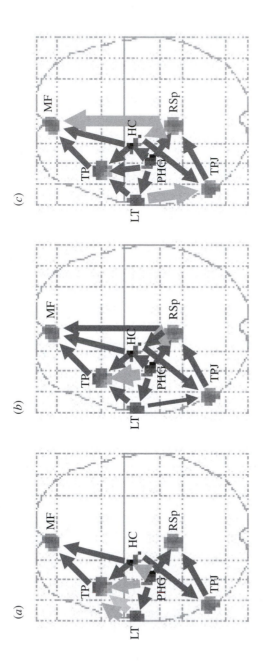

Fig. 10.3. Data from Maguire *et al.* (2001*b*) showing the results of estimation of effective connectivity (§10.4). Transverse views of a glass brain are shown which permits viewing of all significant activations simultaneously. The memory retrieval model comprises the seven brain regions of interest and the connections between them: MF, medial frontal cortex; TP, temporal pole; HC, hippocampus; LT, left anterior middle (lateral) temporal gyrus; PHG, parahippocampal gyrus; RSp, retrosplenial cortex; TPJ, temporo-parietal junction. (*a*) Significant changes in connectivity between regions are shown in green for increased connectivity during retrieval of autobiographical events in particular, in pink for retrieval of public events and in gold for retrieval of general facts. (*b*) The memory retrieval model for the estimation of effective connectivity in patient Jon, with the extra connections required for his model shown in blue. Significant changes in connectivity between regions are shown in green for increased connectivity in particular during retrieval of autobiographical events that Jon remembered. (*c*) Direct comparison of estimates of effective connectivity for control subjects and Jon. In green, the connections where connectivity was increased in Jon compared with the control subjects during retrieval of autobiographical events that were remembered. In gold, the connection where connectivity was increased in Jon compared with the control subjects during retrieval of general facts.

during retrieval of autobiographical event memories that he remembered compared with the other memory tasks, namely increases in connectivity between retrosplenial cortex and hippocampus, and parahippocampal gyrus and temporal pole.

Finally, the estimates of effective connectivity for Jon and the control subjects were directly compared, particularly for the three extra connections that Jon required (Figure 10.3c). In the case of the retrosplenial–hippocampal connection and the retrosplenial–medial frontal cortex connection, effective connectivity was significantly increased for Jon compared with the controls during retrieval of remembered autobiographical events in particular. The lateral temporal–temporo-parietal junction connection was significantly increased in Jon compared with the controls during retrieval of general facts.

Although Jon activates the same network of brain regions as the controls (albeit bilaterally), and with the same pattern of responses in the hippocampus, the communication between regions differs from controls with regard to hippocampal–cortical connectivity. The interplay between regions in response to autobiographical events in particular requires greater interaction in Jon between the hippocampus and retrosplenial cortex, and also increased extra-hippocampal interaction specifically between retrosplenial and medial frontal cortex. That these are possibly not optimal pathways (unlike the parahippocampal–hippocampal pathway as seen in control subjects), and might be capacity-limited, may explain Jon's ability to remember only a limited number of autobiographical events in the context of a general deficit for such memories.

Obviously, there are caveats associated with the estimation of effective connectivity. For example, the models are simple and it is difficult to infer whether changes reflect excitatory or inhibitory influences—and detailed knowledge of human neuroanatomical connectivity is still lacking. Nevertheless, modelling functional integration using neuroimaging may be particularly pertinent in the context of memory breakdown where some clues about impairment may be detectable only at this level.

10.5. Laterality

As mentioned earlier, the balance of findings from functional neuroimaging studies of autobiographical memory show left-sided activations, including left hippocampus. It may be that this is due to the nature of stimulus presentation, e.g. hearing (verbal) statements, although Markowitsch et al. (1997) used a visual stimulus prior to scanning. Recently, we examined personally experienced events but with a less obviously verbal task (Burgess et al. 2001). As described in Table 10.1, in an event-related fMRI study, before scanning, subjects navigated around a virtual reality town and met people who gave them salient objects in different places, these being the autobiographical events, so to speak. During scanning, the subjects again navigated around the town but this time on their way answered forced-choice questions: a content question, namely 'Which object did you get?', then two context questions, namely 'Which object did you get from this person?', and 'Which object did you get in this place?'. Memory for aspects of the context of events resulted in activation of the left hippocampus.

In a parallel behavioural patient study involving left and right temporal lobectomy patients (Spiers et al. 2001), we examined the patients and matched controls using the same virtual reality paradigm. The results confirmed the lateralization. We found that right temporal lobectomy patients were more impaired on several navigation measures, while the left temporal lobectomy patients were more impaired on retrieving aspects of the autobiographical events, such as who they met, when they met them and so on. Of course, these patients had more than just hippocampal tissue removed; nevertheless, the pattern of results is in line with the neuroimaging data outlined. It may be that, in humans, the hippocampal role in spatial memory and navigation (O'Keefe & Nadel 1978) has become more right-hippocampal, while the left human hippocampus has evolved a more general role in supporting autobiographical event memory (Burgess *et al.* 2001; Maguire 2001).

10.6. Conclusions

I have reviewed here the known functional neuroimaging experiments that have examined episodic memory specifically in the form of autobiographical events. As mentioned at the outset, the data perhaps raise more questions than they answer but evidence does seems to suggest a role for the hippocampus in retrieving auto-biographical event memories throughout the lifetime, and a preferential interest of the (possibly left) hippocampus in these memories, in particular. Results from neuro-imaging of a patient with selective bilateral hippocampal pathology underline the need to assess the functionality of remnant tissue as a contributor to the pattern of deficits and preservation seen in such cases. Neuroimaging is well-placed to do this, and in addition is able to examine inter-regional communication where valuable information might also lie. Finally, Jon's data underlines the hippocampal interest in the conscious recollection of events. Whether this reflects the essence of a specifically human memory system remains an open question.

E.A.M. is supported by the Wellcome Trust.

References

Andreasen, N. C., O'Leary, D. S., Cizadlo, T., Arndt, S., Rezai, K., Watkins, G. L., Boles Ponto, L. L. & Hichwa, R. D. 1995 Remembering the past: Two facets of episodic memory explored with positron emission tomography. *Am. J. Psychiatry* **152**, 1576–1585.

Andreasen, N. C., O'Leary, D. S., Paradiso, S., Cizadlo, T., Arndt, S., Watkins, G. L., Ponto, L. L. & Hichwa, R. D. 1999 The cerebellum plays a role in conscious episodic memory retrieval. *Hum. Brain Mapp.* **8**, 226–234.

Brewer, J. B., Zhao, Z., Desmond, J. E., Glover, G. H. & Gabrieli, J. D. E. 1998 Making memories: brain activity that predicts how well visual experience will be remembered. *Science* **281**, 1185–1187.

Büchel, C., Coull, J. T. & Friston, K. J. 1999 The predictive value of changes in effective connectivity for human learning. *Science* **283**, 1538–1541.

Burgess, N., Maguire, E. A., Spiers, H. & O'Keefe, J. 2001 A temporoparietal and prefrontal network for retrieving the spatial context of life-like events. *NeuroImage* **14**, 439–453.

Conway, M. A., Turk, D. J., Miller, S. L., Logan, J., Nebes, R. D., Meltzer, C. C. & Becker, J. T. 1999 A positron emission tomography (PET) study of autobiographical memory retrieval. *Memory* **7**, 679–702.

Crovitz, H. H. & Schiffman, H. 1974 Frequency of episodic memories as a function of their age. *Bull. Psychonom. Soc.* **4**, 517–518.

Dodson, C. S., Koutstaal, W. & Schacter, D. L. 2000 Escape from illusion: reducing false memories. *Trends Cogn. Sci.* **4**, 391–397.

Fink, G. R., Markowitsch, H. J., Reinkemeier, M., Bruckbauer, T., Kessler, J. & Heiss, W. D. 1996 Cerebral representation of one's own past: neural networks involved in autobiographical memory. *J. Neurosci.* **16**, 4275–4282.

Fletcher, P. C. & Henson, R. N. A. 2001 Frontal lobes and human memory—insights from functional neuroimaging. *Brain* **124**, 849–881.

Fletcher, P. C., Shallice, T., Frith, C. D., Frackowiak, R. S. J. & Dolan, R. J. 1998 The functional roles of prefrontal cortex in episodic memory. II. Retrieval. *Brain* **121**, 1249–1256.

Friston, K. J., Frith, C. D. & Frackowiak, R. S. J. 1993 Time-dependent changes in effective connectivity measured with PET. *Hum. Brain Mapp.* **1**, 69–80.

Gadian, D. G., Aicardi, J., Watkins, K. E., Porter, D. A., Mishkin, M. & Vargha-Khadem, F. 2000 Developmental amnesia associated with early hypoxic-ischaemic injury. *Brain* **123**, 499–507.

Gardiner, J. M. & Java, R. I. 1991 Forgetting in recognition memory with and without recollective experience. *Mem. Cognit.* **19**, 617–623.

Hodges, J. R. 1995 Retrograde amnesia. In *Handbook of memory disorders* (ed. A. D. Baddeley, B. A. Wilson & F. N. Watts), pp. 81–107. Chicester: Wiley.

Horwitz, B., Tagamets, M.-A. & McIntosh, A. R. 1999 Neural modelling, functional brain imaging, and cognition. *Trends Cogn. Sci.* **3**, 91–98.

Kapur, N. 1999 Syndromes of retrograde amnesia: a conceptual and empirical synthesis. *Psychol. Bull.* **125**, 800–825.

Knowlton, B. J. & Squire, L. R. 1995 Remembering and knowing: two different expressions of declarative memory. *J. Exp. Psychol.* **21**, 699–710.

Kopelman, M. D., Wilson, B. & Baddeley, A. 1990 *The autobiographical memory interview*. Bury St Edmunds: Thames Valley Test Company.

Lepage, M., Ghaffer, O., Nyberg, L. & Tulving, E. 2000 Prefrontal cortex and episodic memory retrieval mode. *Proc. Natl Acad. Sci. USA* **97**, 506–511.

Liotti, M., Mayberg, H. S., Brannan, S. K., McGinnis, S., Jerabek, P. & Fox, P. T. 2000 Differential limbic–cortical correlates of sadness and anxiety in healthy subjects: implications for affective disorders. *Biol. Psychiatry* **48**, 30–42.

McGuire, P. K., Paulesu, E., Frackowiak, R. S. & Frith, C. D. 1996 Brain activity during stimulus independent thought. *Neuroreport* **7**, 2095–2099.

Maguire, E. A. 2001 Neuroimaging, memory and the human hippocampus. *Rev. Neurol. (Paris)* **157**, 791–794.

Maguire, E. A. & Mummery, C. J. 1999 Differential modulation of a common memory retrieval network revealed by PET. *Hippocampus* **9**, 54–61.

Maguire, E. A., Mummery, C. J. & Büchel, C. 2000 Patterns of hippocampal–cortical interaction dissociate temporal lobe memory subsystems. *Hippocampus* **10**, 475–482.

Maguire, E. A., Henson, R. N. A., Mummery, C. J. & Frith, C. D. 2001a Activity in prefrontal cortex, not hippocampus, varies parametrically with the increasing remoteness of memory. *Neuroreport* **12**, 441–444.

Maguire, E. A., Vargha-Khadem, F. & Mishkin, M. 2001b The effects of bilateral hippocampal damage on fMRI regional activations and interactions during memory retrieval. *Brain* **124**, 1156–1170.

Markowitsch, H. J., Thiel, A., Kessler, J., von Stockhausen, H.-M. & Heiss, W.-D. 1997 Ecphorizing semi-conscious information via the right temporopolar cortex—a PET study. *Neurocase* **3**, 445–449.

Nadel, L. & Moscovitch, M. 1997 Memory consolidation, retrograde amnesia and the hippocampal complex. *Curr. Opin. Neurobiol.* **7**, 217–227.

Nadel, L., Samsonovich, A., Ryan, L. & Moscovitch, M. 2000 Multiple trace theory of human memory: computational, neuroimaging, and neuropsychological results. *Hippocampus* **10**, 352–368.

O'Keefe, J. & Nadel, L. 1978 *The hippocampus as a cognitive map*. Oxford University Press.

Oxbury, S., Oxbury, J., Renowden, S., Squier, W. & Carpenter, K. 1997 Severe amnesia: an unusual late complication after temporal lobectomy. *Neuropsychologia* **35**, 975–988.

Ryan, L., Nadel, L., Keil, K., Putnam, K., Schnyer, D., Trouard, T. & Moscovitch, M. 2001. The hippocampal complex and retrieval of recent and very remote autobiographical memories: evidence from functional magnetic resonance imaging in neurologically intact people. *Hippocampus* **11**, 707–714.

Scoville, W. B. & Milner, B. 1957 Loss of recent memory after bilateral hippocampal lesions. *J. Neurol. Neurosurg. Psychiatry* **20**, 11–21.

Spiers, H. J., Burgess, N., Maguire, E. A., Baxendale, S. A., Hartley, T., Thompson, P. & O'Keefe, J. 2001 Unilateral temporal lobectomy patients show lateralised topographical and episodic memory deficits in a virtual town. *Brain* **124**, 2476–2489.

Squire, L. R. 1992 Memory and the hippocampus: a synthesis from findings with rats, monkeys, and humans. *Psychol. Rev.* **99**, 195–231.

Tulving, E. 1983 *Elements of episodic memory*. Oxford: Clarendon Press.

Tulving, E. 1985 Memory and consciousness. *Can. Psychol.* **26**, 1–12.

Vargha-Khadem, F., Gadian, D. G., Watkins, K. E., Connolly, A., Van Paesschen, W. & Mishkin, M. 1997 Differential effects of early hippocampal pathology on episodic and semantic memory. *Science* **277**, 376–380.

Wagner, A. D., Schacter, D. L., Rotte, M., Koustaal, W., Maril, A., Dale, A. M., Rosen, B. R. & Buckner, R. L. 1998 Building memories: remembering and forgetting of verbal experiences as predicted by brain activity. *Science* **281**, 1188–1191.

Warrington, E. K. 1996 Studies of retrograde memory: a long-term view. *Proc. Natl Acad. Sci. USA* **93**, 13 523–13 526.

11

Episodic-like memory in animals: psychological criteria, neural mechanisms and the value of episodic-like tasks to investigate animal models of neurodegenerative disease

Richard G. M. Morris

The question of whether any non-human species displays episodic memory is controversial. Associative accounts of animal learning recognize that behaviour can change in response to single events but this does not imply that animals need or are later able to recall representations of unique events at a different time and place. The lack of language is also relevant, being the usual medium for communicating about the world, but whether it is critical for the capacity to represent and recall events is a separate matter. One reason for suspecting that certain animals possess an episodic-like memory system is that a variety of learning and memory tasks have been developed that, even though they do not meet the strict criteria required for episodic memory, have an 'episodic-like' character. These include certain one-trial learning tasks, scene-specific discrimination learning, multiple reversal learning, delayed matching and non-matching tasks and, most recently, tasks demanding recollection of 'what, where and when' an event happened. Another reason is that the neuronal architecture of brain areas thought to be involved in episodic memory (including the hippocampal formation) are substantially similar in mammals and, arguably, all vertebrates. Third, our developing understanding of activity-dependent synaptic plasticity (which is a candidate neuronal mechanism for encoding memory traces) suggests that its expression reflects certain physiological characteristics that are ideal components of a neuronal episodic memory system. These include the apparently digital character of synaptic change at individual terminals and the variable persistence of potentiation accounted for by the synaptic tag hypothesis. A further value of studying episodic-like memory in animals is the opportunity it affords to model certain kinds of neuro-degenerative disease that, in humans, affect episodic memory. An example is recent work on a transgenic mouse that over-expresses a mutation of human amyloid precursor protein (APP) that occurs in familial Alzheimer's disease, under the control of platelet derived (PD) growth factor promoter (the PDAPP mouse). A striking age- and amyloid plaque-related deficit is seen using a task in which the mice have to keep changing their memory representation of the world rather than learn a single fact.

11.1. Introduction

The year 1983 witnessed the publication of two important books on learning and memory. One was Mackintosh's monograph *Conditioning and Associative Learning*, which ends with the following passage:

'It should not be forgotten that animals are probably not just machines for associating events. Their ability to represent different attributes of their environments, to respond in terms of spatial, and even of abstract relationships between events, to store and rehearse information for later use, are all important and little-understood capacities whose study requires the development of more sophisticated experimental arrangements than those of simple conditioning experiments.'

(Mackintosh 1983, p. 277.)

The other was Tulving's monograph *Elements of Episodic Memory*, which began with the following (second) sentence:

'As far as we know, members of no other species possess quite the same ability to experience again now, in a different situation and perhaps a different form, happenings from the past, and know that the experience refers to an event that occurred at another time and in another place...'

(Tulving 1983, p. 1.)

Published in the same year, the two passages echo each other's guarded views about the memory capabilities of animals, even to the rhetorical use of 'probably' by Mackintosh and 'quite' by Tulving. Mackintosh's book, a defence of associative conditioning as a theoretical framework for understanding animal learning, leaves the reader in little doubt that he believes principles of conditioning will remain relevant even after the development of the 'more sophisticated experimental arrangements' that his open-minded attitude allows. Tulving also leaves the door open to a more inclusive view of memory in animals, but one is again left with the suspicion, as later articles were to spell out explicitly, e.g. Tulving & Markowitsch (1998), that episodic memory is not for the birds but for man.

Over the nearly 20 years since these books were published, there have been numerous developments in our understanding of the learning and memory capacities of humans and animals, and of the underlying physiological and pharmacological mechanisms that may mediate them. A now widely held view in neuroscience is that there are multiple 'types' of memory and these differ with respect to their psychological characteristics, the anatomical circuits involved and the underlying neural mechanisms of encoding, storage, consolidation and retrieval. Various taxonomic frameworks for thinking about these different forms of memory have been proposed, most having a common generic form (Figure 11.1). All recognize a cardinal distinction between working (short-term) memory and long-term memory. Within the domain of long-term memory, the framework according to Tulving subsumes the further distinction between explicit and implicit memory (Tulving & Schacter 1990; sometimes referred to as 'declarative' and 'non-declarative' memory, Squire 1992). Procedural learning and the formation of perceptual representations are held to be instances of implicit memory; explicit memory encompasses both semantic (fact) and episodic (event) memory. The types of memory specified in this and other taxonomic frameworks are thought to map onto distinct anatomical circuits, although not necessarily in any simple or one-to-one manner.

11.2. Do animals have episodic memory?

The two key problems that confront us in thinking about how to apply Tulving's and other similar taxonomies to animals relate to: (i) the implicit/explicit distinction; and (ii)

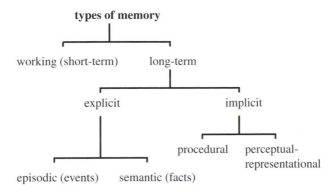

Fig. 11.1. Taxonomy of memory according to Tulving. Working memory is distinguished from long-term memory at the top of the hierarchy. Long-term memory is first subdivided into implicit and explicit forms, with further subdivisions of these into procedural and perceptual representation (implicit), and episodic and semantic (explicit). Other similar taxonomies have been proposed (e.g. Squire 1992).

whether the concepts of semantic knowledge and episodic recollection are relevant to animal memory.

There are several grounds for caution. Assuming the mantle of Morgan (1894) a century before, Macphail (1982, 1998) has long held what he calls an agnostic, others a sceptical, view about the similarities between animal and human cognitive capacities. He argues that the possession of both language and consciousness are two critical differences between humans and animals. As consciousness is central to the distinction between implicit and explicit memory, and as language is the usual medium through which we describe our recollections, this view is also pertinent to episodic memory. Tulving's (1983) definition of it as a mental capacity that requires 'autonoetic' consciousness—a sense of the self—has also to be taken on board. Even if some animal species have forms of awareness that are analogous to particular states of consciousness in humans, Macphail's (1998) review of relevant literature presents cogent arguments for doubting that many (if any) species could possess something as sophisticated as autonoetic consciousness. Were we to accept his view, it would follow that animals cannot, by definition, have anything akin to human episodic memory. We would be left defending the position that all animal learning must be implicit.

There are, however, several grounds for exploring the possibility that some animals may have a form of memory that is explicit and 'episodic' in character, even if we can neither prove that animals are conscious nor be certain that they are not. This category of memory is what Clayton & Dickinson (1998) call 'episodic-like' in which an animal is thought to recall the 'what, where and when' of discrete events and can display this in its overt behaviour. To study this, they have developed an ingenious food-caching paradigm in which scrub jays cache perishable and non-perishable food items (such as worms and peanuts, respectively) and keep track of where they have stored each food type and how long ago. Their work is described more fully in a companion article (Clayton *et al.* 2001). However, before considering this and other experimental paradigms that are potentially 'episodic-like', there are various conceptual issues to consider that provide a basis for believing that the enterprise of studying episodic-like memory in animals is worthwhile.

First, is language as central to episodic memory as Macphail (1998) argues that it is to consciousness? To be sure, language is the usual medium of communication about the events of our lives, but having certain kinds of experiences and recalling them later is surely independent of their overt communication to others. It follows that a species that cannot communicate through language is not logically prevented from having private recollective experiences that may relate to the 'what, where and when' of past events. What is difficult to think about is the nature of this non-human experience—the issue often expressed as 'what might it be like to be a bat'? For, even if we do not communicate our past experience to others, our private recollections of objects and events do generally involve a linguistic code—Macphail's 'aboutness'. The experiential nature of recollection in any animal which lacks language—including, as Macphail discusses at some length, very young infants—cannot be identified with any certainty.

One way forward is to enquire whether there are any aspects of behaviour, other than communication using a representational code, that reflect an animal's knowledge of the world. Here I part company with Macphail for it is my view that non-human vertebrates do segment the world categorically into objects such as food, trees, nests, burrows and so forth. They lack words to describe these entities but it seems to me that they acquire 'factual' knowledge and can display through their behaviour that they 'know' what these and other types of objects are. That is, some animals do have 'aboutness' types of knowledge and they have the neural machinery to acquire it.

Second, is Tulving correct to assert that a particular form of self-consciousness is at the heart of episodic experience—the sense of an event happening to 'me'? A case can be made for seeing the selection pressure that might have led to episodic-like memory, and the brain structures that mediate it, being the need to deal with an important characteristic of the world that applies as much to animals as to humans—dealing with unpredictable events. Events are things that often happen only once and at times when ongoing behaviour is determined by other stimuli, motivational states or incentives. The world is also a dangerous place in which information about the availability of food and the proximity of predators tends not to arrive, as it sometimes does in the laboratory, in the form of ten predictable trials per day. It would therefore be adaptive for a species to evolve a mechanism for enabling its understanding of the world and its behaviour to benefit from encoding information about single events. This 'benefit' need not, as we shall see, necessarily require their explicit recollection—the learning process could be implicit. However, it could be advantageous to encode, store and later recollect events explicitly, and selection pressures must have existed for such memory processes to have evolved. The challenges are: (i) to identify these selection pressures; and (ii) to develop behavioural tasks that can only be carried out effectively were animals to possess a private episodic-like memory system.

This argument leads on to a third reason for being optimistic about identifying episodic-like memory in animals: the ingenuity of comparative and neuropsychologists in developing tasks for exploring animal cognition. When Macphail (1982) first outlined his claim that there were no differences in the learning capacities of vertebrates irrespective of brain size, and that learning by animals was radically different from human learning, he based his argument largely on conditioning tasks—such as habituation, classical conditioning and instrumental conditioning. He did, to be fair, also discuss more complex tasks, such as learning-set and conditional tasks, but the argument felt weaker partly because of frequent appeal to 'contextual' factors to explain away apparent species differences. Since that time, many new perceptual, learning, memory and motor tasks have been invented for animals that a sympathetic reader of Macphail's book at the time might have suspected to be beyond their capabilities. These include tests of mediated conditioning (Holland 1981, 1990), one-trial spatial memory (Foster *et al.* 1999; Steele & Morris 1999) and both scene and object-in-place memory (Gaffan 1994). These and other tasks may be amenable to solution in implicit associative terms, despite their procedural complexity. However, it is unlikely that all of them can be explained in such terms.

One example of this ingenuity is in the perceptual domain: Stoerig and Cowey's (1997) use of a 'commentary key' to reveal that monkeys with unilateral striate cortex lesions can report being unable to see an object that they can accurately reach towards. This is a particularly telling example because the experimental demonstration of 'blindsight' in primates is precisely the kind of phenomenon that a sceptic asserting the importance of language to experience might, until proved otherwise, have expected to be impossible. How could one ever get an animal to 'tell' us about his visual experience unless he had a representational code in which to convey this information? But this experiment suggests that we can.

To summarize this section, cogent arguments have been put forward in relation to the proper definition of episodic memory and the fact that we may never know whether any animal can ever be said to be conscious. Seeking true episodic memory in animals is therefore a forlorn exercise. However, there is value in taking a positive view of the possibility of identifying 'episodic-like' memory in animals: language may not be central to its expression; a sense of the self is not required; and the invention of new behavioural protocols should reveal more about how animals understand and remember their world.

11.3. Does the occurrence of one-trial learning imply that animals form episodic-like memories?

The next step of the argument concerns the issue of whether animals can learn in one trial and what the capacity to do so implies about the types of learning processes they possess.

Many forms of learning, in humans and in animals, require multiple 'trials' before a reliable change in behaviour is seen—the quintessential example being the learning of motor skills. Multiple trials are also a feature of most instances of associative and non-associative conditioning in animals. For example, in habituation (a non-associative waning of responsiveness to repetitive stimulation) and classical conditioning (an associative procedure in which an initially inconsequential stimulus acquires significance by virtue of being repeatedly paired with another stimulus), the overt behavioural change may only become apparent over repeated training trials. In these cases, animal learning theories speak of successive trials causing an incremental change in a parameter specifying the relationship between stimuli, between stimulus and response, or between responses and their outcomes. Formal models exist describing the circumstances in which associative strength changes and accumulates, the parameters affecting the rate of change (Rescorla & Wagner 1972; Mackintosh 1975; Pearce & Hall 1980).

It is important to appreciate that such accounts do not require that an animal encode, store or could ever retrieve information about the separate and unique events that gave rise to that gradual change. Animals have internal representations of stimuli and responses but, formally, the outcome of the learning process is a new value of the parameter that specifies the strength of an association. The value of this parameter may be achieved by several routes and, for that reason, associative learning is said to have the characteristic of 'independence of path' (Figure 11.2). What matters is the value of this parameter at the end of the learning process, like the bottom line of a bank statement, not how it got there.

Newer conditioning paradigms complicate the picture (such as occasion setting), but consideration of this simplest case is sufficient to explore the implications of one versus multitrial learning—for not all types of animal learning do require multiple trials and animals can learn to change their behaviour after a single learning trial. Examples of such rapid learning are poison avoidance, recognition memory, spatial learning and food caching. If a rat is given a single chance to drink saccharin-flavoured water and later made ill by being given a small dose of lithium chloride, it will avoid saccharin-flavoured water for a long time thereafter (Garcia & Koelling 1966). Similarly, if a rat explores one arm of a T-maze during an initial bout of exploration, it will display a strong tendency to explore the other arm of the T-maze later on—the phenomenon of spontaneous alternation (Halliday 1968). Are we to suppose that because learning has taken place so rapidly, an account in terms of implicit associative learning is inapplicable?

The answer to this is 'no'. The occurrence of one-trial learning is not a sufficient condition for asserting that a distinct episodic-like learning process must be engaged. In the case of poison avoidance learning, the value of learning in one trial is obvious—the animal might not survive were learning to take longer. The parameter specifying the

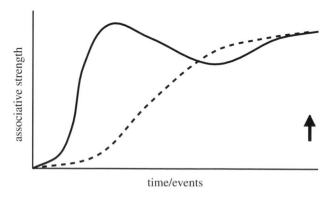

Fig. 11.2. Independence of path assumption of classical associative learning theory. Experience (*x*-axis, time/events) results in increases or decreases of a single parameter, associative strength (*y*-axis). Probing 'memory' at any time point (arrow) involves reading off the value of associative strength without regard to the varied routes taken to the current value. Animals that learn according to the continuous line would display identical performance at the test point to those that learn by the dotted line.

associative relationship between a stimulus (in this case a foodstuff) and its consequence (illness) must increment very rapidly, but the animal is obliged to recall the events associated neither with eating nor with malaise for this learning to be successful. The same is true of humans. Indeed, we may enjoy telling each other stories about the restaurant where we had the oysters and what happened at home later that night, but such stories are what Weiskrantz (1997) calls a 'commentary' on the learning process rather than an integral part of it. For both animals and humans, rapid food-aversion learning and phenomena such as neophobia indicate that learning about what food to eat has evolved to be a conservative specialization (Rozin & Kalat, 1971). Nonetheless, poison avoidance is a curious instance of associative learning for it breaks many of the usual rules—such as the need for the stimulus and its consequence to be closely contiguous in time. Careful analysis has revealed, however, that it displays a number of the properties of other widely studied forms of associative learning and, in the view of most, a sufficient number to obviate the need to invoke any specialized learning process other than that of associative conditioning (Dickinson 1980). Similarly, although the argument will not be laid out in detail, implicit processes such as judgements of familiarity can mediate certain kinds of one-trial object recognition memory. That it also occurs in one trial is not in itself a basis for supposing that a distinct form of learning and memory is involved.

What are the necessary features of episodic-like memory in animals? The key feature, in my view, is not just the occurrence of learning in a single trial but the evolution of some system of explicit encoding and recall. Whereas associative learning theories hold that multiple events have their effect on an animal's later behaviour by incrementing and decrementing a single parameter called associative strength, the possession of episodic-like memory has to do with being able to encode and recall specific features of such events. Not only might an animal be tested with respect to where something has happened, what happened and when, but the implicit/explicit distinction has also to be considered. The experimental test, as I see it, is as follows:

> We need to devise behavioural tasks that somehow distinguish between the changes in behaviour that occur because an animal remembers one or more prior events, and changes in behaviour that occur merely because these prior events have happened.
>
> (Adapted from Morris & Frey 1997, p. 1495.)

This is the challenge and, with the possible exception of the work of Clayton & Dickinson (1998) on food caching, few if any of the behavioural tasks we have at our disposal today yet meet it.

11.4. In what kinds of animal learning and memory tasks might an explicit episodic-like memory system become engaged?

Numerous learning and memory tasks have been developed for animals that are 'episodic-like' in character. Certain tasks relate particularly to an animal's experience of the context in which learning takes place, others to the memory of prior events. Both are sufficiently different from classical associative learning tasks that they merit close attention. In both cases, a strictly implicit learning process may be sufficient for learning, once supplemented by abstract concepts such as recency or familiarity.

However, whether it is always the most effective way of learning is another matter—explicit encoding and recall may sometimes be better.

The first group can be categorized as unusual discrimination learning tasks. These include tasks in which the solution of a series of problems depends upon, or at least could benefit from, memory of the scene against which the discrimination takes place. Prominent amongst these is a range of ingenious tasks developed by Gaffan prompted by a particular theoretical view of episodic memory. Working with monkeys, Gaffan & Harrison (1989) discovered that fornix lesions interfered with the acquisition of ambiguous object discrimination learning tasks when the ambiguity about which of two objects signalled reward could be resolved with respect to the direction an animal was facing in a complex scene. This finding led him to think about the experiential aspects of episodic recall, arguing that:

> 'When a human subject recalls specific information about some discrete, personal experience from the past, the recall process often involves a covert reconstruction of a spatially organised complex scene.'

> (Gaffan 1991, p. 262.)

Because securing propositional descriptions of the experiential aspects of recall in monkeys is not feasible, Gaffan and his colleagues went on to develop touch-screen based tasks in which a large variety of different scenes are projected onto a screen (Gaffan 1994). The role of these scenes is either to provide a set of stimuli to be discriminated in their own right, or to serve as backgrounds for other object discriminations that take place against them. A consistent finding is that such tasks are learned incredibly fast. They are also remembered very well and experimental damage to the hippocampus–fornix–mamillary bodies, a connected group of structures implicated in episodic memory in humans, causes impairments in learning (Gaffan & Parker 1996; Murray *et al.* 1998; Parker & Gaffan 1998; Gaffan & Parker 2000). Gaffan argues that this protocol is a model of episodic memory in the monkey.

The question arises of whether the monkeys are obliged to use explicit memory to encode and store the information necessary to solve these tasks. Both the faster speed of learning and the sensitivity to damage in particular brain areas differ from that seen for more conventional discrimination tasks, but we must also ask the information-processing question of whether the task meets Clayton & Dickinson's (1998) criteria for an episodic-like task, i.e. recall of 'what, where and when'. Leaving aside the issue of self-identity on the part of the monkeys, it is possible that the task involves no more than a combination of recognition and association. The monkey does not have to recall the scene during test trials—it is presented to him and it has only to be recognized. Moreover, it might be recalling which of two typographical 'objects' in the scene was associated with reward, using the background scene as a cue for recall, but as the scenes and objects associated with them are unique, the task can actually be solved through differential association with reward. A strictly implicit solution is therefore possible. In addition, one could argue, in keeping with Warrington and Weiskrantz's classical analysis of the effects of providing recall cues to amnesic persons, that the very provision of the background scenes during test trials would differentially aid the performance of lesioned monkeys (see McCarthy & Warrington 1990). Thus, while fornix-lesioned monkeys showed a deficit in this task, one wonders if that deficit would actually be larger if the distinctive scenes used during training were sometimes omitted during testing. Might normal monkeys be able to recall the scene with which individual typographical characters had been associated and, in doing so, use this explicit recall to help retrieve which of the two objects was associated with reward? Gaffan's scene-specific memory task seems to be neither an instance of memory for 'what, where and when' nor one that requires explicit recall. The task remains a pioneering and valuable approach to thinking about the experiential character of episodic memory in animals and could be adapted further.

The second group of tasks to be considered, this time studied using rodents, are those in which the animal has to keep changing what it should do in the light of what it has just done. A now classical paradigm for looking at this is Olton's 'radial maze' in which rats are required to search for single food items at the ends of each arm of the maze (Olton *et al.* 1979). The animal is confronted with the travelling salesman's problem of visiting all the places at which he can find food while minimizing the distance travelled. It is a task in which the animal must keep track of its own actions. Spontaneous alternation (Halliday 1968), delayed non-matching to place in a T-maze (Rawlins 1985; Aggleton *et al.* 2001) and the delayed matching to place (DMP) task in the water maze (Morris 1983; Steele & Morris 1999) are also examples of conceptually similar tasks that are so readily learned as to be almost spontaneously expressed (Figure 11.3). Although each of these tasks is spatial, analogous non-spatial tasks also exist (Ennaceur & Delacour 1988).

Each of these tasks might be learned using an episodic-like memory system. In delayed non-matching to place in a T-maze, the animal might remember several aspects of what happened on the previous trial—where it went, what food it ate at the end of the maze arm, how long ago this eating happened. Unfortunately, there is an ostensibly more parsimonious solution. This is that the cues associated with turning left or turning right could acquire 'familiarity' through exposure on the sample trial and the animal need do no more than learn the rule, in the case of non-matching to place, of avoiding familiar cues when it confronts them on the choice trial. No explicit recall of prior events is then necessary—the task can be solved implicitly using familiarity.

A similar objection has been raised by Griffiths *et al.* (1999) to an episodic-like account of performance in the DMP task in the water maze (Steele & Morris 1999). In this, rats are trained to find a hidden escape platform that moves location between days. There are several trials each day, usually four, and the rats' behaviour very rapidly settles down to a pattern in which they show a long escape latency on trial one and a short latency on trial two and thereafter (Figure 11.3c). In fact, learning takes place so rapidly that one wonders if the animal has to learn any 'rule' for solution at all. Griffiths *et al.* (1999) argue that this task could also be solved by familiarity—the animal has only to approach the set of cues that are most familiar, these being the ones associated with the last position in which the platform has been placed. This objection cannot be definitively dismissed, but I would make two points:

First, it is not clear that there are any overt cues associated with the most recent goal location, in or around the testing arena, that are more or less familiar than any others. The extra-maze cues provide the basis for the animal forming a representation or 'map' of space. This map is learned rapidly and remains stable over the days or weeks of testing. All that changes is the entry into the map of where the hidden platform has last been located. This location is unmarked by local cues, it is a 'place' within the animal's map that has to be recalled rather than merely recognized at the start of a trial. To

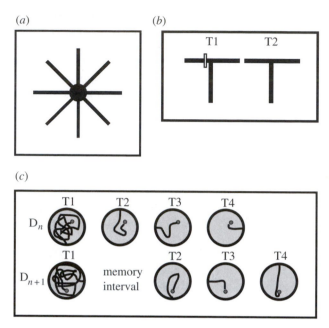

Fig. 11.3. One-trial spatial learning tasks that require an animal to keep changing its memory representation. (*a*) The radial maze: many protocols are possible but the typical procedure involves the rat searching for food at the end of each maze arm. The best solution minimizes revisits to arms from which the food has already been taken. Short periods of confinement in the central area prevent the use of turning algorithms that minimize memory demands. (*b*) T-maze delayed non-matching: on trial 1 (T1), the rat is required to go in one or the other direction from the stem (bottom) to secure food. There is a free choice on T2, but the rat must remember to go to the opposite arm to that just visited. The task has an episodic-like character and is exquisitely sensitive to hippocampal disruption, but can also be solved by familiarity. (*c*) Water maze delayed matching to place (DMP). Rats are given four trials per day to a platform that moves location between days (rows). Memory formed during T1 of each day is tested on T2 and subsequent trials. The memory delay interval can be manipulated. The task is exquisitely sensitive to hippocampal disruption. See §11.4 for discussion of whether this task can be solved by familiarity.

object that performance could rely exclusively on the recognition of what is familiar and what is not also requires us to believe that the rat can recognize, from the starting point, the familiarity of cues that may only be visible from the goal location. Foster *et al.* (1999) have recently modelled performance in this and a standard reference memory task in the water maze using a temporal difference learning algorithm. Their work revealed that an associative solution to both tasks was possible, but the solution of the DMP task relied upon: (i) the formation of a map of space using hippocampal 'place-cells' (O'Keefe 1976); and (ii) the ability of the animal to recall goal locations in the map from start locations at any point in the maze. The model therefore contains a cryptic form of episodic-like recall. Interestingly, Foster *et al.* (1999) show that the standard reference memory task of finding an escape platform that stays in a single location does not require a map of space, nor recall of the goal location. The animal need learn only to execute appropriate approach behaviour at locations that are individuated by place cell firing but these cells are not necessarily part of a map.

Second, performance of the DMP task is exquisitely sensitive to disruption of *N*-methyl-D-aspartic acid (NMDA) receptor-dependent synaptic plasticity (Steele & Morris 1999). Performance of the DMP task is disrupted completely by hippocampal lesions, even at short memory delay intervals, arguably because recall of information from the animal's map of space cannot occur without synaptic transmission in this brain area. Accordingly, to examine the neural mechanisms of episodic-like memory encoding independently of performance, we need a way of disrupting it in a manner that does not, or at least may not, affect retrieval. Work on the underlying neurobiological mechanisms of learning and memory in animals is currently at a transition point. We are moving from studies searching for process dissociations on the basis of discrete lesions which permanently damage brain tissue through to studies that use reversible, pharmacological manipulations (Izquierdo & Medina 1998; Riedel *et al.* 1999; McGaugh 2000). Our developing understanding of glutamate neurobiology has given us a range of tools with which we can manipulate function within discrete brain areas in highly selective ways to investigate learning mechanisms (Danysz *et al.* 1995). Intra-hippocampal infusion of the NMDA receptor antagonist D-2-amino-5-phosphopenta-noic acid (D-AP5) is one way of achieving this. Steele & Morris (1999) found that doing this had no effect on performance at a short memory delay of 15 s between trials 1 and 2 but disrupted performance at the longer interval of 2 h (Figure 11.4). Our preferred interpretation of this finding is that the animal encodes information about the act of escaping from the water and where this happened at the end of each trial using a hippocampal NMDA receptor-dependent mechanism. Navigational performance on the

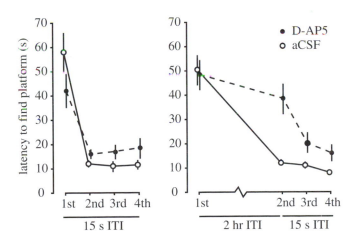

Fig. 11.4. Intra-hippocampal microinfusion of the NMDA antagonist D-AP5 causes a delay-dependent impairment of one-trial spatial memory. Rats implanted with bilateral infusion cannulae aimed at the dorsal hippocampus were trained for on the DMP task to asymptote. They were then tested with D-AP5 or artificial cerebrospinal fluid (aCSF) (vehicle) infusions over a series of days, with these treatments given within-subject on alternate days. The inter-trial memory delay interval (ITI) between trials 1 and 2 was varied between 15 s (short-term memory) and 2 h (long-term memory) with all other trials at 15 s. Averaged across days, there was an impairment on the second trial of the day at the long memory delay. Data from Steele & Morris (1999, experiment 3).

succeeding trial would be guided by recall, not recognition, of this context-event association encoded and stored during the preceding trial.

Unfortunately, the water maze DMP task shares various limitations with Gaffan's scene-memory task. One is that only a single kind of event can ever happen at the end of each trial—escape from the water—and for this reason is an inadequate analytic tool to look at 'what, where and when'. The same limitation applies to the paired comparison object recognition memory task of Ennaceur (Ennaceur & Delacour 1988). What we need are tasks in which several different kinds of events can occur. This is precisely the problem to which Clayton & Dickinson (1998) so successfully turned their attention in their studies of memory for food caches by scrub jays.

11.5. Are there any constraints on the anatomical systems involved in episodic-like memory?

A separate reason for suspecting that mammals, and perhaps all vertebrates have an episodic-like memory system is because of similarities in the structure of particular areas of their brains. Mammals contain all the cortical areas in the human brain that have been implicated in episodic memory from clinical and functional imaging studies on humans—although some comparative anatomists question the development of the frontal cortex in rodents (Preuss 1995). At least one of these structures, the hippocampus, has an evolutionary well-conserved structure. It contains similar cell types and apparently similar connectional architecture in humans and non-human primates—and its structure in rodents is strikingly similar albeit with about 10 times fewer cells (Amaral & Witter 1989; Amaral & Insausti 1990) and more extensive inter-hemispheric connections. Parsimony dictates consideration of the possibility that the same algorithm is being carried out in human and non-human brains in this and other relevant brain structures. Even if the information upon which it is operating is different by virtue of the human possession of language, there are no obvious cellular, connectional or biochemical differences to which we might relate the supposed differences in conscious awareness of animals and humans.

Several neural network models of episodic-like memory have been proposed (Marr 1971; McNaughton & Morris 1987; Gluck & Granger 1993; Granger *et al.* 1996; Rolls & Treves 1998; Redish 1999). Despite differences of emphasis, these generally focus on certain distinctive features of hippocampal excitatory circuitry that may enable particular types of associations to be formed. The architecture of the dentate gyrus, with a much larger number of cells than the layer II neurons of the entorhinal cortex that are afferent to it, has a structure that is ideal for orthogonalizing inputs. The architecture of area CA3 is remarkable, with each cell receiving about 3500 perforant path connections that bypass the dentate gyrus, each receiving around 10 000 feedback connections from other CA3 neurons (the longitudinal-association pathway) and, most intriguing of all, a very limited number of mossy fibre inputs from the dentate gyrus. In the rat brain, mossy fibre axons of individual dentate gyrus cells make a total of 15 ± 2 connections in CA3 as they traverse through the thousands of cells that lie in a single lamella plane, with each CA3 cell receiving about 50 mossy fibre terminals. No one working on the hippocampus can look at this unique neuronal architecture without wondering what algorithm it computes. Other brain areas have architectures that immediately suggest their function, such as the coincidence-detecting 'delay lines' of the nucleus laminaris used for prey localization by the barn owl (Konishi 1986). Yet CA3 remains a mystery. Rolls & Treves (1998), in proposing that CA3 is an autoassociative type of memory device, have made the interesting suggestion that its architecture is ideal for controlling the conditions of memory encoding, via mossy fibre activation, somewhat separately from the determinants of cued recall. Lisman (1999) has proposed a somewhat heretical model consisting of reciprocal interconnections between the dentate gyrus and CA3. Synaptic potentiation in area CA3 of the hippocampus is thought to encode traces relevant to sequences of events occurring within episodes, and maintain sequence order despite the essentially passive nature of trace storage at synapses of the longitudinal-association pathway. During retrieval, CA3 neurons are, speculatively, held to project information retrieved in response to items earlier in a sequence back to the mossy cells of the dentate gyrus. There, pattern completion corrects recall errors, the corrected recall pattern is then projected forward to CA3 to retrieve the next item in the sequence, and so on. Lisman's (1999) model also allows a role for context to bias the firing of CA3 cells (achieved by the direct perforant path input to CA3), with recoding of the hippocampal representation back into a neocortical form accomplished by area CA1.

Area CA1 of the hippocampus also has an architecture whose complexity is often underestimated. Most writers about hippocampal neuroanatomy emphasize the Schaffer-collateral inputs from CA3 which synapse *en passant* as they course through the transverse plane. However, recent research indicates that CA1 may also receive a direct, topographic excitatory input from layer III of the entorhinal cortex. The existence of this pathway is highly controversial (see the articles in *Hippocampus* 1994) but it raises the possibility that information might be recalled from the cortex to the hippocampus by a route that bypasses the orthogonalizing dentate gyrus and associative machinery of CA3. This route may enable representations retrieved from memory to be integrated with other information that has been newly processed. Perhaps their intersection is the basis of context-event associations?

11.6. Are there any constraints on the physiological mechanisms involved in episodic-like memory?

Given current emphasis on the role of the hippocampus in explicit memory, it is also worth considering whether the physiological properties of the activity-dependent synaptic plasticity that has been intensively studied in this brain area relate in any way to episodic-like memory. One well-known idea is that long-term potentiation (LTP) is a suitable model of the synaptic changes that might be involved in the formation of memory traces. Proponents of this hypothesis have often noted that three properties of LTP—input specificity, associativity and persistence—are suitable properties of a physiological memory mechanism. Evidence in favour of the generic 'Synaptic Plasticity and Memory' hypothesis is gradually getting stronger as various objections raised by early critics are addressed by ever more sophisticated experiments (for a review, see Martin *et al.* 2000). For the purposes of the present discussion, however, these basic properties are as suited to a strictly implicit learning machine as to any other.

What may be less well appreciated is that more recent physiological studies have revealed additional properties of LTP (and its companion long-term depression, LTD) that are ideal for mediating a particular form of memory mechanism. These additional properties include metaplasticity, silent synapses, the apparently digital nature of the synaptic change at individual terminals, and synaptic tagging. Two of these properties seem particularly pertinent to episodic-like memory.

First, when LTP is studied in whole animals *in vivo*, as in the classical work of both Bliss & Lomo (1973) and McNaughton *et al.* (1978), successive tetanizations cause an incremental change in the size of evoked field potentials. This graded increase has sometimes been likened to learning which, so the analogy goes, also increments gradually. But is this really what is happening at the level of individual synapses? To study this, Petersen *et al.* (1998) used brain slices *in vitro* and explored the effects of minimal stimulation until, in the limit, they would have been activating only single fibres. In the Schaffer collateral input to CA1, it is known that each fibre makes, on average, one *en passage* synaptic bouton per pyramidal cell as it passes through area CA1. It follows that many fibres were activated at which it was possible to examine the consequences of attempting to induce LTP at single synapses. Using both extra- and intracellular recording in neurons of the target CA1 region of the hippocampus, Petersen *et al.* (1998) observed that the gradual incremental increase in the extracellular field potential that followed successive tetanizations was accompanied by step-like changes at the level of single fibres. Single-fibre potentials jumped from their baseline level to their maximal level at varying times but, once potentiated, could be potentiated no further by later bouts of high frequency stimulation. The implication is that, at the level of individual synapses, LTP in the hippocampus is a digital change in synaptic strength—from zero (or weak) to strong. As activity patterns in CA3 project to CA1 by axons that enable any given CA3 cell to project onto a particular CA1 cell at (on average) only one synaptic terminal, such a system has the potential to change the strength of individual synaptic weights to the maximum allowable level following single events. That is, patterns of neural activity in CA3 could be associated with patterns of firing in area CA1 and, with a single pairing, realize maximal synaptic change at many of the thousands of individual synapses that connect neurons that were firing.

A second of the newer properties of LTP relates to whether synaptic potentiation necessarily results in the formation of a lasting memory trace or is merely creating the potential for creating a lasting trace. Episodic memory occurs continuously and automatically—we cannot decide to turn off what Frey and I have previously described as the 'automatic recording of attended experience' (Morris & Frey 1997). Unpredictable events happen to us and, whatever our separate intentions or concerns at the time such events happen, we necessarily make some record of attended events even if that command of attention has been involuntary. Our theoretical supposition is that this is what LTP in the hippocampus is doing all the time—automatically recording traces of experience. The Frey and Morris hypothesis further suggests that very few of the synaptic changes that occur as part of this ongoing record are preserved. The vast majority decay to baseline.

If this idea is on the right lines, we must then ask what determines whether synaptic potentiation decays, or that it persists and becomes the basis for lasting memory traces in the brain? The recent research revealing additional properties of LTP suggests that the past and future history of postsynaptic neuronal activation is the critical determinant. Importantly, whether a trace lasts a short or a long time does not have to be determined at the time that the trace is first formed—persistence can be influenced heterosynaptically by other activity patterns impinging on the target neuron over a window of time (of about an hour). This cellular property of LTP could be very relevant to episodic-like memory because it provides a potential mechanism for distinguishing between creating the potential for lasting memory traces and ensuring that a lasting trace is actually encoded.

The physiological studies first suggesting this possibility were reported by Frey & Morris (1997, 1998a). Using hippocampal brain slices *in vitro*, they found that application of a weak tetanus (21 pulses, 100 Hz) to one stratum radiatum pathway that ordinarily induced long-term potentiation decaying over 4 h (early LTP) could be made to induce a more persistent LTP (lasting > 8 h). This happened if stimulation with the weak tetanus was closely followed (1998a) or preceded (1997) by the application of three strong tetani (3×100 pulses, 100 Hz) to a separate input that successfully induced late LTP. Our explanation for this result centred on the synthesis of plasticity proteins in the target neurons. On the basis of data secured using the protein synthesis inhibitors anisomycin and emetine, Frey and Morris suggested that 'synaptic tags' set at the postsynaptic terminals of the weakly stimulated pathway sequester plasticity related proteins whose synthesis is induced in response to strong tetanization. These proteins, probably synthesized in the cell body, are presumed to travel in a non-targeted manner via transport mechanisms in the dendrite. Their function is to stabilize or 'consolidate' the otherwise transient synaptic potentiation; elegant studies in culture by Martin *et al.* (1997) have established the mechanism at the single cell level. Put together (see Figure 11.5), the input specificity of transient or lasting synaptic change is determined by the pattern of glutamatergic synaptic activation that, in addition to causing transient potentiation, also sets synaptic tags. The persistence of such changes is, however, determined by the history of activation of the neuron. This history governs the intersection between the availability of plasticity proteins and synaptic tags that have not yet reset to baseline.

At one level of analysis, the synaptic tagging hypothesis of the persistence of LTP is no more than a possible solution to the conceptual problem of targeting plasticity proteins to dendritic sites at which they are needed. However, this molecular machinery also endows the memory system of which it is a part with an almost magical property. This is to allow the memory system to 'keep its options' open with respect to the persistence of memory traces until and if other events occur that might influence whether or not a permanent trace should be created. The 'decision' to make a long-term memory does not have to be made at the time that the event to be remembered actually happens—a key contribution to the decision can occur beforehand or afterwards. The time window of decision making is determined, in part, by the kinetics of the synthesis and intracellular distribution of plasticity proteins. Such a property is ideal within that subset of the episodic memory system that automatically encodes attended experience. To speculate, we might think of the hippocampal formation as mediating this automatic component of episodic memory and the frontal lobes as the substrate of the intentional, executive parts of the system. In the intentional part, the focus of attention is on a limited body of new information that has to be learned—such as a list of paired associates in an experiment on cued recall. In contrast, in the automatic component of episodic memory, the subject has much less control over what gets temporarily

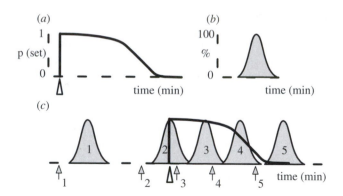

Fig. 11.5. The synaptic tagging hypothesis of long-term potentiation (LTP). (*a*) Synaptic tag. In addition to inducing a transient form of synaptic potentiation (lasting at most a few hours), induction of LTP is also thought to set a 'synaptic tag' at activated terminals, which will reset after a few hours. (*b*) Plasticity proteins. Relevant gene activation, probably through heterosynaptic activation, sets in train the synthesis and intracellular distribution of plasticity proteins. These travel diffusely from their site of synthesis, whether the cell body or at local sites of dendritic synthesis. (*c*) Dynamics of tag–protein interactions. Tag–protein interactions are responsible for stabilizing or consolidating the otherwise transient potentiation. These interactions can occur when the availability of proteins intersects temporally with the activation of synaptic tags (positions 2, 3 and 4 in the diagram). Based on Frey & Morris (1998*b*).

recorded. The hippocampus records the incidentals of life as they happen to us on a minute-by-minute, hour-by-hour basis—we cannot stop ourselves from doing this. However, the mechanism of encoding is one that results in erasure of a very large part of this record of events within a matter of hours unless other events happen that could stabilize memory traces selectively. Behavioural experiments to examine this speculation from the physiological properties of LTP are underway.

11.7. Does episodic-like memory in animals become dysfunctional in models of human disease and, if so, can we use such models to develop new therapies?

One value of working with animals is to develop models of human or animal diseases with a view to understanding them better and developing appropriate therapeutic strategies. Certain brain diseases, such as Alzheimer's disease, are well known to affect episodic memory during an early stage of its insidious progression. The importance of using appropriate behavioural tests of learning and memory is illustrated by recent work using transgenic mice engineered to be 'models' of aspects of the disease.

It has long been known that mice over-expressing human mutant amyloid precursor protein (hAPP) show learning deficits. However, a puzzle that has eluded explanation is the apparent lack of relationship between these deficits and the progressive β-amyloid plaque formation that these mice sometimes display. In the standard reference version of the water maze in which the animals search for a hidden escape platform in a fixed location in space (Morris *et al.* 1982), hAPP mice are impaired throughout the life span—before and after amyloid plaque deposition (D'Hooge *et al.* 1996; Nalbantoglu *et al.* 1997; Moechars *et al.* 1999). Puzzled by the apparent lack of relationship to this striking age-related neuropathological change, Chen *et al.* (2000) wondered whether the water maze reference memory task was the appropriate behavioural assay. They decided to explore whether PDAPP mice, in which a human mutation of amyloid precursor protein is over-expressed under the control of a platelet derived growth factor promoter (Games *et al.* 1995), show age- and amyloid plaque-related learning or memory deficits using a more 'episodic-like' training protocol.

Accordingly, a new water maze training procedure was developed in which the mice had to keep changing their memory representation of the environment in much the same way as in the DMP task. A preliminary study using a version of the DMP task adapted for mice was unsuccessful, partly because performance was so poor in the PDAPP group that they failed to learn to return to the most recent location of the platform. To improve performance, yet retain the important feature that the memory representation of where escape is possible has to be updated frequently, a serial reversal procedure was used. A series of separate spatial learning problems was given to the mice, each of which had to be learned to a pre-set criterion of performance. When the mice reached this criterion, whether transgenic or control, they were then switched to learning a new platform location. Reversal learning, as usually analysed, involves repeatedly switching the reward assignments of two cues with all other cues being irrelevant. This new procedure is analogous excepting that the significance and spatial relationship between the extra-maze cues—the animal's map of space—remains constant; all that changes is the location of the hidden escape platform within this map. Associative learning theory can offer a satisfactory account of varying rates of learning in such a procedure (often couched in terms of varying attention to relevant and irrelevant cues—see Mackintosh 1983, p. 252), but the procedure is 'episodic-like' in the following sense. The animal cannot treat the extra-maze cues as irrelevant and so ignore them because they provide the basis for its successful navigation. Nor can the animal use only its map of space to recall the current platform location. Instead, and as in the DMP task, the animal must either keep updating its map of space by ensuring that only one possible location of the platform can be recalled, or it must use recency as an additional cue for distinguishing the multiple long-term traces of where the platform might be located.

The results revealed that heterozygous PDAPP mice displayed both an age-independent and an age-related deficit in learning. Consistent with previous findings, the age-independent effect was apparent in learning the first of the series of spatial problems. This was to be expected because the training procedure, with the sole exception of training to criterion, is identical to a standard reference memory protocol as previously studied by other groups. However, as training continued on successive problems, an age-related deficit became apparent. Young PDAPP mice became successively better at learning to a point where they were indistinguishable from littermate controls; middle-aged and old PDAPP were even more impaired in an age-related manner (Figure 11.6). This learning impairment was apparent in both a cross-sectional study (in which mice were first trained at different ages) and a longitudinal study (in which mice, first trained when they were young, were re-tested throughout the life span). It also correlated with β-amyloid (Aβ) plaque burden, with age itself removed as a covariate (see Chen *et al.* 2000). Training on other tasks,

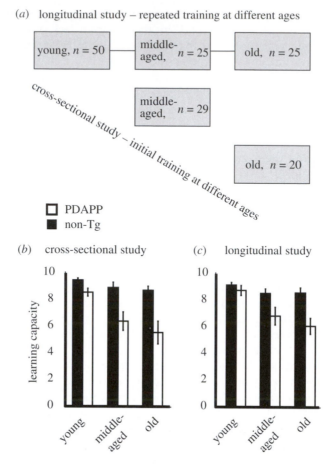

Fig. 11.6. Use of serial-reversal to monitor the age- and plaque-related decline in 'learning capacity' in transgenic mice. (*a*) Longitudinal study—repeated training at different ages. Chen *et al.* (2000) used both a longitudinal and a cross-sectional design to examine the capacity of heterozygous PDAPP mice and their non-transgenic littermate controls to learn a series of spatial problems. (*b*) Cross-sectional study. The results showed that the 'learning capacity' (the total number of problems that could be acquired in a ten-day period) declined in an age-related manner in the PDAPP mice. This decline in learning also correlated with the age-related deposition of amyloid plaques. (*c*) Longitudinal study.

including navigation to a visible escape platform and a test of object recognition memory, revealed a further degree of selectivity to these animals' learning deficit.

These findings have an important practical implication. They indicate that the over-expression of Aβ and/or the frank deposition of Aβ plaques are associated with disturbed cognitive function and, importantly, suggest that some but not all tests of learning and memory are suitable behavioural assays of the progressive cognitive deficits associated with Alzheimer's disease-type pathologies. As disturbances of episodic memory are an early symptom of the disease, there is value in creating animal models of aspects of the disease using 'episodic-like' tests. In addition, two recent reports (Janus *et al.* 2000; Morgan *et al.* 2000) indicate that immunization against human Aβ in closely related hAPP mice can not only protect against the neuropathological deposition of amyloid plaques, as first shown by (Schenk *et al.* 1999), but can also prevent this age-related learning deficit from developing. It is noteworthy that variants of the 'episodic-like' DMP task and this serial reversal procedure were used in these successful vaccination experiments.

11.8. Conclusion

The primary aim of this paper has been to point to reasons for thinking that mammals may possess an 'episodic-like' memory system even though Tulving's formal definition of episodic memory puts the concept outside the realm of experimental study in non-human species. In developing episodic-like memory tests for animals, I have suggested that the current emphasis on one-trial learning may be misplaced; many one-trial tasks are ambiguous with respect to the demands they place on implicit versus explicit memory processes. The focus now needs to be on developing behavioural protocols that capture the essentially 'explicit' nature of recall. An episodic-like system must, to be sure, have the capability of encoding unique events and a newly discovered property of LTP suggests that activity-dependent synaptic plasticity at the level of the individual synapse may be digital. However, the encoding mechanism might also be one in which the creation of a transient but automatic record of attended events does not preclude the selective stabilization of memory traces at other times through heterosynaptic interactions (Frey & Morris 1998*b*; Bailey *et al.* 2000).

In contrast to encoding and storage, episodic recall is primarily about 'mental time travel', reconstructing the past at the point of retrieval and knowing that it is the past. The behavioural criteria for identifying this mental state in animals remain ill-defined but they must be distinguished from the control of behaviour by parameters that merely accumulate value (associative strength, familiarity, etc.) independently of the path taken to that value. There must also be some preservation of the 'what, where and when' of events. Few of the tasks that have been developed to model different types of memory meet these strict definitional criteria. However, certain tasks, such as serial reversal learning, one-trial scene and object-in-place memory, delayed matching and non-matching to place are exquisitely sensitive to hippocampal lesions and to the selective disruption of hippocampal synaptic plasticity. While the argument is circular, it seems likely that these tasks are mediated by the same neural networks that subserve episodic recall in humans—including the hippocampal formation. Pending the development of analytically less ambiguous tasks, their use to investigate animal models of neurodegenerative disease is valuable pragmatically, as they could provide an effective way of evaluating new therapeutic strategies.

There remains at least one key issue where the argument of this paper differs sharply from that of Macphail's (1998) discussion of the evolution of consciousness. We have seen that Macphail asserts that animals have only an implicit learning system, that the development of language by humans is central to our having consciousness, and that animals, lacking language, cannot be conscious as we are. It follows from this argument that they cannot have anything like episodic recall. However, he also suggests that, in humans, the hippocampal formation is one of a group of structures that mediate explicit recall. The problem with this last part of the argument is that it leaves the hippocampal formation in mammals as what he calls a pre-adaptation or, to quote, a 'forerunner of the system used by humans to gain conscious access to memories' (Macphail 1998, p. 173). This is unsatisfactory because there must have been a selective advantage to the possession of this 'forerunner' (*sic*) long before the advent of hominids and the emergence of language. For Macphail, the mammalian hippocampus seems to be left in a kind of no man's land between having nothing to do with the primitive but stable implicit learning mechanisms shared by all vertebrates, but everything to do with the conscious, lateralized, language-based system used by humans. In contrast, the view taken here is that the hippocampus is a system for the automatic recording of attended experience that enables the encoding, storage and private recollection of experience in a form that would be advantageous to an animal but cannot yet be communicated to another. The challenge is to develop new analytically powerful behavioural tasks to study this memory system.

I am grateful to many colleagues and friends for discussing the ideas contained in this paper including Nicola Clayton, Anthony Dickinson, J. Uwe Frey, Susan Healy, Stephen Martin, Edvard Moser, Gernot Riedel and Emma Wood. The experimental work described includes studies conducted with J. Uwe Frey, Robert Steele, Guiquan Chen and colleagues at Elan Pharmaceuticals (Karen Chen, Dora Games and Stephen Freedman). This work was supported by grants from the Cunningham Trust, Medical Research Council, the Human Frontiers Science Programme and the European Union Framework V.

References

Aggleton, J. P. & Pearce, J. M. 2001 Neural systems underlying episodic memory: insights from animal research. *Phil. Trans. R. Soc. Lond.* B **356**, 1467–1482.

Amaral, D. G. & Witter, M. P. 1989 The three dimensional organization of the hippocampal formation: a review of anatomical data. *Neuroscience* **31**, 571–591.

Amaral, D. G. & Insausti, R. 1990 The hippocampal formation. In *The human nervous system* (ed. G. Paxinos), pp. 711–755. San Diego: Academic Press.

Bailey, C. H., Giusetto, M., Huang, Y. Y., Hawkins, R. D. & Kandel, E. R. 2000 Is heterosynaptic modulation essential for stabilizing Hebbian synaptic plasticity and memory? *Nature Neurosci.* **1**, 11–20.

Bliss, T. V. P. & Lomo, T. 1973 Long-lasting potentiation of synaptic transmission in the dentate area of the anaesthetized rabbit following stimulation of the perforant path. *J. Physiol.* (*Lond.*) **232**, 331–356.

Chen, G. (and 10 others) 2000 A learning deficit related to age and β-amyloid plaques in a mouse model of Alzheimer's disease. *Nature* **408**, 975–979.

Clayton, N. S. & Dickinson, A. 1998 What, where and when: episodic-like memory during cache recovery by scrub jays. *Nature* **395**, 272–274.

Clayton, N. S., Griffiths, D. P., Emery, N. J. & Dickinson, A. 2001 Elements of episodic-like memory in animals. *Phil. Trans. R. Soc. Lond.* B **356**, 1483–1491.

D'Hooge, R., Nagels, G., Westland, C. E., Muck, L. & De Deyn, P. P. 1996 Spatial learning deficit in mice expressing human 751-amino acid beta-amyloid precursor protein. *Neuroreport* **7**, 2807–2811.

Danysz, W., Zajaczkowski, W. & Parsons, C. G. 1995 Modulation of learning processes by ionotropic glutamate receptor ligands. *Behav. Pharmacol.* **6**, 455–474.

Dickinson, A. 1980 *Contemporary animal learning theory*. Cambridge University Press.

Ennaceur, A. & Delacour, J. 1988 A new one-trial test for neurobiological studies of memory in rats. 1. Behavioral data. *Behav. Brain Res.* **31**, 47–59.

Foster, D. J., Morris, R. G. M. & Dayan, P. 1999 A model of hippocampally-dependent navigation using the temporal difference learning rule. *Hippocampus* **10**, 1–16.

Frey, U. & Morris, R. G. M. 1997 Synaptic tagging and long-term potentiation. *Nature* **385**, 533–536.

Frey, U. & Morris, R. G. M. 1998*a* Weak before strong: dissociating synaptic-tagging and plasticity-factor accounts of late-LTP. *Neuropharmacology* **37**, 545–552.

Frey, U. & Morris, R. G. M. 1998*b* Synaptic tagging: implications for late maintenance of hippocampal long-term potentiation. *Trends Neurosci.* **21**, 181–188.

Gaffan, D. 1991 Spatial organization of episodic memory. *Hippocampus* **1**, 262–264.

Gaffan, D. 1994 Scene-specific memory for objects: a model of episodic memory impairment in monkeys with fornix transection. *J. Cogn. Neurosci.* **6**, 305–320.

Gaffan, D. & Harrison, S. 1989 Place memory and scene memory: effects of fornix transection in the monkey. *Exp. Brain Res.* **74**, 202–212.

Gaffan, D. & Parker, A. 1996 Interaction of perirhinal cortex with the fornix-fimbria: memory for objects and 'object-in-place memory. *J. Neurosci.* **16**, 5864–5869.

Gaffan, D. & Parker, A. 2000 Mediodorsal thalamic function in scene memory in rhesus monkeys. *Brain* **123**, 816–827.

Games, D. (and 33 others) 1995 Alzheimer-type neuropathology in transgenic mice overexpressing V717F β-amyloid precursor protein. *Nature* **373**, 523–526.

Garcia, J. & Koelling, R. A. 1966 Relation of cue to consequence in avoidance learning. *Psychonomic Sci.* **4**, 123–124.

Gluck, M. A. & Granger, R. 1993 Computational models of the neural bases of learning and memory. *A. Rev. Neurosci.* **16**, 667–706.

Granger, R., Wiebe, S. P., Taketani, M. & Lynch, G. 1996 Distinct memory circuits composing the hippocampal region. *Hippocampus* **6**, 567–578.

Griffiths, D., Dickinson, A. & Clayton, N. 1999 Episodic memory: what can animals remember about their past? *Trends Cogn. Sci.* **3**, 74–80.

Halliday, M. S. 1968 Exploratory behaviour. In *Analysis of behavioural change* (ed. L. Weiskrantz), pp. 107–126. New York: Harper and Row.

Holland, P. C. 1981 Acquisition of representation-mediated conditioned food aversions. *Learning and Motivation* **12**, 1–18.

Holland, P. C. 1990 Event representation in Pavlovian conditioning: image and action. *Cognition* **37**, 105–131.

Izquierdo, I. & Medina, J. H. 1998 On brain lesions, the milkman and Sigmunda. *Trends Neurosci.* **21**, 423–426.

Janus, C. (and 16 others) 2000 Aβ peptide immunization reduces behavioural impairment and plaques in a model of Alzheimer's disease. *Nature* **408**, 979–982.

Konishi, M. 1986 Centrally synthesised maps of sensory space. *Trends Neurosci.* **9**, 163–168.

Lisman, J. E. 1999 Relating hippocampal circuitry to function: recall of memory sequences by reciprocal dentate-CA3 interactions. *Neuron* **22**, 233–242.

McCarthy, R. A. & Warrington, E. A. 1990 *Cognitive neuropsychology.* San Diego: Academic Press.

McGaugh, J. L. 2000 Memory—a century of consolidation. *Science* **287**, 248–251.

McNaughton, B. L. & Morris, R. G. M. 1987 Hippocampal synaptic enhancement and information storage within a distributed memory system. *Trends Neurosci.* **10**, 408–415.

McNaughton, B. L., Douglas, R. M. & Goddard, G. V. 1978 Synaptic enhancement in fascia dentata: cooperativity among coactive afferents. *Brain Res.* **157**, 277–293.

Mackintosh, N. J. 1975 A theory of attention: variations in the associability of stimuli with reinforcement. *Psychol. Rev.* **82**, 276–298.

Mackintosh, N. J. 1983 *Conditioning and associative learning.* Oxford: Clarendon Press.

Macphail, E. M. 1982 *Brain and intelligence in vertebrates.* Oxford: Clarendon Press.

Macphail, E. M. 1998 *The evolution of consciousness*. Oxford University Press.

Marr, D. 1971 Simple memory: a theory for archicortex. *Phil. Trans. R. Soc. Lond.* B **262**, 23–81.

Martin, K. C., Casadio, A., Zhu, H. Y. E., Rose, J. C., Chen, M., Bailey, C. H. & Kandel, E. R. 1997 Synapse-specific, long-term facilitation of aplysia sensory to motor synapses: a function for local protein synthesis in memory storage. *Cell* **91**, 927–938.

Martin, S. J., Grimwood, P. D. & Morris, R. G. M. 2000 Synaptic plasticity and memory: an evaluation of the hypothesis. *Ann. Rev. Neurosci.* **23**, 649–711.

Moechars, D. (and 12 others) 1999 Early phenotypic changes in transgenic mice that overexpress different mutants of amyloid precursor protein in brain. *J. Biol. Chem.* **274**, 6483–6492.

Morgan, C. L. 1894 *An introduction to comparative psychology*. London: Walter Scott.

Morgan, D. G. (and 14 others) 2000 Aβ peptide vaccination prevents memory loss in an animal model of Alzheimer's disease. *Nature* **482**, 982–986.

Morris, R. G. M. 1983 An attempt to dissociate 'spatial mapping' and 'working memory' theories of hippocampal function. In *Neurobiology of the hippocampus* (ed. W. Seifert), pp. 405–432. London: Academic Press.

Morris, R. G. M. & Frey, U. 1997 Hippocampal synaptic plasticity: role in spatial learning or the automatic recording of attended experience? *Phil. Trans. R. Soc. Lond.* B **352**, 1489–1503.

Morris, R. G. M., Garrud, P., Rawlins, J. N. P. & O'Keefe, J. 1982 Place navigation impaired in rats with hippocampal lesions. *Nature* **297**, 681–683.

Murray, E. A., Baxter, M. G. & Gaffan, D. 1998 Monkeys with rhinal cortex damage or neurotoxic hippocampal lesions are impaired on spatial scene learning and object reversals. *Behav. Neurosci.* **112**, 1291–1303.

Nalbantoglu, J. (and 10 others) 1997 Impaired learning and LTP in mice expressing the carboxy terminus of the Alzheimer amyloid precursor protein. *Nature* **387**, 500–505.

O'Keefe, J. 1976 Place units in the hippocampus of the freely moving rat. *Exp. Neurol.* **51**, 78–109.

Olton, D. S., Becker, J. T. & Handelmann, G. E. 1979 Hippocampus, space, and memory. *Brain Behav. Sci.* **2**, 313–365.

Parker, A. & Gaffan, D. 1998 Interaction of frontal and perirhinal cortices in visual object recognition memory in monkeys. *Eur. J. Neurosci.* **10**, 3044–3057.

Pearce, J. M. & Hall, G. 1980 A model for Pavlovian learning: variations in the effectiveness of conditioned but not of unconditioned stimuli. *Psychol. Rev.* **87**, 532–552.

Petersen, C. C., Malenka, R. C., Nicoll, R. A. & Hopfield, J. J. 1998 All-or-none potentiation at CA3-CA1 synapses. *Proc. Natl Acad. Sci. USA* **95**, 4732–4737.

Preuss, T. 1995 The argument from animals to humans in cognitive neuroscience. In *The cognitive neurosciences*, 1st edn (ed. M. Gazzaniga), pp. 1227–1241. Cambridge, MA: MIT Press.

Rawlins, J. N. P. 1985 Associations across time: the hippocampus as a temporary memory store. *Behav. Brain Sci.* **8**, 479–497.

Redish, A. D. 1999 *Beyond the cognitive map: from place cells to episodic memory*. Cambridge, MA: MIT Press.

Rescorla, R. A. & Wagner, A. R. 1972 A theory of Pavlovian conditioning: the effectiveness of of reinforcement and nonreinforcement. In *Classical conditioning. II. Current research and theory* (ed. A. H. Black & W. F. Prokasy). New York: Appleton-Century-Crofts.

Riedel, G., Micheau, J., Lam, A. G. M., Roloff, E. L., Martin, S. J., Bridge, H., De Hoz, L., Poeschel, B., McCulloch, J. & Morris, R. G. M. 1999 Reversible neural inactivation reveals hippocampal participation in several memory processes. *Nature Neurosci.* **2**, 898–905.

Rolls, E. T. & Treves, A. 1998 *Neural networks and brain function*. Oxford University Press.

Rozin, P. & Kalat, J. W. 1971 Specific hungers and poisoning as adaptive specializations of learning. *Psychol. Rev.* **78**, 459–486.

Schenk, D. (and 24 others) 1999 Immunization with amyloid-beta attenuates Alzheimer-disease-like pathology in the PDAPP mouse. *Nature* **400**, 173–177.

Squire, L. R. 1992 Memory and the hippocampus: a synthesis from findings with rats, monkeys, and humans. *Psychol. Rev.* **99**, 195–231.

Steele, R. J. & Morris, R. G. M. 1999 Delay-dependent impairment of a matching to place task with chronic and intrahippocampal infusion of the NMDA antagonist D-AP5. *Hippocampus* **9**, 118–136.

Stoerig, P. & Cowey, A. 1997 Blindsight in man and monkey. *Brain* **120**, 535–559.

Tulving, E. 1983 *Elements of episodic memory*. Oxford: Clarendon Press.

Tulving, E. & Schacter, D. L. 1990 Priming and human memory systems. *Science* **247**, 301–306.

Tulving, E. & Markowitsch, H. J. 1998 Episodic and declarative memory: role of hippocampus. *Hippocampus* **8**, 198–204.

Weiskrantz, L. 1997 *Consciousness lost and found*. Oxford University Press.

12

Neural systems underlying episodic memory: insights from animal research

John P. Aggleton and John M. Pearce

Two strategies used to uncover neural systems for episodic-like memory in animals are discussed: (i) an attribute of episodic memory (*what*? *when*? *where*?) is examined in order to reveal the neuronal interactions supporting that component of memory; and (ii) the connections of a structure thought to be central to episodic memory in humans are studied at a level of detail not feasible in humans. By focusing on spatial memory (*where*?) and the hippocampus, it has proved possible to bring the strategies together. A review of lesion, disconnection and immediate early-gene studies in animals reveals the importance of interactions between the hippocampus and specific nuclei in the diencephalon (most notably the anterior thalamic nuclei) for spatial memory. Other parts of this extended hippocampal system include the mammillary bodies and the posterior cingulate (retrosplenial) cortex. Furthermore, by combining lesion and immediate early-gene studies it is possible to show how the loss of one component structure or tract can influence the remaining regions in this group of structures. The validity of this convergent approach is supported by new findings showing that the same set of regions is implicated in anterograde amnesia in humans.

12.1. Introduction

The anterograde amnesic syndrome demonstrates that specific brain structures are necessary for episodic memory. Once these individual structures are identified, the next goal will be to identify neural systems that are necessary for this form of memory, as no brain structure operates in isolation. A potentially vital piece of information associated with both research goals is that pathology in either the medial temporal lobe or the medial diencephalon can lead to similar amnesic syndromes. This raises the possibility that structures in these regions form part of a common system that is compromised in amnesia, a proposal first made explicitly by Delay & Brion (1969) following their analyses of Korsakoff's syndrome (principally a form of diencephalic amnesia) and examples of medial temporal lobe amnesia.

There are, however, severe limitations in using clinical findings to identify neural systems for memory processes. A persistent problem is that the pathology in clinical cases of amnesia is almost never confined to a single structure, making it impossible to be definitive about the necessary and sufficient pathologies for anterograde amnesia. Furthermore, studying the effects of pathology in the medial temporal lobe will not reveal whether that region is functionally linked in a vital way with the diencephalon, or vice versa. While there is little doubt that functional imaging (e.g. functional magnetic resonance imaging) will offer more and more clues as to the circuitry of different functions (e.g. when combined with structural equation modelling), this approach is not without its drawbacks. Anatomical resolution remains a problem for many sites, and null results (i.e. the lack of an overall change in a measure of activity) are difficult to interpret. As a consequence, attempts to assess the interdependence of different brain structures remain problematic. More general limitations arise from the fact that in order to identify and specify the full extent of a functional system, it is necessary to have a comprehensive knowledge of the connectivity of the structures under investigation. As has been observed (Crick & Jones 1993), our knowledge of the connectivity of the human brain is in fact very poor. This is principally because axonal transport techniques, widely used with animals, are not applicable with humans.

Research with animals provides a way of overcoming some of these problems as it offers the opportunity for high anatomical precision set within a detailed background knowledge of not only the connections of the target area but also its physiological, pharmacological and molecular properties. Furthermore, by applying disconnection techniques it is possible to address the issue of functional connectivity in a way that is simply not possible in humans. Animal research is not, however, without its own limitations. The most obvious is that brains have been subject to evolution, and the consequent variability means that generalizing across species can be fraught with problems. A less obvious, but even more fundamental problem, is whether it is possible to assess episodic memory in animals. Memory for a particular episode assumes retrieval of information concerning what happened, when it happened, and where it happened. To examine these combined facets of memory in a single behavioural task has required especially ingenious solutions (see Clayton 2001), and the practicality and generality of such tests for detailed neuroscientific examination remain to be determined. Even if it is possible to examine these combined aspects of memory, this will still fall short of demonstrating 'episodic memory' if inherent in the definition is a sense of conscious or active retrieval associated with mentally travelling back in time to recollect (Tulving 1983). By applying the principle of parsimony or Lloyd Morgan's canon (Morgan 1894), it is evident that the involvement of processes such as deliberate access rather than automatic access cannot be assumed in animals and, hence, episodic memory cannot be demonstrated.

This review examines two strategies used in animal research to address these problems. It then considers how the resultant information has helped to identify functional systems for the processing of episodic-like memory. In the first approach, a particular component of episodic memory that can be examined in animals is identified and the neural systems underlying that facet of episodic memory identified. Relevant to this approach is the acknowledgement that 'the presence or absence of episodic memory is no more an all-or-none matter between species than it is within them' (Tulving 1984, p. 258). Accordingly, it should be possible to break down episodic memory into a number of simpler components and examine them separately. Given that an event in episodic memory will characteristically contain information concerning *what*? *when*? and *where*? these components form obvious targets for animal research. These attributes can then be examined singly or even in pairs (Gaffan 1992). Of these attributes, the question *where*? is not only the most amenable to behavioural testing, but there are also theoretical grounds for believing that some forms of spatial memory are especially pertinent for the analysis of episodic-like memory (see § 12.2).

The second approach is to focus on a brain structure that clinical studies have implicated in episodic memory, and then to explore the functional connectivity of that structure in animals. In fact, if both approaches are valid then the two sets of findings should intersect. This prediction is supported by studies into the neural basis of spatial memory. While a number of brain regions are important for the acquisition of new spatial knowledge (the *where*? component of episodic memory), the hippocampal formation is thought to be pre-eminent (O'Keefe & Nadel 1978; Morris *et al.* 1982; Maguire *et al.* 1996; Riedel *et al.* 1999; Holdstock *et al.* 2000; Rosenbaum *et al.* 2000). At the same time, clinical research into temporal lobe amnesia has shown that hippocampal damage is not only necessary but is almost certainly sufficient to induce anterograde amnesia in humans. Thus, the hippocampus is necessary for episodic memory as well as spatial processing. This intersection of evidence may reflect specific features of spatial memory.

12.2. Stimulus binding and the relevance of spatial memory

There are conceptual reasons why the study of episodic-like memory in animals (and especially rodents) has focused on spatial memory (Gaffan 1991). The notion that the episodic memory of an event can be regarded as a 'mental snapshot' (Tulving 1983; Gaffan 1992) underlines the importance of linking or binding elements that are in memory. Thus, to create a 'snapshot' it is not sufficient to encode just the component items, but it is also necessary to have them arranged in a unique, spatial array. In a similar way, the cues that are used for allocentric spatial processes have to be combined in a manner that involves not just the identity of the component cues but also their relative positions. (Allocentric processing refers to the use of the relative positions of distal cues to aid spatial location and navigation.) By this view, episodic memory entails a record not just of a list of items but of how those items are linked or bound together.

The possible relationship of episodic memory processes to the binding of cues in configural groups has been noted before (Sutherland & Rudy 1989; Rudy & Sutherland 1995; Gaffan 1998), and has led to numerous studies that have attempted to identify brain regions that are critical for the acquisition of configural tasks such as negative patterning, positive patterning, transverse patterning and biconditional discriminations. The diagnostic feature of these tasks is that they cannot be solved by merely learning about the significance of an individual cue or element, rather the animal must also learn about the significance of combinations of cues. In positive patterning, for example, an outcome occurs when two stimuli, A and B, are presented together but not when they are presented separately i.e. AB + , A−, B− (Figure 12.1*a*). Such tasks have been used to test the importance of the hippocampus in configural memory, and while the data are not entirely consistent it is clear that rats with hippocampal or hippocampal system damage can still acquire many configural tasks (Gallagher & Holland 1992; Davidson *et al.* 1993; Rudy & Sutherland 1995; Bussey *et al.* 1998, 2001*b*). At first sight, this pattern of results would appear to contradict the premise described above, as hippocampal lesions consistently disrupt allocentric tasks yet are able to spare configural tasks. In fact, a key aspect of both 'snapshot' memories and 'allocentric' processing is that the elements have a structural component. That is, they have a specific spatial relationship to one another. This is not a demand of most configural tasks. It therefore appears that the closest parallel to mental snapshots may be found in a subclass of configural learning, known as 'structural' learning.

(*a*)

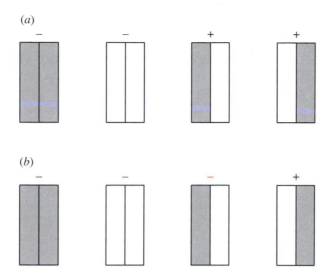

(*b*)

Fig. 12.1. Design of a configural learning task (*a*) 'positive patterning', and (*b*) a 'structural learning' task. The grey and white bars depict elements of a discriminative stimulus that is always composed of two elements. The symbols + and − indicate which stimuli are associated with reward and non-reward, respectively. Neither discrimination can be solved by reference to a single element (white or grey) and, hence, are configural. The structural task has the added feature that the geometrical position of the cues is relevant.

For a structural discrimination, the signals for reward and non-reward are composed of the same features, or elements, but they are assembled in different ways. Hence, a rat might be required to respond in one way when it is shown a black rectangle to the left of a white rectangle, and in a way different from the mirror image of this pattern (Figure 12.1*b*). Animals can solve this type of problem (Wodinsky *et al.* 1952; George *et al.* 2001) and there are good reasons for believing that it might require processes additional to those normally considered necessary for the solution of other discriminations. According to a number of connectionist theories of discrimination learning (e.g. Gluck & Bower 1988; Pearce 1994) when a pattern of stimulation is presented to a network, it is decomposed into its components which then have the opportunity to enter either directly or indirectly into an association with the trial outcome. Because the two black and white patterns that have just been mentioned are composed of the same features, it follows that they will be indistinguishable to the network and a discrimination between them will not be possible. George *et al.* (2001) have argued that in order for the network to solve a structural discrimination, it must be extended to allow it to be sensitive to structural information—that is, information about the relationships among the features within a particular pattern of stimulation. Perhaps it is this aspect of discrimination learning that depends upon an intact hippocampus. If this is correct, then there would be no need for an intact hippocampus if animals are to solve a positive patterning discrimination. Although the same features are presented on both reinforced and non-reinforced trials, even a relatively simple network can solve a negative patterning discrimination because a different set of features is presented on each type of trial (Gluck 1991; Pearce 1994).

An ability to appreciate the structure among features to create unique scenes or snapshots would seem to be an important attribute of episodic memory. Suppose a rat must locate a goal that is hidden near one corner of a featureless, rectangular test arena. In order to find the goal the rat must appreciate that the rectangle is composed of long and short walls, and that the goal is, say, near one of the two corners where the short wall is to the left of the long wall. If animals were unable to respond on the basis of the relationship between the short and long wall they would be forced to search indiscriminately among all four corners. In fact, in a preliminary study, Good *et al.* (2001) have shown that rats can be trained to search preferentially in the correct corners in this task. Furthermore, they have shown that if the rats have received bilateral lesions to the hippocampus then they are no longer able to discriminate the correct from the incorrect corners. The implication of these results is that normal rats are able to appreciate the structure of the rectangular test arena, and that this appreciation depends upon an intact hippocampus. Of course, it is not just for finding goals in rectangular environments that an appreciation of structure might be beneficial. Orientation in many spatial tasks is likely to depend on this ability. If an animal is required to use two landmarks to identify the position of a goal, then the manner in which it searches for the goal will depend very much, say, on whether one landmark is to the left or right of the other landmark. It is thus quite possible that the disruptive effect of hippocampal damage on spatial tasks, such as the Morris swimming pool, is due to the effect it has on the ability of the animal to appreciate the way in which the many landmarks in the environment are positioned with respect to each other.

There is a parallel between the foregoing proposals and findings from research with humans. Kroll *et al.* (1996) presented subjects with a list of two-syllable words, and occasionally presented recognition test trials with new words composed of the syllables from previously shown words. Thus they might be presented with 'valley' and 'barter' and then asked if they had been shown 'barley'. Normal subjects made relatively few errors on this task, but those with damage to the left hippocampus showed a strong tendency to respond to the novel test words as if they had seen them previously. According to Kroll *et al.* (1996), the hippocampus is important for binding together information about pairs of syllables that occur in the same word. Damage to this structure disrupts this process and results in subjects classifying stimuli as familiar simply on the basis of whether or not they are composed of familiar syllables. Related data come from two studies of amnesic individuals with pathology thought to be largely confined to the hippocampus (Vargha-Khadem *et al.* 1997; Mayes *et al.* 1999; Mayes 2001). In both studies there was striking evidence of a sparing of recognition when individual items were used as stimuli. In contrast, more consistent deficits appeared when subjects were given tests of associative recognition, in which the component stimuli were familiar but their arrangements were novel (Vargha-Khadem *et al.* 1997; Mayes *et al.* 1999).

The starting point for this analysis was the notion of a mental snapshot, but this is not sufficient of itself. Not only is it necessary to bind items within a scene but it is also necessary to combine scenes in the correct temporal order. Unfortunately we lack appropriate ways of testing this process in rodents, although experiments with pigeons have formally demonstrated that animals can distinguish between sequences of stimuli in which the choice cannot be made on the basis of the final stimulus alone (Weisman *et al.* 1980). It would clearly be of great interest to know whether the hippocampus, or structures connected with the hippocampus, are critical for this function in rats.

12.3. Lesion studies of allocentric spatial processes

Although it is not yet possible to identify brain sites necessary for 'structural discriminations', we can identify neural systems underlying spatial (allocentric) processing. Thus, in this section we will review evidence from lesion studies that have sought to identify the brain structures necessary for the acquisition and performance of allocentric spatial tasks. The resulting evidence reveals a group of interconnected structures that all have extensive links with the hippocampus. The final part of this section describes a number of disconnection studies that test whether these brain regions function in an interlinked way. These are of especial relevance as this class of task can be conducted experimentally in animals but will rarely, if ever, occur in clinical cases.

(a) Hippocampus

Studies with rats have shown that the hippocampus (dentate gyrus, CA1–4 and subiculum) is essential for allocentric spatial processing (O'Keefe & Nadel 1978; Morris *et al.* 1982, 1990). The involvement of this structure appears to occur at more than one stage of spatial learning and performance (Riedel *et al.* 1999; see Morris 2001) making it difficult to tease out individual component processes. Furthermore, both anatomical and electrophysiological evidence suggest that within the hippocampus there are functional changes along the longitudinal axis and, consistent with this, some lesion studies point to a greater contribution to spatial learning from the rat dorsal than the ventral hippocampus (Moser *et al.* 1995; Moser & Moser 1998).

Studies of spatial memory in non-human primates present a slightly more complex picture for several reasons. First, there are problems of task comparability as spatial tasks for monkeys typically involve little if any ambulation and so often differ from those given to rats (but see Murray *et al.* 1989). Second, the surgical approach used for aspiration lesions involves additional damage to subicular and parahippocampal regions, and this may contribute to the outcome of the study. Consistent with this, current data on selective neurotoxic hippocampal lesions in monkeys indicate that these may have more limited effects on tests of spatial memory (Murray & Mishkin 1998; Murray *et al.* 1998) than aspiration lesions (Jones & Mishkin 1972; Parkinson *et al.* 1988). Athough the cause of this discrepancy remains unproven, the most likely explanation is that conventional lesions disconnect the subicular, presubicular and parasubicular cortices. These regions are of especial significance as they provide hippocampal outputs to other regions implicated in spatial memory (Aggleton *et al.* 1986; Swanson *et al.* 1987; Naber *et al.* 2000).

(b) Cortical regions

The anatomical connections of the hippocampus can be used to guide assessments of the contribution made to spatial memory by additional brain structures (Figure 12.2).

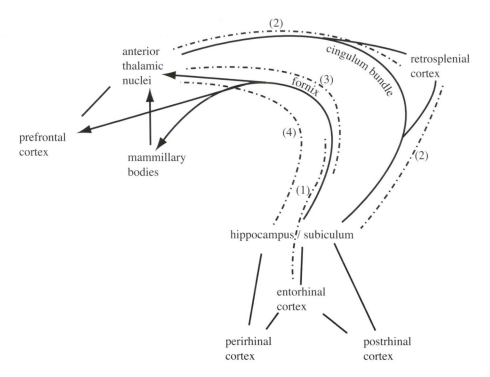

Fig. 12.2. Schematic diagram showing the interconnections (solid lines) linking some of the key structures implicated in spatial memory in the rat. The dashed lines indicate where functional linkages have been established by disconnection studies, while the numbers refer to the relevant study ((1) Olton *et al.* 1982; (2) Sutherland & Hoesing 1993; (3) Warburton *et al.* 2000; (4) Warburton *et al.* 2001).

The principal cortical input to the hippocampus comes from the entorhinal cortex, but there is also a complex pattern of both direct and indirect inputs from other parahippocampal cortices and from the retrosplenial cortex (Burwell *et al.* 1995; Witter *et al.* 1989). Careful anatomical studies in the rat have recently revealed that the perirhinal cortex preferentially projects to the lateral entorhinal cortex, while the postrhinal cortex projects to the medial entorhinal cortex (Witter *et al.* 1989). Furthermore, these two entorhinal divisions have different projection fields within the hippocampus (Witter *et al.* 2000), suggesting that there are at least two functional processing streams, one via the perirhinal cortex and one via the postrhinal cortex. The functional nature of these streams and the ways in which they interact remain to be uncovered, but the visuospatial nature of the inputs to the postrhinal cortex (Burwell & Amaral 1998) suggest that this may be the more important for spatial processes.

Lesion studies have confirmed that entorhinal lesions can disrupt tests of spatial memory in rats, deficits being most consistent in studies using conventional lesions (Ramirez & Stein 1984; Hunt *et al.* 1994; Kirby & Higgins 1998). A common finding, however, is that the deficits are appreciably less severe than those observed after hippocampectomy. This is most evident in the case of cytotoxic lesions where studies have typically observed mild or even no apparent deficit on tasks sensitive to hippocampectomy (Bouffard & Jarrard 1988; Galani *et al.* 1998; Kesner & Giles 1998; Pouzet *et al.* 1999; Aggleton *et al.* 2000*b*). Thus although the entorhinal cortex is involved in spatial memory, it also appears that fibres passing through the entorhinal cortex have a contribution. This conclusion suggests that the remaining parahippocampal cortices (the perirhinal and postrhinal cortices in the rat) may have an additional role in spatial processes.

The consequences of perirhinal cortex lesions in rats have been varied. Removal of this area has been reported to have either no effect (Ennaceur *et al.* 1996; Ennaceur & Aggleton 1997; Mumby & Glenn 2000; Bussey *et al.* 2001*a*) or relatively mild, disruptive effects (Wiig & Bilkey 1994*a,b*; Liu & Bilkey 1998*a,b*; Mumby & Glenn 2000) on spatial tasks sensitive to hippocampal damage. What is consistent is that the deficits (when present), are considerably less severe than those following hippocampectomy. Fewer studies have examined the postrhinal cortex, but the removal of this region appears to have no effect on standard spatial tasks sensitive to hippocampectomy (Bussey *et al.* 1999, 2000). The conclusion to be drawn from these studies on the parahippocampal cortices is that while the entorhinal, perirhinal and postrhinal cortices may contribute to spatial memory processing, their involvement is poorly revealed by standard spatial memory tasks (Aggleton *et al.* 2000*b*). As an example of this, perirhinal lesions will impair a conditional task in which spatial information must be used to solve a visual discrimination, but more standard spatial tasks remain unaffected (Bussey *et al.* 2001*a*).

A third cortical region to be considered is the cingulate cortex, and in particular the retrosplenial cortex (in the rat there is no posterior cingulate cortex, area 23, but an extended retrosplenial cortex, area 29). This region projects directly to the parahippocampal cortices and parts of the subicular complex, and has extensive reciprocal connections with the anterior thalamic nuclei (Wyss & Van Groen 1992). Like the parahippocampal cortices, the effects of lesions in this region have been varied and when deficits are found they are more often associated with conventional rather than cytotoxic lesions (Sutherland *et al.* 1988; Sutherland & Hoesing 1993; Warburton *et al.* 1998; Aggleton *et al.* 2000*b*). The interpretation of cingulate lesion effects is complicated by the fact that the cingulum bundle passes immediately adjacent to much of the retrosplenial cortex and this tract is compromised by conventional lesions. Not only does the cingulum bundle provide connections for the retrosplenial cortex itself, but it also contains afferents to and from the hippocampal formation (Mufson & Pandya 1984). It is therefore not surprising that selective lesions of the cingulum bundle can produce mild, but significant, deficits on spatial tasks (Neave *et al.* 1996, 1997; Warburton *et al.* 1998). Furthermore, the lack of effect of cytotoxic retrosplenial lesions on spatial tasks would seem to suggest that the cingulum bundle deficit does not include the consequences of retrosplenial disconnection. In fact, recent evidence (Vann and Aggleton, 2002) shows that unusually complete cytotoxic lesions of the full length of the retrosplenial cortex, that spare the cingulum bundle, can produce clear deficits on a variety of tests that tax allocentric spatial memory (Figure 12.3). It would therefore appear that the retrosplenial cortex does contribute to the performance of tasks that tax allocentric memory and that this accounts for some of the effects of cingulum bundle damage.

The hippocampus is also connected to parts of the frontal cortex, and in the rat these connections are principally with the prelimbic cortex in the medial prefrontal cortex

(Jay & Witter 1991). While lesions of this medial prefrontal region produce deficits on tasks sensitive to hippocampal dysfunction, the impairments are qualitatively different. Thus prefrontal deficits are often independent of retention interval (Aggleton *et al.* 1995*b*), and can often be characterized as reflecting a tendency to perseverate with inefficient strategies (Chudasama & Muir 1997; Ragozzino *et al.* 1999; Kesner 2000; Dias & Aggleton 2000). In this regard, they clearly mirror some of the consequences of prefrontal cortex damage in primates (Passingham 1993). Thus although these prefrontal regions appear to have an important role in the execution of spatial tasks, presumably via an interaction with the hippocampal system, their contribution appears to be of a more general nature.

(c) Subcortical areas

The fornix provides the principal route for the subcortical connections of the hippocampus. As fornix lesions disrupt an array of spatial tasks in both rodents and primates (Mahut 1971, 1972; Olton *et al.* 1979; Murray *et al.* 1989), it has been assumed that subcortical regions linked to the hippocampus are involved. At the same time, fornix lesion deficits are sometimes not as severe as those associated with hippocampectomy (Eichenbaum *et al.* 1990; but see Whishaw & Jarrard 1995). For example, on reference memory tests in the Morris water maze, rats with fornix lesions are slower at learning than normal rats but they are still able to learn the approximate location of a hidden platform (Whishaw *et al.* 1995; Warburton & Aggleton 1999). In contrast, rats with hippocampal lesions require considerable overtraining to show a place preference in the Morris water maze (Morris *et al.* 1990).

Subcortical sites directly connected with the hippocampus via the fornix include the mammillary bodies, the anterior thalamic nuclei and the septum. All three have been implicated in supporting hippocampal function and, hence, supporting spatial processing. There are very close anatomical links between the mammillary bodies and the anterior thalamic nuclei, and it is not surprising that the effects of lesions in these two sites on tests of spatial memory are often similar (Sutherland & Rodriguez 1989; Aggleton *et al.* 1995*b*; Byatt & Dalrymple-Alford 1996). The effects of anterior thalamic lesions are, however, the more disruptive (Aggleton *et al.* 1995*b*; Warburton *et al.* 1997, 1999). This difference is consistent with their respective anatomical relationships with the hippocampus. While the mammillary bodies receive direct inputs from the hippocampus, the anterior thalamic nuclei receive both direct inputs from the hippocampus and indirect inputs via the mammillary bodies (Figure 12.2). The anterior thalamic nuclei are composed of three major nuclei and all three appear to contribute to spatial processes (Aggleton *et al.* 1996; Byatt & Dalrymple-Alford 1996). A more caudal nucleus, the lateral dorsal nucleus is often added to this group as it has similar anatomical properties including direct connections with the hippocampus (Bentivoglio *et al.* 1993). Consistent with this, there is evidence that disruption of this nucleus exacerbates the effects of anterior thalamic damage (Mizumori *et al.* 1994; Warburton *et al.* 1997). Although the adjacent medial dorsal thalamic nucleus appears to modulate a range of tasks, including those taxing spatial memory, there is less direct evidence for a specific role in spatial memory (Hunt & Aggleton 1998*a,b*).

Other sites linked to the hippocampus, via the fornix, include the septum and the nucleus accumbens. Interpreting the consequences of septal damage has proved difficult as conventional lesions inevitably involve fornix fibres of passage. Nevertheless, studies using increasingly selective cytotoxic lesions of the region have found comparatively mild deficits on tasks in the Morris water maze (McAlonan *et al.* 1995; McMahan *et al.* 1997). Similarly, the effects of nucleus accumbens lesions on place learning in the water maze arm are very mild (Sutherland & Rodriguez 1989).

This review of the effects of selective lesions on tasks that tax spatial processing has provided a series of candidate regions that may function in an integrated manner with one another (Figure 12.2). The hippocampus appears at the centre of this group, and associated with it are the anterior thalamic nuclei, the mammillary bodies, the septum, the retrosplenial cortex, and the entorhinal cortex. Of these, only removal of all of the anterior thalamic nuclei appears to produce deficits as severe as those associated with hippocampectomy (Warburton *et al.* 1997). Next it is necessary to test the extent to which these structures depend on each other. This will reveal whether these lesions studies have identified a number of disparate deficits or whether they reflect common components in an extended hippocampal system.

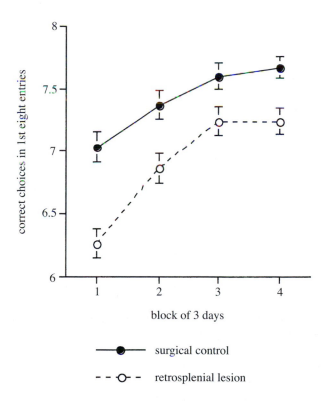

Fig. 12.3. Performance of rats with complete neurotoxic lesions of the retrosplenial cortex on the eight arm radial arm maze task (Vann and Aggleton 2002). The graph shows the significantly greater number of errors made by rats with retrosplenial lesions on this test of spatial working. Standard errors are shown by vertical bars.

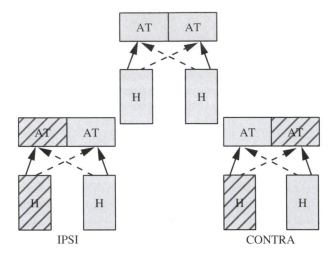

Fig. 12.4. Pattern of ipsilateral (IPSI) and contralateral (CONTRA) lesions used in a disconnection study (Warburton *et al.* 2001) to examine whether the hippocampus (H) and anterior thalamic nuclei (AT) function in concert for the acquisition and performance of spatial memory tasks. For simplicity, the connections from the anterior thalamic nuclei to the hippocampus have not been added.

(d) Disconnection studies

Standard lesion approaches may reveal striking similarities between the effects of lesions in two or more sites, but this alone does not show that these sites are functionally interdependent. For this it is necessary to turn to disconnection studies. The rationale is that if area A is a critical source of inputs for area B, then a unilateral lesion in area A combined with a unilateral lesion in area B in the contralateral hemisphere will result in a disconnection of the spared half of area B (Figure 12.4). The consequence will be an impairment that mimics the effect of bilateral loss of area B (and of area A). This prediction assumes that there are few, if any, crossed connections between areas A and B. Comparisons are then made with pairs of unilateral lesions, both lesions in the same (ipsilateral) hemisphere. In this latter group the total amount of tissue damage is the same as that in the disconnection case, but one hemisphere should remain functional. Thus the ipsilateral condition should have much milder disruptive effects.

The disconnection approach has been used with rats to identify interlinked systems necessary for the performance or acquisition of a number of spatial memory tests, all of which tax allocentric memory processes. These studies provide direct evidence for a link from the entorhinal cortex to the fornix (Olton *et al.* 1982), and from the fornix to the anterior thalamic nuclei (Warburton *et al.* 2000). In both cases, the hippocampal commissures had to be cut to induce a clear deficit, highlighting the involvement of interhippocampal transfer in normal performance. It should also be noted that the study by Olton *et al.* (1982) used conventional lesion methods and so it may be more accurate to say that it demonstrated a functional linkage between the parahippocampal cortex and fornix.

Other disconnection studies using the Morris water maze have provided evidence for a functional interaction between the hippocampus and anterior thalamic nuclei (Warburton *et al.* 2001), the anterior thalamic nuclei and the retrosplenial cortex (Sutherland & Hoesing 1993), and the hippocampus and retrosplenial cortex (Sutherland & Hoesing 1993). Once again, the retrosplenial lesions were made by aspiration, raising the likelihood that damage to the cingulum bundle contributed to the deficits (Neave *et al.* 1996, 1997; Warburton *et al.* 1998). Nevertheless, when combined these disconnection studies provide direct evidence for a linked system that involves the parahippocampal (entorhinal) cortex, the hippocampus, the fornix, the anterior thalamic nuclei, and the retrosplenial cortex and cingulum bundle (Figure 12.2). This system closely corresponds to the Papez (1937) circuit, which was originally regarded as a substrate for emotional interactions. The original ideas of Papez have long since been discarded, but his 'circuit' interlinks a set of regions (hippocampus, fornix, mammillary bodies, anterior thalamic nuclei, posterior cingulate cortex and retrosplenial cortex) via substantial tracts that are evident not only in rats, but also in monkeys and humans.

12.4. Immediate early gene (IEG) studies

Lesion studies do not directly measure the contribution of a target region, rather they measure how the rest of the brain functions in its absence. As a consequence, there is a need to complement lesion data with those from techniques examining normal brain tissue. Measuring the activity of IEGs (Dragunow & Faull 1989; Herrera & Robertson 1996; Herdegen & Leah 1998) provides a novel form of functional imaging that permits activity in many sites to be compared in the same brain. Recent discoveries using this technique accord with the results of lesion studies, thus adding further support to the extended hippocampal system underlying spatial memory processes.

IEGs have low basal transcription rates, but they can be quite rapidly activated. This activation is, however, transient. Their gene product is thought to regulate the more long-term production of other proteins. Although there is evidence that IEGs may have an integral role in plastic processes that accompany learning (Tischmeyer & Grimm 1999), this remains unproven. There is more general agreement that IEGs can provide a more general measure of neuronal activity. As it is possible to compare the activity of multiple regions within the same brain this technique offers a form of functional mapping with exceptional anatomical resolution (down to the level of single neurons). There is, however, relatively low temporal resolution as IEG measurement occurs at the point of peak production either of mRNA or of the gene product itself. As this will be many minutes after the experimental (activating) event it is often impossible to tease apart component processes within a form of learning or performance.

*(a) c-*fos *imaging in normal animals*

In a series of experiments we have mapped the activity of an IEG, c-*fos*, during the performance of spatial memory tasks. Rats were tested in the radial arm maze (Olton *et al.* 1979), where they performed a test of spatial working memory that taxes allocentric spatial processing (Bussey *et al.* 1999) and is sensitive to hippocampal dysfunction.

Comparisons with yoked control rats, matched for their perceptual, motor and reward experiences, have made it possible to identify a network of cortical and subcortical sites that show enhanced c-*fos* activity during such tests of spatial memory (Vann *et al.* 2000*a,b*). Evidence that the control procedure was appropriate came from the lack of difference in Fos levels in primary motor and sensory regions. In contrast, increased c-*fos* activity was found in all hippocampal and subicular subfields, the entorhinal cortex, postrhinal cortex, retrosplenial cortex, prelimbic cortex, septum, nucleus of the diagonal band, nucleus reuniens, and all three of the anterior thalamic nuclei (Figure 12.5). This list includes many of the same sites revealed by lesion studies.

In a second experiment, rats were moved to a novel room for the final radial arm maze session, so requiring the animals to remap the external world in order to perform the task (Vann *et al.* 2000*a,b*). Comparisons were made with animals also performing the radial arm maze task, but in the same room that had always been used for training. The novel room manipulation should prove more demanding since the animal has to learn new distal room cues, in addition to maintaining its memory of which arms had been entered. This remapping is of especial interest as it is presumably allocentric and so is likely to tax aspects of structural learning. Increased c-*fos* activity was found in fewer sites, but these were always labelled in Experiment 1. Thus structures showing increased Fos production in both conditions included nearly all of the hippocampal subfields, the dorsal and caudal subiculum, postsubiculum, presubiculum, and parasubiculum, the prelimbic cortex, entorhinal cortex, postrhinal cortex, lateral septum, supramamillary nuclei, the three anterior thalamic nuclei, and nucleus reuniens (Figure 12.5). Among the regions showing a Fos increase in Experiment 1 but not in Experiment 2 were the cingulate and retrosplenial cortices. The implication is that these latter regions contribute to radial arm maze task performance, but not to the creation and use of new cognitive maps. Two notable regions that did not show increased Fos levels in either condition were the perirhinal cortex and nucleus accumbens. This is of interest as both have strong anatomical links with the hippocampus, yet there is uncertain lesion evidence over their involvement in spatial learning (see § 12.3). While the present IEG data indicate that the perirhinal cortex is not directly involved in spatial mapping tasks, the adjacent postrhinal cortex did show increased Fos production in both experiments. Although loss of the postrhinal cortex does not appear to affect radial arm performance (Bussey *et al.* 1999), there are good grounds for believing that this region is normally involved in spatial processing. Most notably, it is the postrhinal cortex rather than the perirhinal cortex that receives the majority of sensory inputs associated with spatial information in the rat (Burwell *et al.* 1995).

A further manipulation provides an even more direct examination of the processes likely to be involved in structural discriminations (Wan *et al.* 1999). In this task rats were shown a series of visual stimuli, each composed of three objects in a specific location. These compound 'scenes' were shown simultaneously to the left and right eyes of the rat over a series of successive sessions, so that they could become familiar. On the final test day the stimuli shown to one eye remained unchanged, while those shown to the other eye were rearranged so that for each scene the component objects were the same but their locations were swapped, i.e. novel (Figure 12.6). Levels of Fos were then measured and compared between the two hemispheres. Fos increases were found in the postrhinal cortex and in parts of the hippocampus in the hemisphere that first received visual inputs from the eye viewing the rearranged objects (Wan *et al.* 1999). No

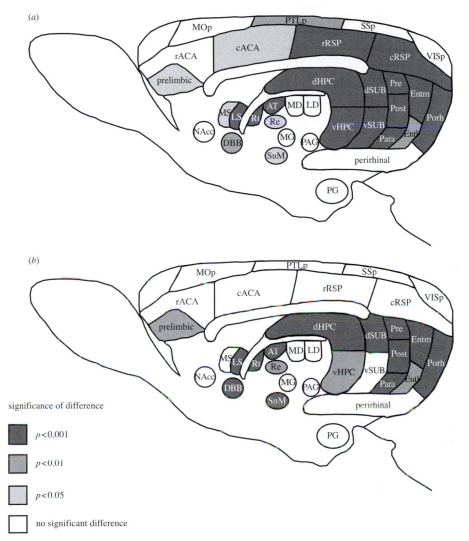

Fig. 12.5. Summary of results from two c-*fos* experiments, depicting sites that show a significant increase in activity (Vann *et al.* 2000*a*,*b*). Experiment 1 (*a*) shows Fos increases following the performance of the radial arm maze task (compared with running up and down just one arm of the same maze). Experiment 2 (*b*) shows Fos increases when the radial arm maze task is performed in a novel room (compared with animals in a familiar room). Abbreviations: AT, anterior thalamic nuclei; cACA, caudal anterior cingulate cortex; cRSP, caudal retrosplenial cortex; DBB, diagonal band of Broca; dHPC, dorsal hippocampus; dSUB, dorsal subiculum; Entl, lateral entorhinal cortex; Entm, medial entorhinal cortex; LD, lateral dorsal thalamic nucleus; LS, lateral septum; MD, medial dorsal thalamic nucleus; MG, medial geniculate; MOp, primary motor cortex; MS, medial septum; NAcc, nucleus accumbens; PAG, periaqueductal grey; Para, parasubiculum; PG, pontine grey; Porh, postrhinal cortex; Post, postsubiculum; Pre, presubiculum; PTLp, parietal cortex; rACA, rostral anterior cingulate cortex; Re, nucleus reunions; rRSP, rostral retrosplenial cortex; Rt, rostral reticular thalamic nucleus; SSp, primary somatosensory cortex; SuM, supramammillary nucleus; vHPC, ventral hippocampus; VISp, primary visual cortex; vSUB, ventral subiculum.

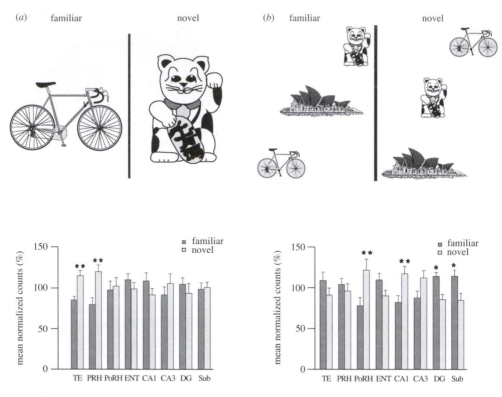

Fig. 12.6. Paired-viewing study (Wan *et al.* 1999) that compared Fos activity in the two hemispheres following the presentation of a novel single stimulus (left) or the presentation of a novel arrangement of familiar individual stimuli (right). Note the different regions showing significant activations in the two versions of the task ($^{*}p < 0.05$, $^{**}p < 0.01$). The item to the left of the vertical line can be regarded as the familiar stimulus (seen by the left eye only), while the item to the right of the vertical line is novel and only seen by the right eye. Fos levels are then compared across hemispheres in the same animal. Fos counts have been normalized so that that equal counts in the two hemispheres would be 100%. Abbreviations: CA, hippocampal fields CA1 and CA3; DG, dentate gyrus; ENT, entorhinal cortex; PoRH, postrhinal cortex; PRH, perirhinal cortex; Sub, subiculum; TE, area TE. Standard errors are indicated by the vertical lines.

increases were found in the perirhinal cortex. In contrast, a comparison condition that involved showing novel versus familiar single objects (i.e. no structural component) led to increased activation in the perirhinal cortex, but not in the hippocampus or postrhinal cortex (Wan *et al.* 1999). These data implicate the hippocampus and postrhinal cortex in structural learning, i.e. learning about the way in which objects are located with respect to each other. They also provide a further parallel with studies of allocentric learning and c-*fos* imaging (Vann *et al.* 2000*b*).

(b) c-fos *imaging in animals with lesions*

In order to understand how a lesion in one structure can have detrimental effects on other sites, we have extended the c-*fos* procedure to examine how damage to a specific part of the circuit revealed by lesion studies can affect other putative members of that system. The first study measured the consequences of a unilateral fornix lesion upon c-*fos* activation during radial arm maze performance (Vann *et al.* 2000*c*). This tract was chosen since (i) clinical studies have increasingly indicated that damage to the fornix may be sufficient to induce anterograde amnesia (Aggleton *et al.* 2000*a*), and (ii) the fornix lies at the heart of connections between temporal and diencephalic regions implicated in spatial memory processes in rats. The radio-frequency lesion led to decreased Fos production in an array of sites including all of the hippocampal subfields, most of the subicular complex, the entorhinal cortex, anterior cingulate cortex, retrosplenial cortex and postrhinal cortex. Subcortical regions showing decreased Fos included the anterior thalamic nuclei, the supramamillary nucleus, the lateral septum and diagonal band of Broca. Not only are many of these same sites implicated in spatial memory processes from electrophysiological and lesion data, but there is also striking overlap between those regions that show increased Fos production in the intact brain following performance of a spatial memory task (Vann *et al.* 2000*a,b*) and those that show abnormal production following fornix damage (Vann *et al.* 2000*c*). It is evident that fornix transection has widespread consequences that extend far beyond the hippocampus, and these will need to be considered when trying to understand why fornix lesions can impair memory processes (Gaffan & Gaffan 1991; Gaffan *et al.* 1991; Aggleton *et al.* 2000*a*).

The same approach, i.e. lesioning a specific site and then measuring the disruption of c-*fos* activity throughout the brain, has also been applied to the anterior thalamic nuclei. Bilateral neurotoxic lesions of the anterior thalamus resulted in hypoactivity in the hippocampus, as well as in the retrosplenial cortex and prelimbic cortex (Dias *et al.* 2000). This finding not only suggests that anterior thalamic damage might affect memory via its disruptive consequences on the hippocampus and other limbic regions, but also helps to explain why medial temporal lobe and medial diencephalic lesions might have similar consequences on memory.

12.5. Object recognition memory

A quite different approach to the study of episodic-like memory has come from the study of recognition memory in animals. This approach has been very influential (Mishkin 1978; Squire & Zola-Morgan 1991) and is intuitively extremely attractive. Recognition memory is often closely equated with episodic memory (Squire & Knowlton 1995; LePage *et al.* 2000; but see Yonelinas 2001) and, consistent with this, amnesic individuals almost always show a recognition memory deficit. As a consequence, it is quite common to see clinical deficits of recognition simply described as episodic memory impairments (e.g. Collie & Maruff 2000). Thus the testing of object recognition should provide an unusually direct means of testing episodic-like memory in animals. Furthermore, one might expect to discover that systems linked to the hippocampus that are important for spatial memory are also important for recognition memory. In fact, a surprisingly different set of key structures emerge when recognition memory is analysed in animals.

Before considering recognition in animals it is helpful to consider recognition by humans. If, in order to recognize an item as having previously been presented, a subject must mentally travel back in time in an active fashion, then tests of recognition memory can indeed be thought to test episodic memory. There is, however, considerable controversy over the nature of human recognition memory. The principal area of debate is whether it comprises a single process directly linked to other forms of episodic recall or whether it is a dual process in which recognition can stem from two (or more) independent processes (see Gardiner (2001) and Yonelinas 2001). While one of these processes does indeed appear to be episodic, as it involves actively remembering the repeated event, the other simply involves the detection of familiarity (Mandler 1980). This dichotomy helps to highlight a fundamental problem for tests of recognition memory in animals.

This problem can best be considered in the light of Lloyd Morgan's 'canon' (Morgan 1894). The most parsimonious account of recognition by animals is that objects are distinguished on the basis of their relative familiarity, rather than to suppose that the animal is actively engaged in recalling the event when one of the test objects was previously presented. This of course assumes that animals do have access to a signal that permits a judgement based on familiarity. Direct evidence that a familiarity signal exists comes from single unit recording studies in both monkeys and rats. Such studies have uncovered cells, most typically in the perirhinal cortex, that show differential responding to novel versus previously exposed visual stimuli (Brown et al. 1987; Zhu et al. 1995a; Brown & Aggleton 2001). Furthermore, lesion experiments have confirmed the critical importance of the same brain region for behavioural tests of recognition (Murray & Mishkin 1986; Zola-Morgan et al. 1989b; Murray 1996). The perirhinal cortex also shows increased c-fos activation when novel stimuli are presented (Zhu et al. 1995b, 1996). This convergence of data makes it increasingly likely that these electrophysiological signals do have an important role in the judgement of novelty (Brown & Aggleton 2001).

It is necessary to consider next the ways in which recognition is tested behaviourally in animals. Although there is a surprising range of potential tests (Steckler et al. 1998), two classes of task have had the most impact. The first is delayed non-matching-to-sample (DNMS). For this, the animal receives a food reward for selecting the novel item when offered a choice between a novel and a familiar item. Thus the animal must make a choice based on prior information (the familiarity of the item that had already been presented). Although this may superficially look like a test of recall, there is no demand on the animal to recall the episode of first seeing the now familiar stimulus. While it is the case that human amnesics are typically impaired on recognition tasks that have deliberately been made comparable with the animal DNMS task (Aggleton et al. 1988; Squire et al. 1988; but see Holdstock et al. 1995), this does not show that the task taxes episodic memory in animals. If judgements based on relative familiarity can effectively solve DNMS problems (which they presumably can), then the mere performance of this task does not demonstrate episodic memory in animals.

The second class of task involves tests of spontaneous exploration or viewing of novel versus familiar items (Zola-Morgan et al. 1983; Ennaceur & Delacour 1988; Bachevalier et al. 1993). This form of paired comparison task takes advantage of the fact that many animals show a spontaneous preference for novel objects or locations. The behavioural measure is not a single choice, but the difference in time spent examining the items within the pair of objects. The advantage of this task is that it requires no pretraining, making it arguably a purer test of recognition, while the absence of a specific reward removes a potential source of variance. Disadvantages include the fact that it is disrupted by any manipulation that affects levels or patterns of exploration, while the final choice measure is dependent on rates of habituation. This latter factor presents a problem for testing hippocampal lesions as these can disrupt habituation (Honey & Good 2000). Although, human amnesics are impaired on analogues of the visual paired comparison task (McKee & Squire 1993), for the same reasons as noted above this does not show that the task taxes the recall of prior episodes by animals.

In view of these concerns, it is instructive to compare what is known about brain systems underlying object recognition and spatial learning. Lesions studies in animals have pointed to three principal regions associated with recognition deficits: the perirhinal cortex, the medial dorsal nucleus of the thalamus and the prefrontal cortex (Aggleton & Mishkin 1983; Zola-Morgan & Squire 1985; Murray & Mishkin 1986; Zola-Morgan et al. 1989b; Bachevalier & Mishkin 1986; Mumby & Pinel 1994; Murray 1996). In contrast, lesions of the fornix or mammillary bodies have little or no effect on tests of object recognition (Aggleton & Mishkin 1985; Bachevalier et al. 1985; Zola-Morgan et al. 1989a; Shaw & Aggleton 1993). There has, however, been much debate over the consequences of hippocampal damage on tests such as DNMS, but a recent meta-analysis helps to show that the effects are typically mild and consistently less severe than those observed after perirhinal cortex lesions (Baxter & Murray 2001).

The group of regions that appear most critical for object recognition (perirhinal cortex, prefrontal cortex, medial dorsal thalamic nucleus) are directly linked anatomically. Furthermore, by using disconnection procedures it has been possible to show that both the medial dorsal thalamus and the perirhinal cortex interact with the frontal cortex for the performance of recognition tasks by monkeys (Parker & Gaffan 1998). At the same time, these regions provide surprisingly little overlap with the key regions required for allocentric spatial memory processes, with the hippocampus providing a potential point of overlap. Nevertheless, comparisons between the perirhinal cortex and the hippocampus provide a series of double dissociations when the magnitude of lesion effects on DNMS and spatial learning are considered in rats (Brown & Aggleton 2001). Similar double dissociations are found for c-*fos* activation studies (Aggleton & Brown 1999).

While it is self-evident that tests of object recognition and spatial memory should not tax precisely the same neural substrates, the lack of overlap is surprising if both provide insights into episodic memory. One possibility is that standard tests of recognition as performed by animals assess familiarity judgements and, hence, do not depend on any episodic-like component of recognition memory. This explanation accounts for the different distribution of key structures for recognition and spatial memory, and accords with evidence that familiarity information is available in the perirhinal cortex. A second possibility is that, as in humans, there are dual processes for recognition and that one of these is familiarity-based while the other is a form of episodic memory. While it is the case that ingenious new behavioural tasks have shown that birds have access to memory functions that can be described as episodic-like (Clayton et al. 2001) and it is quite conceivable that this form of memory can help animals solve behavioural tests of recognition, there is no a priori case for assuming that animals do use this more complex form of memory when performing standard versions of tasks such as DNMS. To do this it will be necessary to derive independent measures that distinguish between these processes. This has proved extremely difficult in humans, and is likely to be even more challenging for research with animals.

A quite different way of thinking about object recognition is to assume that by monitoring object familiarity the same system is also able to provide information concerning item identity i.e. the *what?* element of episodic memory. This provides a more constructive way to consider the anatomical links between the perirhinal cortex and hippocampus, namely that they enable *what?* and *where?* information to be combined (Gaffan 1998). This view is supported by lesion data (Gaffan & Parker 1996; Bussey *et al.* 1999, 2001*a*), and helps to highlight the importance of the functional interactions between the hippocampus and parahippocampal cortices in both humans and animals (Squire & Zola-Morgan 1991; Eichenbaum 2000). At the same time, the analyses of spatial memory strongly suggest that these interactions are not sufficient and that connections with diencephalic sites are also required in order to combine these classes of information (Parker & Gaffan 1997).

12.6. Conclusions and caveats

In spite of the logical problems of assessing episodic memory in animals, it is possible to examine the neural basis of the key aspects of this form of memory, namely the *what?* *where?* and *when?* of an event. Furthermore, research with animals can determine how structures function in an integrated manner to support each of these attributes, e.g. by disconnection techniques. Using these approaches in rodents it has been possible to uncover an interlinked group of cortical and subcortical structures for spatial learning. The hippocampus is central to this group and, at the same time, is dependent upon other regions within it. It has also been proposed that aspects of spatial memory make it especially pertinent for the study of episodic-like processes. This is because a particular type of processing described as 'structural learning' may provide a precursor to the creation of 'mental snapshots'. As allocentric processing can be seen as a form of structural learning, the study of this aspect of spatial memory should be of especial value.

In order to examine the neural basis of spatial learning we have described how selective lesions can disrupt the performance of tasks that tax allocentric processing. Care must be taken, however, to exclude deficits that are not spatial but reflect more general disruptions of behaviour such as hyperactivity or response perseveration (Chudasama & Muir 1997). A more challenging problem is the fact that animals have multiple strategies to aid performance in tasks taxing allocentric processing. As a consequence, other structures may provide quite different forms of spatial information that also promote successful navigation. Examples include 'egocentric information' (mapping external space with respect to your own body position, e.g. to the right or to the left) and 'path integration' (using self-movement cues such as motor and vestibular information to track a path through space). Of these, path integration is likely to be of particular relevance as there is growing evidence that the hippocampus is involved in this form of spatial tracking as well as allocentric mapping (Whishaw *et al.* 1995; Whishaw 1998). Note, however, that it is very difficult to understand how successful performance in spatial tasks such as the Morris pool can be explained solely by reference to path integration. Likewise, the similar effects on scene discrimination learning in rats following lesions of the fornix, anterior thalamic nuclei or mammillary bodies (Gaffan *et al.* 2001) cannot be interpreted as a deficit in path integration.

Disentangling systems for path integration and allocentric processing is likely to prove demanding as the same region might be involved in both spatial mechanisms. Examples include not only the hippocampus but also the retrosplenial cortex (Whishaw *et al.* 2001). Similarly, inputs in the rat from the anterior thalamic nuclei to the hippocampal formation provide head direction information (Taube 1995; Goodridge & Taube 1997), and this may prove to be relevant for both allocentric processing and path integration (Sharp 1999). At the same time, head direction information arises from only specific subregions within the anterior thalamic nuclei, yet both lesion and IEG data show that all of these nuclei contribute to spatial activity (Aggleton *et al.* 1996; Byatt & Dalrymple-Alford 1996; Vann *et al.* 2000*a*). Thus the anterior thalamic nuclei appear to have an additional, as yet unknown, contribution to the extended hippcampal system. Similarly, while the lateral mammillary nuclei are involved in providing head direction information for the anterior thalamic nuclei (Blair *et al.* 1999), the medial mammillary nuclei have a different function that also remains to be determined. Thus the 'extended hippocampal system' in the rat cannot be regarded as having a unitary function, even as regards spatial processing. There appears to be a much finer degree of anatomical specificity within the component structures as regards different functions. Furthermore, these different forms of spatial information need to be integrated so that they can be used in the most effective manner. Indeed, it has been argued that it is this process of integration, which enables an animal to monitor and remember its movements in space, that should be regarded as a more direct precursor of episodic memory in primates (Wise & Murray 1999).

Although it is increasingly evident that the Papez circuit has multiple influences on spatial learning, we have argued that this circuit is important because it allows animals to appreciate the structure of complex stimuli, a fundamental component of episodic memory. By highlighting the role of 'structural learning' we have provided a new starting point that incorporates the contribution of configural learning within a more specific framework. This now requires testing, and a vital step will be the development of formal tests of structural learning by animals. At a more general level, it is possible to assess the validity of the approach adopted in this review by considering the pathologies responsible for anterograde amnesia in humans. This immediately shows that there is a very clear concordance between sites responsible for anterograde amnesia and those critical for tests of spatial memory in animals. In both cases the hippocampus is the most prominent site. Although clinical studies have persistently suffered from a lack of cases with circumscribed pathology, there is considerable evidence indicating that hippocampal damage is sufficient to induce amnesia (e.g. Penfield & Mathieson 1974; Squire 1992; Rempel-Clower *et al.* 1996). Of especial relevance is evidence that hippocampal damage in humans can result not only in amnesia, but also in a loss of spatial memory that is selective for allocentric memory (Holdstock *et al.* 2000). Establishing the importance of other single structures for anterograde amnesia has been more difficult, but a number of recent group studies have provided convincing evidence for the importance of the fornix, the mammillothalamic tract (and thus the mammillary bodies), and the anterior thalamic nuclei (Aggleton & Brown 1999; Aggleton *et al.* 2000*a*; Harding *et al.* 2000; Van der Werf *et al.* 2000). Similarly there is growing evidence that damage to the retrosplenial region can disrupt episodic memory

(Valenstein *et al.* 1987; Maguire 2001), and this is supported by recent brain imaging data (Maguire 2001). These results highlight the same extended hippocampal system for spatial processing in rats and for episodic memory in humans. This concordance strongly supports the general approach outlined in this review.

The authors thank L. Awcock, N. Thomas and S. Vann (Cardiff University) for assistance, as well as the support of the UK Medical Research Council.

References

Aggleton, J. P. & Brown, M. W. 1999 Episodic memory, amnesia and the hippocampal–anterior thalamic axis. *Behav. Brain Sci.* **22**, 425–444.

Aggleton, J. P. & Mishkin, M. 1983 Memory impairments following restricted medial thalamic lesions in monkeys. *Exp. Brain Res.* **52**, 199–209.

Aggleton, J. P. & Mishkin, M. 1985 Mamillary-body lesions and visual recognition in monkeys. *Exp. Brain Res.* **58**, 190–197.

Aggleton, J. P., Desimone, R. & Mishkin, M. 1986 The origin, course, and termination of the hippocampo–thalamic projections in the macaque. *J. Comp. Neurol.* **243**, 409–422.

Aggleton, J. P., Nicol, R. M., Huston, A. E. & Fairbairn, A. F. 1988 The performance of amnesic subjects on tests of experimental amnesia in animals: delayed matching-to-sample and concurrent learning. *Neuropsychologia* **26**, 265–272.

Aggleton, J. P., Neave, N., Nagle, S. & Hunt, P. R. 1995*a* A comparison of the effects of anterior thalamic, mamillary body and fornix lesions on reinforced spatial alternation. *Behav. Brain Res.* **68**, 91–101.

Aggleton, J. P., Neave, N., Nagle, S. & Sahgal, A. 1995*b* A comparison of the effects of medial prefrontal, cingulate cortex, and cingulum bundle lesions on tests of spatial memory: evidence of a double dissociation between frontal and cingulum bundle contributions. *J. Neurosci.* **15**, 7270–7281.

Aggleton, J. P., Hunt, P. R., Nagle, S. & Neave, N. 1996 The effects of selective lesions within the anterior thalamic nuclei on spatial memory in the rat. *Behav. Brain Res.* **81**, 189–198.

Aggleton, J. P., McMackin, D., Carpenter, K., Hornak, J., Kapur, N., Halpin, S., Wiles, C. M., Kamel, H., Brennan, P. & Gaffan, D. 2000*a* Differential effects of colloid cysts in the third ventricle that spare or compromise the fornix. *Brain* **123**, 800–815.

Aggleton, J. P., Vann, S. D., Oswald, C. J. P. & Good, M. 2000*b* Identifying cortical inputs to the hippocampus that subserve allocentric spatial processes: a simple question with a complex answer. *Hippocampus* **10**, 466–474.

Bachevalier, J. & Mishkin, M. 1986 Visual recognition impairment follows ventromedial but not dorsolateral prefrontal lesions in monkeys. *Behav. Brain Res.* **20**, 249–261.

Bachevalier, J., Saunders, R. C. & Mishkin, M. 1985 Visual recognition in monkeys; effects of transection of fornix. *Exp. Brain Res.* **57**, 547–553.

Bachevalier, J., Brickson, M. & Hagger, C. 1993 Limbic-dependent recognition in monkeys develops early in infancy. *Learn. Mem.* **4**, 77–80.

Baxter, M. G. & Murray, E. A. 2001 Opposite relationship of hippocampal and rhinal cortex damage to delayed nonmatching-to-sample deficits in monkeys. *Hippocampus* **11**, 61–71.

Bentivoglio, M., Kultas-Ilinsky, K. & Ilinsky, I. 1993 Limbic thalamus: structure, intrinsic organisation and connections. In *Neurobiology of cingulate cortex and limbic thalamus* (ed. B. A. Vogt & M. Gabriel), pp. 71–122. Boston, MA: Birkhäuser.

Blair, H. T., Cho, J. & Sharp, P. E. 1999 The anterior thalamic head direction signal is abolished by bilateral but not unilateral lesions of the lateral mammillary nucleus. *J. Neurosci.* **19**, 6673–6683.

Bouffard, J. P. & Jarrard, L. E. 1988 Acquisition of a complex place task in rats with selective ibotenate lesions of hippocampal formation: combined lesions of subiculum and entorhinal cortex versus hippocampus. *Behav. Neurosci.* **102**, 828–834.

Brown, M. W. & Aggleton, J. P. 2001 Recognition memory: what are the roles of the perirhinal cortex and hippocampus? *Nature Rev. Neurosci.* **2**, 51–61.

Brown, M. W., Wilson, F. A. W. & Riches, P. 1987 Neuronal evidence that inferomedial temporal cortex is more important than hippocampus in certain processes underlying recognition memory. *Brain Res.* **409**, 158–162.

Burwell, R. D. & Amaral, D. G. 1998 Cortical afferents of the perirhinal, postrhinal, and entorhinal cortices of the rat. *J. Comp. Neurol.* **398**, 179–205.

Burwell, R. D., Witter, M. P. & Amaral, D. G. 1995 Perirhinal and postrhinal cortices of the rat: a review of the neuroanatomical literature and comparison with findings from the monkey brain. *Hippocampus* **5**, 390–408.

Bussey, T. J., Warburton, E. C., Aggleton, J. P. & Muir, J. L. 1998 Fornix lesions can facilitate acquisition of the transverse patterning task: a challenge for 'configural' theories of hippocampal function. *J. Neurosci.* **18**, 1622–1631.

Bussey, T. J., Muir, J. L. & Aggleton, J. P. 1999 Functionally dissociating aspects of event memory: the effects of combined perirhinal and postrhinal lesions on object and place memory in the rat. *J. Neurosci.* **19**, 495–503.

Bussey, T. J., Duck, J. D., Muir, J. L. & Aggleton, J. P. 2000 Distinct patterns of behavioural impairments resulting from fornix transection or neurotoxic lesions of the perirhinal and postrhinal cortices in the rat. *Behav. Brain Res.* **111**, 187–202.

Bussey, T. J., Dias, R., Amin, E., Muir, J. L. & Aggleton, J. P. 2001a Perirhinal cortex and place-object conditional learning. *Behav. Neurosci.* **115**, 776–785.

Bussey, T. J., Dias, R., Redhead, E. S., Pearce, J. M., Muir, J. L. & Aggleton, J. P. 2001b Intact negative patterning in rats with fornix or combined perirhinal and postrhinal cortex lesions. *Exp. Brain Res.* **134**, 506–519.

Byatt, G. & Dalrymple-Alford, J. C. 1996 Both anteromedial and anteroventral thalamic lesions impair radial-maze learning in rats. *Behav. Neurosci.* **110**, 1335–1348.

Chudasama, Y. & Muir, J. L. 1997 A behavioural analysis of the delayed non-matching to position task: the effects of scopolamine, lesions of the fornix and of the prelimbic region on mediating behaviours by rats. *Psychopharmacology* **134**, 73–82.

Clayton, N. S., Griffiths, D. P., Emery, N. J. & Dickinson, A. 2001 Elements of episodic-like memory in animals. *Phil. Trans. R. Soc. Lond.* B **356**, 1483–1491.

Collie, A. & Maruff, P. 2000 The neuropsychology of preclinical Alzheimer's disease and mild cognitive impairment. *Neurosci. Biobehav. Rev.* **24**, 365–374.

Crick, F. & Jones, E. 1993 The backwardness of human neuroanatomy. *Nature* **361**, 109–110.

Davidson, T. L., McKernan, M. G. & Jarrard, L. E. 1993 Hippocampal lesions do not impair negative patterning: a challenge to configural association theory. *Behav. Neurosci.* **107**, 227–234.

Delay, J. & Brion, S. 1969 *Le syndrome de Korsakoff*. Paris: Masson.

Dias, R. & Aggleton, J. P. 2000 Effects of excitotoxic prefrontal lesions on acquisition of nonmatching- and matching-to-place in the T-maze: evidence for intact spatial working memory but differential involvement of the prelimbic–infralimbic and anterior cingulate cortices in providing behavioural flexibility. *Eur. J. Neurosci.* **12**, 1–12.

Dias, R., Morgan, A., Brown, M. W. & Aggleton, J. P. 2000 Anterior thalamic lesions disrupt hippocampal activity measured by c-*fos* imaging: implications for temporal lobe memory processes and amnesia. *Eur. J. Neurosci.* **12**(Suppl. 11), 42.2.

Dragunow M. & Faull R. 1989 The use of c-*fos* as a metabolic marker in neuronal pathway tracing. *J. Neurosci. Meth.* **29**, 261–265.

Eichenbaum, H. 2000 A cortical-hippocampal system for declarative memory. *Nature Rev. Neurosci.* **1**, 41–50.

Eichenbaum, H., Stewart, C. & Morris, R. G. M. 1990 Hippocampal representation in place learning. *J. Neurosci.* **10**, 3531–3542.

Ennaceur, A. & Aggleton, J. P. 1997 The effects of neurotoxic lesions of the perirhinal cortex combined to fornix transection on object recognition memory in the rat. *Behav. Brain Res.* **88**, 181–193.

Ennaceur, A. & Delacour J. 1988 A new one-trial test for neurobiological studies of memory in rats. I Behavioural data. *Behav. Brain Res.* **31**, 47–59.

Ennaceur, A., Neave, N. & Aggleton, J. P. 1996 Neurotoxic lesions of the perirhinal cortex do not mimic the behavioural effects of fornix transection in the rat. *Behav. Brain Res.* **80**, 9–25.

Gaffan, D. 1991 Spatial organization of episodic memory. *Hippocampus* **1**, 262–264.

Gaffan, D. 1992 The role of the hippocampus–fornix–mammillary system in episodic memory. In *Neuropsychology of memory*, 2nd edn (ed. L. R. Squire & N. Butters). New York: Guilford Press.

Gaffan, D. 1998 Idiothetic input into object-place configuration as the contribution to memory of the monkey and human hippocampus: a review. *Exp. Brain Res.* **123**, 201–209.

Gaffan, D. & Gaffan, E. A. 1991 Amnesia in man following transection of the fornix. *Brain* **114**, 2611–2618.

Gaffan, D. & Parker, A. 1996 Interaction of perirhinal cortex with the fornix-fimbria: memory for objects and 'object-in-place' memory. *J. Neurosci.* **16**, 5864–5869.

Gaffan, E. A., Gaffan, D. & Hodges, J. R. 1991 Amnesia following damage to the left fornix and to other sites. *Brain* **114**, 1297–1313.

Gaffan, E. A., Bannerman, D. M., Warburton, E. C. & Aggleton, J. P. 2001 Rat's processing of visual scenes: effects of lesions to fornix, anterior thalamus, mamillary nuclei or the retrohippocampal region. *Behav. Brain Res.* **121**, 103–117.

Galani, R., Weiss, I., Cassel, J. C. & Kelche C. 1998 Spatial memory, habituation, and reactions to spatial and nonspatial changes in rats with selective lesions of the hippocampus, the entorhinal cortex or the subiculum. *Behav. Brain Res.* **96**, 1–12.

Gallagher, M. & Holland, P. 1992 Preserved configural learning and spatial learning impairments in rats with hippocampal damage. *Hippocampus* **2**, 81–88.

Gardiner, J. M. 2001 Episodic memory and autonoietic consciousness: a first-person approach. *Phil. Trans. R. Soc. Lond.* B **356**, 1351–1361.

George, D., Ward-Robinson, J. & Pearce, J. M. P. 2001 The discrimination of structure. I Implications for connectionist theories of discrimination learning. *J. Exp. Psychol. Anim. Behav. Process.* **27**, 206–218.

Gluck, M. A. 1991 Stimulus generalization and representation in adaptive network models of category learning. *Psychol. Sci.* **2**, 50–55.

Gluck, M. A. & Bower, G. H. 1988 From conditioning to category learning: an adaptive network model. *J. Exp. Psychol. Gen.* **117**, 225–244.

Good, M. A., Haywood, A., McGregor, A., Muir, J. L. & Pearce, J. M. A unique role for shape in spatial navigation in the watermaze: evidence from overshadowing manipulation and hippocampal lesion. *Soc. Neurosci. Abstracts* 2001.

Goodridge, J. P. & Taube, J. S. 1997 Interaction between the postsubiculum and anterior thalamus in the generation of head direction cell activity. *J. Neurosci.* **17**, 9315–9330.

Harding, A., Halliday, G., Caine, D. & Kril, J. 2000 Degeneration of anterior thalamic nuclei differentiates alcoholics with amnesia. *Brain* **123**, 141–154.

Herdegen, T. & Leah, J. D. 1998 Inducible and constitutive transcription factors in the mammalian nervous system: control of gene expression by Jun, Fos and Krox, and CREB/ATF proteins. *Brain Res. Rev.* **28**, 379–490.

Herrera, D. G. & Robertson, H. A. 1996 Activation of c-*fos* in the brain. *Prog. Neurobiol.* **50**, 83–107.

Holdstock, J. S., Shaw, C. & Aggleton, J. P. 1995 The performance of amnesic subjects on tests of delayed matching-to-sample and delayed matching-to-position. *Neuropsychologia* **33**, 1583–1596.

Holdstock, J. S., Mayes, A. R., Cezayirli, E., Isaac, C. L., Aggleton, J. P. & Roberts, J. N. 2000 A comparison of egocentric and allocentric spatial memory in a patient with selective hippocampal damage. *Neuropsychologia* **38**, 410–425.

Honey, R. C. & Good, M. 2000 Associative modulation of the orientating response: distinct effects revealed by hippocampal lesions. *J. Exp. Psychol. Anim. Behav. Process.* **26**, 3–14.

Hunt, M. E., Kesner, R. P. & Evans, R. B. 1994 Memory for spatial location: functional dissociation of entorhinal cortex and hippocampus. *Psychobiology* **22**, 186–194.

Hunt, P. R. & Aggleton, J. P. 1998a An examination of the spatial working memory deficit following neurotoxic medial dorsal thalamic lesions in rats. *Behav. Brain Res.* **97**, 129–141.

Hunt, P. R. & Aggleton, J. P. 1998b Neurotoxic lesions of the dorsomedial thalamus impair the acquisition but not the performance of delayed matching to place by rats: a deficit in shifting response rules. *J. Neurosci.* **18**, 10 045–10 052.

Jay, T. M. & Witter, M. P. 1991 Distribution of hippocampal CA1 and subicular efferents in the prefrontal cortex of the rat studied by means of anterograde transport of *Phaeolus vulgaris* leucoagglutinin. *J. Comp. Neurol.* **313**, 574–586.

Jones, B. & Mishkin, M. 1972 Limbic lesions and the problem of stimulus-reinforcement associations. *Exp. Neurol.* **36**, 362–377.

Kesner, R. P. 2000 Subregional analysis of mnemonic functions of the prefrontal cortex in the rat. *Psychobiology* **28**, 219–228.

Kesner, R. P. & Giles, R. 1998 Neural circuit analysis of spatial working memory: role of pre- and parasubiculum, medial and lateral entorhinal cortex. *Hippocampus* **8**, 416–423.

Kirby, D. L. & Higgins, G. A. 1998 Characterization of perforant path lesions in rodent models of memory and attention. *Eur. J. Neurosci.* **10**, 823–838.

Kroll, N. E. A., Knight, R. T., Metcalfe, J., Wolf, E. S. & Tulving, E. 1996 Cohesion failure as a source of memory illusions. *J. Mem. Lang.* **35**, 176–196.

Lepage, M., Ghaffar, O., Nyberg, L. & Tulving, E. 2000 Prefrontal cortex and episodic memory retrieval mode. *Proc. Natl Acad. Sci. USA* **97**, 506–511.

Liu, P. & Bilkey, D. K. 1998a Lesions of perirhinal cortex produce spatial memory deficits in the radial maze. *Hippocampus* **8**, 114–121.

Liu, P. & Bilkey, D. K. 1998b Perirhinal cortex contributes to performance in the Morris water maze. *Behav. Neurosci.* **112**, 304–315.

McAlonan, G. M., Dawson, G. R., Wilkinson, L. O., Robbins, T. W. & Everitt, B. J. 1995 The effects of AMPA-induced lesions of the medial septum and vertical limb nucleus of the diagonal band of Broca on spatial delayed non-matching to sample and spatial learning in the water maze. *Eur. J. Neurosci.* **7**, 1034–1049.

McKee, R. D. & Squire, L. R. 1993 On the development of declarative memory. *J. Exp. Psychol. Learn. Mem. Cogn.* **19**, 397–404.

McMahan, R. W., Sobel, T. J. & Baxter, M. G. 1997 Selective immunolesions of hippocampal cholinergic input fail to impair spatial working memory. *Hippocampus* **7**, 130–136.

Maguire, E. A. 2001 The retrosplenial contribution to human navigation: a review of lesion and neuroimaging findings. *Scand. J. Psychol* **42**, 225–238.

Maguire, E. A., Frackowiak, R. S. J. & Frith, C. D. 1996 Learning to find your way: a role for the human hippocampal formation. *Proc. R. Soc. Lond.* B **263**, 1745–1750.

Mahut, H. 1971 Spatial and object reversal learning in monkeys with partial temporal lobe ablations. *Neuropsychologia* **9**, 409–424.

Mahut, H. 1972 A selective spatial deficit in monkeys after transection of the fornix. *Neuropsychologia* **10**, 65–74.

Mandler, G. 1980 Recognizing: the judgment of previous occurrence. *Psychol. Rev.* **87**, 252–271.

Mayes, A. R., Van Eijk, R., Gooding, P. A., Isaac, C. L. & Holdstock, J. S. 1999 What are the functional deficits produced by hippocampal and perirhinal lesions? *Behav. Brain Sci.* **22**, 460–461.

Mayes, A. R. & Roberts, N. 2001 Theories of episodic memory. *Phil. Trans. R. Soc. Lond.* B **356**, 1395–1408.

Mishkin, M. 1978 Memory in monkeys severely impaired by combined, but not by separate removal of amygdala and hippocampus. *Nature* **273**, 297–298.

Mizumori, S. J. Y., Miya, D. Y. & Ward, K. E. 1994 Reversible inactivation of the lateral dorsal thalamus disrupts hippocampal place representation and impairs spatial learning. *Brain Res.* **644**, 168–174.

Morgan, C. L. 1894 *An introduction to comparative psychology*. London: Scott.

Morris, R. G. M. 2001 Episodic-like memory in animals: psychological criteria, neural mechanisms and the value of episodic-like tasks to investigate animal models of neurodegenerative disease. *Phil. Trans. R. Soc. Lond.* B **356**, 1453–1465.

Morris, R. G. M., Garrud, P., Rawlins, J. N. P. & O'Keefe, J. 1982 Place navigation impaired in rats with hippocampal lesions. *Nature* **297**, 681–683.

Morris, R. G. M, Schenk, F., Tweedie, F. & Jarrard, L. E. 1990 Ibotenate lesions of hippocampus and/or subiculum: dissociating components of allocentric spatial learning. *Eur. J. Neurosci.* **2**, 1016–1028.

Moser, M.-B. & Moser, E. I. 1998 Functional differentiation in the hippocampus. *Hippocampus* **8**, 608–619.

Moser, M.-B., Moser, E. I., Forrest, E., Andersen, P. & Morris, R. G. M. 1995 Spatial learning with a minislab in the dorsal hippocampus. *Proc. Natl Acad. Sci. USA* **92**, 9697–9701.

Mufson, E. J. & Pandya, D. N. 1984 Some observations on the course and composition of the cingulum bundle in the rhesus monkey. *J. Comp. Neurol.* **225**, 31–43.

Mumby, D. G. & Glenn, M. J. 2000 Anterograde and retrograde memory for object discriminations and places in rats with perirhinal cortex lesions. *Behav. Brain Res.* **114**, 119–134.

Mumby, D. G. & Pinel, J. P. J. 1994 Rhinal cortex lesions and object recognition in rats. *Behav. Neurosci.* **108**, 1–8.

Murray, E. A. 1996 What have ablation studies told us about the neural substrates of stimulus memory? *Semin. Neurosci.* **8**, 13–22.

Murray, E. A. & Mishkin, M. 1986 Visual recognition in monkeys following rhinal cortical ablations combined with either amygdalectomy or hippocampectomy. *J. Neurosci.* **7**, 1991–2003.

Murray, E. A. & Mishkin, M. 1998 Object recognition and location memory in monkeys with excitotoxic lesions of the amygdala and hippocampus. *J. Neurosci.* **18**, 6568–6582.

Murray, E. A., Davidson, M., Gaffan, D., Olton, D. S. & Suomi, S. 1989 Effects of fornix transection and cingulate coritical ablation on spatial memory in rhesus monkeys. *Exp. Brain Res.* **74**, 173–186.

Murray, E. A., Baxter, M. G. & Gaffan, D. 1998 Monkeys with rhinal cortex damage or neurotoxic hippocampal lesions are impaired on spatial scene learning and object reversals. *Behav. Neurosci.* **112**, 1291–1303.

Naber, P. A., Witter, M. P. & Lopes da Silva, F. H. 2000 Networks of the hippocampal memory system of the rat. The pivotal role of the subiculum. *Ann. NY Acad. Sci.* **911**, 392–403.

Neave, N., Nagle, S., Sahgal, A. & Aggleton, J. P. 1996 The effects of discrete cingulum bundle lesions in the rat on the acquisition and performance of two tests of spatial working memory. *Behav. Brain Res.* **80**, 75–85.

Neave, N., Nagle, S. & Aggleton, J. P. 1997 Evidence for the involvement of the mamillary bodies and cingulum bundle in allocentric spatial processing by rats. *Eur. J. Neurosci.* **9**, 101–115.

O'Keefe, J. & Nadel, L. 1978 *The Hippocampus as a cognitive map*. Oxford University Press.

Olton, D. S., Becker, J. T. & Handelman, G. E. 1979 Hippocampus, space, and memory. *Behav. Brain Sci.* **2**, 313–365.

Olton, D. S., Walker, J. A. & Woolf, W. A. 1982 A disconnection analysis of hippocampal function. *Brain Res.* **233**, 241–253.

Papez, J. W. 1937 A proposed mechanism of emotion. *Arch. Neurol. Psychiatry* **38**, 725–743.

Parker, A. & Gaffan, D. 1997 The effects of anterior thalamic and cingulate cortex lesions on 'object-in-place' memory in monkeys. *Neuropsychologia* **35**, 1093–1102.

Parker, A. & Gaffan, D. 1998 Interaction of frontal and perirhinal cortices in visual object recognition memory in monkeys. *Eur. J. Neurosci.* **10**, 3044–3057.

Parkinson, J. K., Murray, E. A. & Mishkin, M. 1988 A selective mnemonic role for the hippocampus in monkeys: memory for the location of objects. *J. Neurosci.* **8**, 4159–4167.

Passingham, R. E. 1993 *The frontal lobes and voluntary action.* Oxford University Press.

Pearce, J. M. 1994 Similarity and discrimination: a selective review and a connectionist model. *Psychol. Rev.* **101**, 587–607.

Penfield, W. & Mathieson, G. 1974 Memory: autopsy findings and comments on the role of the hippocampus in experiential recall. *Arch. Neurol.* **31**, 145–154.

Pouzet, B., Welzl, H., Gubler, M. K., Broersen, L., Veenman, C., Feldon, J., Rawlins, J. N. P. & Yee, B. K. 1999 The effects of NMDA-induced retrohippocampal lesions on performance of four spatial memory tasks known to be sensitive to hippocampal damage in the rat. *Eur. J. Neurosci.* **11**, 123–140.

Ragozzino, M. E., Detrick, S. & Kesner, R. P. 1999 Involvement of the prelimbic–infralimbic areas of the rodent prefrontal cortex in behavioral flexibility for place and response learning. *J. Neurosci.* **19**, 4585–4594.

Ramirez, J. J. & Stein, D. G. 1984 Sparing and recovery of spatial alternation performance after entrohinal cortex lesions in rats. *Behav. Brain Res.* **13**, 53–61.

Rempel-Clower, N. L., Zola, S. M., Squire, L. R. & Amaral, D. G. 1996 Three cases of enduring memory impairment after bilateral damage limited to the hippocampal formation. *J. Neurosci.* **16**, 5233–5255.

Riedel, G., Micheau, J., Lam, A. G. M., Roloff, E. V. L., Martin, S. J., Bridge, H., de Hoz, L., Poeschel, B., McCulloch, J. & Morris, R. G. M. 1999 Reversible neural inactivation reveals hippocampal participation in several memory processes. *Nature Neurosci.* **2**, 898–905.

Rosenbaum, R. S., Priselac, S., Kohler, S., Black, S. E., Gao, F., Nadel, L. & Moscovitch, M. 2000 Remote spatial memory in an amnesic person with extensive bilateral hippocampal lesions. *Nature Neurosci.* **3**, 1044–1048.

Rudy, J. W. & Sutherland, R. J. 1995 Configural association theory and the hippocampal formation: an appraisal and reconfiguration. *Hippocampus* **5**, 375–389.

Sharp, P. E. 1999 Complimentary roles for hippocampal versus subicular/entorhinal place cells in coding place, context, and events. *Hippocampus* **9**, 432–443.

Shaw, C. & Aggleton, J. P. 1993 The effects of fornix and medial prefrontal lesions on delaying nonmatching-to-sample by rats. *Behav. Brain Res.* **54**, 91–102.

Squire, L. R. 1992 Memory and the hippocampus: a synthesis from findings with rats, monkeys, and humans. *Psychol. Rev.* **99**, 195–231.

Squire, L. R. & Knowlton, B. J. 1995 Memory, hippocampus, and brain systems. In *The cognitive neurosciences* (ed. M. Gazzinaga), pp. 825–835. Cambridge, MA: MIT Press.

Squire, L. R. & Zola-Morgan, S. 1991 The medial temporal lobe memory system. *Science* **253**, 1380–1386.

Squire, L. R., Zola-Morgan, S. & Chen, K. S. 1988 Human amnesia and animal models of amnesia: performance of amnesic patients on tests designed for the monkey. *Behav. Neurosci.* **102**, 210–221.

Steckler, T., Drinkenburg, W. H. I. M., Sahgal, A. & Aggleton, J. P. 1998 Recognition memory in rats. I Concepts and classification. *Prog. Neurobiol.* **54**, 289–311.

Sutherland, R. J. & Hoesing, J. M. 1993 Posterior cingulate cortex and spatial memory: a microlimnology analysis. In *Neurobiology of cingulate cortex and limbic thalamus* (ed. B. A. Vogt & M. Gabriel), pp. 461–477. Boston, MA: Birkhäuser.

Sutherland, R. J. & Rodriguez, A. J. 1989 The role of the fornix/fimbria and some related subcortical structures in place learning and memory. *Behav. Brain Res.* **32**, 265–277.

Sutherland, R. J. & Rudy, J. W. 1989 Configural association theory: the role of the hippocampal formation in learning, memory, and amnesia. *Psychobiology* **17**, 129–144.

Sutherland, R. J., Whishaw, I. Q. & Kolb, B. 1988 Contributions of cingulate cortex to two forms of spatial learning and memory. *J. Neurosci.* **8**, 1863–1872.

Swanson, L. W., Kohler, C. & Bjorklund, A. 1987 The limbic region. I The septohippocampal system. In *Handbook of chemical neuroanatomy, vol. 5: integrated systems of the CNS*, part 1 (ed. A. Bjorklund, T. Hokfelt & L. W. Swanson), pp. 125–277. New York: Elsevier.

Taube, J. S. 1995 Head direction cells recorded in the anterior thalamic nuclei of freely moving rats. *J. Neurosci.* **15**, 70–86.

Tischmeyer, W. & Grimm, R. 1999 Activation of immediate early genes and memory formation. *Cell. Mol. Life Sci.* **55**, 564–574.

Tulving, E. 1983 *Elements of episodic memory.* New York: Oxford University Press.

Tulving, E. 1984 Precis of *Elements of episodic memory. Behav. Brain Sci.* **7**, 223–268.

Valenstein, E., Bowers, D., Verfaellie, M., Heilman, K. M., Day, A. & Watson, R. T. 1987 Retrosplenial amnesia. *Brain* **110**, 1631–1646.

Van der Werf, Y. D., Witter, M. P., Uijlings, H. B. M. & Jolles, J. 2000 Neuropsychology of infarctions in the thalamus: a meta-analysis. *Neuropsychologia* **38**, 613–627.

Vann, S. D. & Aggleton, J. P. 2002 Extensive cytotoxic lesions of the rat retrosplenial cortex reveal consistent deficits on tasks that tax allocentric spatial memory. *Behav. Neurosci.* (In the press.)

Vann, S. D., Brown, M. W. & Aggleton, J. P. 2000a Fos expression in the rostral thalamic nuclei and associated cortical regions in response to different spatial memory tasks. *Neuroscience* **101**, 983–991.

Vann, S. D., Brown, M. W., Erichsen, J. T. & Aggleton, J. P. 2000b Fos imaging reveals differential patterns of hippocampal and parahippocampal subfield activity in response to different spatial memory tasks. *J. Neurosci.* **20**, 2711–2718.

Vann, S. D., Brown, M. W., Erichsen, J. T. & Aggleton, J. P. 2000c Using Fos imaging in the rat to reveal the anatomical extent of the disruptive effects of fornix lesions. *J. Neurosci.* **20**, 8144–8152.

Vargha-Khadem, F., Gadian, D. G., Watkins, K. E., Connelly, A., Van Paesschen, W. & Mishkin, M. 1997 Differential effects of early hippocampal pathology on episodic and semantic memory. *Science* **277**, 376–380.

Wan, H., Aggleton, J. P. & Brown, M. W. 1999 Different contributions of the hippocampus and perirhinal cortex to recognition memory. *J. Neurosci.* **19**, 1142–1148.

Warburton, E. C. & Aggleton, J. P. 1999 Differential effects in the Morris water maze following cytotoxic lesions of the anterior thalamus and fornix transection. *Behav. Brain Res.* **98**, 27–38.

Warburton, E. C., Baird, A. L. & Aggleton, J. P. 1997 Assessing the magnitude of the allocentric spatial deficit associated with complete loss of the anterior thalamic nuclei in rats. *Behav. Brain Res.* **87**, 223–232.

Warburton, E. C., Aggleton, J. P. & Muir, J. L. 1998 Comparing the effects of selective cingulate cortex and cingulum bundle lesions on a spatial navigation task. *Eur. J. Neurosci.* **10**, 622–634.

Warburton, E. C., Morgan, A., Baird, A. L., Muir, J. L. & Aggleton, J. P. 1999 Does pretraining spare the spatial deficit associated with anterior thalamic damage in rats? *Behav. Neurosci.* **113**, 956–967.

Warburton, E. C., Baird, A. L., Morgan, A., Muir, J. L. & Aggleton, J. P. 2000 Disconnecting hippocampal projections to the anterior thalamus produces deficits on tests of spatial memory in rats. *Eur. J. Neurosci.* **12**, 1714–1726.

Warburton, E. C., Morgan, A., Baird, A., Muir, J. L. & Aggleton, J. P. 2001 The importance of the anterior thalamic nuclei for hippocampal function: evidence from a disconnection study in rats. *J. Neurosci.* **21**, 7323–7330.

Weisman, R. G., Wasserman, E. A., Dodd, P. W. D. & Larew, M. B. 1980 Representation and retention of two event sequences in pigeons. *J. Exp. Psychol. Anim. Behav. Process.* **6**, 312–325.

Whishaw, I. Q. 1998 Place learning in hippocampal rats and the path integration hypothesis. *Neurosci. Biobehav. Rev.* **22**, 209–220.

Whishaw, I. Q. & Jarrard, L. E. 1995 Similarities vs. differences in place learning and circadian activity in rats after fimbria-fornix section or ibotenate removal of hippocampal cells. *Hippocampus* **5**, 595–604.

Whishaw, I. Q., Cassel, J-C. & Jarrard, L. E. 1995 Rats with fimbria-fornix lesions display a place response in a swimming pool: a dissociation between getting there and knowing where. *J. Neurosci.* **15**, 5779–5788.

Whishaw, I. Q., Maaswinkel, H., Gonzalez, C. L. R. & Kolb, B. 2001 Deficits in allothetic and idiothetic spatial behavior in rats with posterior cingulate cortex lesions. *Behav. Brain Res.* **118**, 67–76.

Wiig, K. A. & Bilkey, D. K. 1994a Perirhinal cortex lesions in rats disrupt performance in a spatial DNMS task. *NeuroReport* **5**, 1405–1408.

Wiig, K. A. & Bilkey, D. K. 1994b The effects of perirhinal cortical lesions on spatial reference memory in the rat. *Behav. Brain Res.* **63**, 101–109.

Wise, S. P. & Murray, E. A. 1999 Role of the hippocampal system in conditional motor learning: mapping antecedents to action. *Hippocampus* **9**, 101–117.

Witter, M. P., Groenewegen, H. J., Lopes da Silva, F. H. & Lohman, A. H. M. 1989 Functional organization of the extrinsic and intrinsic circuitry of the parahippocampal region. *Prog. Neurobiol.* **33**, 161–253.

Witter, M. P., Naber, P. A., Van Haeften, T., Machielsen, W. C. M., Rombouts, S. A. R. B., Barkhof, F., Scheltens, P. & Lopes da Silva, F. H. 2000 Cortico–hippocampal communication by way of parallel parahippocampal–subicular pathways. *Hippocampus* **10**, 398–410.

Wodinsky, J., Varley, M. A. & Bitterman, M. E. 1952 Situational determinants of the relative difficulty of simultaneous and successive discriminations. *J. Comp. Physiol. Psychol.* **47**, 337–340.

Wyss, J. M. & Van Groen, T. 1992 Connections between the retrosplenial cortex and the hippocampal formation in the rat: a review. *Hippocampus* **2**, 1–12.

Yonelinas, A. P. 2001 Components of episodic memory: the contribution of recollection and familiarity *Phil. Trans. Roy. Soc. Lond.* B **356**, 1363–1374.

Zhu, X. O., Brown, M. W. & Aggleton, J. P. 1995a Neuronal signalling of information important to visual recognition memory in rat rhinal and neighbouring cortices. *Eur. J. Neurosci.* **7**, 753–765.

Zhu, X. O., Brown, M. W., McCabe, B. J. & Aggleton, J. P. 1995b Effects of the novelty or familiarity of visual stimuli on the expression of the intermediate early gene c-*fos* in the rat brain. *Neuroscience* **69**, 821–829.

Zhu, X. O., McCabe, B. J., Aggleton, J. P. & Brown, M. W. 1996 Mapping recognition memory through the differential expression of the immediate early gene c-*fos* induced by novel or familiar visual stimulation. *NeuroReport* **7**, 1871–1875.

Zola-Morgan, S. & Squire, L. R. 1985 Amnesia in monkeys after lesions of the mediodorsal nucleus of the thalamus. *Ann. Neurol.* **17**, 558–564.

Zola-Morgan, S., Dabrowska, J., Moss, M. & Mahut, H. 1983 Enhanced preference for perceptual novelty in the monkey after section of the fornix but not after ablation of the hippocampus. *Neuropsychologia* **21**, 433–454.

Zola-Morgan, S., Squire, L. R. & Amaral, D. G. 1989a Lesions of the hippocampal formation but not lesions of the fornix or the mammillary nuclei produce long-lasting memory impairments in monkeys. *J. Neurosci.* **9**, 898–913.

Zola-Morgan, S., Squire, L. R., Amaral, D. G. & Suzuki, W. A. 1989b Lesions of perirhinal and parahippocampal cortex that spare the amygdala and hippocampal formation produce severe memory impairment. *J. Neurosci.* **9**, 4355–4370.

13

Elements of episodic-like memory in animals

N. S. Clayton, D. P. Griffiths, N. J. Emery and A. Dickinson

A number of psychologists have suggested that episodic memory is a uniquely human phenomenon and, until recently, there was little evidence that animals could recall a unique past experience and respond appropriately. Experiments on food-caching memory in scrub jays question this assumption. On the basis of a single caching episode, scrub jays can remember when and where they cached a variety of foods that differ in the rate at which they degrade, in a way that is inexplicable by relative familiarity. They can update their memory of the contents of a cache depending on whether or not they have emptied the cache site, and can also remember where another bird has hidden caches, suggesting that they encode rich representations of the caching event. They make temporal generalizations about when perishable items should degrade and also remember the relative time since caching when the same food is cached in distinct sites at different times. These results show that jays form integrated memories for the location, content and time of caching. This memory capability fulfils Tulving's behavioural criteria for episodic memory and is thus termed 'episodic-like'. We suggest that several features of episodic memory may not be unique to humans.

13.1. Introduction

In the latter half of the nineteenth century, Charles Darwin suggested that mental characteristics are subject to natural selection in much the same way as morphological traits, and that human mental capabilities therefore share many features in common with those of other animals (Darwin 1871). Inspired by Darwin's thesis that we should be able to learn about our mental lives by studying those of other animals, comparative psychologists began to develop animal models of learning and memory and have spent the past hundred years and more in the scientific study of animal memory. Of the many categories of memory that humans possess (e.g. Squire *et al.* 1993; Schacter & Tulving 1994), there is only one form of memory that is thought to differentiate us from other animals—the ability to episodically recall unique past experiences (e.g. Suddendorf & Corballis 1997; Tulving 1983; Tulving & Markowitsch 1998). The argument is derived from the fact that language-based reports of episodic recall suggest that the retrieved experiences are explicitly located in the past ('mental time travel') and are accompanied by the conscious experience of recollection, so-called 'autonoetic consciousness' (Tulving & Markowitsch 1998).

This definition makes it impossible to demonstrate episodic memory in animals because there are no agreed non-linguistic behavioural markers of conscious experience (Griffiths *et al.* 1999). The dilemma can be resolved to some degree by adopting Tulving's (1972) original definition in which he states that episodic memory 'receives and stores information about temporally dated episodes or events, and temporal-spatial relations among these events' (p. 385). Thus, episodic memory provides information about the 'what' and 'when' of events ('temporally dated experiences') as well as 'where' they happened ('temporal-spatial relations'). The merit of this definition is that the simultaneous retrieval and integration of information about these three features of a single, unique experience may be demonstrated behaviourally in animals without the need for language. We therefore refer to an animal's ability to fulfil the behavioural criteria regardless of autonoetic consciousness as 'episodic-like' memory (Clayton & Dickinson 1998, 1999*a*).

To date, most studies of animal memory have not distinguished between episodic recall of events from semantic knowledge for facts that can be acquired over multiple trials. Typically, the memory tasks require the animal to retrieve information about only a single feature of the episode as opposed to testing its ability to form an integrated memory of 'temporal-spatial relations'. It is also common for the animal to be given multiple training experiences thereby removing the trial-uniqueness of the task (see Griffiths *et al.* 1999). Furthermore, in many of the tasks that have been used, the animal does not need to recall the 'what, where and when' of an event. Instead, the task may be solved by discriminating on the basis of relative familiarity, a process which is dissociable both psychologically (Mandler 1980; Jacoby & Dallas 1981; Jacoby 1991) and neurobiologically (Aggleton & Brown 1999) from episodic memory recall.

Most of the tasks that have been used to investigate animal memory can be explained in terms other than episodic recall. A different strategy of testing whether or not animals are capable of episodic memory is to adopt an ethological perspective and consider cases in nature in which an animal might need simultaneously to retrieve and integrate information about what happened, where and when during a specific previous experience. The ability to remember the 'what, where and when' of individual past episodes is probably met by several behaviours.

When considering the evolutionary history of episodic-like memory in animals, it might seem intuitively logical to focus on the abilities of non-human primates. The study of non-human primate coalition or alliance formation might provide a useful starting point, given that the social partners need to keep track of cognitively complex social relationships. Social status is at the core of monkey and ape society. Males are distinguished from each other on the basis of size, strength, fighting ability, etc., and the greater these attributes, the higher the individual's social status, and the greater their access to resources such as food and mating partners (Tomasello & Call 1997). Alliances are predominantly formed after a number of conflicts, usually between subordinate animals in attempts to gain access to those resources unavailable to them when alone, and are more long-term and more stable than coalitions (Van Schaik & Aureli 2000). Alliance formation may be more reliant on episodic-like memory processes than coalition formation because of the need to keep track of a number of different trial-unique events concerning who did what and to whom. Less certain are the roles of the 'where' and 'when' components of episodic-like memory in alliance formation, as there is still little known about the mechanisms of this behaviour.

An alternative strategy would be to look to the behavioural ecology of an animal that may provide important clues to which species may make use of, or require, an episodic-like memory. One potential candidate may be brood parasitism. Brood parasitic birds, such as cuckoos and cowbirds, deposit eggs in the nests of other species and the young are then cared for by the host species. This is a mechanism by which the parasitic birds may remove the high costs associated with parental care (by getting another bird to pay the costs). There are two types of brood parasite: specialists and generalists (Krebs &

Davies 1993). Cuckoos (*Cuculus canorus*) are specialist parasites in that they lay eggs in the nest of one species of host—they observe the host building a nest and then wait for them to begin their clutch, laying their egg during the host's laying period. Secrecy is of the essence, for fear of discovery by the host, and the total time spent at the host nest is thought to be less than 10 s in this species (Davies & Brook 1988). By contrast, brown-headed cowbirds (*Molothrus ater*) are generalist parasites because they lay their eggs in the nests of many species of host birds, each of which will produce clutches at different times. Both generalist and specialist parasites 'must remember where potential victims have started their nests in order to return to them one to several days later when the time is ripe for the cowbird to add her egg to those already laid' (Alcock 1998, pp. 112–113). A successful brood parasite may use information concerning the location of the host nest ('where'), the status of the clutch ('what') and the time of laying ('when'), although the memory load may be greater for generalist parasites in terms of the number of different host nests they visit. Episodic-like memory would be important for this form of parasitism, not only because the parasite would need to remember the 'what', 'where' and 'when', but also because these events are likely to be trial-unique. The parasite would not be able to keep returning to each host nest to see whether the clutch had been laid through fear of discovery by the host. Thus every discovery of a possible host nest would be a trial-unique event and the calculation of the relative time to parasitize each nest would be essential.

Another potential candidate for a natural use of episodic-like memory may be present in animals that have a polygynous mating system, such as some species of vole. Meadow vole (*Microtus pennsylvanicus*) males mate with multiple females and have larger home range sizes than females of the same species, and of other species of voles that form long-term pair-bonds with only one partner (Jacobs *et al.* 1990). Male meadow voles control a large number of females through mate guarding at the time of oestrus and the females mate exclusively with that male. The females are distributed over a wide area and come into oestrus at different times. One potential mechanism by which the male can keep track of the females' reproductive state, and ensure that the females do not reproduce with other males, may be through the use of episodic-like memory. Again, this form of behaviour could benefit from the ability to remember the 'what' (female identity), 'where' (location of female') and 'when' (changing reproductive state and relative time of states between females) components of episodic-like memory. This form of behaviour would also be trial-unique because every female would be encountered during a particular reproductive state at a particular location.

The final example we will consider in more detail is food caching. The advantage of food caching is that it can be studied in the laboratory as well as in the field, and is easily amenable to experimentation. Scatter hoarding birds hide hundreds of seeds throughout the territory and rely on memory to recover their food caches, weeks or even months later (for a comprehensive review, see Shettleworth 1995). It is well established that food caching species remember cache locations. There are good reasons to believe that they would need to encode much richer representations of the caching event, however. It is known, for example, that some food-caching species do not return to sites from which they have retrieved all the food, which suggests that they can remember whether or not they have emptied a cache site (Clayton & Dickinson 1999*b*; Shettleworth & Krebs 1986). Some of these species, including scrub jays (*Aphelocoma* *coerulescens*) cache insects and other perishable items as well as seeds (Vander Wall 1990). It may be adaptive, therefore, for them to encode and recall information about what has been cached when as well as where.

In order to fulfil the behavioural criteria for episodic memory, animals would need to be able to encode the information about the caching or recovery episode based on a specific past experience, and then accurately recall the information about what, where and when a particular past event occurred. In the remainder of this paper, we will describe a series of experiments on episodic-like memory in scrub jays and discuss how these studies may provide a working model for testing episodic-like memory in animals in the absence of language (Clayton & Dickinson 1998). To test the jays' ability to retrieve and integrate information simultaneously about the 'what, where and when' of a specific caching episode we capitalized on the jays' natural propensity to cache perishable and non-perishable food items, and rely on memory to search for their caches at a later date. In this way, we could test their ability to remember the contents and location of their caches and the relative time of caching in terms of whether or not the cached items should have perished by the time of recovery.

13.2. Episodic-like memory in food-storing birds

To test whether scrub jays are capable of episodic-like memory, birds were allowed to cache perishable foods, such as mealworms and crickets, and non-perishable peanuts in sand-filled caching trays on Monday morning. The scrub jays were divided into two groups, 'degrade' and 'replenish', which differed in whether or not they had the opportunity to learn that some foods are perishable and therefore degrade over time. Both groups of birds were given the opportunity to recover their caches on Monday afternoon (i.e. 4 h later), Tuesday afternoon (i.e. following a 28 h retention interval) or on Friday afternoon (i.e. after a 100 h retention interval). The logic is as follows. Jays show a strong preference to cache, recover and eat the perishable foods when they are fresh, and prefer both mealworms and crickets to peanuts, but prefer mealworms to crickets. Both mealworms and crickets degrade rapidly over time, however, so that if they are left for several days they become rotten and unpalatable. If birds in the degrade group can remember when they cached as well as what they cached and where, then they should recover the perishable foods when they were cached just a few hours ago. They should avoid them, however, and instead search for peanut caches, if the mealworms and crickets were cached several days ago and have had time to degrade. To ensure that the perishable items were thoroughly degraded, we coated them in washing up liquid and left them to rot in the sun. A supply of these degraded mealworms and crickets was kept in the refrigerator. We arranged for the mealworms to degrade more quickly than the crickets: mealworms were only fresh 4 h later and had degraded by both the middle and the long retention intervals, whereas the crickets were still fresh after 28 h, but were rotten 100 h after caching (Clayton *et al.* 2001).

To ensure that each episode was unique, the birds cached and recovered from trial-unique plastic, sand-filled ice-cube trays that contained two rows of eight ice cube moulds that served as individual cache sites. Each tray was attached to a wooden board and surrounded by a visuo-spatially distinct Lego Duplo structure that was placed next to one of the long sides of the tray (see Clayton & Dickinson 1998, 1999*a,b*). The jays cached the perishable items in one side of the tray and then cached non-perishable items in the opposite side of the same tray, or vice versa. Birds were given access to only half of a tray at a time by attaching a transparent Perspex cover over one half of the tray with bulldog clips, thereby restricting access to one column of eight cache sites parallel to the Lego structure.

The 'degrade' group received a series of training trials in which they had the opportunity to learn when the mealworms and crickets degrade. They were allowed to cache two food types and then recover them after retention intervals of 4, 28 and 100 h. They cached peanuts (P) in one side of a caching tray on every trial and then either mealworms (M) or crickets (C) in the other side so that each bird received alternating P/M and P/C trials at each of the three retention intervals. The six different types of training trials are illustrated in Figure 13.1, as are the predicted choices for the 'degrade' group. The birds should selectively recover mealworms on P/M trials and crickets on P/C trials, when those items are fresh. They should switch their preference to peanuts, however, when the mealworms were cached 28 or 100 h ago on P/M trials, and when the crickets were cached 100 h ago on P/C trials.

The birds were given only four P/C and P/M trials at each retention interval because the 'degrade' group birds acquired this information about rates of perishability after just two or three trials of each type. To assess the extent to which their recovery searches depended on memory, the experiment concluded with six test trials (P/M and P/C trials at each retention interval) in which all the food items had been removed prior to recovery. The trays were filled with fresh sand so that no extraneous cues were present and the birds therefore had to rely on their memory of where and when the worms and peanuts had been cached. As predicted, the results of both training and test trials showed that the 'degrade' group jays reversed their search preference when the retention interval was such that the perishable foods would have degraded. The fact that this switch in search preference was observed even on test trials in which no food was present at recovery shows that the jays relied on memory as opposed to visual, olfactory or tactile cues that may emanate directly from the sand covering the hidden food.

Finally, to ensure that the preference profile depended on learning about the perishability of the mealworms and crickets, the performance of the 'degrade' group was compared with that of the 'replenish' group in which both mealworms and crickets were fresh on every trial. As predicted, birds in the 'replenish' group searched preferentially for mealworms and crickets at all retention intervals on both training and test trials. The fact that the 'replenish' group did not show the switch in search preference on P/M and P/C trials rules out a simple explanation in terms of differential rates of forgetting for the different types of food caches. It also rules out the possibility that jays use some intrinsic, unlearned sensory properties of the food, such as texture or shape, to guide their preference to search for perishable foods after the short retention interval but to avoid them when a long time had elapsed between caching and recovery. The results of this first experiment suggest that the 'degrade' group scrub jays can rapidly learn to remember temporal information about when the items were cached relative to recovery, as well as which items were cached where.

Without further training, the birds were given a new caching condition that they had not experienced previously: the birds cached mealworms in one side of the tray and crickets in the other side of the same tray. We gave them a test trial (i.e. no food present

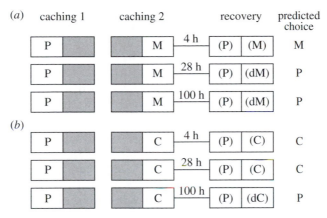

Fig. 13.1. The caching and recovery conditions during each type of training trial for the two sides of the caching tray during the two caching periods and the recovery period for experiment 1; (*a*) P/M trials, (*b*) P/C trials. Also shown are the predicted choices for the degrade group at recovery. The shaded areas represent the non-accessible side of the tray and the non-shaded areas the accessible side. P, peanuts; M, fresh mealworms; C, fresh crickets; dM, decayed mealworms; dC, decayed crickets; ( ), food items present on training trials but absent on test trials. h = hour. Reprinted by permission of Clayton *et al.* (2001, fig. 1).

during recovery) in which they were allowed to search for these caches either 4 h (when both foods are still fresh) or 28 h later (when the mealworms have decayed but the crickets are still fresh). Since the birds prefer fresh mealworms to crickets, the 'replenish' group should always search preferentially in the sites in which they had cached the mealworms. If birds in the 'degrade' group can apply their knowledge about the relative perishability profiles of mealworms and crickets derived from earlier P/M and P/C trials to this novel M/C trial, then they should search selectively for mealworms when they had been cached 4 h ago but switch to searching for crickets when the mealworms had been cached 28 h previously. The results confirmed these expectations, demonstrating that the birds can remember where and when they hid their caches. The birds also possess sufficient information about the contents of the caches to allow them to distinguish between mealworm and cricket cache sites. Furthermore, the results suggest that the birds can flexibly use the information learned in one context and apply it to a new caching condition.

In order to search preferentially for mealworms during the four-hour test trials and for crickets during the 28-hour test trials, at the time of recovery birds in the 'degrade' group must have been able to recognize the trays in which they had cached mealworms and crickets earlier. Like many other tests of memory, the problem is that this task can be solved either by recollection or by familiarity. Familiarity is an automatic process based on the perceptual characteristics of the stimuli that allow the individual to distinguish previously experienced stimuli from novel ones, but it does not require the birds to remember any of the details of the original presentation of the stimuli (Mandler 1980; Jacoby & Dallas 1981; Jacoby 1991). Thus the jays may have based their decision of when to search for mealworms on the relative familiarity of the two trays as opposed to recalling what they cached where and when. If this were the case then 'degrade' group birds could have learned to search in mealworm sites on the four-hour trials when the tray was relatively familiar, and learned to search in cricket sites when the tray had not been seen for 28 h and was therefore relatively unfamiliar.

We therefore tested whether the jays could remember what, where and when in the absence of using tray familiarity as a cue. The same birds were given a further pair of test trials in which they cached mealworms in one side of the tray and crickets in the other side of the same tray. On the M/C trial, birds cached mealworms first and then, instead of caching crickets immediately afterwards, there was a retention interval of 24 h between the two caching events followed by a further gap of 4 h before the recovery test phase (in which no food was present, so we could test for memory). Thus, the mealworms were 28 h old and the crickets were only 4 h old at the time of recovery on the M/C trial. The reverse order of caching was enforced on the C/M trial so that the crickets were 28 h old, and the mealworms were still fresh, having been cached only 4 h ago. If the 'degrade' group birds were relying on familiarity to solve the task then they should preferentially search for mealworms on both M/C and C/M trials because on both recovery test trials the tray had been seen only 4 h ago. By contrast, if the birds remembered how long ago each type of food had been cached then they should only search for mealworm cache sites on C/M trials (when the mealworms had been cached 4 h ago) and switch to cricket caches on M/C trials (when the mealworms had been cached 28 h ago and should therefore have degraded). The 'degrade' group birds showed this switch in preference from mealworm sites on C/M trials to cricket sites on M/C trials and, as expected, the 'replenish' group always searched in mealworm sites. We therefore conclude that the 'degrade' group birds must have remembered the time at which they cached the mealworms and in a way that cannot be explained by relative familiarity of the trays (Clayton *et al.* 2001).

Taken together, the results of this series of experiments show that jays can remember the 'what, where and when' of specific past caching episodes. We believe that the specific 'what–where–when' information encoded during each trial-unique caching period is episodic in nature. By contrast, the information about the decay properties of the food that the birds acquired during training can be characterized as non-episodic (semantic-like) declarative memory as opposed to procedural memory because of the flexible way in which the birds use this information about the decay properties of the food. The jays used information about the decay profiles of mealworms and crickets learned during training on P/M and P/C trials in the first experiment to control searching in C/M and M/C trials in which the jays were given a direct choice between mealworm and crickets cache sites for the first time.

13.3. Remembering the 'what' of an event

The results in the previous section suggest that food-caching scrub jays can remember some information about the contents of their caches, as well as the relative time since caching and the locations in which the items were cached. Stronger support for this claim that birds remember the 'what' of an event comes from a second study in which we assessed how richly the events that occur during a caching episode are encoded by contrasting memory for caching with that for recovery (Clayton & Dickinson 1999*b*). The fact that some food-caching species do not return to sites from which they have retrieved all the food (e.g. Shettleworth & Krebs 1986) suggests that they can remember whether or not they have emptied a cache site. In order to do so, the birds would need to distinguish between the actions of placing the bill in the sand to cache, and placing the bill in the sand to recover the cache. Of course, these caching and recovery episodes involve memory for the location and content of the same food items. The episodes differ in terms of the type of actions performed, namely caching or recovering caches, and whether the food cache is intact at the end of the episode (after caching) or whether the cache site is now empty (after recovery).

The study consisted of four caching phases and two recovery phases followed by a recovery test phase. Birds cached three peanuts in the left-hand sides, and three dog-food kibbles in the right-hand sides, of two visuo-spatially distinct caching trays. They were then allowed to recover all three peanuts from one tray and all three kibbles from the other tray 3 h later. This meant that at the end of these recovery phases, one tray contained only kibbles and the other tray contained only peanuts. As in the previous experiment, the birds had access to only half a tray at a time during caching and recovery. In a final test, both sides of both trays were presented to the bird simultaneously. The caches were removed prior to this test trial and the trays were filled with fresh sand so that no extraneous cues were present and the birds therefore had to rely on their memory. If they can remember what type of food they had cached in each of the sites, what they had recovered from each site, and can integrate these two sources of information, then during the test trial birds ought to go to the tray that should still contain their preferred food (Clayton & Dickinson 1999b).

The relative preference of the foods at recovery was manipulated by pre-feeding the jays with one of the two food types because pre-feeding of a specific food selectively reduces the subsequent value of that food in terms of both eating and caching (Clayton & Dickinson 1999c). They were pre-fed peanuts or dog biscuits in powdered form to ensure they could not cache during the pre-feeding phase. Those that had been pre-fed peanuts preferentially searched in the cache sites in which they had cached dog biscuits and selectively searched only in those sites from which the birds had not recovered dog biscuits during the previous recovery phase (i.e. the intact dog biscuit sites). Likewise, those birds that had been pre-fed dog biscuits preferentially searched in the intact peanut sites. This ability to encode what action occurred, and whether the cache site still contains food, enables the animal to keep track of 'what' is cached and 'where' across a series of caching and recovery episodes (Clayton & Dickinson 1999b).

The results of this second study confirm the finding described in the previous section that scrub jays encode information about the contents of their caches. Without this knowledge they could not have directed their searches selectively to the tray that should still have contained the non-pre-fed food. The results also show that the birds can integrate information of the content of a cache at recovery with information about the specific location of the cache. Without the capacity for such integration, the birds could not have directed their searches selectively to the intact sides of the tray, let alone to the particular cache sites in which they had stored the food items. Furthermore, their ability to encode what action occurred, and whether the cache site still contains food, enables the animal to keep track of 'what' is cached and 'where' across a series of caching and recovery episodes (Clayton & Dickinson 1999b).

In a third study we tested whether scrub jays can remember where a conspecific has cached and then subsequently recover (pilfer) them more accurately than conspecifics who are not given the opportunity to observe food caching (D. P. Griffiths, A. L.

Duarte and N. S. Clayton, unpublished data). Although other studies have suggested that corvids have this ability, this study introduced a novel control for the use of other potential cues that may signal the location of food, thereby limiting the difference between the groups to the opportunity to observe caching. Storer birds cached in a sand-filled caching tray in their home cage. The control and observer birds' cages were equidistant from the storer's cage, but differed in whether or not they could see the storer as well as hear the bird caching. The observer bird had the opportunity to see where the storer cached by observing through a Plexiglas screen that divided the two cages. The control could not see the storer because the divider between the control's and storer's cage was made of aluminium. The control group could therefore listen but not look.

After a retention interval of approximately 4 h, each subject had the opportunity to search in the caching tray in which the storer had cached. During recovery, none of the other birds could observe the subject as a dark cloth was placed between the cages to entirely cover the back of the cage. We then compared accuracy of recovery when each of the three groups of birds had the opportunity to search for the storer's caches. As in the previous studies, there was no food available during the recovery phase of the test trial so the birds had to rely on memory. Although scrub jays that stored food were the most accurate at cache recovery, the results of this experiment also showed that observer birds made fewer searches to discover the cached food, relative to control birds that could hear but not watch the items being stored. These results suggest that observation is an effective mechanism by which a bird can increase its pilfering success.

Taken together, the results of the experiments described in this section demonstrate that the bird's ability to encode and recall 'what' memories is not limited to information about the contents of the caches. Jays can also remember other types of 'what' information such as whether or not the food has been recovered and whether that information has been gained by a personal experience of caching or as a result of observing another individual's food-caching behaviour.

13.4. Keeping track of time

The ability to accurately encode and recall trial-unique spatial locations has been well established across a variety of spatial memory tasks, from the performance of rats in radial arm mazes (e.g. Olton & Samuelson 1976) to the caching behaviour of food-storing birds (e.g. Shettleworth 1995). The results described in the previous sections provide strong evidence for the claim that scrub jays can also remember 'what' occurred during caching: our results suggest the birds can recall information about the type of food item cached and the nature of the behavioural transaction in terms of whether it was cached or recovered. It is also clear that the jays can remember the relative time since caching, in the absence of using tray familiarity as a cue. What is less clear, however, is the mechanism by which the jays keep track of time and the nature of the temporal representation of caching episodes.

In order to characterize the nature of this temporal control, Clayton and colleagues conducted a further experiment to assess the temporal generalization of search preferences for birds that had received the peanut and cricket caching trials (N. S. Clayton, K. Yu and A. D. Dickinson, unpublished data). Having been trained with 4,

28 and 100 h retention interval trials, both 'degrade' and 'replenish' group birds were given probe tests in which no food was present during recovery to test whether the pattern of searching was based upon memory for the caching episode. Birds cached peanuts and crickets as usual but then received these recovery tests at untrained retention intervals of 52, 76 and 124 h, i.e. after two, three and five days. These generalization tests were conducted in pairs. The first pair assessed the recovery preference after two- and three-day retention intervals, whereas the second reassessed recovery after the three-day interval and compared the preference with that observed after a five-day retention interval.

The replenish group showed a consistent preference to search in the cricket cache sites across variations in the retention interval. By contrast, the proportion of searches varied with retention interval for the degrade group. After the one-, two- and three-day intervals, birds in the 'degrade' group also showed a strong preference to search in cricket cache sites. The four- and five-day intervals produced a marked divergence between the groups with the 'degrade' group searching preferentially in the peanut cache sites. This generalization of search preferences across variations in retention interval suggests that the 'degrade' group scrub jays treated the perishability of crickets categorically. Having been trained that crickets are fresh and palatable at 4 h and one-day intervals, but decayed and disgusting after a four-day interval, these birds showed a stable preference for the crickets at intervals shorter than four days but a marked preference for peanuts at intervals of four days or longer.

The fact that the search preferences of the replenish group were independent of the retention interval also provides strong support for the claim that the jays were not simply forgetting the locations of the various food types at different rates. Clearly, the temporal control of searching by the 'degrade' group could not have reflected more rapid forgetting of the perishable caches. This temporal control could have been mediated by the strength of a decaying trace of a 'what–where' memory, however, without any direct encoding of the time of caching. In his review of memory for the time of past events, Friedman (1993) identified the strength of a decaying memory trace for an episode as one of the possible processes by which humans judge the time of the episode. An account in terms of strength of a memory trace assumes that the jays in the 'degrade' group learn to search mealworm or cricket sites if a retrieved 'what–where' memory is strong and to search for the peanuts sites if the memory trace is weak. This account rests on the implausible assumption that the discriminability of memory traces does not vary with their strength. Using a specific satiety devaluation procedure, Clayton & Dickinson (1999b) reported that the difference between searching for caches of the devalued and non-devalued food was just as strong after a 172 h retention interval as after one of 4 h, thereby demonstrating that the discriminability of the 'what–where' memories for the two foods was just as good after one week as after a few hours. The overall level of searching did not decrease with retention interval in any of the aforementioned jay experiments, as might be expected if the strength of the memory trace for a cache episode determines searching activity.

There is no doubt that animals can time elapsed intervals (Bradshaw & Szababi 1997). Interval timing has been studied mainly using operant conditioning procedures in rats and pigeons and there is now an extensive body of data and theory about the processes underlying interval timing (for a review, see Shettleworth 1998). Essentially, the encoding event is thought to start an internal 'clock' in the form of a pacemaker (e.g. Gibbon *et al.* 1984) or a series of oscillators (e.g. Church & Broadbent 1990). To time events, the animal compares the current state of its clock with a stored reference value that was acquired during training. In evaluating the relevance of such models to the temporal control of cache recovery, it is important to note that these models are based on tests using operant conditioning procedures in which the elapsed intervals are a matter of seconds, minutes and at most a few hours (Gibbon *et al.* 1997), rather than days involved in cache recovery. The fact that jays in the 'degrade' group showed a switch in preference from mealworms to peanuts at both the 28 h and 100 h retention intervals, yet showed a switch from crickets to peanuts after only the 100 h interval, requires the bird to use multiple timers simultaneously, each associated with a particular cache location. Furthermore, the birds could not simply use the passing of a night as a cue for when to switch their search preference because the degrade group birds discriminated between one and four diurnal cycles in their searches for crickets and peanuts. There are, however, a number of other processes that could have mediated the temporal control observed in these caching studies. For example, Gallistel (1990) has argued that animals automatically encode the time of an experience in memory with some form of time tag. In addition to trace strength and automatic time tagging, Friedman (1993) identifies six further processes that could play a role in human temporal memory.

13.5. The structure of integrated 'what, where and when' memories

The experiments described in the previous sections suggest that scrub jays form integrated memories of the 'what, where and when' of a caching episode, but they do not address the structure of this integrated memory. It has been suggested that the retrieval of information about a discrete event, such as a caching episode, depends on multiple, complex mnemonic structures and processes (e.g. Gallistel 1990; McClelland *et al.* 1995; Teylor & DiScenna 1986). The aim of the final experiment was to attempt to specify the minimal memory structure required to support the cache recovery observed in the present studies (see Clayton *et al.* 2001).

One possibility is that the presentation of the caching tray at recovery activates 'where' representations of the cache sites, which in turn retrieves both 'what' representations of the food items cached at those locations and 'when' representations of how long ago the caching event occurred in that location. We shall refer to this memory structure as a 'what–*where*–when' structure to illustrate that the 'what' and 'when' information is integrated into the memory of the caching episode through the 'where' representation of the cache sites. Figure 13.2*a* illustrates the structure of such 'what–*where*–when' memories in the case in which peanuts were cached in the left side of a caching tray and mealworms were cached in the right-hand side relatively recently. Note that there is no direct association between 'what' and 'when'. At retrieval, the bird can recall what type of food it cached in a particular location and when it stored the food in that location, but it has no direct access to temporal information from the content representation or *vice versa*. Only the 'where' information provides access to both 'what' and 'when' memories.

An alternative structure is a 'where–*what*–when' memory in which binding occurs through the 'what' representation, which retrieves information about where and when those food items were cached but in this case there is no direct association between the 'where' and 'when' representations. Figure 13.2*b* illustrates the structure of the 'where–*what*–when' memories for the same caching episode as shown in Figure 13.2*a*, namely when peanuts were cached in the left and mealworms were cached in the right side of a caching tray just a few hours previously.

The final possibility is a 'what–*when*–where' structure. In this case, the information about 'what' and 'where' are integrated indirectly as a result of both being bound by a 'when' representation of the time of caching. This structure is not illustrated in Figure 13.2 because it cannot support the patterns of recovery already described in the previous studies. Consider the case in which the birds cached crickets and mealworms, and then searched for their caches either 4 h or 28 h later. According to this 'what–*when*–where' structure, both the recent and remote temporal representations would both retrieve 'what' representations of the two foods. The recent and remote temporal representations would also retrieve 'where' representations of the two sides of the caching tray but, without a direct link between the 'what–where', the bird would be precluded from knowing which type of food item was stored where. Consequently, this memory structure would not allow selective searching for the two food types depending on whether the foods had been cached 4 or 28 h ago. The patterns of recovery observed in those previous experiments can be explained by both a 'what–*where*–when' (Figure 13.2*a*) and a 'where–*what*–when' structure (Figure 13.2*b*), however. In the final experiment we therefore distinguished between the two structures.

The design capitalized on the fact that, under certain circumstances, the 'where–*what*–when' memory cannot support appropriate search patterns for a single type of food item depending upon the time since caching. Consider the following scenario in which jays cache mealworms in tray 1 on a Thursday morning, then cache mealworms in tray 2 on a Friday morning and are allowed to search for their caches 4 h later on a Friday afternoon. Whether or not the birds should search for mealworms depends upon which tray is presented at recovery. The birds should avoid mealworm sites when presented with tray 1 because the mealworms were cached 28 h previously and should have already decayed. When tray 2 is presented, however, they should search for the mealworm caches because those mealworm caches are only 4 h old and should still be fresh.

A 'where–*what*–when' memory cannot support this search pattern, however, because the birds can remember what was cached where, and what was cached when, but there is no direct memory for when and where (Figure 13.2*c*). According to this memory structure, the bird should retrieve the 'what' representation of mealworms when presented with either tray and this mealworm representation should then retrieve 'when' representations for both the 24 h and the 4 h retention intervals. Consequently, the bird would have conflicting temporal information about when the mealworms had been cached and would not be able to use its knowledge about perishability to search for the relatively fresh mealworms and avoid searching for the older ones. To do so, 'when' and 'where' representations must be bound directly. A 'what–*where*–when' memory structure (Figure 13.2*d*) can support the appropriate search pattern, however, because the 'where' representation retrieves

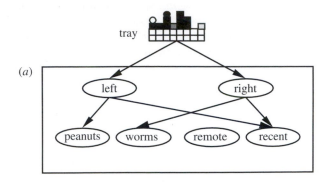

(a)

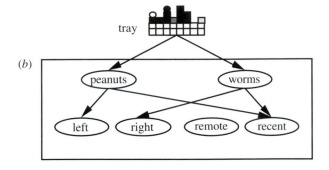

(b)

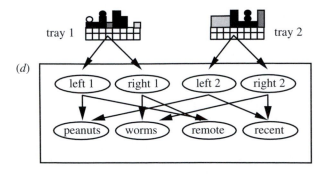

(c)

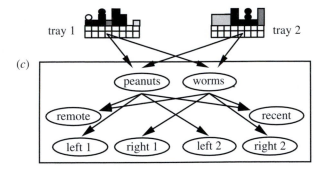

(d)

information about both the time of caching in that location as well as the contents of those caches.

We therefore allowed the birds in both the 'degrade' and 'replenish' groups to cache peanuts in one side of a tray and mealworms in the other, on two occasions separated by a day. Different trays were used on each day. Four hours after the second caching period, the jays were given two recovery periods in succession, first with the tray in which they cached on the first day and then with the tray in which they cached on the second day. No food was present during recovery in order to test for memory. As expected, birds in the replenish group that always received fresh mealworms irrespective of retention interval consistently searched in the mealworm sites in both trays. It is the birds in the 'degrade' group, however, that provide the critical test concerning the type of memory structure jays might use when encoding a caching episode. As predicted, birds in the 'degrade' group searched preferentially in the peanut side of the first tray but searched mainly in the mealworm side of the second tray. This result is therefore consistent with a 'what–*where*–when' memory structure in which the animals can remember both the 'what and where' and also the 'when and where' (Figure 13.2*d*). It should be noted, however, that this structure is only the most parsimonious one warranted by the present studies and that the same performance could, of course, be supported by more complex mnemonic structures and processes. Gallistel (1990), for example, has also argued that feeding-related experiences set up multiple memory records that encode and integrate what, where and when information.

13.6. Conclusions

The results of this series of experiments show that jays possess an episodic-like memory of the 'what, where and when' of specific caching events that have occurred in the past. The jays can also remember what they recovered and from where, they can differentiate between memories of caching and recovering, and update information about the current status of their caches, based on whether or not they have already recovered from that particular cache. In addition, they can remember information about the social context of the caching event, based on whether they have a personal experience of food caching or have observed another bird doing so. When integrated, the jay has sufficient information to isolate 'what', 'where' and 'when' and thus is able to recall the episode of caching a specific item (Griffiths *et al.* 1999). These results fulfil Tulving's original behavioural criteria for episodic memory by providing information about 'temporally-dated experiences' and their 'temporal-spatial relations' (Tulving 1972).

There is a large gap between human and animal studies of memory and, in particular, the extent to which non-human animals possess episodic-like memory. This is principally

---

Fig. 13.2. (*opposite*) The memory structures for caching episodes (see text). (*a*) the 'what–*where*–when' structure for peanuts cached in the left side of the tray and mealworms in the right side of the tray relatively recently. (*b*) The 'where–*what*–when' structure for the same caching episodes as in (*a*). (*c*) The 'where–*what*–when' structure for peanuts cached in the left sides of the trays and mealworms in the right sides when caching occurred in tray 1 at a time remote from recovery and in tray 2 more recently. (*d*) The 'what–*where*–when' structure for the same caching episodes as in (*c*). Reprinted from Clayton *et al.* (2001, fig. 7).

due to the absence of suitable tasks that can isolate episodic memory without the reliance on language for testing episodic recall. We now believe, however, that the food-caching paradigm can test the ability of an animal to recall episodic-like information about a specific past experience and is mediated by an integrated or bound memory with at least a 'what–where–when' structure. A challenge for the future will be to develop other tasks that capture some of the critical features of episodic memory that do not rely on language, which in turn may provide invaluable insights into how space, time and events are represented and remembered in the brain.

Griffiths *et al.* (1999) have argued that unlike the food-caching jay paradigm, previous demonstrations of trial-unique memory in animals could have been mediated by relative familiarity rather than the temporal encoding of the episode and, hence, do not require an integrated memory of the features of the episode. Based on the results of a recent experiment, Menzel (1999) suggests that chimpanzees can remember the location and content of food sources. It remains to be seen whether the chimpanzees can also form integrated 'what–where–when' memories. As we suggested at the outset, the ecological approach to animal cognition (e.g. Real 1993; Healy & Braithwaite 2000) suggests that there may be a number of other naturally occurring situations in which an animal's ability to encode and recall integrated memories of specific past events are of vital importance to its survival. Potential candidates include brood parasitism, mate guarding in polygynous species where females come into oestrus at different times, and possibly social signalling systems such as the ability to form coalitions and maintain alliances in some monkeys and apes. The capacity for episodic-like memory is unlikely to be unique to humans and food-storing birds, and is probably important for survival in a number of animals.

References

Aggleton, J. P. & Brown, M. W. 1999 Episodic memory, amnesia and the hippocampal-anterior thalamic axis. *Behav. Brain Sci.* **22**, 425–444.

Alcock, J. 1998 The development of behavior: role of the environment. In *Animal behavior* (J. Alcock), 6th edn, chapter 4, pp. 87–125. Sunderland, MA: Sinauer.

Bradshaw, C. M. & Szabadi, E. 1997 *Time and behavior: psychological and neurobehavioral analyses.* Amsterdam: Elsevier.

Church, R. M. & Broadbent, H. A. 1990 Alternative representations of time, number, and rate. *Cognition* **37**, 55–81.

Clayton, N. S. & Dickinson, A. D. 1998 Episodic-like memory during cache recovery by scrub jays. *Nature* **395**, 272–274.

Clayton, N. S. & Dickinson, A. D. 1999*a* Scrub jays (*Aphelocoma coerulescens*) remember when as well as where and what food items they cached. *J. Comp. Psychol.* **113**, 403–416.

Clayton, N. S. & Dickinson, A. D. 1999*b* Memory for the content of caches by scrub jays. *J. Exp. Psychol. Anim. Behav. Process.* **25**, 82–91.

Clayton, N. S. & Dickinson, A. D. 1999*c* Motivational control of food storing in the scrub jay *Aphelocoma coerulescens. Anim. Behav.* **57**, 435–444.

Clayton, N. S., Yu, K. & Dickinson, A. D. 2001 Scrub jays (*Aphelocoma coerulescens*) can form integrated memory for multiple features of caching episodes. *J. Exp. Psychol. Anim. Behav. Process.* **27**, 17–29.

Darwin, C. 1871 *The descent of man, and selection in relation to sex.* London: John Murray. Second edition 1874; facsimile reproduction of first edition with an introduction by John Tyler Bonner and Robert M. May, 1981. Princeton University Press.

Davies, N. B. & Brooke, M. de L. 1988 Cuckoos versus reed warblers: adaptations and counteradaptations. *Anim. Behav.* **36**, 262–284.

Friedman, W. J. 1993 Memory for the time of past events. *Psychol. Bull.* **113**, 44–66.

Gallistel, C. R. 1990 *The organization of learning.* Cambridge, MA: MIT Press.

Gibbon, J., Church, R. M. & Meck, W. H. 1984 Scalar timing in memory. In *Timing and time perception* (ed. J. Gibbon & L. Allan), pp. 52–77. New York Academy of Sciences.

Gibbon, J., Fairhurst, S. & Goldberg, B. 1997 Cooperation, conflict and compromise between circadian and interval clocks in pigeons. In *Time and behavior: psychological and neurobehavioral analyses* (ed. C. M. Bradshaw & E. Szabadi), pp. 329–384. Amsterdam: Elsevier.

Griffiths, D. P., Dickinson, A. & Clayton, N. S. 1999 Declarative and episodic memory: what can animals remember about their past? *Trends Cogn. Sci.* **3**, 74–80.

Healy, S. D. & Braithwaite, V. 2000 Cognitive ecology: a field of substance? *Trends Ecol. Evol.* **15**, 22–26.

Jacobs, L. F., Gaulin, S. J. C., Sherry, D. F. & Hoffman, G. E. 1990 Evolution of spatial cognition: sex-specific patterns of spatial behavior predict hippocampal size. *Proc. Natl Acad. Sci. USA* **87**, 6349–6352.

Jacoby, L. L. 1991 A process dissociation framework: separating automatic from intentional uses of memory. *J. Mem. Lang.* **30**, 513–541.

Jacoby, L. L. & Dallas, M. 1981 On the relationship between autobiographical memory and perceptual learning. *J. Exp. Psychol. Gen.* **3**, 306–340.

Krebs, J. R. & Davies, N. B. 1993 Predators versus prey: evolutionary arms races. In *An introduction to behavioural ecology* (ed. J. R. Krebs & N. B. Davies), 3rd edn, chapter 4, pp. 77–101. Oxford: Blackwell Science Ltd.

McClelland, J. L., McNaughton, B. L. & O'Reilly, R. C. 1995. Why there are complementary learning systems in the hippocampus and neocortex: insights from successes and failures of connectionist models of learning and memory. *Psychol. Rev.* **102**, 419–457.

Mandler, G. 1980 Recognising: the judgement of previous experience. *Psychol. Rev.* **87**, 252–271.

Menzel, C. R. 1999 Unprompted recall and reporting of hidden objects by a chimpanzee (*Pan troglodytes*) after extended delays. *J. Comp. Psychol.* **113**, 1–9.

Olton, D. A. & Samuelson, R. J. 1976 Remembrance of places past: spatial memory in rats. *J. Exp. Psychol. Anim. Behav. Process.* **2**, 97–116.

Real, L. A. 1993 Toward a cognitive ecology. *Trends Ecol. Evol.* **8**, 413–417.

Schacter, D. L. & Tulving, E. 1994 What are the memory systems of 1994? In *Memory systems* (ed. D. L. Schacter & E. Tulving), pp. 1–38. Cambridge, MA: MIT Press.

Shettleworth, S. J. 1995 Memory in food-storing birds: from the field to the skinner box. In *Behavioral brain research in naturalistic and semi-naturalistic settings* (ed. E. Alleva, A Fasolo, H.-P. Lipp & L. Nadel), pp. 158–179. Proceedings of NATO Advanced Study Institute Series Maratea, Italy. The Hague, The Netherlands: Kluwer.

Shettleworth, S. J. 1998 Timing and counting. In *Cognition, evolution and behavior* (S. J. Shettleworth), pp. 333–378. Oxford University Press.

Shettleworth, S. J. & Krebs, J. R. 1986 Stored and encountered seeds: a comparison of two spatial memory tasks in marsh tits and chickadees. *J. Exp. Psychol. Anim. Behav. Process.* **3**, 248–257.

Squire, L. R., Knowlton, B. & Musen, G. 1993 The structure and organization of memory. *A. Rev. Psychol.* **44**, 453–496.

Suddendorf, T. & Corballis, M. C. 1997 Mental time travel and the evolution of the human mind. *Genet. Soc. Gen. Psychol. Monogr.* **123**, 133–167.

Teyler, T. J. & DiScenna, P. 1986 The hippocampal memory indexing theory. *Behav. Neurosci.* **100**, 147–154.

Tomasello, M. & Call, J. 1997 *Primate cognition.* New York: Oxford University Press.

Tulving, E. 1972 Episodic and semantic memory. In *Organisation of memory* (ed. E. Tulving & W. Donaldson), pp. 381–403. New York: Academic Press.

Tulving, E. 1983 *Elements of episodic memory.* Oxford: Clarendon Press.

Tulving, E. & Markowitsch, H. J. 1998 Episodic and declarative memory: role of the hippocampus. *Hippocampus* **8**, 198–204.

Van Schaik, C. P. & Aureli, F. 2000 The natural history of valuable relationships in primates. In *Natural conflict resolution* (ed. F. Aureli & F. B. M. de Waal), pp. 306–333. Berkeley, CA: University of California Press.

Vander Wall, S. B. 1990 *Food hoarding in animals*. Chicago: University of Chicago Press.

14

Memory for events and their spatial context: models and experiments

Neil Burgess, Suzanna Becker, John A. King and John O'Keefe

The computational role of the hippocampus in memory has been characterized as: (i) an index to disparate neocortical storage sites; (ii) a time-limited store supporting neocortical long-term memory; and (iii) a content-addressable associative memory. These ideas are reviewed and related to several general aspects of episodic memory, including the differences between episodic, recognition and semantic memory, and whether hippocampal lesions differentially affect recent or remote memories. Some outstanding questions remain, such as: what characterizes episodic retrieval as opposed to other forms of read-out from memory; what triggers the storage of an event memory; and what are the neural mechanisms involved? To address these questions a neural-level model of the medial temporal and parietal roles in retrieval of the spatial context of an event is presented. This model combines the idea that retrieval of the rich context of real-life events is a central characteristic of episodic memory, and the idea that medial temporal allocentric representations are used in long-term storage while parietal egocentric representations are used to imagine, manipulate and re-experience the products of retrieval. The model is consistent with the known neural representation of spatial information in the brain, and provides an explanation for the involvement of Papez's circuit in both the representation of heading direction and in the recollection of episodic information. Two experiments relating to the model are briefly described. A functional neuroimaging study of memory for the spatial context of life-like events in virtual reality provides support for the model's functional localization. A neuropsychological experiment suggests that the hippocampus does store an allocentric representation of spatial locations.

14.1. Introduction

One of the brain's most important and self-defining functions is to provide memory for the personally experienced events in our daily lives. The function of this 'episodic' memory system has been studied for many years. Much of this work, both experimental and theoretical, has focused on: how functionally to dissociate episodic memory from other forms of memory; which behavioural measures most purely reflect its operation; how and if it breaks down into component processes; the time courses over which these processes act; and which brain regions support them. These issues are discussed at length elsewhere in this issue. This article focuses on how these processes happen in the brain, i.e. how the actions of neurons and synapses in different brain regions conspire to produce an episodic memory system. Of course, the success of this enterprise depends crucially on both the interpretation of the above ideas and experiments, and on the ability to make predictions regarding them. It is worth noting at this stage that we will pay particular attention to one of the brain regions involved in episodic memory (the hippocampus), and to one of the distinguishing characteristics of episodic memory (the ability to retrieve the rich spatial context of an event). These choices reflect biases

hippocampus

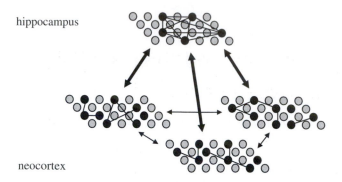

neocortex

Fig. 14.1. The generic hippocampo-neocortical model of long-term memory. Relatively dense recurrent connections and sparse representations in the hippocampus enable efficient pattern completion. Connections between neocortex and hippocampus allow the hippocampal representation of an event to be associated with its sensory details, including reactivation of the representations in different neocortical areas dealing with different sensory modalities. Abstracted semantic representations may also be learned over time in neocortex. The recurrent connections within each neocortical area allow unimodal recognition.

of the authors: that the hippocampus is the central player in the neural support of episodic memory; that it is important to consider the spatial locations of the protagonists in an event in understanding both its encoding and retrieval; and that computational modelling benefits from knowledge of the neuronal representations involved—for which the spatial domain provides the richest data.

The article is organized as follows. We start with a brief review of what has become a generic framework for modelling the hippocampal and neocortical roles in long-term memory for personal experience, following from the work of David Marr (1971). We consider some of the ways in which this model has been developed over the years in terms of general theoretical issues concerning memory, such as time-courses, capacities, representations and interference. We attempt to relate these issues to questions regarding the nature of episodic memory as compared with other forms of memory. In § 14.3 we discuss a neural-level model of the medial temporal and parietal processes involved in the retrieval of the spatial context of an event (Becker & Burgess 2001). This model relates to the Marr-type models given that the subject's spatial location provides one way for the hippocampus to index events. It also relates to the idea that allocentric (i.e. world-centred) representations are used in long-term storage of the spatial locations of the landmarks forming the event's spatial context, while egocentric (i.e. body-centred) representations are used in imagery.

The final section (§ 14.4) concerns experiments testing some of the model's assumptions and predictions. The first experiment is a functional neuroimaging study of retrieval of the spatial context of lifelike events using virtual reality to provide a rich spatial context (Burgess *et al.* 2001), supporting the model's suggested mapping of functions onto structures in the brain. The second experiment is a neuropsychological study of a single case of hippocampal pathology, Jon (Vargha-Khadem *et al.* 1997), providing evidence that the hippocampus supports an allocentric representation of the locations of objects (King *et al.* 2001).

14.2. A generic hippocampo-neocortical model of long-term memory

As the inspiration for a host of models of the hippocampal and neocortical roles in memory, Marr's (1971) paper 'Simple memory: a theory for archicortex' is the starting point for this section (see Willshaw & Buckingham 1990 for an excellent synopsis and evaluation). In brief, Marr suggests that the hippocampus provides a mechanism for rapidly storing the day's events for later transfer to the neocortex, whose role (described in his 1971 paper) is to reorganize and classify this information as relevant to the animal. During encoding, the neocortical representation of an event is mapped onto a 'simple representation' in the hippocampus via connections with modifiable synapses (the reverse mapping also being learned in modifiable return connections). He notes that this simple representation 'needs to be formed only of those parts of [the event]...through which [it] will later be addressed' (p. 32). Modifiable synapses on the hippocampus's recurrent collaterals also play a role—associating together elements of the simple representation so as to enable subsequent pattern completion (the 'collateral effect'). During retrieval, a subset of the neocortical event representation can cause reactivation of the entire 'simple representation' in the hippocampus and thence reactivation of the entire neocortical representation. The majority of the paper concerns physiological details and capacity considerations, assuming that the hippocampus must be able to store, at minimum, one day's events for transfer during the night's sleep.

The general scheme envisaged by this model, and the many subsequent related models, is illustrated in Figure 14.1. Below, we use this generic model as a framework to illustrate various computational issues concerning episodic memory, and how they have been addressed by the model and the developments to it proposed over the years.

(a) The hippocampal representation: indexes, content and context

The nature of the 'simple representations' of events stored in the hippocampus has some implications for the functioning of an episodic memory system. Below, we refer to these representations as 'event codes' or 'codes' for brevity. Such codes might be purely abstract representations, or might include elements of the context or content of an event, as discussed below. The separation of information relating to an event into 'context' and 'content' is made in several models, often without definition. If an event is defined as a temporally localized change in the state of the world (e.g. 'she dropped her ticket'), then the change in the world that forms the event is the content, while the remaining ongoing state of the world forms the event's external context.

One way to avoid interference during the retrieval of neocortical event representations would be to ensure that the event codes are unique to each event. The process of generating unique codes from potentially similar events is known as 'pattern separation', a role that has been ascribed to the dentate gyrus with its large numbers of cells and very sparse activity (McNaughton & Morris 1987). In the limit of completely unique codes for each event, the hippocampus essentially provides an index (see Teyler & DiScenna 1986), i.e. a set of codes that can be used to reactivate the content of the memory via the return projections to the neocortex. Sparse coding also ameliorates the problem of 'catastrophic interference' that can occur during rapid learning of distributed representations (McClelland et al. 1995). This problem can also be avoided in other ways, such as limiting the maximum size of connection weights in an associative network (Hopfield 1982).

The retrieval of stored codes is aided by the collateral effect: incomplete patterns of activation can be completed by a process of 'pattern completion' ascribed to region CA3 with its long-range recurrent collaterals. In this process, region CA3 acts an 'auto-associative memory' in which stored patterns of activity are attractor states such that the system will return to the most similar stored pattern from any initial state (Willshaw *et al.* 1969; Kohonen 1972; Gardner-Medwin 1976; Hopfield 1982). Another advantage of distinct (i.e. orthogonal) event codes is to reduce interference during this process of pattern completion. For this reason, Marr suggests that the simple representations be formed by populations of cells with very sparse activity.

Note that the operation of pattern completion and pattern separation in the same system can cause conflicting effects (see e.g. McClelland *et al.* 1995). When a pattern of activity in the neocortex gives rise to a pattern of activity in the hippocampus, hippocampal pattern completion will tend to map that activity onto the most similar stored event code. However, this code will not necessarily represent the event with the most similar neocortical representation due to the pattern separation in the mapping from neocortex to hippocampus. These effects can give rise to counter-intuitive results, e.g. enabling models to fit the confusing experimental data that shows hippocampal dependence in some tasks requiring event-unique codes but not in other similar tasks (O'Reilly & Rudy 2000).

The alternative to abstracted event-unique codes is codes that reflect the content or context of the event itself in some way. A simple associative memory in which the elements of the representation of the event are associated equally with all other elements of the representation provides one way to achieve this. However, as implied by Marr's description of simple representations, some aspects of an event seem better able to cue associative retrieval than others, while other aspects of an event can be associatively retrieved more easily than others. The name of someone one met on a single occasion is a good example of both asymmetries (a good cue, but sometimes hard to retrieve), while the location of the meeting is often both a good cue and relatively easy to retrieve. The sequential position of an item in a list of items is another example of a good cue that is relatively hard to retrieve itself (Jones 1976). Considerations such as these demand at least asymmetrical associations, and have fuelled the theoretical distinctions made between the context and content of an event (e.g. Raaijmakers & Shiffrin 1981) and between the stored record and the 'header' by which it is referenced (Morton *et al.* 1985). Other approaches to generating event codes have included using an efficient compression of the event representations (Gluck & Myers 1996) and endogenously generated temporally varying codes (Levy 1996). One idea to which we will return is that the hippocampal role in episodic memory might relate to the provision of the spatio-temporal context of the event (O'Keefe & Nadel 1978).

(b) Learning rates, cross-modal binding and consolidation

Marr suggests that the hippocampus provides a mechanism for rapidly capturing the day's events as they happen, so as to allow the relevant information to be appropriately categorized in the neocortex. This process may occur overnight, freeing up the memory capacity of the hippocampus for the next day's events. Many subsequent models have elaborated on this basic idea, proposing different time-scales and mechanisms by which relevant information is abstracted and incorporated into neocortical systems (see e.g. McClelland *et al.* 1995; Murre 1996). The proposed transfer of episodic information from hippocampus to neocortex, such that memory for this information would then be immune to subsequent hippocampal damage, remains controversial to this day. Such a process acting over days or weeks is clearly at odds with the human neuropsychological data, and it is questionable whether such a process could occur even over several decades (see e.g. Cipolotti *et al.* 2001). One recent development of the model proposes that, over time, events can be rehearsed, creating new event-codes on each rehearsal (Nadel & Moscovitch 1997). This allows for the possibility that, while a complete lesion of the medial temporal lobe impairs retrieval of all memories, the older the memory, the more robust it will be to partial damage.

A related distinction, between fast hippocampal learning and slower neocortical learning, has arisen from consideration of the physical constraints on learning to associate information from different sensory modalities represented in disparate cortical areas. Damasio's (1989) solution was that 'convergence zones' must exist in the brain to enable such long-range associations to be formed via association with representations in such a convergence zone. Many subsequent models have identified the hippocampus (or, less specifically, the medial temporal lobe) as a convergence zone, so that rapid learning of hippocampal simple representations can allow subsequent, slower, learning of long-range associations between the different neocortical areas (Alvarez & Squire 1994; Murre 1996; Moll & Miikkulainen 1997). Again, it is questionable whether or not the slower process of cross-modal association can, in time, render the hippocampal representations completely redundant.

(c) Implications for encoding versus retrieval and functional subdivisions of memory

The encoding of episodic memories in this type of model raises some interesting considerations. The presence of the collateral effect in CA3 means that the activation of neurons participating in an event code will depend both on the afferent input from the neocortical representation and on the feedback received from other neurons in CA3. This has the advantage, during retrieval, of encouraging the system to settle on a previously learned event-code. However, when a new event has to be encoded, a new hippocampal event-code needs to be generated in the absence of interference from previously stored information. One solution is that the mossy fibre synapses from the dentate gyrus onto the CA3 pyramidal cells act as 'detonator' synapses (being physically large and near to the cell body) that impose the new pattern of activity during encoding, while recurrent collaterals dominate retrieval (McNaughton & Morris 1987; see also Treves & Rolls 1992). An alternative proposal, and a mechanism, for the switching between encoding and retrieval modes concerns the supply of acetylcholine (ACh) to the hippocampus by the medial septum (Hasselmo *et al.* 1996; see also Murre 1996). On this account, increased delivery of ACh suppresses the feedback excitation in CA3, allowing encoding of new information. This increased delivery of ACh is effectively determined by the novelty of the neocortical inputs to the hippocampus compared with previously stored events. One very positive aspect of this idea is that it captures some of the importance of the fornix (an enormous fibre bundle connecting the hippocampus to the medial septum and other subcortical structures). In the model, sectioning the fornix will prevent the learning of new memories due to lack of ACh, corresponding to the experimental observation that sections of the fornix produce similar impairments to lesioning the hippocampus (see *e.g.* Aggleton & Pearce 2001; Gaffan & Hornak 1997; Aggleton & Brown 1999). Interestingly, lesions to the fornix often spare memories encoded prior to the lesion (Spiers *et al.* 2001*b*).

With regard to distinctions between different types of memory, it is interesting to consider the idea that event-unique simple representations are rapidly stored in the hippocampus, while the meaning of an event in relation to the animal's lifetime experience is abstracted into the neocortex over a longer period of time. This would suggest that semantic memories arise from combinations of hippocampal event-unique memories but eventually they can become independent of the hippocampus. This corresponds well with the idea that memory for the unique content and context of a specific event (episodic memory) depends on the hippocampus, while semantic memory depends on other areas of the temporal lobe (see e.g. Graham & Hodges 1997). However, it does not correspond so well with the idea that semantic information can be acquired despite bilateral hippocampal pathology (Vargha-Khadem *et al.* 1997). The possibility of partial sparing of the hippocampus and episodic memory (Squire & Zola 1998), or the use of external rehearsal of information (Baddeley *et al.* 2001), might provide explanations in these cases.

Similarly it is interesting to consider the implications of the idea that the hippocampus mediates associations between disparate cortical areas for the neural bases of different types of memory. Clearly, effects mediated by the familiarity of single stimuli might be supported by the association of elements within each of the neocortical areas alone. Thus recognition of previously presented stimuli would depend on neocortical rather than hippocampal areas, while correct recognition of a pair of cross-modal associates amongst equally familiar distractors would require the hippocampus. Recent evidence indicates that simple recognition memory does not depend on the hippocampus but on nearby neocortical areas (Vargha-Khadem 2001; Zhu *et al.* 1996; Murray & Mishkin 1998; Vargha-Khadem *et al.* 1997; Wan *et al.* 1999; Aggleton & Brown 1999; Holdstock *et al.* 2000; Baxendale *et al.* 1997; Baddeley *et al.* 2001; but see also Manns & Squire 1999; Zola *et al.* 2000), whereas there is some evidence that recognition of cross-modal associations is impaired by bilateral damage restricted to the hippocampus (Holdstock *et al.* 2000; Vargha-Khadem *et al.* 1997). More extensive unilateral damage may also impair the binding of elements within the same modality (Kroll *et al.* 1996). The logical extension of this idea is that episodic memory requires the full recollection of an event and its context in all of its multimodal detail and so will require an intact hippocampus.

14.3. A model of retrieval of the spatial context of an event

The models reviewed in § 14.2 provide insights into some of the general computational issues behind the construction of a long-term memory system, some of which we have related to the nature of episodic memory in particular. Other issues specifically concerning episodic memory remain to be fully addressed by computational models. One such issue is the nature of episodic encoding, such as how (or if) experience is chopped up into discrete events and what aspects of an event contribute to context or index representations as opposed to content representations. We return to this issue in the final part of § 14.5.

A second issue concerns the details of the mechanism of episodic retrieval, as opposed to other forms of read-out from memory, e.g. pattern completion might equally well apply to recognition or semantic memory.

A third issue concerns the nature of the neural representations involved in the processes of episodic memory, something not addressed by models of the retrieval of purely abstract binary codes.

In this section we consider the specific problem of remembering the spatial layout of a familiar environment. As well as being an important aspect of memory in its own right, this problem serves as an instructive example of context-dependent memory (retrieval of the spatial context of an event) for which detailed experimental data exists regarding the neural representations and mechanisms involved. Thus we hope to relate the insights of the more general attempts to model memory both to a specifically episodic task and to the vast literature regarding the functional neuroanatomy of spatial information processing in the mammalian brain.

There are three ideas behind the rationale for this model. First, that the ability to retrieve the rich spatio-temporal context of real-life events, as opposed to simply recognizing their content, is a determining characteristic of episodic memory (Gardiner & Java 1993). Second, that allocentric (i.e. world-centred) representations are suited to long-term storage of spatial locations (as the subject's body will have moved between presentation and recall) while egocentric (i.e. body-centred) representations are suited to imagining, manipulating and re-experiencing the products of retrieval (as sensory perception is egocentric and any actions must be specified egocentrically) (Goodale & Milner 1992; Milner et al. 1999; Burgess et al. 1999). Third, that the allocentric spatial representations of the hippocampus in rats have become co-opted to form part of the episodic memory system in humans by providing spatial context and making use of the additional inputs of a linear sense of time (on the right) and language (on the left) (O'Keefe & Nadel 1978). For further discussion of the model and details of simulations see Becker & Burgess (2001). Recce & Harris (1996) describe an alternative model in which a hippocampal place code indexes spatial maps permanently stored in the parietal cortex. The functional architecture of the model is shown in Figure 14.2. Below we describe the various components of the model and how it works.

(a) Medial temporal areas

The ventral visual processing stream encodes the visual features of the subject's environment and terminates in the perirhinal cortex. The parahippocampus encodes the distance and allocentric direction of any landmarks (large objects or barriers) around the subject. Each neuron here is broadly tuned to respond to the presence of any landmark at a specific distance and bearing from the subject in a manner analogous to the likely functional inputs to the rat hippocampus (O'Keefe & Burgess 1996; Hartley et al. 2000). The hippocampus provides a representation of the current location of the subject, each neuron responding in a manner analogous to hippocampal place cells in the rat (O'Keefe & Nadel 1978). In primates, this might become a representation of the current location of gaze (Robertson et al. 1998) without further change to the model. The hippocampus is simply simulated as a single layer of recurrently connected neurons, i.e. ignoring the

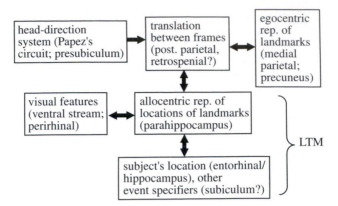

Fig. 14.2. The functional architecture of the model of the encoding and retrieval of the spatial context of an event (see also Becker & Burgess 2001). LTM, long-term memory; post., posterior; rep., representation.

functional contributions of areas other than CA3 such as the entorhinal cortex, dentate gyrus and CA1, but taking advantage of the bidirectional connectivity to subiculum and parahippocampus that they provide. Bidirectional associations exist between the perirhinal and parahippocampal areas (associating landmark locations and visual features), and between the parahippocampus and hippocampus, allowing the para-hippocampal representation to drive the hippocampus, as in Hartley *et al.* (2000), and *vice versa* (see Figure 14.3). Recurrent connections within the hippocampus are arranged to form a continuous attractor (Samsonovich & McNaughton 1997), to enable pattern completion in the firing of place cells such that the firing rates of all of the place cells are always consistent with the subject being in a single location.

Evidence for this assignment of structure to function includes the following. The perirhinal cortex is the crucial structure for matching or non-matching to the visual features of an object (Murray & Mishkin 1998). As well as being implicated in a specific scheme for encoding the spatial locations of environmental boundaries by deductions from the activation of place cells (O'Keefe & Burgess 1996), this role for the parahippocampus has also been supported by functional neuroimaging of the human parahippocampal response to spatial scenes (Epstein & Kanwisher 1998). Evidence that the human hippocampus provides an allocentric representation of location is presented in § 14.4. We also note that the 'spatial context' represented in the medial temporal system includes landmarks such as environmental boundaries but does not necessarily include all of the objects found within an environment. This is consistent with experiments showing which environmental features affect place cell firing (O'Keefe & Burgess 1996; Cressant *et al.* 1997). It is also consistent with behavioural data suggesting that the structural features of a room are represented within a single spatial framework while the room's contents are not (Wang & Spelke 2000).

(b) Encoding the location of an event

In previous models of rat navigation (Burgess *et al.* 1994; Burgess & O'Keefe 1996) we postulated the existence of 'goal cells' that could encode the location of a reward site

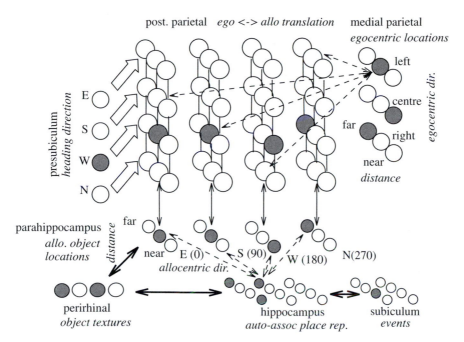

Fig. 14.3. Detail of the model of encoding and retrieval of the spatial context, with an illustration of possible cell activations when facing west, with landmarks nearby to the west, farther away to the east and south and far away to the north (see also Becker & Burgess 2001). allo., allocentric; auto-assoc., auto-associative; dir., direction; ego, egocentric; post., posterior; rep., representation.

after one instance of encountering the reward (e.g. the submerged platform in a water maze, or a location containing food or water). These cells are associated to the specific non-spatial attributes of different types of reward, causing the appropriate cell to be activated by the reward. They should be located immediately downstream of the place cells, e.g. in the subicular complex or the nucleus accumbens. In the 'simple model' of Burgess & O'Keefe (1996), Hebbian learning in the projections to a goal cell from active place cells at the moment the rat encounters the goal cause the goal cell's firing rate to subsequently indicate the rat's proximity to the goal location. This occurs simply because more place cells with potentiated connections to the goal cell will be active the closer the rat gets to the goal location in its subsequent perambulations (see Figure 14.4).

To encode the location of an event, we postulate a similar mechanism: 'event cells' in the subiculum associated with non-spatial aspects of the event. These cells would be activated by the specific non-spatial attributes of an event so that Hebbian learning causes a bidirectional association with the place cells representing the location of the event. In this way, activating an event cell via some non-spatial characteristic of the event can cause reactivation of the place cell representation of its location. Likewise, activating the place cell representation of a location can cause the activation of cells representing the events that happened there. Note that to produce a more general model of retrieval of non-spatial information would require changes throughout the model, perhaps reflecting a generalization of hippocampal

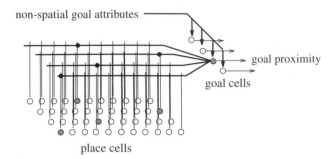

Fig. 14.4. A simple model for encoding and retrieving a spatial location, adapted from Burgess & O'Keefe (1996). When a goal is encountered, synapses between active place cells and a 'goal cell' associated with the particular attributes of the goal are potentiated (active cells are shown as grey circles, potentiated synapses as black circles). The subsequent firing of the goal cell indicates the similarity of the current place cell representation to the representation of the goal location and thus indicates the proximity of the rat to the goal. A similar mechanism can be used to store the spatial location of an event.

function from spatial memory in the right hemisphere to episodic memory in the left hemisphere (Spiers *et al.* 2001*a*).

(c) Parietal areas and the head-direction circuit

Neurons in the medial parietal area (the precuneus) encode the distance and egocentric directions (angle relative to the head) of environmental landmarks so as to form a fully-egocentric imageable representation. Different parts of this image can be inspected via foveation or covert shifts of attention. The mappings between allocentric and body-centred and between body-centred and head-centred representations occur in the posterior parietal area. For simplicity, simulations (as shown in Figures 14.3 and 14.5) consider only the translation between allocentric and body-centred representations (i.e. the simulated subject cannot rotate its head relative to its body). The two types of representation are translated into each other by making use of the subject's orientation in the world (encoded in a set of 'head-direction cells'). This occurs via an expanded set of cells whose responses are modulated by both the position of the stimulus relative to the body and the orientation of the body in the world—see Pouget & Sejnowski (1997) for successful use of this type of model of parietal coordinate transforms. The posterior parietal area consists of layers of neurons repeating the parahippocampal representation (the neurons in each layer have a bidirectional connection to the corresponding neurons in the parahippocampus). The activity of the neurons in each layer is modulated by the activity of a particular head-direction cell. Given the correct representation of head direction, this allows parietal egocentric representations of the set of environmental landmarks to activate the allocentric parahippocampal representation and *vice versa*.

Evidence for this assignment of structure to function includes the following. Neurons in parietal area 7a have been shown to have the correct 'gain field' modulation of response to the egocentric (retinal) location of a stimulus by the position of the animal's eyes (Andersen *et al.* 1985), head (Duhamel *et al.* 1992) or body (Snyder *et al.* 1998) to effect the appropriate coordinate transformations. The precuneus has been found to be activated by imagery of the products of retrieval from memory (see e.g. Fletcher *et al.* 1996). Neurons encoding the current head direction have been recorded in rats in the mammillary bodies, anterior thalamus and presubiculum (see e.g. Taube 1998). It is interesting to note that the circuit of regions known to be involved in encoding the current head direction in the rat corresponds closely with the circuit (known as Papez's circuit since the 1930s) that has been closely associated with human episodic memory (see e.g. Aggleton & Pearce 2001; Aggleton & Brown 1999; Gaffan & Hornak 1997; Delay & Brion 1969).

(d) Functional overview

During exploration of an environment, egocentric sensory input is translated into the allocentric parahippocampal representation of landmark locations via the posterior parietal cortex. As each landmark is foveated, the association between the perirhinal representation of the visual features of a landmark and its parahippocampal representation is learned. The association between the patterns of parahippocampal and hippocampal activations at given positions within the environment could also be learned during exploration (Burgess *et al.* 1994), or might simply be already hard-wired (Hartley *et al.* 2000). Similarly, the recurrent connections between place cells, such that cells representing similar locations support each other, might also be learned, or be already hard-wired (Samsonovich & McNaughton 1997). In the cases of hard-wired connection existing before exposure to the environment, these connections effectively determine that the appropriate place cells are active at the appropriate locations.

During retrieval of a spatial scene from a particular point of view, partial input is supplied to the medial temporal system, such as the presence of a particular visual feature in a particular direction. Retrieval of the spatial context of a specific event occurs as described above (see 'encoding the location of an event'). In either case, pattern completion occurs, involving the bidirectional associations between all three areas and within the hippocampus, such that the system settles on a place, landmark and visual feature representation consistent with the specifying inputs. An imageable egocentric representation is then produced in the precuneus via translation in the posterior parietal cortex, making use of the current head direction. Finally, inspecting (i.e. attending to) one part of the imageable representation is modelled by boosting the activation of neurons in that part of the image. This extra activation flows back through the posterior parietal and parahippocampal parts of the model to activate the perirhinal representation of the visual features at that part of the image.

(e) Simulation of the effect of parietal lesions

In their famous experiment on representational neglect, Bisiach and Luzzatti (1978) asked patients with hemispatial neglect following right parietal damage to imagine standing in the familiar Piazza del Duomo from their home town of Milan. Interestingly, when asked to imagine facing towards the cathedral they neglected to describe the buildings to the left of that viewpoint, while, when asked to imagine facing away from the cathedral they neglected the buildings to the left of that viewpoint. Their ability to describe the buildings on both sides of the Piazza over the two trials is

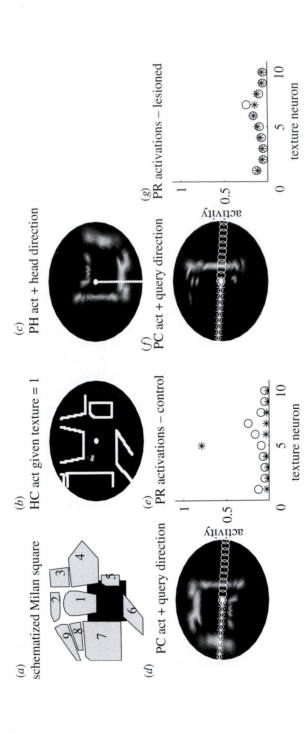

Fig. 14.5. Simulation of retrieval of spatial information in the Milan square experiment of Bisiach & Luzzatti (1978) (adapted from Becker & Burgess 2001). (*a*) Training consists of simulated exploration of the square (shaded area, north is up). The system is cued to imagine being near to the cathedral (i.e. the perirhinal cell for the texture of building 1 and parahippocampal cell for a building at a short distance north are activated) and the hippocampal-parahippocampal-perirhinal system settles. (*b*) The hippocampus settles to a location in the north-west corner of the square (hippocampal cell activity shown as the brightness of the pixel corresponding to the location of each cell's place field). (*c*) The parahippocampus correctly retrieves the locations of the other buildings (parahippocampal cell activity shown as the brightness of the pixel for the location encoded by each cell, relative to the subject at the centre). A line indicates that the imagined head-direction is south. (*d*) Medial parietal cell activity: the parahippocampal map has been correctly rotated given head-direction south (straight ahead is up), stars indicate a direction of inspection to the left, circles to the right. (*e*) Perirhinal cell activations correctly showing building 5 to the left and building 7 to the right. (*f*) Effect of a right parietal lesion on the medial parietal representation (note lack of activation on the left) and (*g*) PR activations (note decrease in activation of building 5 when inspection is to the left). HC, hippocampal; act, activation; PH, parahippocampal; PC, parietal cortex; PR, perirhinal.

consistent with having an intact viewpoint-independent representation of the Piazza, but an impaired mechanism for extracting a viewpoint-dependent representation for imagery (see also Baddeley & Lieberman 1980). This experiment can be simulated by our model, by making a selective lesion to the neurons on the left side of the egocentric representation, the posterior parietal neurons that project to them, or by biasing the inspection of this representation so that its left side is neglected (see Figure 14.5 and Becker & Burgess 2001). We note that caloric irrigation, or other means of manipulating the head-direction signal, causes a mistranslation between egocentric and allocentric representations. In some circumstances this can rotate part of the left of the scene that would otherwise be neglected further to the right, ameliorating the neglect of this part of the scene—consistent with some experimental data (Guariglia *et al.* 1998).

14.4. Experimental support for the spatial model

(a) Localization of retrieval functions

In a recent functional neuroimaging study (Burgess *et al.* 2001) we examined the neural systems involved in the retrieval of the spatial context of an event. In brief, subjects followed a route through a town (presented using virtual reality), meeting one of two characters in one of two places along the route. During each of 16 encounters a different object was passed from the character to the subject. Scanning occurred during retrieval which was tested by returning the subject to the scene of an event, in the presence of one of the characters, and giving them a forced choice of two objects. Two conditions are of interest here: 'place', in which the object that had been received in the current location had to be chosen; and 'width', in which the widest object had to be chosen. The areas activated in the place condition relative to the width condition are shown in Figure 14.6. They show good correspondence with the areas predicted by the model, with the additional feature of a continuous strip of activation running from medial temporal to medial parietal areas, through the retro-splenial cortex and up the parieto-occipital sulcus. We suppose that this activation reflects the buffering of the locations of scene elements in the successively translated frames of reference (allocentric, body-centred, head-centred) between the parahippocampus and the precuneus.

Additionally, we saw activation of all of the prefrontal areas usually activated in previous experiments on memory for laboratory stimuli such as lists of words, etc. (bilateral anterior, dorso- and ventro-lateral prefrontal cortex, anterior cingulate). We ascribed these activations to sorting out the interference caused by the highly similar context of the events used in our study (16 events occurring in two places) and in previous experiments on lists of items presented in the scanner but not in studies of the richly diverse events in autobiography (Maguire *et al.* 2000). This would be broadly consistent with neuropsychological studies of the medial temporal and prefrontal roles in memory (see e.g. Incisa-della & Milner 1993; Smith *et al.* 1995).

(b) Allocentric representation of space in the human hippocampus

To test whether or not the hippocampus is specifically involved in storing allocentric (or viewpoint-independent) representations we designed a test for this (King *et al.* 2001)

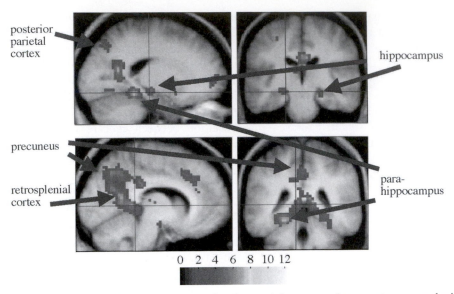

Fig. 14.6. Regions of activation in memory for the spatial context of an event compared with a non-memory control condition (adapted from Burgess *et al.* 2001). In the memory condition subjects had to choose which of two objects was received in the current location in a virtual reality town. In the non-memory condition they had to choose the widest. The figure shows the results of an event-related random-effects functional magnetic resonance imaging (fMRI) analysis of 13 subjects with threshold $P < 0.01$ uncorrected. The colour bar shows Z-score equivalents. See text for details.

and administered it to a patient with bilateral hippocampal pathology, Jon (Vargha-Khadem *et al.* 1997). In brief, the subject was given a viewpoint from the rooftops surrounding a small town square, using a virtual reality presentation. During presentation, *n* objects appeared sequentially in different locations around the square. During testing, *m* copies of each object were presented in different locations, with the subject asked to indicate which was in the same location as at presentation. Between presentation and testing, the subject's viewpoint might be changed to another location overlooking the square.

Compared with previous tests (e.g. Abrahams *et al.* 1997; Holdstock *et al.* 2000; Roskos *et al.* 1998), this test included several features to favour the use of an allocentric representation and checks to rule out the use of alternative egocentric strategies. The most notable features were that: (i) a single representation of all object locations would have to be constructed cumulatively due to their sequential presentation; (ii) instantaneous transfer between viewing locations prevents gradual updating of an initial egocentric representation using 'path integration'; and (iii) reaction times were recorded and two different angular changes of position used so that any signs of mental rotation could be monitored (none were found). Thus, although both allocentric and egocentric representations could be used to solve the same viewpoint condition, solution of the changed viewpoint condition solely on the basis of storing egocentric snapshots at presentation would be difficult.

Patient Jon's performance as a function of list length (tested using two foils) indicated a massive deficit in performance in the changed viewpoint condition. His span was over 13 items in the same viewpoint condition, but he was at chance at all list lengths greater than one in the changed viewpoint condition. As expected, healthy controls performed slightly better than Jon in the same viewpoint condition and vastly better in the changed viewpoint condition. By increasing the number of foils to five, so that controls performed as well as or worse than Jon in the same viewpoint condition but still significantly better in the different viewpoint condition, we formally demonstrated Jon's additional impairment for allocentric representation.

14.5. Discussion

The model of hippocampo-neocortical interaction proposed by Marr (1971), and its subsequent development by many authors, has provided a computational framework within which to consider the processes involved in long-term memory. A strict interpretation of its principal motivation, that the hippocampus acts as a temporary store from which useful information is transferred into neocortical long-term memory, remains unsupported by convincing experimental data to this day. Nonetheless, it has provided computational insights into several aspects of the functioning of the episodic memory system and its relationship to other memory systems. It supports the utility of rapidly storing a high-level representation that can be used to recall the detailed multimodal information comprising an event. It suggests an explanation for the presence of long-range recurrent collaterals in area CA3 of the hippocampus—to provide pattern completion of the hippocampal representations during retrieval. Most interestingly for the concerns of this paper, it provides computational explanations for the separation of processes supporting episodic, semantic and recognition memory, and suggests some neurophysiological mechanisms relating to the encoding of new memories.

  This type of model can be applied to the specifically episodic task of retrieving the spatial context of an event. This provides an additional set of constraints for modelling, given the detailed current state of knowledge regarding the neural representation of spatial information in the mammalian brain. In the model we have presented, the location of the subject during the event forms the hippocampal representation used to retrieve other information and in which pattern completion occurs (see also Recce & Harris 1996). Both this hippocampal representation and the parahippocampal representation of landmark locations are 'allocentric', in being independent of the orientation of the subject. The use of allocentric representations, in long-term storage makes sense, in that the orientation and position of body parts will change between presentation and recall (see also Goodale & Milner 1992; Burgess et al. 1999) and links the spatial role of the hippocampus in rats to its role in episodic memory in humans (see also O'Keefe & Nadel 1978). However, sensory perception produces egocentric representation, and the ability to perform visual imagery on the products of retrieval also requires an egocentric representation. The model proposes that egocentric imagery occurs in medial parietal areas, while translation of information between egocentric and allocentric representations is supported by the posterior parietal cortex. Interestingly, this translation requires knowledge of the subject's heading direction, linking the role of mammillary body–anterior thalamic–presubicular circuit in encoding head-direction in the rat (see e.g. Taube 1998) to the apparent role of this circuit in episodic memory in humans (see e.g. Aggleton & Brown 1999; Gaffan & Hornak 1997). The model provides a computational framework for understanding the operation of several brain areas within the retrieval of episodic information and predicts the effects of parietal lesions, hippocampal lesions and manipulations of the subject's perceived head-direction on the retrieval of the spatial context of episodic memories.

The assumptions of the spatial model can be tested experimentally. In § 14.4 we described two experiments regarding these assumptions. The proposed localization of the processes involved in the retrieval of episodic memory were examined in a functional neuroimaging study of memory for the spatial context of an event (Burgess *et al.* 2001). For this study, a virtual reality presentation was used to provide both a rich spatial context for the events and a controllable way to simulate lifelike events in which the subject can actively participate. The areas activated in this experiment were surprisingly consistent with the model's proposed functional localization, with the addition of a continuous stream of activation from parahippocampus to medial parietal areas, running through the retrosplenial cortex. We hypothesize that this activation corresponds to buffering of the intermediate representations between the allocentric parahippocampal representation and the head-centred medial parietal one.

The proposed role for the hippocampus, particularly the proposal that it stores an allocentric representation of location, was tested in a patient with focal bilateral hippocampal pathology, Jon (Vargha-Khadem *et al.* 1997). For this we used virtual reality to present objects located in three-dimensional space and tested recognition memory for their locations. By changing the subject's viewpoint between presentation and recall, and controlling for alternative, egocentric, strategies we attempted to test directly for the storage of viewpoint-independent information. Jon's enormous impairment when the viewpoint was changed but only mild impairment from the same viewpoint strongly indicates a role for the hippocampus in storing allocentric representations of object locations. It is possible that this rare deficit in recognition memory (at which he generally performs well) is related to Jon's wider problems in episodic memory, possibly via a role for hippocampal storage of allocentric information as outlined in the spatial model.

If at least part of the index to episodic memory (be it hippocampal or otherwise) relates to the spatial context of an event, it should be possible to test experimentally. Indirect evidence can be found in considering the effect of completing a task involving moving from one location to another on the storage of that event in memory (Barreau 1997). Young children (around four years old) showed a more robust memory for such events when tested after their completion than when tested in transit. Interestingly, the pattern of errors made by these children depended on the order in which different events were questioned. These data can largely be captured by a surprisingly simple model of the interaction of short- and long-term storage systems in supporting episodic memory (Morton & Barreau 2001).

In conclusion, we have discussed how attempts to model the hippocampal and neocortical roles in long-term memory have provided insights into some of the features of episodic memory. To further investigate the neural mechanisms specifically relevant to episodic memory, we have proposed a detailed model of an example of contextually cued recall—the retrieval of the spatial context of an event. This has enabled us to tie together findings from neurophysiology, functional neuroanatomy and neuropsychology relating to episodic memory. The model also makes experimental predictions regarding the interaction of space and memory in all of these fields. To illustrate the types of experiment addressed by the model, we described a functional neuroimaging study of the retrieval of spatial context and a neuropsychological study of the representation of location stored by the human hippocampus.

We thank our collaborator in functional imaging, Eleanor Maguire, and in the study on patient Jon, Faraneh Vargha-Khadem. We also thank John Morton, Sofi Barreau, Tom Hartley, Hugo Spiers, Mick Rugg, David Shanks and Rick Henson for useful discussions. This work was supported by a Medical Research Council (MRC) project grant to N.B., J.O'K. and F Vargha-Khadem, an MRC program grant to J.O'K. and a National Science and Engineering Research Council (NSERC), Canada, grant to S.B. N.B. is a Royal Society University Research Fellow.

References

Abrahams, S., Pickering, A., Polkey, C. E. & Morris, R. G. 1997 Spatial memory deficits in patients with unilateral damage to the right hippocampal formation. *Neuropsychologia* **35**, 11–24.

Aggleton, J. P. & Brown, M. W. 1999 Episodic memory, amnesia, and the hippocampal–anterior thalamic axis. *Behav. Brain Sci.* **22**, 425–490.

Aggleton, J. P. & Pearce, J. M. 2001 Neural systems underlying episodic memory: insights from animal research. *Phil. Trans. R. Soc. Lond.* B **356**, 1467–1482.

Alvarez, P. & Squire, L. R. 1994 Memory consolidation and the medial temporal lobe: a simple network model. *Proc. Natl Acad. Sci. USA* **91**, 7041–7045.

Andersen, R. A., Essick, G. K. & Siegel, R. M. 1985 Encoding of spatial location by posterior parietal neurons. *Science* **230**, 456–458.

Baddeley, A. D. & Lieberman, K. 1980 Spatial working memory. In *Attention and performance VIII*, pp. 521–539. Hillsdale, NJ: Lawrence Erlbaum Associates.

Baddeley, A., Vargha-Khadem, F. & Mishkin, M. 2001 Preserved recognition in a case of developmental amnesia: implications for the acquisition of semantic memory? *J. Cogn. Neurosci.* (In the press.)

Barreau, S. 1997 Developmental constraints on a theory of memory. PhD thesis, Department of Psychology, University College London, UK.

Baxendale, S. A., Van Paesschen, W., Thompson, P. J., Duncan, J. S., Shorvon, S. D. & Connelly, A. 1997 The relation between quantitative MRI measures of hippocampal structure and the intracarotid amobarbital test. *Epilepsia* **38**, 998–1007.

Becker, S. & Burgess, N. 2001 A model of spatial recall, mental imagery and neglect. *Adv. Neural Inf. Processing Sys.* **13**. (In the press.)

Bisiach, E. & Luzzatti, C. 1978 Unilateral neglect of representational space. *Cortex* **14**, 129–133.

Burgess, N. & O'Keefe, J. 1996 Neuronal computations underlying the firing of place cells and their role in navigation. *Hippocampus* **6**, 749–762.

Burgess, N., Recce, M. & O'Keefe, J. 1994 A model of hippocampal function. *Neural Networks* **7**, 1065–1081.

Burgess, N., Jeffery, K. J. & O'Keefe, J. 1999 Integrating hippocampal and parietal functions: a spatial point of view. In *The hippocampal and parietal foundations of spatial cognition* (ed. N. Burgess, K. J. Jeffery & J. O'Keefe), pp. 3–29. Oxford University Press.

Burgess, N., Maguire, E. A., Spiers, H. J. & O'Keefe, J. 2001 A temporoparietal and prefrontal network for retrieving the spatial context of lifelike events. *Neuroimage* **14**, 439–453.

Cipolotti, L., Shallice, T., Chan, D., Fox, N. C., Scahill, R., Harrison, G., Stevens, J. & Rudge, P. 2001 Long term retrograde amnesia. The crucial role of the hippocampus. *Neuropsychologia* **39**, 151–172.

Cressant, A., Muller, R. U. & Poucet, B. 1997 Failure of centrally placed objects to control the firing fields of hippocampal place cells. *J. Neurosci.* **17**, 2531–2542.

Damasio, A. R. 1989 The brain binds entities and events by multiregional activation from convergence zones. *Neural Comput.* **1**, 123–132.

Delay, J. & Brion, S. 1969 *Le syndrome de Korsakoff.* Paris: Masson.

Duhamel, J. R., Colby, C. L. & Goldberg, M. E. 1992 The updating of the representation of visual space in parietal cortex by intended eye movements. *Science* **255**, 90–92.

Epstein, R. & Kanwisher, N. 1998 A cortical representation of the local visual environment. *Nature* **392**, 598–601.

Fletcher, P. C., Shallice, T., Frith, C. D., Frackowiak, R. S. & Dolan, R. J. 1996 Brain activity during memory retrieval. The influence of imagery and semantic cueing. *Brain* **119**, 1587–1596.

Gaffan, D. & Hornak, J. 1997 Amnesia and neglect: beyond the Delay–Brion system and the Hebb synapse. *Phil. Trans. R. Soc. Lond.* B **352**, 1481–1488.

Gardiner, J. M. and Java, R. I. 1993 In *Theories of memory* (ed. A. Collins, S. Gathercole & P. Morris), pp. 168–188. Hillsdale, NJ: Erlbaum.

Gardner-Medwin, A. R. 1976 The recall of events through the learning of associations between their parts. *Proc. R. Soc. Lond.* B **194**, 375–402.

Gluck, M. A. & Myers, C. E. 1996 Integrating behavioral and physiological models of hippocampal function. *Hippocampus* **6**, 643–653.

Goodale, M. A. & Milner, A. D. 1992 Separate visual pathways for perception and action. *Trends Neurosci.* **15**, 20–25.

Graham, K. S. & Hodges, J. R. 1997 Differentiating the roles of the hippocampus complex and the neocortex in long-term memory storage: evidence from the study of semantic dementia and Alzheimer's disease. *Neuropsychology* **11**, 77–89.

Guariglia, C., Lippolis, G. & Pizzamiglio, L. 1998 Somato-sensory stimulation improves imagery disorders in neglect. *Cortex* **34**, 233–241.

Hartley, T., Burgess, N., Lever, C., Cacucci, F. & O'Keefe, J. 2000 Modeling place fields in terms of the cortical inputs to the hippocampus. *Hippocampus* **10**, 369–379.

Hasselmo, M. E., Wyble, B. P. & Wallenstein, G. V. 1996 Encoding and retrieval of episodic memories: role of cholinergic and GABAergic modulation in the hippocampus. *Hippocampus* **6**, 693–708.

Holdstock, J. S., Mayes, A. R., Cezayirli, E., Isaac, C. L., Aggleton, J. P. & Roberts, N. 2000 A comparison of egocentric and allocentric spatial memory in a patient with selective hippocampal damage. *Neuropsychologia* **38**, 410–425.

Hopfield, J. J. 1982 Neural networks and physical systems with emergent collective computational abilities. *Proc. Natl Acad. Sci. USA* **79**, 2554–2558.

Incisa-della, R. A. & Milner, B. 1993 Strategic search and retrieval inhibition: the role of the frontal lobes. *Neuropsychologia* **31**, 503–524.

Jones, V. J. 1976 A fragmentation hypothesis of memory: cued recall of pictures and of sequential position. *J. Exp. Psychol. Gen.* **105**, 277–293.

King, J. A., Burgess, N., Hartley, T., Vargha-Khadem, F. & O'Keefe, J. 2001 (In preparation.)

Kohonen, T. 1972 Correlation matrix memories. *Institute of Electrical and Electronics Engineers Trans. Comp.* **C-21**, 353–359.

Kroll, N. E., Knight, R. T., Metcalfe, J., Wolf, E. S. & Tulving, E. 1996 Cohesion failure as a source of memory illusions. *J. Mem. Lang.* **35**, 176–196.

Levy, W. B. 1996 A sequence predicting CA3 is a flexible associator that learns and uses context to solve hippocampal-like tasks. *Hippocampus* **6**, 579–590.

McClelland, J. L., McNaughton, B. L. & O'Reilly, R. C. 1995 Why there are complementary learning systems in the hippocampus and neocortex: insights from the successes and failures of connectionist models of learning and memory. *Psychol. Rev.* **102**, 419–457.

McNaughton, B. L. & Morris, R. G. 1987 Hippocampal synaptic enhancement and information storage within a distributed memory system. *Trends Neurosci.* **10**, 408–415.

Maguire, E. A., Mummery, C. J. & Buchel, C. 2000 Patterns of hippocampal–cortical interaction dissociate temporal lobe memory subsystems. *Hippocampus* **10**, 475–482.

Manns, J. R. & Squire, L. R. 1999 Impaired recognition memory on the Doors and People Test after damage limited to the hippocampal region. *Hippocampus* **9**, 495–499.

Marr, D. 1970 A theory for cerebral neocortex. *Proc. Roy. Soc. Lond.* B **176**, 161–234.

Marr, D. 1971 Simple memory: a theory for archicortex. *Phil. Trans. R. Soc. Lond.* B **262**, 23–81.

Milner, A. D., Dijkerman, H. C. & Carey, D. P. 1999 Visuospatial processing in a case of visual form agnosia. In *The hippocampal and parietal foundations of spatial cognition* (ed. N. Burgess, K. J. Jeffery & J. O'Keefe), pp. 443–466. Oxford University Press.

Moll, M. & Miikkulainen, R. 1997 Convergence-zone episodic memory: analysis and simulations. *Neural Networks* **10**, 1017–1036.

Morton, J. & Barreau, S. 2001 (In preparation.)

Morton, J., Hammersley, R. H. & Bekerian, D. A. 1985 Headed records: a model for memory and its failure. *Cognition* **20**, 1–23.

Murray, E. A. & Mishkin, M. 1998 Object recognition and location memory in monkeys with excitotoxic lesions of the amygdala and hippocampus. *J. Neurosci.* **18**, 6568–6582.

Murre, J. M. 1996 TraceLink: a model of amnesia and consolidation of memory. *Hippocampus* **6**, 675–684.

Nadel, L. & Moscovitch, M. 1997 Memory consolidation, retrograde amnesia and the hippocampal complex. *Curr. Opin. Neurobiol.* **7**, 217–227.

O'Keefe, J. & Burgess, N. 1996 Geometric determinants of the place fields of hippocampal neurons. *Nature* **381**, 425–428.

O'Keefe, J. & Nadel, L. 1978 *The hippocampus as a cognitive map.* Oxford University Press.

O'Reilly, R. C. & Rudy, J. W. 2000 Computational principles of learning in the neocortex and hippocampus. *Hippocampus* **10**, 389–397.

Pouget, A. & Sejnowski, T. J. 1997 A new view of hemineglect based on the response properties of parietal neurones. *Phil. Trans. R. Soc. Lond.* B **352**, 1449–1459.

Raaijmakers, J. G. & Shiffrin, R. M. 1981 Search of associative memory. *Psychol. Rev.* **88**, 93–134.

Recce, M. & Harris, K. D. 1996 Memory for places: a navigational model in support of Marr's theory of hippocampal function. *Hippocampus* **6**, 735–748.

Robertson, R. G., Rolls, E. T. & Georges-Fran, O. P. 1998 Spatial view cells in the primate hippocampus: effects of removal of view details. *J. Neurophysiol.* **79**, 1145–1156.

Roskos, E. B., McNamara, T. P., Shelton, A. L. & Carr, W. 1998 Mental representations of large and small spatial layouts are orientation dependent. *J. Exp. Psychol. Learn. Mem. Cogn.* **24**, 215–226.

Samsonovich, A. & McNaughton, B. L. 1997 Path integration and cognitive mapping in a continuous attractor neural network model. *J. Neurosci.* **17**, 5900–5920.

Smith, M. L., Leonard, G., Crane, J. & Milner, B. 1995 The effects of frontal- or temporal-lobe lesions on susceptibility to interference in spatial memory. *Neuropsychologia* **33**, 275–285.

Snyder, L. H., Grieve, K. L., Brotchie, P. & Andersen, R. A. 1998 Separate body- and world-referenced representations of visual space in parietal cortex. *Nature* **394**, 887–891.

Spiers, H. J., Burgess, N., Maguire, E. A., Baxendale, S. A., Hartley, T., Thomson, P. & O'Keefe, J. 2001*a* Unilateral temporal lobectomy patients show lateralised topographical and episodic memory deficits in a virtual town. *Brain.* (In the press.)

Spiers, H. J., Maguire, E. A. & Burgess, N. 2001*b* Hippocampal amnesia. *Neurocase.* (In the press.)

Squire, L. R. & Zola, S. M. 1998 Episodic memory, semantic memory, and amnesia. *Hippocampus* **8**, 205–211.

Taube, J. S. 1998 Head direction cells and the neuropsychological basis for a sense of direction. *Prog. Neurobiol.* **55**, 225–256.

Teyler, T. J. & DiScenna, P. 1986 The hippocampal memory indexing theory. *Behav. Neurosci.* **100**, 147–154.

Treves, A. & Rolls, E. T. 1992 Computational constraints suggest the need for two distinct input systems to the hippocampal CA3 network. *Hippocampus* **2**, 189–199.

Vargha-Khadem, F., Gadian, D. G., Watkins, K. E., Connelly, A., Van Paesschen, W. & Mishkin, M. 1997 Differential effects of early hippocampal pathology on episodic and semantic memory. *Science* **277**, 376–380.

Vargha-Khadem, F., Gadian, D. G. & Mishkin, M. 2001 Dissociations in cognitive memory: the syndrome of developmental amnesia. *Phil. Trans. R. Soc. Lond.* B **356**, 1435–1440.

Wan, H., Aggleton, J. P. & Brown, M. W. 1999 Different contributions of the hippocampus and perirhinal cortex to recognition memory. *J. Neurosci.* **19**, 1142–1148.

Wang, R. F. & Spelke, E. 2000 Updating egocentric representations in human navigation. *Cognition* **77**, 215–250.

Willshaw, D. J. & Buckingham, J. T. 1990 An assessment of Marr's theory of the hippocampus as a temporary memory store. *Phil. Trans. R. Soc. Lond.* B **329**, 205–215.

Willshaw, D. J., Buneman, O. P. & Longuet-Higgins, H. C. 1969 Non-holographic associative memory. *Nature* **222**, 960–962.

Zhu, X. O., McCabe, B. J., Aggleton, J. P. & Brown, M. W. 1996 Mapping visual recognition memory through expression of the immediate early gene *c-fos*. *Neuroreport* **7**, 1871–1875.

Zola, S. M., Squire, L. R., Teng, E., Stefanacci, L., Buffalo, E. A. & Clark, R. E. 2000 Impaired recognition memory in monkeys after damage limited to the hippocampal region. *J. Neurosci.* **20**, 451–463.

15

Episodic memory and common sense: how far apart?

Endel Tulving

Research has revealed facts about human memory in general and episodic memory in particular that deviate from both common sense and previously accepted ideas. This paper discusses some of these deviations in light of the proceedings of The Royal Society's Discussion Meeting on episodic memory. Retrieval processes play a more critical role in memory than commonly assumed; people can remember events that never happened; and conscious thoughts about one's personal past can take two distinct forms—'autonoetic' remembering and 'noetic' knowing. The serial—dependent—independent (SPI) model of the relations among episodic, semantic and perceptual memory systems accounts for a number of puzzling phenomena, such as some amnesic patients' preserved recognition memory and their ability to learn new semantic facts, and holds that episodic remembering of perceptual information can occur only by virtue of its mediation through semantic memory. Although common sense endows many animals with the ability to remember their past experiences, as yet there is no evidence that humanlike episodic memory—defined in terms of subjective time, self, and autonoetic awareness—is present in any other species.

15.1. Introduction

Much of science begins as exploration of common sense, and much of science, if successful, ends if not in rejecting it then at least going far beyond it. The science of memory, although still in its early formative years, is no exception to the general rule. Many findings yielded by research, and theoretical interpretations of them that were brought up at the Royal Society discussion meeting on episodic memory and appearing in print here, neatly illustrate this point. They transcend traditional thought.

Here I organize my comments on the discussion meeting around the theme of how the science of memory has departed, or is in the process of distancing itself, not only from common sense but also from what have been standard views of memory—what Alan Baddeley in his introductory paper refers to as 'status quo' or 'received wisdom'. In doing so I rely heavily on a simple model—the serial–parallel–independent (SPI) model—of the relations among three memory 'systems' because it embodies a number of active issues around which the battle of old versus newer ideas about memory currently revolves.

15.2. What is episodic memory?

Let us begin with the very theme of the meeting, 'episodic memory'. Episodic memory, very roughly speaking, is the kind of memory that allows one to remember past happenings from one's life. The definition implies that there are other 'kinds' of memory that do not have the same properties that episodic memory does, and that do not serve the same function.

The (postulated) existence of different 'kinds' of memory (or 'memory systems') represents the first departure from traditional thought because in traditional thought, as in common sense, memory is 'unitary' in the sense that there is only one 'kind' of memory, as there is only one kind of water, or blood or forget-me-nots. In the world of memory, for a long time, just about everyone accepted the idea of a fundamental unity of learning and memory as a basic given. It was seldom questioned and, when it was, it was affirmed without hesitation. At an unusual, small conference in 1962 that had been explicitly organized to consider the 'taxonomy' of learning, most participants blithely ignored the central issue of the meeting: the possibility of different kinds of learning. Only Benton Underwood, one of the pre-eminent verbal learning researchers of the era, confronted it and succinctly put the credo of the field as follows:

> 'Are we to accept a conclusion that we will have different principles of learning for different species? Most of us would not accept this any more than we would accept the idea that we will have fundamentally different principles for different forms of human learning.' (Underwood 1964, p. 74).

Alan Baddeley, in his introductory paper in this issue, provides a pithy summary of how the idea of 'unitary' memory was shattered. The first breach came with the revelation that the laws and principles governing primary ('short-term') memory are not quite the same as those that apply to secondary ('long-term') memory (Waugh & Norman 1965; Atkinson & Shiffrin 1968). Although the split between primary and secondary memory was initially vigorously resisted by Underwood and others, it was not long before it was considered standard fare in all textbooks. Today, the break between primary memory, or its more theoretically meaningful successor, 'working memory' (Baddeley & Hitch 1974), on the one hand, and secondary memory ('long-term memory') on the other, is as sharp as one can find anywhere in nature.

The second breach took the form of the division of secondary memory into 'episodic' and 'semantic' (Tulving 1972). The division did not emerge out of the blue; similar ideas had been proposed before. These earlier ideas about different kinds of memory, however, were largely ignored. As pointed out by Baddeley, the idea of episodic memory stayed alive, grew, changed, matured and is now under intense scrutiny. It is one member of the family of 'multiple memory systems' (Foster & Jelicic 1998; Schacter & Tulving 1994). It has traditionally been categorized as one of the two subsystems of 'declarative' (or 'cognitive' or 'explicit') memory, semantic memory being the other one (Squire 1992; Tulving & Markowitsch 1998; Griffiths *et al.* 1999).

Episodic memory is 'memory for *personally experienced events*' or '*remembering* what happened where and when', whereas semantic memory is 'memory for *general facts* of the world.' A somewhat more elaborate definition holds that episodic memory has to do with one's 'autonoetic' awareness of one's experiences in the continuity of subjectively apprehended time that extends both backward into the past in the form of 'remembering' and forward into the future, in the form of 'thinking about' or imagining or 'planning for' the future. This definition emphasizes the conjunction of three ideas: self, autonoetic awareness, and subjectively sensed time. The definition of semantic memory at the corresponding level would refer to 'one's "noetic" awareness of the existence of the world and objects, events, and other regularities in it', independently of self, autonoetic awareness and (subjective) time. In this case, the less familiar terms used—such as autonoetic awareness and subjective time—then need to be explicated, as has been done elsewhere (Tulving 1993; Wheeler *et al.* 1997).

Critics have persistently questioned the concept of episodic memory, for a variety of reasons (for a summary, see Tulving 2002*a*). In this issue, Conway has taken the more constructive step of refining the concept by drawing a substantial distinction between episodic and autobiographical memory. Until now most students of memory have thought of autobiographical memory in the way that Kopelman and Kapur do:

> Autobiographical memory refers, characteristically, to a person's recollection of past incidents and events, which occurred at a specific time and place. Episodic memory is a somewhat broader term, encompassing autobiographical memories as well as performance on certain learning tasks such as recall of a word-list. However, the terms "autobiographical" and "episodic" are often used interchangeably. (Kopelman & Kapur 2001.)

Conway's concept of autobiographical memory (see also Conway & Pleydell-Pearce 2000) retains some features previously associated with episodic memory, but also includes some novel ideas—such as the temporal duration of episodic memory (short) and autobiographical memory (long), and different kinds of recollective experience: recollection and familiarity in episodic, and feelings of 'knowing' in autobiographical memory. Conway's proposal is wide in scope and rich in detail. It should generate a lively debate in the future.

15.3. Storage and retrieval

Common sense and everyday thinking about memory, honouring a long tradition that goes back all the way to Plato's aviary metaphor of memory, conceptualize memory in terms of a single measurable capacity, frequently identified with memory 'storage'. Thus, when a lay person, or even an expert, speaks of encoding information 'into' memory, the 'memory' in the expression designates the metaphorical 'store' in which 'memories' are held. 'Good memory' is a store with a large capacity for holding information. Once the remembered stuff ('memories') has been effectively acquired, or stored, it can be used ('retrieved') at will.

In the science of memory too, there is, of course, a great deal of interest in encoding and storage, but these two concepts are only a part of the story. Another part, some go as far as to say a more important part (Roediger 2000), has to do with the problem of how the successfully encoded information can be used ('retrieved'). Retrieval consists in a complex and elaborate set of processes; it is not simply a matter of 'reading the contents of memory store'. Every educated person, to give a homely example, knows the names of two capital cities in Europe which have two initial letters and three final letters in common. Although the required memory information is clearly 'in' the memory store, few people can produce the names thus described. This kind of a retrieval failure points to the existence of the 'problem' of retrieval in both semantic and episodic memory, which is independent of the 'problem' of storage, and leads to experiments in which the two sets of processes can be examined and measured separately (Brown & Craik 2000; Koriat 2000). The earlier tradition, which still rules supreme in some quarters, consisted in measuring 'memory' in memory 'tasks' and psychometric 'tests' in which encoding, storage and retrieval were thoroughly conflated (Tulving 1983, pp. 219–220).

Because of the historical tendency to identify memory with information storage, the problem of retrieval escaped the attention of memory researchers for a long time. In some branches of the science of memory it still does. But the concept of retrieval, and its relation to storage (and encoding), played a central role in the proceedings of the discussion meeting, and were especially prominent in the papers in this issue by Conway 2001; Gardiner 2001; Kopelman & Kapur 2001; Maguire 2001; Mayes 2001; and Yonelinas 2001. Without the distinction between storage and retrieval, many ideas that one can have about episodic memory would not arise. This simple even if surprising fact shows again how the science of memory goes beyond common sense.

Consider two relevant examples. The first one is provided by neuropsychological research on retrograde amnesia—severe impairment in the ability to remember or make use of knowledge acquired before the onset of the brain damage that causes such amnesia. The topic is thoroughly aired in the papers by Kopelman & Kapur (2001) and elsewhere (Wheeler & McMillan 2001). In the absence of the concept of retrieval one would necessarily have to conclude that retrograde amnesia stems from the loss of relevant information from the memory store. Now an interesting and serious possibility is that we are dealing with a special kind of failure of retrieval, and the existence of alternative explanations provides the kind of guidance for research that would not exist otherwise.

Second, in research designed to explore the similarities and differences in functional neuroanatomy of episodic and semantic memory—a topic of central concern in Maguire's paper (2001), and actively pursued in a number of laboratories in a number of countries—it turns out that it has been difficult to differentiate between encoding and storage processes in episodic and semantic memory but relatively easy to do so with respect to retrieval. This whole rich research area, which has contributed greatly to the neuroanatomical differentiation of episodic from semantic memory, either would not exist or would have been quite different in the world of 'memory tests', i.e. in the absence of the concept of retrieval.

15.4. False memories

Let us next consider another departure from conventional wisdom, put in the form of a question: 'If a person clearly and vividly remembers a particular event, does that mean that the event in fact happened?' In other words, can we make safe inferences about the past on the basis of what people remember about it? Common sense says 'yes', of course, and wonders how it could be otherwise. Is it not self-evident? Surely we make use of this simple truth—'I remember it, therefore it happened'—all the time. Much of our legal system operates on the premise that eyewitness's testimony, if given in good faith, provides true evidence of what happened. Physicians take a patient's history and believe that the patient correctly remembers when a symptom first appeared. People take great delight in telling stories of what they did, saw or heard, and others take equal delight in listening to them. Storytelling and listening are some of the oldest and most common forms of entertainment. The listeners naturally believe that the storyteller describes what actually happened. The element of entertainment would be marred if one had no idea whether the story was true or just so much imagination.

Scientific research has clearly established that it is not always possible to determine what happened in the past on the basis of a person's recollection, regardless of whom the person is, and regardless of how strongly—and genuinely—the person believes that he or she is telling the truth. This research shows that it is perfectly possible for even completely sane, intelligent and honest people to clearly remember and strongly believe something that never happened. Such 'false memories' or 'memory illusions' do not happen all the time, of course. Usually what we remember is true to a larger or smaller extent. Memory can also be absolutely veridical—think of all the memorized poems, speeches, dates, addresses, phone numbers and passwords that we can recall (most of the time). Nevertheless, a good part of the activity of memory consists not in reproduction, or even in reconstruction, but in sheer construction. And constructed memories do not always correspond to reality. One need not suffer from any neurological or psychiatric dysfunction, nor need one be very young or very old, to have false memories and to remember events that never happened. Thus, thanks to research, we now know something that does not readily fit into common sense: sometimes people remember events, say the 'miniature' event of a word or picture having appeared in a visually presented to-be-remembered list, that in fact did not appear. This is a fact. The relevant research is discussed in this issue at some length by Schacter & Dodson (2001) and touched on by Gardiner (2001).

Now, however, what about the situation where there is available completely objective verification of the fact that an event did happen, and the person being tested (the 'subject' participant in the experiment) correctly indicates his or her knowledge of the fact. Can we infer that the subject now actually does remember seeing the word? Again, for an outsider, it must be very difficult not to say 'yes,' and imagine why anyone would want to even raise the question. Yet research shows that the question is appropriate and the answer to it more complex than what was suspected in traditional thinking. Much of the relevant data come from a widely used method of observing and measuring retrieval known as the yes–no recognition test.

15.5. Remembering and knowing

Recognition tests are no doubt the most frequently used tests of memory today. The reason for their popularity lies in their apparent common-sense face value, assumed theoretical simplicity, ease of administration and employability across different kinds of stimulus materials as well as subject populations. What is a more direct way of testing someone's memory than presenting a stimulus item now for (intentional or casual) study or inspection and then later on asking the subject to indicate whether it is an item that was previously encountered? The 'remembered' item is responded to in one way, a 'non-remembered' item in another. All sorts of items can be used: words, pairs of words, line drawings, photographs of scenery or faces, actual three-dimensional objects. The test subjects can be people—infants, young, old, healthy, brain damaged or whatever—as well as non-human animals of a great variety—goldfish, rats, pigeons, monkeys and many others. Subjects in recognition tasks can be instructed about the rules of the game through verbal instructions, if they possess language, or through appropriate training procedures if they do not.

Common sense and traditional thought about yes–no recognition is that it measures memory, or, with the advent of the episodic–semantic distinction, that it measures episodic memory: 'Did you see this item in the list that you studied earlier?'. Again, it is a perfectly natural assumption to make. How well the experimental subject can distinguish between old and new test items clearly depends on, and hence reflects, how well the subject remembers what she or he previously studied. As with much if not all wisdom inherent in common sense, there seems nothing debatable about these kinds of thoughts.

However, research suggests that the idea that 'episodic' recognition tests assess episodic memory is only partially correct. The relevant research has been carried out under the banner of the remember–know (RK) paradigm. It is of central concern in Gardiner's paper (2001; see also Gardiner & Richardson-Klavehn 2000; Knowlton & Squire 1995; Rajaram & Roediger 1997). The RK paradigm is also involved in the evaluation of Yonelinas's (2001) dual-signal detection model of recognition that he discusses in his paper in this issue.

In a typical application of the RK paradigm, experimental subjects participate in a standard yes–no recognition test, with an additional twist: whenever they judge a test item to be 'old' (they think it was a member of the studied collection) they make a further judgement about whether they 'remember' the event of the item's occurrence in studied collection or whether they have some other grounds (such as a feeling of 'familiarity') for 'knowing' that the item did occur in the collection.

There is surprisingly good agreement between the conclusions drawn by Gardiner and Yonelinas, despite several differences in their overall approach to the issue. Thus, Gardiner concentrates on the RK paradigm, Yonelinas includes Jacoby's process-dissociation procedure (Jacoby 1991) in his analyses. Gardiner is interested in the conscious aspects of recognition, whereas Yonelinas keeps his focus on measurement of behaviour. Gardiner is very much in tune with the idea of multiple memory systems; Yonelinas concentrates on processes and can do without multiple systems. Gardiner roams over a wide territory in his coverage of empirical evidence, Yonelinas sticks more closely to traditional cognitive psychology and neuropsychological procedures.

Given all these differences, it is most satisfying to see how well the conclusions drawn by the two converge on a common bottom line: there are indeed two, rather different components (modes of retrieval, processes, memory systems) that feed into performance on yes–no recognition tests. This means that the standard measures of recognition memory that have served the field so well for a very long time—hit rates, false alarm rates and their derivatives—can no more be regarded as sufficiently analytical. Anyone who wishes to study nature, rather than theories about nature, will have to start worrying about the meaning of old-fashioned recognition tests.

Additional convergent evidence for the existence of two component processes of recognition is provided by event related potential (ERP) studies (Düzel *et al.* 1997; Mangels *et al.* 2001) and functional magnetic resonance imaging (fMRI) studies (Henson *et al.* 1999; Eldridge *et al.* 2000) that have revealed neural correlates of the two processes. Especially interesting converging evidence is provided by the ERP findings on the young amnesic patient Jon, who has a severely impaired episodic memory but performs quite normally on standard yes–no recognition tests. These findings show that he has a normal N400 ERP effect, which is known to be associated with the familiarity component of recognition, whereas the late-positive effect, known to reflect episodic recollection, is completely absent in Jon's ERP waveform (Düzel *et al.* 1999). These findings suggest that, unlike healthy people, Jon relies largely if not wholly on his intact, perhaps enhanced, ability to distinguish between novel and familiar test items in performing the recognition test.

A new idea about recognition memory is that, in addition to reflecting 'remembering' and 'knowing,' it can also reflect familiarity that is purely perceptual. Aggleton & Pearce (2001) as well as Morris (2001), in their respective papers in this issue, cogently argue in considerable detail that recognition tests may, but need not, depend on episodic memory. Many animals do perfectly well on a variety of recognition tests and one need not assume that they have episodic memory.

The idea that successful performance on recognition tests can occur at different levels of memory—episodic, semantic, and perceptual—may help to clarify outstanding issues and help understand a number of memory phenomena.

15.6. Knowledge through experience? The SPI model

In everyday thinking about memory it is often assumed that new facts about the world are learned through experience, i.e. through observing happenings in everyday life, through being exposed to statements about the facts (as in learning from teachers or books), or observing happenings in real life and drawing appropriate conclusions about the 'facts of the world' from them. This means that when we wonder which came first—episodic memory (experiences) or semantic memory (facts)—common sense tells us that the answer is episodic memory. Information gets into semantic memory 'through' episodic memory: first an individual has a particular experience in the course of which he, say, learns a new fact, and later on he can use the knowledge thus acquired independently of any remembering of the original learning episode as such.

This is what many experts in the area of memory have believed (and many still do) ever since the distinction between episodic and semantic memory was drawn. The careful reader of papers in this issue will be able to spot statements to this effect in various chapters. Nevertheless, although the jury is still out on this question, and although the final answer may turn out to be of a kind that almost always is reached at the end of debates ('well, it all depends'), I believe that the correct view is the reverse of common sense: information gets into episodic memory through semantic memory.

This belief has been formalized in a very simple model of the relations among memory systems. The central idea is that the relations among systems are process-specific: encoding is serial (S), storage is parallel (P) and retrieval is independent (I); hence the model is referred to as SPI (Tulving 1995; Tulving & Markowitsch 1998). Figure 15.1 presents a sketch of the SPI model, applied to three kinds of memory or memory systems: perceptual, semantic and episodic. The three memory systems are arranged hierarchically (or 'monohierarchically'). The perceptual system is at the lowest level and episodic at the highest. The perceptual system (also called 'perceptual representation system' or PRS; Tulving & Schacter 1990) receives, stores and makes available to other systems information about perceptual features of physical objects. It makes possible associative (e.g. stimulus–response) learning by furnishing one ingredient (the stimulus) for the basic unit of such learning. The perceptual system is also assumed to be involved in 'perceptual priming' in that experience-based changes in it may manifest themselves as enhancement in the perceptual identification of objects (Tulving & Schacter 1990). The other two levels are as already specified: the semantic system does with 'facts' what PRS does with perceptual features of objects, and the episodic system extends the processing of objects and facts to the 'self' in 'subjective time'. (Note that semantic memory concerns knowledge of the world in general; despite its label it does not require language for its operations.)

Encoding of information into these systems proceeds serially. At any level of the monohierarchy, the products of processing of a given system can be either transmitted to the next higher level, or 'stored' at that level, or both. Whatever is stored at a given level of processing is potentially retrievable at that level, provided that the other conditions of efficient retrieval are fulfilled. Thus, information from the perceptual system can be, but need not be, transmitted to the semantic system and stored 'in' the perceptual memory system.

Not all perceptually processed information, of course, needs to 'reach' the semantic system, and not all of the information processed at the semantic level needs to reach the episodic system. It all depends on other factors that influence encoding: 'bottom-up' factors, such as novelty of the incoming information (Tulving *et al.* 1994); and 'top-down' factors, such as 'levels of processing' (Craik & Lockhart 1972).

The parallel storage assumption of SPI holds that different aspects of incoming information are stored separately in different systems: information about the perceptual features of the input are stored in the perceptual system, information about conceptual and semantic aspects is stored in the semantic system, and information about the involvement of the self in the experiencing of the input is stored in the episodic system. This assumption also goes against traditional thought, and perhaps common sense, which holds that a single event leaves a 'single' trace in the memory store. The idea in SPI is that the trace is a 'bundle' of widely but systematically dispersed features organized hierarchically.

The third process in SPI, retrieval, is assumed to be independent between the systems. This assumption follows directly from the assumption of parallel storage. It holds that what is retrieved from one system need not have any implications for retrieval of information from any other system. Frequently, the information from different systems is used jointly in a given act of retrieval, or separately but additively on individual components of a task. However, because of separate storage, it is perfectly possible, although not necessary of course, for retrieval to occur from only one system.

The SPI model goes against traditional thought in several ways. But because it is not only testable but falsifiable, it is worth attention and analysis.

15.7. SPI and traditional thought

It may be worth emphasizing five points about this simple model that illustrate how what was held by many to be true for a long time (and by some still is) should no more be so, or how at least it is now being challenged.

First, the organizational structure of SPI makes explicit that 'memory' can operate perfectly well at lower levels independently of higher levels in a given kind of brain—as well as in brains in which higher levels do not exist, either because they never evolved or in which they have been lost through brain damage. Thus, learning and memory may occur at the perceptual level alone, in the absence of any intervention by semantic and episodic memory. A great deal of memory research in non-human animals, for example, is essentially concerned with perceptual (recognition) memory (Aggleton & Pearce 2001), as is research done with pre-verbal human infants (Rovee-Collier & Hayne 2000). The widely used delayed non-matching to sample (DNMS) and other kinds of 'object recognition' tasks can be effectively executed without relying on semantic memory. It is this feature that allows a meaningful comparative analysis of 'memory' across species at the same level (Wright *et al.* 1985). Because comparisons in situations where memory operates at non-corresponding levels in different species are difficult to interpret, it is always important to establish what level of memory in species *X* is compared with what level of memory in species *Y*.

A great deal of learning and memory may occur at the semantic (general knowledge) level alone, without any intervention by episodic memory. Young children can acquire knowledge about the world efficiently and rapidly long before they develop the ability to recollect specific happenings from their past (Nelson 1993; Perner & Ruffman 1995; for more detailed discussion see Wheeler *et al.* 1997). Some amnesic patients, who have severely impaired or no functional episodic memory, can nevertheless acquire new semantic information (Hamann & Squire 1995; Kitchener *et al.* 1998; Tulving *et al.* 1991), especially when associative interference in learning is minimized (Hayman *et al.* 1993) or when 'errorless learning' procedures are used (Baddeley & Wilson 1994).

An especially striking demonstration of massive semantic learning in the absence of episodic memory is provided by cases of developmental amnesia, such as the young man Jon, described by Vargha-Khadem *et al.* 1997; 2001). Such cases present a serious challenge to conventional theory (Squire & Zola 1998; Tulving & Markowitsch 1998). The important point in the present context, however, is that all these cases illustrate how memory can successfully work below the level of episodic, even in the human brain.

Second, there is no provision in SPI for 'direct' encoding of perceptual information into episodic memory: the information must first go 'through' the semantic memory system. This proposal goes very much against common sense and against my own earlier thinking (Tulving 1972). Recently, the assumption that there is 'no direct line' from perceptual to episodic memory has been questioned by Simons and his colleagues in Cambridge (Graham *et al.* 2000; Simons *et al.* 2001). The issue represents one of the central topics of the paper by Hodges & Graham (this issue). I will return to it later in this paper.

Third, the SPI model explicitly allows—one might even say 'predicts'—double dissociations between episodic and semantic memory in retrograde amnesia (RA). If an individual suffers brain damage that causes RA, it can consist only (or at least primarily) in impairment of episodic memory (Kitchener *et al.* 1998; Kapur 1999; Tulving *et al.* 1988; Wheeler & McMillan 2001), only (or primarily) in semantic memory (De Renzi *et al.* 1987; Grossi *et al.* 1988; Wheeler & McMillan 2001; Yasuda *et al.* 1997), or more or less evenly in both, as in the majority of reported cases of amnesia. This feature of SPI is directly contrary to the widely accepted views of amnesia, advocated by Squire and Zola and their colleagues (Squire 1992; Squire & Zola 1998),

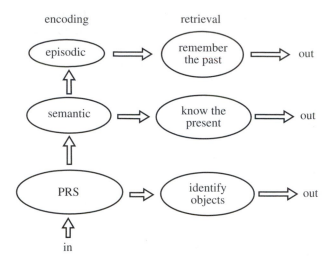

Fig. 15.1. A schematic rendering of a model of process-specific relations (serial–parallel–independent; SPI) among three large memory systems—perceptual (PRS), semantic and episodic.

which do not readily allow for exceptions to the more-or-less even impairment of memory for facts (semantic memory) and memory for events (episodic) memory.

Fourth, although double dissociations are allowed in RA or even 'predicted' by SPI, because of the serial encoding assumption they are strictly ruled out in anterograde amnesia (AA). When a healthy individual suffers brain damage and develops AA, it can consist in impairment of both semantic and episodic memory (the 'standard' form of AA) or impairment in episodic memory alone. What cannot happen, according to SPI, is AA in semantic memory alone. The matter is of considerable interest because, according to a widely accepted alternative view, anterograde memory for facts (semantic memory) and memory for events (episodic memory) are expected to be impaired more-or-less evenly (Squire 1992; Squire & Zola 1998).

Finally, SPI can be used to account for the many facts generated by the RK paradigm, which constitutes the central theme of Gardiner's paper (this issue) and figures prominently in Yonelinas's dual-process model of signal detection in recognition memory (this issue), as discussed in § 15.8.

The SPI model, when first proposed, was meant to be a purely 'psychological theory', an abstract model in keeping with the hypothetical, abstract nature of the concepts of episodic and semantic memory. No suggestions were offered about its neural correlates. Some recent developments, however, allow us to postulate parallels between the abstract SPI model and conclusions drawn from neuropsychological studies of both humans and animals. Aggleton & Brown (1999; see also Aggleton & Pearce, this issue) point out that, in animals, the brain structures involved in spatial memory are surprisingly different from those involved in recognition memory. In Aggleton's model, two partially overlapping medial–temporal and diencephalic systems mediate performance on different memory tasks. Recall, and episodic memory, depend on the hippocampus, the fornix and several structures in the diencephalon, whereas non-episodic recognition and familiarity are highly dependent on the perirhinal cortex and the medial dorsal nucleus of the thalamus, and do not require the hippocampus. The logic of this model would fit SPI if we assumed that the performance on recognition memory tests, in animals, is mediated by the perceptual (PRS) systems whereas performance on spatial memory tests is mediated by the declarative ('semantic' in Tulving & Markowitsch, 1998) system.

Mishkin and his colleagues (Mishkin *et al.* 1997; Vargha-Khadem & Mishkin, this issue) have suggested a hierarchical model of the organization of medial–temporal lobe structures in the service of episodic and semantic memory that also agrees neatly with the abstract SPI model. In Mishkin's model, the hippocampus operates at the highest level of the medial–temporal lobe (MTL) hierarchy and is associated with episodic memory, whereas the subjacent cortical regions operate at lower levels and are associated with semantic memory. The model is compatible with what is known about the psychology and neuroanatomy of the case of Jon and other perinatal amnesia patients (Vargha-Khadem *et al.* 1997) who fit SPI.

The idea that episodic recollection is not needed for recognition of 'old' and 'new' items is relevant to two other issues discussed at the meeting. First, the test of one of the most counter-intuitive features of the SPI model discussed earlier, namely the idea that there is no direct encoding of perceptual information into episodic memory and that perceptual information can enter episodic memory only through semantic memory. Second, the question of whether animals have episodic memory. I discuss these two issues in the remainder of this paper.

15.8. Is there direct encoding of perceptual information into episodic memory?

The SPI model, as already mentioned, rules out any direct encoding of perceptual information into episodic memory. As shown in Figure 15.1, for perceptual information to be stored in episodic memory it needs to be processed not only in the perceptual system but also in the semantic system. The idea that it is not possible for people to recollect consciously what they have perceived unless it has been first 'interpreted' by semantic memory sounds counter-intuitive, perhaps even strongly so. However, the matter is testable and therefore the model is capable of being rejected in its present form. Surprisingly, the demonstration of direct entry of perceptual information into episodic memory has turned out to be difficult.

Recently, Jon Simons and his colleagues in Cambridge (Graham *et al.* 2000; Simons *et al.* 2001) have questioned the validity of the assumption of serial encoding in the SPI model. This assumption implies that individuals with dysfunctional semantic memory should have difficulty storing information in episodic memory. Even if such individuals have intact perceptual systems, their remembering of recent experiences should be deficient because there is no direct input from perceptual systems to episodic memory. Simons and his colleagues have tested this assumption with their semantic dementia patients who are selectively deficient in semantic memory, attributed to (usually asymmetrical) temporal lobe atrophy (Graham *et al.* 1997, 1999, 2000).

In one experiment, Simons and his colleagues (2001, experiment 2) tested two such patients for their ability to recognize recently seen faces. Two kinds of faces were initially presented for inspection: celebrities that were known and celebrities who were not known to the patients. After study, the patients were given two kinds of yes–no episodic recognition tests. In one, the test faces were identical with those seen initially; in the other, the test faces of the celebrities encountered at encoding were presented in different orientations.

The logic of the experiment rested on two assumptions: (i) the subjects' semantic memory would contribute to the recognition of known celebrities but not, or less so, to the recognition of unknown faces, and (ii) the problem of recognizing faces presented in the same orientation at study and test could be solved by relying on perceptual features alone, whereas recognizing faces in changed orientations would require, or at least would benefit from, semantic knowledge of the people whose faces were shown.

In the experimental situation used by Simons *et al.* (2001), the SPI model implies that the patients' impaired semantic memory should make it impossible, or at least more difficult, to remember the previous (virtual) encounter with unknown individuals than the encounter with known celebrities. The findings of this study agreed with this implication in the test condition in which different views of faces were used, but not in the condition in which test faces were changed. Simons and colleagues claimed this latter finding to be contrary to the SPI model, and proposed, therefore, that the SPI model, needs to be rejected and replaced with a more appropriate model, one they call 'multiple input' (MI) model or hypothesis. According to this revised model, episodic memory normally receives information from both the perceptual and conceptual (semantic) systems of the brain. These sentiments were echoed by Andrew Mayes and Neil Roberts (2001).

The Cambridge group's suggested revision of the SPI is attractive for several reasons:

(i) The SPI model is currently very crude. It is difficult to imagine that as such it could capture the essence of the encoding–retrieval relations of complex memory systems, such as PRS, semantic and episodic.

(ii) All good scientists know that all current models and theories are wrong—in the sense that sooner or later they all will be modified or replaced by better ones— and therefore any explicitly proposed revision of the crude SPI model represents a step in the right direction.

(iii) The proposed MI model makes good common sense. What could be more natural than to believe that a person can remember 'purely perceptual' events?

It is to be hoped, therefore, that the MI model of the Cambridge group will turn out to be a better idea about the encoding relations of PRS, semantic memory and episodic memory than the SPI model. There are, however, a couple of problems that need attention before we can certify the MI as the current 'front runner'.

One problem has to do with the claimed critical finding that patients with semantic dementia show equally good recognition memory for semantically familiar and unfamiliar faces (Simons *et al.* 2001), or recognition memory comparable with that of healthy controls (Graham *et al.* 2000), when test items have the same format as studied items. The validity of the claim is uncertain because of the observed ceiling effects in relevant conditions in both experiments. Thus, in the Simons *et al.* (2001) study, it is simply not known whether the critical interaction between type of recognition test (identical versus perceptually different test objects) and type of test items (familiar versus unfamiliar faces) came about because of the processes postulated in the MI model or because of ceiling effects. The Cambridge group are aware of the problems caused by ceiling effects but are willing to overlook them and to assume that the interaction would occur even in the absence of the ceiling effects. Nevertheless, the matter requires attention especially because other experiments have shown that even healthy individuals (young, old and very old) show better recognition memory for familiar than unfamiliar faces tested in their original form (Bäckman 1991; see also Bäckman & Herlitz 1990). A clear demonstration of the absence of the same effect in patients with semantic dementia, under conditions where the patients' recognition performance is free to vary, would settle this particular matter convincingly, leaving only the second problem.

This second problem has to do with the discrepancy between the concepts of episodic memory in the SPI and the MI models. In the formulation of the SPI model, 'episodic memory' refers to the episodic 'system', which has a certain set of process-specific relations to other systems. The critical findings that Simons and his colleagues use to reject the SPI model were obtained in yes–no recognition memory tests. Although such tests are frequently treated as 'tests of episodic memory'—I myself have done it regularly—as mentioned earlier, we now know that this is an oversimplification. The current understanding is that the extent to which episodic memory influences performance on recognition tests can vary, sometimes greatly, with conditions. In the absence of corroborating evidence there is no need to assume that semantic dementia patients relied on their episodic memory in the recognition test for faces. It is conceivable that they relied on their perceptual memory alone.

The assumption is that it is quite possible for any kind of subjects to do well on recognition memory tests in the absence of episodic memory. The most glaring example is provided by recognition memory tests in experiments with non-human animals as subjects.

15.9. Do animals remember past events?

Do animals, such as rats, cats, dogs and monkeys, have episodic memory? That is, do they remember their own life experiences the same way that humans do? Common sense would say 'yes' and perhaps again be perplexed at the questions. Surely there could be no doubt that they do. Surely, all one needs to do is watch one's pet cat or dog to be convinced that the cat has excellent episodic memory. Why even bother raising the question?

Indeed, more often than not, the question has not been raised—because the answer to it has been clear without any need for thought. The earlier quote by Underwood said it all. Besides, there have been literally thousands of research reports on the close similarity of learning and memory data for non-human animals and humans. So, what is the reason for wanting to raise the question about episodic memory in animals?

The question about episodic memory in animals is a part of a larger issue—the nature of continuity of forms of learning and memory across the species. On the one hand, it is an unassailable fact that humans share a very large proportion of their genome with other animals, that their brains are built on the same basic plan as those of rats and monkeys and other mammals, and that, as far as we know, the molecular mechanisms and synaptic changes assumed to underlie learning and memory are the same across the species. These facts make thinking of continuity natural and non-controversial. On the other hand, the fact that humans engage in many unique forms of learned behaviour that are found in no other species—language and literature, art and music, religion and philosophy, science and technology, to mention the most obvious ones—should also encourage thoughts about differences in learning and memory. It would be unreasonable to assume that these uniquely human forms of self-expression are based on features of the evolved human brain that it shares with other animals.

The issue of episodic memory in animals is discussed thoroughly by three sets of authors: Aggleton & Pearce (2001; Aggleton & Brown 1999); Clayton and her colleagues (2001; Clayton & Dickinson 1998; Griffiths *et al.* 1999); and Morris (2001; Morris & Frey 1997). All three come to the conclusion, put by Clayton *et al.* (2001), as follows. In many of the tasks used in studies of animal memory, presumably including various 'recognition' tasks:

> '... the animal does not need to recall the "what, where and when" of an event. Instead, the task may be solved by discriminating on the basis of relative familiarity, a process which is dissociable both psychologically (Mandler 1980; Jacoby & Dallas 1981; Jacoby 1991) and neurobiologically (Aggleton & Brown 1999) from episodic memory recall.' (Clayton *et al.* 2001, § 1).

More broadly, the common verdict is that the answer to the question about episodic memory in animals is not obvious and it cannot be settled by common sense. At the present time, all agree that the weight of evidence seems to lie with the absence of human-like episodic memory in animals. However, because interesting analogues of episodic memory exist in non-human animals ('episodic-like' memories), future research may topple the current received wisdom.

The ingenious and convincing demonstrations of the 'what, where, when' memory in scrub jays by Clayton and her colleagues come very close to clinching the case for the jays' episodic memory. The only thing missing is evidence that they have human-like conscious recollections of their worm and nut caching activities. They may just 'know' what kind of food is where, and what state it is in—fresh or rotten—without knowing how or why they know it; hence, most appropriately, the use of the term 'episodic-like' memory. Clayton's scrub jay experiments clearly take us beyond what was known about non-human animals' ability to handle the 'when?' part of episodic memory—the 'what' and 'where' in animal learning and memory has been known for a long time (e.g. Shettleworth 1998). However, the nature of the information—is it 'remembered' or just 'known'—remains an open question. Richard Morris, in his talk at the meeting, expressed his hope (conviction?) that this question will be answered through the ingenuity of comparative psychologists who may be able to invent ways of communicating with animals that are almost as good as Dr Doolittle's. A wise scientist would not even dream of doubting the reality of the hope.

It is interesting, as Clayton *et al.* (2001) point out, that scrub jays do have episodic memory by the standards of 1972: their performance in the various tasks that Clayton and her team have posed for them clearly implies that they remember what happened where and when. In 1972, I (and I suspect just about everybody else) was convinced that remembering particular events, such as occurrences of words in a list, necessarily depended on remembering the general event of which the particular ones had been a part, namely the learning the list. For example, for a subject in a verbal learning experiment to be able to respond with the word 'gallant' to the word 'legend', which she had learned in a paired-associate learning task, she had to remember that she had learned the list. I and others thought it was impossible to remember that 'legend' and 'gallant' appeared together in the list if one did not remember having learned the list. This is very similar to the demonstrated capabilities of scrub jays.

The scrub jays' problem, therefore, is that our concept of episodic memory has changed since 1972. Unlike then, the main emphasis is now on three concepts: subjectively apprehended time, self and autonoetic consciousness. The combination of the three supports activities that can be subsumed under the category of 'mental time travel', activities such as remembering past experiences as such and imagining possible future personal happenings as such. It is the uncertainty about the animals' possession of these kinds of experiential capabilities that makes it difficult to attribute human-type episodic memory to them.

Another feature of episodic (as well as semantic) memory that has been mentioned but has not been systematically explored, but which may turn out to be relevant to the issue of episodic and episodic-like memories in animals, is that retrieval of information 'from' episodic memory does not oblige the rememberer to any kind of overt behaviour. Any 'conversion' (Tulving 1983) of retrieved ('ecphoric') information is optional rather than obligatory: there is no fixed relation between thought and action. This fact is sometimes said to illustrate a property of cognitive or declarative memory called 'flexibility,' although the term has been used in other senses as well.

In animal studies of episodic-like memory, it would be interesting to see whether it would be possible to persuade the subjects to demonstrate their ability to act 'flexibly' upon the information that they have about a given 'what–where–when'. For example, could Clayton and her colleagues (or someone else) get their scrub jays, who remember what kind of food is where, to do something other with that information than act on it 'inflexibly', i.e. something other than approach the preferred food in order to eat it? Could the internally generated knowledge of a state of the world ('rotten worms on the left') serve as a Skinnerian discriminative stimulus for some other behaviour that produces some other reward that the birds appreciate? Convincing demonstrations of the decoupling of what appears a hard-wired connection between fixed behaviour prompted by fixed knowledge would constitute another step in the emancipation of birds, or other animals, as episodic creatures.

Another kind of a situation that is unrelated to mediation by or communication through language, and which, if it yielded appropriate results, I would find supportive of the idea of 'real' episodic (not just episodic-like) memory in animals is the following. Systematic observation shows that animals, at some point $T1$ in their 'spare time,' engage in a given behaviour X which is not controlled (instigated and maintained) by any physiological stimulus, external or internal, but which can be shown to be of benefit to the animal at some future time $T2$. The argument here is, first, that humans engage in these kinds of (foresightful, 'planning') behaviours all the time—indeed, a surprisingly large proportion of all human activities is orientated towards the future—and, second, at the root of such an ability to travel mentally into the future is an 'autonoetic' time sense of episodic memory (for more on these kinds of ideas see Tulving 2002a,b). Therefore, if animals would also exhibit intelligent and purposeful behaviour that is not prompted by present stimuli, it becomes reasonable to assume that they are doing so on the same basis as humans. Lloyd Morgan's canon, emphasized by both Morris (2001) and Aggleton & Pearce (2001) would no longer apply.

At the present time the rational consensus is that episodic memory is unique to humans. Lest someone worry about the current political correctness of such an assertion, let me hasten to remind such a person that many behavioural and cognitive capabilities of many non-human species are equally unique to those species: echolocation in bats, electrical sensing in fish and genetically determined navigational capabilities of migratory birds are examples that come quickly to mind, but there are many, many others. Indeed, it is these kinds of abilities—unfathomable by common sense, but very real in fact—that allow one to remain a sceptic about episodic memory in birds and animals: evolution is an exceedingly clever tinkerer who can make its creatures perform spectacular feats without necessarily endowing them with sophisticated powers of conscious awareness.

Endel Tulving's research is supported by the Natural Sciences and Engineering Research Council of Canada, and by an endowment by Anne and Max Tanenbaum in support of research in cognitive neuroscience.

References

Aggleton, J. P. & Brown, M. W. 1999 Episodic memory, amnesia and the hippocampal–anterior thalamic axis. *Behav. Brain Sci.* **22**, 425–444.

Aggleton, J. P. & Pearce, J. M. 2001 Neural systems underlying episodic memory: insights from animal research. *Phil. Trans. R. Soc. Lond.* B **356**, 1467–1482.

Atkinson, R. C. & Shiffrin, R. M. 1968 Human memory: a proposed system and its control processes. In *The psychology of learning and motivation: advances in research and theory*, vol. 2 (ed. K. W. Spence & J. T. Spence), pp. 89–195. New York: Academic Press.

Bäckman, L. 1991 Recognition memory across the adult life span: the role of prior knowledge. *Mem. Cogn.* **19**, 63–71.

Bäckman, L. & Herlitz, A. 1990 The relationship between prior knowledge and face recognition memory in normal aging and Alzheimer's disease. *J. Gerontol. Psychol. Sci.* **45**, 94–100.

Baddeley, A. D. & Hitch, G. J. 1974 Working memory. In *Recent advances in learning and motivation,* vol. 8 (ed. G. H. Bower), pp. 47–89. New York: Academic Press.

Baddeley, A. & Wilson, B. A. 1994 When implicit learning fails—amnesia and the problem of error elimination. *Neuropsychologia* **32**, 53–68.

Brown, S. C. & Craik, F. I. M. 2000 Encoding and retrieval of information. In *The Oxford handbook of memory* (ed. E. Tulving & F. I. M. Craik), pp. 93–107. New York: Oxford University Press.

Clayton, N. S. & Dickinson, A. 1998 Episodic-like memory during cache recovery by scrub jays. *Nature* **395**, 272–274.

Clayton, N. S., Griffiths, D. P., Emery, N. J. & Dickinson, A. 2001 Elements of episodic-like memory in animals. *Phil. Trans. R. Soc. Lond.* B **356**, 1483–1491.

Conway, M. A. & Pleydell-Pearce, C. W. 2000 The construction of autobiographical memories in the self memory system. *Psychol. Rev.* **107**, 261–288.

Conway, M. A. 2001 Sensory-perceptual episodic memory and its context: autobiographical memory. *Phil. Trans. R. Soc. Lond.* B **356**, 1375–1384.

Craik, F. I. M. & Lockhart R. S. 1972 Levels of processing: a framework for memory research. *J. Verbal Learn. Verbal Behav.* **11**, 671–684.

De Renzi, E., Liotti, M. & Nichelli, P. 1987 Semantic amnesia with preservation of autobiographic memory: a case report. *Cortex* **23**, 575–597.

Düzel, E., Yonelinas, A. P., Mangun, G. R., Heinze, H. J. & Tulving, E. 1997 Event-related brain potential correlates of two states of conscious awareness in memory. *Proc. Natl Acad. Sci. USA* **94**, 5973–5978.

Düzel, E., Vargha-Khadem, F., Heinze, H. J. & Mishkin, M. 1999 ERP evidence for recognition without episodic recollection in a patient with early hippocampal pathology. *Soc. Neurosci. Abstr.* **25**, 259.11.

Eldridge, L. L., Knowlton, B. T., Furmanski, C. S., Bookheimer, S. Y. & Engel, S. A. 2000 Remembering episodes: a selective role for the hippocampus during retrieval. *Nature Neurosci.* **3**, 1149–1152.

Foster, J. K. & Jelicic, M. (eds) 1998 *Memory: systems, process or function?* pp. 31–65. Oxford University Press.

Gardiner, J. M. & Richardson-Klavehn, A. 2000 Remembering and knowing. In *The Oxford handbook of memory* (ed. E. Tulving & F. I. M. Craik), pp. 229–244. New York: Oxford University Press.

Gardiner, J. M. 2001 Episodic memory and autonoetic consciousness: a first-person approach. *Phil. Trans. R. Soc. Lond.* B **356**, 1351–1361.

Graham, K. S., Becker, J. T. & Hodges, J. R. 1997 On the relationship between knowledge and memory for pictures: evidence from the study of patients with semantic dementia and Alzheimer's disease. *J. Int. Neuropsychol. Soc.* **3**, 534–544.

Graham, K. S., Patterson, K. & Hodges, J. R. 1999 Episodic memory: new insights from the study of semantic dementia. *Curr. Opin. Neurobiol.* **9**, 245–250.

Graham, K. S., Simons, J. S., Pratt, K. H., Patterson, K. & Hodges, J. R. 2000 Insights from semantic dementia on the relationship between episodic and semantic memory. *Neuropsychologia* **38**, 313–324.

Griffiths, D. P., Dickinson, A. & Clayton, N. S. 1999 Declarative and episodic memory: what can animals remember about their past? *Trends Cogn. Sci.* **3**, 74–80.

Grossi, D., Trojano, L., Grasso, A. & Orsini, A. 1988 Selective 'semantic amnesia' after closed-head injury. A case report. *Cortex* **24**, 457–464.

Hamann, S. B. & Squire, L. R. 1995 On the acquisition of new declarative knowledge in amnesia. *Behav. Neurosci.* **109**, 1027–1044.

Hayman, C. A. G., Macdonald, C. A. & Tulving, E. 1993 The role of repetition and associative interference in new semantic learning in amnesia. *J. Cogn. Neurosci.* **5**, 375–389.

Henson, R. N. A., Rugg, M. D., Shallice, T., Josephs. O. & Dolan, R. J. 1999 Recollection and familiarity in recognition memory: an event-related functional magnetic resonance imaging study. *J. Neurosci.* **19**, 3962–3972.

Jacoby, L. L. 1991 A process dissociation framework: separating automatic from intentional uses of memory. *J. Mem. Lang.* **30**, 513–541.

Jacoby, L. L. & Dallas, M. 1981 On the relationship between autobiographical memory and perceptual learning. *J. Exp. Psychol. Gen.* **3**, 306–340.

Kapur, N. 1999 Syndromes of retrograde amnesia: a conceptual and empirical analysis. *Psychol. Bull.* **125**, 800–825.

Kitchener, E. G., Hodges, J. R. & McCarthy, R. 1998 Acquisition of post-morbid vocabulary and semantic facts in the absence of episodic memory. *Brain* **121**, 1313–1327.

Knowlton, B. J. & Squire, L. R. 1995 Remembering and knowing: two different expressions of declarative memory. *J. Exp. Psychol. Learn. Mem. Cogn.* **21**, 699–710.

Kopelman, M. D. & Kapur, N. 2001. The loss of episodic memories in retrograde amnesia: single-case and group studies. *Phil. Trans. R. Soc. Lond.* B **356**, 1409–1421.

Koriat, A. 2000 Control processes in remembering. In *The Oxford handbook of memory* (ed. E. Tulving & F. I. M. Craik), pp. 333–346. New York: Oxford University Press.

Maguire, E. A. 2001 Neuroimaging studies of autobiographical event memory. *Phil. Trans. R. Soc. Lond.* B **356**, 1441–1451.

Mandler, G. 1980 Recognizing: the judgment of previous occurrence. *Psychol. Rev.* **97**, 252–271.

Mangels, J. A., Picton, T. W. & Craik, F. I. M. 2001 Attention and successful episodic encoding: an event-related potential study. *Cogn. Brain Res.* **11**, 77–95.

Mayes, A. R. & Roberts, N. 2001 Theories of episodic memory. *Phil. Trans. R. Soc. Lond.* B **356**, 1395–1408.

Mishkin, M., Suzuki, W. A., Gadian, D. G. & Vargha-Khadem, F. (1997) Hierarchical organization of cognitive memory? *Phil. Trans. R. Soc. Lond.* B **352**, 1461–1467.

Morris, R. G. M. & Frey, U. 1997 Hippocampal synaptic plasticity: role in spatial learning or the automatic recording of attended experience? *Phil. Trans. R. Soc. Lond.* B **352**, 1489–1503.

Morris, R. G. M. 2001 Episodic-like memory in animals: psychological criteria, neural mechanisms and the value of episodic-like tasks to investigate animal models of neurodegenerative disease. *Phil. Trans. R. Soc. Lond.* B **356**, 1453–1465.

Nelson, K. 1993 The psychological and social origins of autobiographical memory. *Psychol. Sci.* **4**, 7–14.

Perner, J. & Ruffman, T. 1995 Episodic memory and autonoetic consciousness: developmental evidence and a theory of childhood amnesia. *J. Exp. Child Psychol.* **59**, 516–548.

Rajaram, S. & Roediger III, H. L. 1997 Remembering and knowing as states of consciousness during recollection. In *Scientific approaches to the question of consciousness* (ed. J. D. Cohen & J. W. Schooler), pp. 213–240. Hillsdale, NJ: Erlbaum.

Roediger III, H. L. 2000 Why retrieval is the key process in understanding memory. In *Memory, consciousness and the brain: the Tallinn conference* (ed. E. Tulving), pp. 52–75. Philadelphia: The Psychology Press.

Rovee-Collier, C. & Hayne, H. 2000 Memory in infancy and early childhood. In *The Oxford handbook of memory* (ed. E. Tulving & F. I. M. Craik), pp. 267–282. New York: Oxford University Press.

Schacter, D. L. & Dodson, C. S. 2001 Misattribution, false recognition and the sins of memory. *Phil. Trans. R. Soc. Lond.* B **356**, 1385–1393.

Schacter, D. L. & Tulving, E. 1994 What are the memory systems of 1994? In *Memory systems 1994* (ed. D. L. Schacter & E. Tulving), pp. 1–38. Cambridge, MA: MIT Press.

Shettleworth, S. 1998 *Cognition, evolution, and behavior.* New York: Oxford University Press.

Simons, J. S., Graham, K. S., Galton, C. J., Patterson, K. & Hodges, J. R. 2001 Semantic knowledge and episodic memory for faces in semantic dementia. *Neuropsychology* **15**, 101–114.

Squire, L. R. 1992 Memory and the hippocampus: a synthesis from findings with rats, monkeys and humans. *Psychol. Rev.* **99**, 195–231.

Squire, L. R. & Zola, S. M. 1998 Episodic memory, semantic memory, and amnesia. *Hippocampus* **8**, 205–211.

Tulving, E. 1972 Episodic and semantic memory. In *Organization of memory* (ed. E. Tulving & W. Donaldson), pp. 381–403. New York: Academic Press.

Tulving, E. 1983 *Elements of episodic memory.* Oxford: Clarendon Press.

Tulving, E. 1993 What is episodic memory? *Curr. Persp. Psychol. Sci.* **2**, 67–70.

Tulving, E. 1995 Organization of memory: quo vadis? In *The cognitive neurosciences* (ed. M. S. Gazzaniga), pp. 839–847. Cambridge, MA: MIT Press.

Tulving, E. 1998 Study of memory: processes and systems. In *Memory: systems, process, or function?* (ed. J. K. Foster & M. Jelicic), pp. 11–30. Oxford University Press.

Tulving, E. 2002*a* Episodic memory: from mind to brain. *Ann. Rev. Psychol.* (In the press.)

Tulving, E. 2002*b* Chronesthesia: awareness of subjective time. In *Principles of frontal lobe function* (ed. D. T. Stuss & R. C. Knight). New York: Oxford University Press. (In the press.)

Tulving, E. & Markowitsch, H. J. 1998 Episodic and declarative memory: role of the hippocampus. *Hippocampus* **8**, 198–204.

Tulving, E. & Schacter, D. L. 1990 Priming and human memory systems. *Science* **247**, 301–306.

Tulving, E., Schacter, D. L., McLachlan, D. R., & Moscovitch, M. 1988 Priming of semantic autobiographical knowledge: a case study of retrograde amnesia. *Brain Cogn.* **8**, 3–20.

Tulving, E., Hayman, C. A. G. & Macdonald, C. A. 1991 Long-lasting perceptual priming and semantic learning in amnesia: a case experiment. *J. Exp. Psychol. Learn. Mem. Cogn.* **17**, 595–617.

Tulving, E., Markowitsch, H. J., Kapur, S., Habib, R. & Houle, S. 1994 Novelty encoding networks in the human brain: positron emission tomography data. *Neuroreport* **5**, 2525–2528.

Underwood, B. J. 1964 The representativeness of rote verbal learning. In *Categories of human learning* (ed. A. W. Melton), pp. 48–78. New York: Academic Press.

Vargha-Khadem, F., Gadian, D. G., Watkins, K. E., Connelly, A., Van Paesschen, W. & Mishkin, M. 1997 Differential effects of early hippocampal pathology on episodic and semantic memory. *Science* **277**, 376–380.

Vargha-Khadem, F., Gadian, D. G. & Mishkin, M. 2001 Dissociations of cognitive memory: the syndrome of developmental amnesia. *Phil. Trans. R. Soc. Lond.* B **356**, 1435–1440.

Waugh, N. C. & Norman, D. A. 1965 Primary memory. *Psychol. Rev.* **72**, 89–104.

Wheeler, M. A. & McMillan, C. T. 2001 Focal retrograde amnesia and the episodic–semantic distinction. *Cogn. Affect. Behav. Neurosci.* **1**, 22–37.

Wheeler, M., Stuss, D. T. & Tulving, E. 1997 Toward a theory of episodic memory: the frontal lobes and autonoetic consciousness. *Psychol. Bull.* **121**, 331–354.

Wright, A. A., Santiago, H. C., Sands, S. F., Kendrick, D. F. & Cook, R. G. 1985 Memory processing of serial lists by pigeons, monkeys, and people. *Science* **229**, 287–289.

Yasuda, K, Watanabe, O. & Ono, Y. 1997 Dissociation between semantic and autobiographical memory: a case report. *Cortex* **33**, 623–638.

Yonelinas, A. P. 2001 Components of episodic memory: the contribution of recollection and familiarity. *Phil. Trans. R. Soc. Lond.* B **356**, 1363–1374.

Index